"At the beginning of everything is the word.
It is a miracle to which we owe the fact that we are human.
But at the same time it is a pitfall and a test, a snare and a trial.
More so, perhaps, than it appears to you who have enormous
freedom of speech, and might therefore assume that words are
not so important.
They are.
They are important everywhere."

Václav Havel, author, playwright, and
President of Czech and Slovak Federative Republic

Excerpted from *Open Letters* (Alfred A. Knopf, New York, 1991)
with permission from President Václav Havel and the publisher.

For Shelley Bell,
Um diversity lies
in the richness of life!
Best Wishes
Helen Foster
Nov. 6, 1993

WRITING

FOR THE

ETHNIC
MARKETS

Books in the Writers Connection Press
Marketplace Series

*California and Hawaii Publishing
Marketplace*
Southwest Publishing Marketplace
Northwest Publishing Marketplace

WRITING

FOR THE

ETHNIC MARKETS

SSSSSSSSSSSSSSSSSS

MEERA LESTER

Printed and Bound in the United States of America

The author gratefully acknowledges permission from the following sources to reprint material in their control: Random House, Inc., for material from *The Journey* by Indira Ganesan (Alfred A. Knopf 1990) and University of Chicago Press for material from *Intimate Relations, Exploring Indian Sexuality* by Sudhir Kakar (The University of Chicago Press, Chicago 60637, Penguin Books India, Ltd. New Delhi, India. Copyright 1989 by the University of Chicago. All rights reserved. Published 1990. Printed in the United States of America.) Author's failure to obtain the necessary permission for the use of any other copyrighted material included in this work is inadvertent and will be corrected in future printings following notification in writing to the Publisher of such omission accompanied by appropriate documentation.

Cover Illustration: Sherrie Smith

Art Director: Detta Penna

Publisher's Cataloging in Publication
(Prepared by Quality Books, Inc.)

Lester, Meera.
 Writing for the ethnic markets / Meera Lester.
 p. cm.
 Includes bibliographical references and index.
 ISBN 0-9622592-4-1

  1. Authorship--Handbook, manuals, etc. 2. Ethnic groups--United States. I. Title.

PN165.L4 1991   808.02
                QBI91-1699

Writers Connection books are available at special discounts for bulk purchases for sales promotions, fund-raising, or educational purposes. For details, contact:

Special Book Sales Director
Writers Connection
1601 Saratoga-Sunnyvale Road, Ste. 180
Cupertino, CA 95014
(408) 973-0227 Fax: (408) 973-1219

For Steve,
who taught me about roots, family,
and Jewish cultural traditions

and

For Dhyanyogi Madhusudandas,
who continues to teach me that Truth
transcends cultural, political, and religious boundaries

ACKNOWLEDGEMENTS

My most heartfelt thanks go to my editor Jan Stiles. If writers and critics judge this book useful, interesting, and to the point, it will be due largely to her efforts and unfailing vision. While supporting my tendency to meander, she always gently but firmly brought me back on course, back in focus.

Thanks also to Marjorie Gersh Young for her insights on format issues, diligence in data entry, and unmatched know-how in creating the various indexes.

My deepest affection and gratitude goes to Carolyn Foster, who widened my perspective of the inner world by teaching me how to tap the creative well of dreams and discover other pathways to empowerment.

A special thanks goes to *Writers Connection* staff writer Nancy Tamburello and photojournalist Mardeene Mitchell, who maintained a vigilant watch for resources and information that I could use in this and other ethnic writing projects.

I'm indebted to Dean Stark for his technical savvy and support. Without his troubleshooting skills and computer expertise, we couldn't have finished the book on schedule.

The work on this project was made significantly lighter by the support and contributions of the staff of Writers Connection.

I gratefully acknowledge the assistance, insights, and information provided by Julee Samuli, Audry Lynch, Pat Kaspar, Pamela Jekel, Norma Majumdar, Ray Faraday Nelson, Phyllis Taylor Pianka, and Kathie Fong Yoneda.

Meera Lester
Cupertino, California

TABLE OF CONTENTS

PART ONE

Introduction   1

Chapter One   Cultural Diversity: A Theme for Writers   5

Chapter Two   Sizing Up the Market   15

Chapter Three   Putting Power in Your Prose   29

Chapter Four   Writing Short, Ethnic-Oriented Nonfiction   39

Chapter Five   Ethnicity in Film   47

PART TWO

Book Publishers   57

Periodical Publishers   111

Film and TV Markets   159

Protection, Trademarks, and ISBNs   169

A Writer's Glossary   173

Multicultural Resources   179

Books for Writers   185

Book Subject Index   195
Periodical Subject Index   217
Film and TV Markets Index   241
Comprehensive Index   245
Author's Biography   251
About Writers Connection   253
Writers Connection Newsletter   255
Writing/Scriptwriting Resources from Writers Connection   256
Order Form   259

Introduction

For years, I have been writing material for ethnic markets in order to better understand aspects of other cultures, expand my knowledge about the people of our world, establish a diverse portfolio of clips, and increase my income.

I leave to the experts the debate of whether or not immigrants, interracial couples, and mixed-race children are assimilating into the proverbial American melting pot. As a writer, I celebrate ethnic and cultural diversity in my country and in my world. I believe that assimilation does not mean having to give up ties to one's cultural traditions and ethnic origins. Never before has multicultural awareness been so high and the demand for multicultural stories so great. Multiculturalism is here to stay—good news for writers interested in writing material for ethnic markets.

At the start of this project, I sent out thousands of questionnaires to newspapers, organization and association newsletters, magazine publishers, book publishers, and film and TV production companies. I asked publishers and producers if they felt ethnicity in publishing and film would increase, decrease, or stay the same over the next few years. Most said it would increase, citing such factors as an increased demand from readers and viewers (who are themselves of varying backgrounds and races) for stories about different races, cultures, and classes of people.

With the proliferation of ethnic markets, not only nationally but globally, the timing seems right for a book specifically for writers interested in learning how to evaluate, write, target, and sell their material to markets that accept manuscripts dealing with ethnic themes, issues, and elements.

This book is divided into two parts. Part One features chapters filled with information on how to write and market ethnic material, while Part Two lists specific information on each market, including the names of publications, the editors, and the publications' addresses; editorial guidelines; the ethnic audience the publication targets; types of ethnic material accepted; acceptance policies; preferred method of query; rights purchased; and tips directed specifically to writers from the respective editors or publishers.

Other sections in Part Two provide information on copyright, trademarks, and ISBNs; a glossary of terms writers should be familiar with; an annotated bibliography of how-to-write books and publishing resources; and a list of multicultural sources.

The listings include only that information sent to us by book or periodical publishers or film producers. If publishers or producers are not listed, it is likely that their surveys were not returned, they requested deletion, or their information could not be verified.

It is my hope that writers will draw from within these pages inspiration, practical tips, and hard-hitting, current information about ethnic markets in order to share the rich ethnic and cultural legacy of stories that exists all around us.

Meera Lester, author

PART ONE

CHAPTER ONE
Cultural Diversity: A Theme for Writers

America's image as a melting pot is evolving into a complex ethnic stew where plurality replaces total assimilation. In a pluralistic society, numerous distinct ethnic, religious, and cultural groups coexist within one nation. For many multi-ethnic nations like the Soviet Union, the United States, and Canada, the idea of complete and total assimilation (all ethnic groups blending into one and abandoning cultural traditions and languages) is out. Cultural pluralism is in. Throughout America, many cities are witnessing an unparalleled population shift as various ethnic groups now make up the majority of the total population within those cities. Births and immigration primarily account for the swelling numbers of ethnic populations in our country, and experts have said that the shift toward pluralism will become more commonplace in the coming years because of immigration and the high birth-rate traditions immigrants may bring with them.

Who are these ethnic groups? According to Jerry Wong, Information Specialist at the United States Bureau of the Census, Los Angeles office, "Of the 248,709,873 total U. S. population counted by the Census Bureau in 1990, 29,986,060 are Afro-Americans, 22,354,059 are of Hispanic origin, 7,273,662 are Asian/Pacific Islanders, and 1,959,234 are American Indians/Eskimo/Aleut."

In California, Asians are the third largest ethnic group in the state, ahead of Afro-Americans, the so-called "shrinking minority." Hispanics—people from such countries as Mexico, Cuba, Puerto Rico, and Central and South America—now comprise a fourth of the population of that state. Besides Hispanics, Afro-Americans, and Asians, many other ethnic groups account for a large percentage of the population in California as well as other states across the country.

What does this mean to writers?

Opportunities lie within our backyards. By mining the rich cultural diversity found within our own communities, we will find powerful stories to be told—stories that will resonate deeply within the hearts of all humans; stories with connections to other worlds, other times, ancient and modern history; stories that sing with cultural clarity and beauty.

Increasing cultural diversity also means a proliferation of new markets—ethnic markets. In the United States, there are literally hundreds of places to sell ethnic stories. As the ethnic population increases, writers will find a wealth of new ethnic markets springing forth from within these communities as they establish small presses to publish newspapers, magazines, and books. Additional markets will emerge from within older, established publishing houses as they, too, become more cognizant of and responsive to ethnicity in manuscripts.

Ethnic, according to dictionary definitions, is that which relates to a religious, racial, national, or cultural group. Ethnic communities in the United States are comprised of people who are newly arrived immigrants, the offspring of generations of those who came here long ago (as with Afro-Americans), or mixed-race children who choose to remain close to the cultural traditions of one or both of their parents. Using our powers of observation and sense of curiosity about the ethnic origins of our own history, culture, and religion as well as the cultural backgrounds of others, we will discover an abundance of ideas for ethnic-oriented stories.

Former Atlanta Mayor Andrew Young, speaking at a conference on Racism and Ethnic Polarization, referred to ethnicity in our country not as homogeneous soup, but as a kind of stew where "everything wants to maintain its own identity." Writing about these cultures and ethnic identities may present a challenge to some writers. Prejudices and stereotypical notions may surface, unwelcome. Such reactions can represent opportunities for new growth, greater vision, expanded horizons. Knowledge and tolerance build bridges to understanding and peace.

Developing an Ethnic Lens

Your choice of a literary form for ethnic subjects is determined by how you view your material. Social commentary can target issues of concern to a particular ethnic community; travel pieces can focus on an ethnic locale, festival, or holy day; food articles can identify the ethnic origins of certain dishes; art and architectural pieces can trace the cultural elements that influenced the work; short stories or novels can be set in other lands or incorporate foreign historical events or cultural philosophies and practices; first-person essays can explore your personal views of an ethnic issue. The possibilities are endless.

The stories that will become the focus of your own ethnic lens will reflect your personal interests, background, and experience. My own story ideas are often triggered by dreams, memories, meditations, conversations, and sensory stimulation—taste, touch, hearing, smell, and sight. Because I'm intrigued by other cultures, especially India, a land rich in ethnic diversity, my story ideas lead me to write ethnically focused pieces.

A visual stimulus can pique interest or evoke a memory that can lead to an ethnic story idea. For example, watching the sun set over the Santa Cruz Mountains near my home in California triggered the memory of a Gujarati village I visited in India, where the blood-red sun oozes right into the earth and disappears. Its hue reappears daily in the tilak mark on the forehead of young Indian women or in the parts of their onyx-colored hair, in freshly strung flower necklaces adorning murthis (statues of deities), in spice heaps, or in the intricately stitched borders of silk saris. The vibrantly colored Santa Cruz sunset triggered visual images for me that led naturally to memories of other sunsets in India—one on a mountain I climbed barefoot because it was considered the abode of a goddess and the other at a mystic's shrine at Fatehpur Sikri. From those memories I wrote an article that sold as a travel piece.

Smells evoke memory, too. The scent of gardenia in bloom might trigger the memory of a garden on Ocho Rios, Jamaica, and of sun-baked huts along rutted roads. Men in their prime, who under different circumstances might be at work, sit in darkened doorways, waiting for the sun and life to pass. The image is the perfect launching point for a social commentary on poverty and joblessness in Jamaica.

Scents can trigger ideas about food or native eating customs. The smell of rose water and mint might evoke the image of a cup of steaming North African tea being poured, whereas coriander and chili might produce the image of a large silver thali mounded with Indian delicacies.

Pay attention also to the scents of the Earth. Soil types smell differently in different seasons. If you love forests, the next time you're standing in a misty grove of towering trees, concentrate on the smell alone for a time. What other images does it call forth? What feelings? Are the images and feelings associated with your childhood or adulthood? With contacts to people of other cultures or visits to other lands? You might wonder if your grove of trees smells like Germany's Black Forest or South America's rain forest or the American Rockies;

thoughts that may lead you to ponder the cultures of Gypsies, South American Indians, or Native Americans.

Concern for the environment and fears about the possible extinction of many plants and animals lead naturally to thoughts of Botswana's Kalahari desert or Tanzania's Serengeti plain and the living things that call those places home. An awareness of the rhythm and cycles of life on our planet, the phases of the moon, and the seasons of planting and harvesting can point toward ethnic subjects. Picture villagers in any Third World country threshing millet ears or wheat or rice in steady rhythm, their bodies united in the task at hand, their voices united in song.

Singing suggests another source for ethnic ideas—sound. It is said music can transcend language and speak directly to the heart. There is no lack of markets for articles about music or musicians, and that applies to ethnic music as well.

Music can be found in all cultures of the world and certainly occupies a place in all the great religious traditions. After reading about ancient musical instruments and discussing the topic with an editor, I was assigned to write a profile piece on G. S. Sachdev, world-renowned master of the bansuri flute. Besides having fun researching and writing the article, I learned a great deal on a subject I knew little about and gained some insights into how cultural and environmental factors might shape musical genius. I learned not only about the bansuri, but about drone boxes, the role ragas played in ancient temple life, and music as a path to higher consciousness.

Articles on the origins of creative musical genius with slants toward particular ethnic communities and their musicians could be done a dozen times over for different magazines. Pieces exploring how the Chinese, Haitians, Native Americans, Afro-Americans, or other ethnic communities use music in ancient cultural or religious practices would be interesting to research and write. Such articles would no doubt sell to targeted ethnic publications, in-flight magazines of airlines serving the country being written about, and general interest publications as well.

Your often-overlooked tactile sense can also open your mind to ethnic topics. Visit any import store and touch the textiles and crafts from other countries. By stroking delicate beaded pillows from Burma or silky handwoven Persian rugs, you can be transported to another place and time. You might want to know if these objects are created in the same way that they have been crafted for centuries. In India, for example, youngsters dye, weave, and trim wool carpets, employing ages-old techniques. In Agra, stonecutters squat on their haunches and ply their craft in the same method as their forefathers who created the Taj Mahal. In Nepal, Tibetan refugees sit for hours on a plank floor in front of looms, creating their masterpieces for tourists who may admire the workmanship and beauty but not realize how each was made. In Africa, spears are fashioned by modern-day tribal warriors using essentially the same materials and tools used by their ancestors.

Articles about textiles indigenous to ethnic communities of the world or pieces about the individual artisans who produce them would be of interest to the general American market as well as to the American immigrants who now reside in the United States. *National Geographic*, for example, in its January 1991 issue, ran a piece titled "Masters of Traditional Arts" that featured profiles of, among others, a Kiowa Indian regalia maker, a Pueblo Indian potter, and a Hispanic weaver from the Southwest who uses the ancient methods passed down through her Anasazi lineage. A piece on ancient techniques still used today takes on added interest when contrasted to the automation and technology common to modern production.

Dreams, too, can suggest ideas for your writing. As Carl G. Jung noted, we pass almost half of our lives in a more or less unconscious state—the level of consciousness at which dreams occur. Jung called dreams the utterance of the unconscious and pointed out that dreams are a way of expressing telepathic vision, philosophical ideology, memories, inescapable truths, and much more. Dreams play an important role in many cultures of the world. Native Americans believe that dreams are gifts of the Great Spirit to guide and inspire the soul.

Many of the great creative geniuses of our civilization have tapped the wellspring of dreams and altered states of consciousness. Writers such as Goethe, Calderon, Cervantes, Marquez, Fuentes, Blake, and a host of others translated their deep visionary experiences into literary expression. Another writer, Robert Louis Stevenson, wrote in his autobiography that he received, among other stories, the plot for *Dr. Jekyll and Mr. Hyde* from a dream.

As writers we can draw upon the creative images and symbols of our dreams and from them decipher and translate messages of personal and universal truth. Dreams with strong multicultural overtones may be cultivated for expression into novels, articles, short stories, and poetry. I know of at least one writer who has written a book entirely from her dreams and another who is simultaneously allowing her dreams to guide her through a healing process and the writing of a book about her experience.

Find an ethnic symbol dictionary, as I did, and it will put an ethnic slant on your interpretation. My article "Dreams, Meditation, and Vedic Symbolism" was the result of a particularly vivid dream that finally made sense when I interpreted it using symbols found in the ancient Vedic literature of the Indians. The article sold to a worldwide newspaper.

My own nightly excursions into the subconscious have led me to multicultural dreaming. Often my dream stories feature people of other races, and I interact with them. However, sometimes I am myself of another culture and perform a role in the ethnic story of my dream. Upon awakening, I record and analyze the dream. I also mine it for ethnic stories, ideas, or relevance to other writing projects.

If you are a voracious reader, you may find the books you read for enjoyment or research can lead to ideas for books or articles that you could write. A few years ago I began reading novels with an India tie-in. I wrote a query to the editor of a local magazine for Indo-Americans, asking if he'd be interested in having me review a book about the armies of the British Raj. He said yes, and I've been reviewing books for his magazine ever since.

Finally, look to your hobbies for ethnic ideas. Collectibles such as stamps from around the world or baseball and football cards can trigger ethnic ideas. Jim Thorpe, a mixed-blood Sauk and Fox Indian dubbed by the King of Sweden as the best athlete in the world, Jackie Robinson, son of black sharecroppers, and Hank Greenberg, legendary Jewish big league slugger, are notable among many outstanding athletes in the annals of sports. In basketball, soccer, boxing—virtually all fields of athletics—you'll find incredible people from widely different cultural backgrounds to write about.

In the field of stamp collectibles, look for the history behind the stamp. My own interest in the British occupation of India led me to search out the first Indian stamp released when India gained independence from England. From there, I sought pre-independence stamps and discovered a number of miniature envelopes embossed with the seal of the maharajas and nawabs who ruled the princely territories before the departure of the Raj. Later I came upon an article in *Linn's Stamp News* about a Nazi-backed issue of a rare Azad Hind Indian Legion stamp and another trivia article on Indian states stamps that some writer had parlayed out of a philatelic interest.

You might find equally fascinating the old envelopes that have passed through censors during World War II. Each envelope represents a fragment of world history as well as the personal histories of the letter writer and receiver. A myriad of ideas will come to mind when you read the countries of origin on the envelopes and wonder what life was like at that juncture of history, in that particular country, within that family.

Follow your senses, heart, and mind as they lead you to uncover new ways of looking at life, people, and our planet. Once you begin to develop your own ethnic lens—a way of looking at or seeing the ethnic potential and slant for your ideas—you'll literally find your writing topics expanding globally.

Capturing Inspiration

You never know when you'll get a flash of inspiration, and you must be prepared to capture their ideas or risk losing them. Keep a notebook near you at all times. Jot down ideas as they surface. You might even want to keep a notepad mounted on the dashboard of your car. Driving a monotonous highway or well-known route invariably calls forth the Muse.

Daily notes recorded in a dream or meditation journal; scribbled character sketches of people at airports, bus stations, and public parks; notes penned while eavesdropping in the grocery check-out line or in a crowded cafe; or photographs and anecdotes from fashion shows, cultural beauty contests, or folk dances sponsored by local ethnic organizations, associations, or churches can yield a bounty of material that can be developed into stories. Cultural festivals like Cinco de Mayo, India Republic Day, Scandinavian Heritage Festival, Chinese New Year, Scottish Highlands Festival, Mardi Gras, Tet—the Vietnamese New Year Festival, and the Japanese Obon Festival can be mined for ethnic material, too.

It's important to capture the information when it presents itself. Don't wait to do it from memory. Writing impressions down immediately preserves the freshness and richly textures your stories when those impressions are interwoven later.

The process of creating and capturing ideas for ethnic material is not really different than that for any other kind of writing. Books like Alex Haley's *Roots*, James Clavell's *Shogun* and *Tai Pan*, Alice Walker's *The Color Purple* and *Her Blue Body Everything We Know*, Sonia Sanchez's *Under a Soprano Sky*, Gus Lee's *China Boy*, or Laurence Durrell's classic Alexandria Quartet, which is set in Egypt and includes *Justine, Clea, Balthazar*, and *Mountolive*, can be good starting places for "opening the tap." Another technique might be to use folktales, musical lyrics, collections of short stories, or poetry by authors of different ethnic backgrounds as a departure point from which to formulate, incubate, and write ideas. Who can read tales from the *Arabian Nights* and not picture turbaned men, veiled dancing girls, and exotic scenes? The image of dancing girls may remind you of the great Mogul emperor Akbar, who had a stone board built that was large enough to accommodate real dancing girls as the playing pieces for the ancient game of *pachisi*. Like Akbar, historical figures from other cultures are immensely interesting to readers, and the research and writing can be fascinating as well.

You may find yourself wanting to know more about Native Americans after seeing the film *Tell Them Willie Boy Is Here* (a story based on a historical incident that occurred in 1909), or *House Made of*

Dawn (based on F. Scott Momaday's Pulitzer Prize-winning book) or, more specifically, the Sioux after seeing the film *Dances with Wolves*, the Cheyenne after seeing *Windwalker*, or the Navajo after reading the mysteries of Tony Hillerman. You may develop a new interest in the people of the Soviet Union, England, or Portugal after viewing *Russia House*; in African-Americans after watching *Glory*; or in the people of India after viewing *Gandhi, Heat and Dust, Salaam Bombay*, or *The Jewel in the Crown*, a miniseries based on the book in Paul Scott's series of novels known as The Raj Quartet.

Ethnic film festivals, fairly commonplace in America's big cities and university towns, are another great resource for generating ideas for stories. Watch for information about them in local newspapers and ethnic publications.

Capture your impressions or ideas by jotting down general subject areas of interest and then listing in descending order the specific topics that you'd like to know more about. Beneath each of those topics, write specific subpoints. From them, list other subheadings, each more specific than the preceding. For example, descending from the main subject of Egypt might be Egyptian Christian Copts, Egyptian Christian Coptic art, then Egyptian Christian Coptic artifacts, iconography, and collections. When you've arrived at the last specific entry under that heading, list all the possible markets for that story idea.

Another way to create a path from general to specific is through free association and the mapping of your ideas. If you are seeking specific techniques for releasing the ideas within and getting them on paper, read Gabriele L. Rico's book, *Writing the Natural Way: Using Right Brain Techniques to Release Your Expressive Powers*, Natalie Goldberg's *Writing Down the Bones, Freeing the Writer Within*, and her latest, *Wild Mind*. Goldberg's insights into writing and creativity are rooted in her experience in Zen meditation.

Techniques may vary, but the goal is the same: to get the ideas on paper and to move from general to specific. After you've accomplished that, fine-tune and decide whether to write out your ideas as short stories, scripts, books, or articles. If an article is your choice, decide on the form—profile, spiritual or inspirational piece, first-person essay, how-to or self-help, personal experience, nostalgia, critical review, round-up, or question and answer interview.

Locating Ethnic Sources and Experts

To find resources or experts that can provide the information you need, begin with the comprehensive list of ethnic periodicals and book publishers elsewhere in this book. Request copies of magazines, newspapers, or book catalogs from those that intrigue you. After perusing the material, subscribe to those periodicals that appeal to you most. Cull them for upcoming events, guest speakers, performing artists, cooking demonstrations, cultural festivals, and classes. From these sources, you'll find excellent interview candidates.

With the help of your librarian, locate ethnic associations in your state or city. Make use of books like *Encyclopedia of Associations*, published by Gale Research, which lists information about cultural institutes (African, Irish American, Lithuanian, etc.), cultural societies (Sinhala [Sri Lanka], Inter-Celtic Arts, Pennsylvania Dutch Folk, etc.), cultural associations, public affairs organizations, cultural centers, councils, exchanges, commissions, foundations, heritage and historical societies, studies, and training. Another valuable resource is the ethnic section of *Writer's Resource Guide* (Writer's Digest Books). And the *Guide to Multicultural Resources*, published by Praxis Publications, Inc., lists addresses, phone numbers, contacts, and descriptive information for the Asian, Afro-American, Hispanic, and American Indian communities. You can purchase the hardcover comprehensive version or the individual guides targeting a specific ethnic community.

Libraries are veritable mines for obscure and sometimes precious collections. For example, a PBS research team seeking the lyrics to a ballad about the black Fifty-Fourth Massachusetts Regiment featured in *Glory*, found them in the Buffalo and Erie County Public Library. The ballad titled "The Colored Volunteer" by Tom Craig is among 2,200 items in a the library's collection dating from 1850 to 1900.

Other sources that should prove helpful include colleges and universities with designated centers for particular fields of study, such as the Centers for South Asian and Southeast Asian Studies and Center for Slavic and East European Studies at the University of California at Berkeley. The Association for the Study of Afro-American Life and History, located in Washington, D. C, and the Great Plains Black Museum/Archives and Interpretive Center in Omaha, Nebraska, provide historical information and resources for those interested in the study of black people.

If you are seeking information on the ethnology of Native Americans, you will want to contact Arizona State Museum in Tucson, the Cherokee National Historical Society, Inc., in Tahlequah, Oklahoma, or the Chickasaw Council House and Historic Site and Museum in Tishomingo, Oklahoma, among others. The Balch Institute for Ethnic Studies in Philadelphia, Pennsylvania, provides information on America's multicultural history through its educational programs, museum, and library. Two excellent sources that often provide insights into ethnic communities are *National Geographic* and *Smithsonian* magazines. Other resources are listed at the back of this book.

For almost every writing subject, there's an ethnic slant. Learn to look for the cultural or ethnic elements of any story, from family relationships to politics to human interest articles. By emphasizing and seeking more depth in the ethnic aspects or overtones of more general subjects, you tap the potential for additional sales to new markets.

No matter what your background, you can find ethnic themes for your writing. It's up you as a writer to prime the pump for ideas, develop an ethnic lens, write down your insights and impressions, and develop them into articles, short stories, or books.

CHAPTER TWO
Sizing Up the Market

Is there really a market for ethnic material? You bet. You'll find markets in all areas of writing and publishing, including articles, books, audio publishing, and film.

Publisher's Weekly, one of the most widely read magazines of the book trade, announced earlier this year the titles of forthcoming books from many U. S. publishers. In 1991, in virtually every area of writing and publishing, listings included titles that dealt in greater or lesser degree with ethnic subject matter—from hardcover and mass market paperback fiction to such nonfiction areas as art, cookbooks, health and fitness, history, performing arts, psychology, poetry, reference, social science, travel, war, and women's studies.

The following is a random sampling: *Mennonite Foods and Folk-ways from South Russia* (Good Books); *Screenplays of the African American Experience* (Indiana University Press); *Buried Treasures of the Appalachians* (August House); *Jewish Heroes of America* (Shapolsky); *The Cherokee* (University of Oklahoma Press); *The Black Anglo Saxons* (Third World Press); *Indian Affairs*, a novel about a couple drawn into Native American life (Farrar, Straus & Giroux); *Coromandel Sea Change*, a novel about a young woman in India (Knopf); *The Batak: Peoples of the Island of Sumatra* (Thames and Hudson); *The Kitchen God's Wife*, Amy Tan's new novel (Putnam); and *Between Heaven and Earth: A Guide to Chinese Medicine* (Ballantine).

If you are just getting started as a writer of fiction books, you should welcome the fact that the publishing of first novels rose in 1991. According to *Library Journal*, a national trade publication for librarians, only 85 first novels were published in the fall 1990 season, "fewer than in any season in the last decade." However, the book season spanning February 1 through August 31, 1991, featured 147 first novelists, and of those, 31 were authors with cultural backgrounds outside the United States. Several of those first novels by U. S. authors such as *China Boy* by Gus Lee (Dutton), *The Loud Adios* by Ken Kuhlken (St. Martin's), and *Refugio, They Named You Wrong* by Susan C. Schofield (Algonquin Books) have titles that suggest ethnicity.

In "Creating Authentic Ethnic Characters," an article featured in the January-February 1991 issue of *Romance Writer's Report*, the magazine of the Romance Writers of America national organization, author Suzanne Ellison provided information on how to incorporate ethnic characters in romance novels. Ellison, who created protagonist Rosie Moreno, a third-generation Mexican-American, for her mainstream novel *Every Kindred, Every Tribe*, urged romance writers to draw upon "the depth and richness of America's diverse heritage and the variety of ethnic experiences which occur in our country today." Markets for romances that tap that heritage and experience include Marron Publishers, Odyssey Books (Afro-American only), and Harlequin/ Silhouette. More specific information on what these publishers are looking for can be found in the book publisher's section of this book.

In a marketplace that is reflecting a deepening interest in Judaism and the American Jewish community, Holmes and Meir is one of several publishers dedicated to producing books that meet the need of that audience. As publishers of Judaic material, Holmes and Meir scheduled a number of Jewish-interest books in a new series called *New Perspectives: Jewish Thought and Experience* for publication beginning in 1992.

Focusing on stories dealing with the Native American culture is Parabola Audio Library, an imprint of the Society for the Study of Myth and Tradition. The company announced early in 1991 that it would produce a series of Native American stories on audio. The first offering in the company's Storytime Series was *The Boy Who Lived with the Bears and Other Iroquois Stories*, narrated by Joe Bruchac, an Iroquois storyteller. Parabola, dedicated to "exploring the wisdom and beauty of traditional cultures in relation to myth and the modern quest for meaning," uses storytellers whose stories have appeared in *Parabola* magazine. Plans for forthcoming tapes include Native American tales from the Southwestern Navajo and Hopi to Southeastern Cherokee.

Even encyclopedia publishers are getting into the multicultural act. G. K. Hall is publishing the *Encyclopedia of World Cultures*, a ten-volume set. *North America*, Volume One, already out, covers the cultures of ethnic groups such as Native Americans and Afro-Americans in the United States, Canada, and Greenland. Cultural and historical data is presented on ethnic groups and folk cultures such as the Amish.

As the call for more ethnically focused stories is sounded from the educational and political arenas, the heightened awareness within the film and publishing sector will translate into product to meet the demand. I believe markets that recognize and celebrate ethnicity in story will flourish in the years to come. The question then, is not whether ethnic markets exist, but rather, how to sell to them.

Marketing Tools, Tips, and Techniques

Articles are typically sold on the basis of a powerful, compelling query letter directed to a specific editor of a publication. Short stories are sold on the basis of the entire manuscript and a cover letter to the editor.

Novels, with the exception of first novels, are accepted or rejected by an editor only after he or she has read a synopsis and sample chapters. First novels, except in rare instances, must be completed before a publisher will consider buying them, largely because of unknown factors. The publisher may be from a non-Anglo background and be producing material for an ethnic audience, or the publisher may be an Anglo depending on you, the writer, to write authoritatively about a particular culture. Either way, because you are the writer of a first novel, he or she does not know your integrity, credibility, writing skill, or ability to manage a book-length work. As a publisher, he or she will wonder if you have the staying power to see the project to completion. Will the second half of the book be as well-conceived and executed as the first half? Will the book remain true to the synopsis? Will you correctly and sensitively portray the ethnic background, characters, or culture?

In a business where there are no guarantees, editors and publishers want to know as much as possible about you and your project and want to do everything they can to tip the scales toward success for you both.

Targeting the Ethnic Article Market

Perhaps you have some great ideas for ethnically focused articles and you've found a list of appropriate markets, but you don't know how to tell if your pieces will fit the editorial content of the newspapers and magazines you've selected? If you haven't seen the publications, you stand a good chance of wasting your postage and your time.

How do you get copies? Check bookstores, newsstands, and libraries. If they can't be found in the library's holdings, ascertain the address of the publication by checking sources like *Reader's Guide to Periodical Literature*. Request sample copies from the publications' editorial offices. Offer to pay for the copies, and at the same time request writers' guidelines. The guidelines will provide you with important information about payment rates for articles and photographs, rights purchased, desired word length, demographics of the readership, and much more.

Once you have copies of the publications, peruse them carefully to see if they include article subject areas and formats such as the one you have in mind. Look at typical word lengths and style. The words a writer uses to tell a story also create a tone and style that can be folksy or pretentious, technical or breezy, soft and soothing or somber and serious.

Some magazines and newspapers will print stories in both English and the native language of their readers. If you can write in the native language that a particular publication uses, let the editor know. However, unless otherwise advised by the publication's guidelines, use non-English words sparingly—even in ethnic publications. Those publications may also have an Anglo readership and possibly individuals from other ethnic backgrounds as well reading the publication.

Finally, if you're writing in English, apply the rules governing English grammar, punctuation, and style. To guide you in determining whether to underline or quote the titles of plays, books, of songs or to italicize foreign words and phrases, consult one of several excellent style guides on the market today, such as *The Chicago Manual of Style, The Associated Press Stylebook and Libel Manual*, or the *Government Printing Office Style Manual*.

For seasonal or holiday-related material, examine a year or more of back issues to see what types of seasonal or holiday stories have run in the past. Stories like "Celebrating the Summer Solstice in the Old Scandinavian Tradition," "The First Cinco de Mayo," or "A Passover Meal in the Cochin Judaic Tradition" are often welcome but sometimes need to be sent several months ahead of the targeted holiday.

By studying the guidelines and the publication, you'll increase your chances for acceptance and avoid sending inappropriate material such as how to celebrate Chanukah to *Hinduism Today* or how to barbecue chicken to *Vegetarian Times*. You'll also discover the correct timetable for submitting your work and learn about any particular requirements such as quotes from experts or the need for photographs.

Creating a Professional Query

The purpose of a query is to get an article assignment from the editor. A good query letter accomplishes several things simultaneously. Its appearance, subject content, tone, organization of ideas, and flow probably say more about you as a writer than the brief paragraph about yourself that you'll include at the end of your letter. Its appearance may say it was created by someone who takes writing seriously—a professional. If it is attractive, well targeted, well conceived, and well executed, you'll probably get the assignment. Conversely, a query that looks like it was dashed off without much thought inevitably ensures rejection.

As an editor over the years, I've had the occasion to read and respond to hundreds of queries. Oddly enough, the best ones faded from my memory after I called the writers of those queries and assigned the articles. I do, however, remember the worst one. It came in a white envelope with my name and address scrawled by a pen in dire need of a refill. The query, repeatedly folded and creased so that it could have passed for a piece of rejected origami, sported coffee stains and wreaked of tobacco smoke. With a certain amount of trepidation, I peeled open the folds, skimmed over the salutation—my misspelled name—and proceeded to the first sentence: "I'm not really a writer."

I felt a certain consternation for that person. Where was the pride in that presentation? The substance in the query? The future for that person as a writer? The point is this: If you can't think of yourself as a writer, then why should the editor?

Your query should be typewritten, double-spaced, on white paper stock (20-pound bond is nice) with one-inch margins. If possible, keep the length of the query to one page. Include your name and address along with your phone number, as some editors will often call to make an assignment. In any correspondence with an editor, it's a good idea to always enclose a self-addressed, stamped envelope (SASE) for his or her response. In fact, some editors will not respond to your query if a SASE is not provided. On the other hand, there are writers who will tell you that unless the manuscript is hefty, a SASE is not necessary. Their attitude is that they are providing a service to a buyer. The buyer should be able to afford to make the order over the phone or through the mail. My preference is to send the SASE. After the relationship with the editor is established, you can ask whether or not the SASE is necessary. I've discovered that the editors I've worked with in ethnic communities have appreciated getting my SASEs and have used them not only for letters of assignment, but for sending tear sheets of the article to me after publication.

When creating your query letter, remember to present the information succinctly. Keep it to one page if possible. Indicate the ethnic connection if it's not obvious. Show the editor that you (1) are familiar his or her publication, (2) have carefully chosen an appropriate article idea and know how to develop it into an interesting piece that will intrigue or resonate with the publication's readers, and (3) understand ethnic make-up of the publication's readership.

Be selective in the information you provide about yourself and, if possible, make it relative to the ethnic audience you've chosen to write for. If you've never published a sentence before, you can still present author information that sounds professional and upbeat and reassuring to the editor. For example, don't say you've never been published. Instead, state that you are a freelance writer (which you are if you are not writing as a full-time occupation) based in (your city) with special interest in writing about (your ethnic interest to reflect the publication you are writing for). Any tidbit of information that supports your "special interest" and adds to the credibility of your knowledge on that subject should be added. Do hone your skills, learn the craft, and write to the best of your ability.

Creating Powerful Openings

Begin your query with a hook. It could be an interesting fact, quote, anecdote, a colorful description of a destination (often seen in travel pieces), statement of a problem, (for which your article will provide solutions or resources), or the juxtaposition of two opposites (people, situations, or things). Or you can hook with word-portraits of universal archetypes or symbols. For example, the writer of one article that caught my attention opened with a powerful image of the 600-year-old Solovetski Monastery standing as a symbol of opposites in the course of Russian history. His language picture would have worked equally as well (and, indeed, may have) in a query letter proposing the article. You can also use statistics illustrating a point. However, a caveat: Statistics can be exceedingly boring if they're not set up as part of an unusual or startling lead into a story.

The hook must grab the reader and compel him or her to read on. For an ethnic publication, always ensure that your hook is somehow anchored in ethnicity appropriate to that publication. If, for example, your story is about apparitions of light occurring in Hispanic communities around Los Angeles and you've chosen to write about the occurrences for a Hispanic Catholic publication, you might want to tie the apparitions of light to a specific Biblical predication, use a quote from the local parish priest, or cite statistics of how often, when, and where it's happened.

The book jacket copy for *Intimate Relations, Exploring Indian Sexuality* by Sudhir Kakar, published by the University of Chicago Press, stated that "in India's lore and tradition, complex symbols abound—snakes take the shape of sensual women or handsome men, celibates sleep with naked women, gods rape their daughters, and a goddess fries a king in oil." Intrigued? Want to read on? The publisher, editor, and author are counting on it.

It is a powerful sentence that titillates the reader to want to know more. It is that kind of response your queries and articles need to evoke from editors and, subsequently, readers.

Coming Up with the Slant

The slant of an article is the direction you're going to take with the material. Consider, for example, the topic of Afro-American slavery—a broad subject area. One slant might be to look at it from the perspective of health. What was the level of medical care afforded slaves in a particular part of the country? Another slant might focus on women and slavery, such as a piece on the legacy of textile art by Afro-American women. Yet another might explore how the pain of social injustices suffered by Afro-Americans manifested itself in their artistic expression—their songs, writing, and artwork.

Developing the Body of the Query

You have the editor's interest because you've established a powerful opening hook and indicated the slant of the piece. Now you must add in specific points or issues to be explored. This is not the time to go off on tangential topics. Stay focused on your particular subject and slant and build upon them. Mention your research sources, including interviews with experts in your subject area. Also indicate your proposed word-length, turnaround time, and your writing credits, if you have them. And always ask for the assignment.

The editor is going to accept or reject your idea based on his or her impression of your writing skill. How well have you presented your idea? Is there a logical progression through major points and subpoints to the conclusion. Is the tone right. How well are transitions handled? How skillful is your use of grammar, punctuation, and style. Does the writing flow?

Spending a little extra time on transition sentences will ensure that your writing flows seamlessly from one group of ideas into the next. Editors might not notice that your letter or article flows seamlessly, but they will always notice if it's choppy, disconnected, or disorganized.

The query makes your first impression and sells your idea. It behooves you to give it as much attention as your article. You'll find an abundance of specific information on how to write queries in *Query Letters/Cover Letters* by Gordon Burgett (Communication Unlimited).

Sell It with Pictures

Great photographs will enhance the value and desirability of your article. There are so many varieties of cameras on the market today that even if you have no experience in photography, you can produce quality pictures with a minimum of understanding about how to operate a camera.

If, however, you prefer to buy professionally produced photographs to complement your articles, there are many sources from which to choose. At a local level, begin by contacting local tourist bureaus, state and city archives, metropolitan newspaper archives, ethnic associations' historical archives, places of worship such as churches or temples or mosques; and, of course, libraries. The San Francisco Public Library, for example, maintains a history room with old photos of historic San Francisco, its landmarks, and its cultural heritage. There is a small charge for copies of the photos, and it takes about two weeks to get them.

Check the yellow pages of your local phone book under the heading Photographic-Photography. The ad for American Stock Photography in Los Angeles, for example, says the company is the West Coast representative for many freelance photographers as well as for many well-known professional photographers (whose names are listed).

The ad for Underwood Photo Archives, Ltd., in San Francisco notes that its holdings, based on an original collection of black-and-white photographs from the Underwood News Photo Service founded in 1882, has historical photos of everything from everywhere in 1,193 worldwide categories.

In New York City there are several commercial agencies with enormous collections on virtually any topic. The two best known are The Bettman Archive and Culver Pictures. Bettman's Director David Greenstein told me Bettman's holdings include 15 to 20 million photos in virtually any category, including ethnic topics. He stated that the company has a team of researchers who can conduct a photo search for a minimum fee of $50 and within a turnaround time of as little as one day. Bettman is the photo library for Reuter and United Press International and has on file the negatives of historical photos from those wire services.

Culver Pictures specializes in images of historical personalities and events, and the company's holdings include some 12 million photos. Peter Tomlinson, researcher with Culver Pictures, said a sampling of categories might include the Civil War, French Revolution, World

Wars I and II, movie stills, and the history and daily life of people of other cultures like the Chinese working on the railroads in the American West. The historical images date from the years prior to 1950. The company will conduct a search for photos for a $50 service fee and will send a selection of photos, charging you only for those that are used.

The United States Government Printing Office publishes catalogs for its collections of photos housed in The National Archives and Library of Congress. The United States Armed Forces maintains a large collection of photographs, as do virtually all departments of government. Check the wire services such as United Press International and Associated Press for photographs they may have on file. Find other listings in *Photographer's Market* (Writer's Digest Books) and in *Stock Photo and Assignment Source* (R.R. Bowker). For photos of specific celebrity musicians, actresses and actors, writers, et al., try contacting their management companies, agents, publishers, recording companies, etc., for publicity photos.

Selling Nonfiction Books with a Proposal

The proposal for a nonfiction ethnic book performs much the same function as the article query. Writing a proposal should begin only after you do the following: (1) determine that your subject is long enough to warrant a book rather than a long article, (2) check the spines of books in local libraries and bookstores as well as resources such as *Books in Print* to determine that your book won't be redundant in the marketplace, (3) justify the need for such a book, (4) determine your primary audience and how to sell to that audience through various avenues such as print and electronic media, speaking engagements, books signings, direct mail, advertising, articles, and other publicity or promotional avenues.

A typical book proposal will include a table of contents, an introduction, a chapter-by-chapter breakdown or short narrative summary of the content to be included within each chapter, information on the potential market for the book, and your interest and authority on the subject as well as your writing credits.

Before you begin work on your proposal, get a copy of *How to Write a Book Proposal* (Writer's Digest Books) by San Francisco author and well-known literary agent Michael Larsen. The book is the most comprehensive and useful guide on the subject and evolved from Larsen's work as a literary agent and consultant guiding authors through the process of writing their book proposals.

Selling Novels with a Synopsis

The synopsis, a powerful sales piece for a novel, must grab an agent's or editor's interest at once. Described as a brief summary of a topic as in an abstract, is presents a prose narrative of your story written in present or past tense. In an industry where thousands of new novels are written each year, it is unrealistic to expect that editors and agents have time to read every manuscript that comes across their desks. In 1990, new fiction titles, including hardcover and paperback, totaled 5,010, according to findings reported in *Publishers Weekly*. On the other hand, a compelling synopsis with sample chapters can be quickly read, and if the material sufficiently entrances them, they will ask for the entire manuscript.

For a 100,000-word novel, the synopsis may typically run between six and fifteen pages, single-spaced. Best-selling author Pamela Jekel (*Sea Star, Columbia, Bayou,* among others) suggests that if the book is a fairly big one with a complex plot, as with a multigenerational saga, a longer synopsis may be required.

A synopsis should include truncated descriptions of the novel's plot points and dramatic situations as well as reveal the identities of your primary characters along with their faults, redeeming qualities, and character growth. The best synopsis, in my opinion, weaves in snippets, if not actual scenes, from the novel itself. If you decide to intersperse your synopsis with actual scenes from your novel (like a love scene or an action scene), prepare the reader with a strong transition and then double space between the present-tense synopsis narrative and the actual scene from the novel. This alerts the reader that a major transition is occurring. Some novelists single space the narrative and double space actual scenes in the synopsis.

Some aspiring novelists may fall into the trap of thinking, "If I don't tell them how the story ends, they'll be so intrigued and want so badly to find out that they'll call me right up and ask me to send the manuscript." The truth, in fact, may be just the opposite. You may alienate or offend the editor or agent by using this tact. If that happens, no one is going to ask to see your manuscript and you've wasted your time, postage, and chances of achieving what you wanted from that person in the first place.

You must reveal your ending in a synopsis. If an agent is going represent your story to publishers and if an editor is going to buy it, both have a right to know how the story ends. Agents and editors are on the author's side—all want a great book worthy of publication. No one is going to buy your story without knowing the ending.

In a synopsis as in a novel, your protagonist must be so alive—so real—that he or she can literally engage the reader in a emotional commitment to join forces for a journey of several hundred pages. Your protagonist must be vital and memorable, more real than real. Readers want to spend time with characters who are fascinating, ones that will lead them into a world they might never otherwise choose to enter.

Avoid stereotypical characters. Humans beings, regardless of their cultural backgrounds and sometimes because of them, are complex creatures. Readers want to identify or sympathize with complex, fully developed characters who are more beautiful or ugly, pure or despicable, noble or sensuous than those they meet every day. Your characters are the most important ingredient in your recipe for story. They will flavor it, spice it up, dish it out, and either satisfy you or make you sick to your stomach, but no story will go anywhere without them.

Putting Sizzle into Your Synopsis

Making your synopsis stand out among all others isn't easy, but there are some techniques you can use to enhance its chances. First, write well. Cut out all passive verbs and replace them with strong, action verbs. Use evocative language that creates the mood and tone of your novel. Open with a bang—seize the reader's attention within the first sentence, if possible, or at least within the first paragraph, and don't let go. Indira Ganesan in her first novel, *The Journey* (Knopf 1990), provides such an opening in her first paragraph.

> The women of her mother's village say that if one twin dies by water, the other will die by fire. Renu's cousin Rajesh died on a train. During the crossing from Madhupur to Chombatore, a storm swelled and rode in from the coast, stripping leaves off drenched branches, tangling long-armed bushes and shrubs, uprooting entire palms. The bridge swung back and forth, the rice paddies flooded, and the train, soot-covered and mud-spattered, trembled its way forward, shuddered, and slipped off the tracks into the water below. Her cousin, the Gogal diving from his pocket, his ugly slippers crushed, must have spun like a Catherine wheel in the air, tumbling, his glasses flying as the train fell. It took two days for the news to reach the family in America, two days for them to untwist his body from that unholy and anonymous death. Renu's mother wept and kept her away from the stove all day.

Ganesan's opening sets the novel's tone and moves us swiftly into the story. Her very first sentence raises a question in the reader's mind. Renu and her cousin are connected like twin souls. He has died by water. Will she die by fire?

Within that opening paragraph there is much symbolism that makes sense as the reader embarks upon the "journey" through the story. The journey, a multilevel one established in the opening (the train on the track, the train off the track, the train below the track in the water), corresponds with inner levels of the conscious, subconscious, and unconscious sojourn of the protagonist as she outwardly journeys to reconnect with her relatives and ancient cultural traditions on Pi, an island in the Bay of Bengal.

Don't spend pages and pages explaining the background of the story in order to get to a place to start your tale. Get right to the *raison d'être*; plunge the reader into the heart of the story and weave in the background piecemeal as the story moves forward. And finally, don't outline a business agenda with the editor or agent in the pages of your synopsis. Save that for your cover letter.

Selling Your Script

My advice is simple. Write the whole thing. The film industry is changing. Gone are the good old days when studios and independent producers were willing to risk fortunes on ideas, high concept or otherwise. Today, a completed script—better still, several completed scripts—serve as your calling card. According to several industry agents, scriptwriters, and producers, a writer won't get a foot in the door without at least one completed script.

Once the screenplay is completed, register it with Writers Guild of America and then try to entice an agent to represent you. If you choose to represent your work yourself, you may first need to request release forms from the studios or production companies where you are sending your script. Releases allow personnel at those companies to read your script without liability, and they help protect companies against nuisance suits filed for ideas or elements claimed stolen from literary properties.

Many professionals believe that in the film industry of the '90s, some of the best opportunities lie in selling book manuscripts, published or unpublished, for adaptation to the screen. Some agents represent manuscripts simultaneously to book publishers and film companies. Others work directly with West Coast agencies that offer literary projects to Hollywood. And in some cases, you can find an agent in Hollywood who will first get an option for film rights and use that to promote your book to publishing houses. But none of these strategies will work for a manuscript that doesn't meet the criteria and quality demanded by producers and others.

Summing Up

By using the tools and techniques outlined in this chapter to sell your writing projects, you will accomplish several things: (1) you save time because you won't be writing an article or book until it is accepted for publication; (2) you may get feedback on your project from an editor or agent before you entirely commit yourself to the writing and that kind of valuable input may allow you to shift direction or focus to make the project more desirable and saleable; and (3) even if don't sell the particular project you're circulating, you may garner the interest of an editor, agent, or producer for other writing projects you're working on or plan to write.

The competition for selling your writing to the publishing and film industries has never been greater. The tools you have to increase your chances for success include finding a niche (targeting a specific cultural or ethnic component, theme, or subject area), acquiring the knowledge (not only about your chosen subject area but about the process of writing), and doing your craft well enough to elicit the attention of a buyer (whether editor or producer).

CHAPTER THREE
Putting Power in Your Prose

Powerful writing, the kind that evokes feelings rather than just informs, fills up readers and satisfies their need to know, to learn, and to grow. It fulfills their heightened sense of expectation. It provides the emotional experience they seek when they willingly suspend their disbelief. People, when they read, consciously choose to become receptive to what the writer has written, to acquire information, to participate in the fictional experience, to be entertained. They want and expect to have their emotions tugged at and touched by a story.

Scriptwriter Bruce Joel Rubin (*Ghost*), in an interview appearing in the May 1991 issue of the *Journal* (magazine of the Writers Guild of America, West), echoed a sentiment felt by many writers when he said he believes that over the next five years, efforts will be made to make movies that appeal to the emotions.

As writers, we have to be in touch with our own emotions and understand how our stories touch us before we'll be able to communicate that to a reader. I believe that powerful writing begins with the writer's understanding of self. A conscious effort to acknowledge, honor, and respect our own passions and obsessions, along with the vision and determination to express those often deeply guarded feelings and urges, is a priori to powerful writing. Writing powerfully is easiest when we first find the points of power within ourselves.

Determination

Miguel de Cervantes, one of Spain's greatest writers, wrote in spite of circumstances that might have broken the spirit and dampened the passions of a lesser writer. Lack of stability (his father, a poor barber/surgeon in search of a community that needed his services, moved the family frequently), the loss of his left hand as a result of a naval battle, his kidnap by pirates (who took him to Algiers as a slave), and his imprisonment twice for tax collection troubles must have fueled Cervantes' determination, for he continued undaunted to write a number of plays, short stories, and his masterpiece *Don Quixote*.

Vision

English poet and artist William Blake, son of simple working folk, used to see angels among the men working in the hay fields. His father, who castigated the youngster for lying, did not realize how vivid and passionately real were the inner creations of the young boy's imagination. Virtually ignored by the literati of his day, Blake nevertheless did not suppress his visionary tendencies and continued to write from his passions. Today he is considered a creative genius, and his poems, prose, and hand-colored engravings constitute a treasured legacy.

The trials of Cervantes illustrate the degree of determination we must have in life, especially in the writing life. Blake, too, had determination. He was determined not to hide or bury his visions, but to honor them through creative expression.

Native American Black Elk said that a man who has had a vision is not able to use the power of it until after he has performed the vision on Earth for people to see. If we pursue our dreams with the determination of a Cervantes and the receptivity and passion of a Blake, we stand a better chance of realizing our dreams than if we make only half-hearted efforts. Through the expression of our visions comes our power.

Hard Work

Paramahansa Yogananda, an Indian yogi, author of *Autobiography of a Yogi* and other works, and founder of the worldwide Self Realization Fellowship, counseled his charges to do some productive work toward their goals every day in order to actualize them. A transient thought or idea for a project won't get it written. Visualizing the project may help, but that isn't the same as using will or determination to hold a powerful inner vision and to "give birth" to your idea by applying psychic energy and sheer physical labor to it every day. In the immortal words of Thomas Edison, "There is no substitute for hard work."

Sometimes when you are working hard to birth a story, elements of it insinuate themselves into your dreams. A dream can reflect the germ of an idea, reveal a plot, or unveil an incident for your narrative.

A dream can point to your story's progress: a lush, fecund garden—healthy, growing, evolving—or a dry, barren landscape—dead, silent, and without movement. A dream can project symbols that obfuscate meaning or reveal mystery.

In the Sufi tradition of ancient Persian culture, dreams were thought to be the place of the unfolding of many mysteries. Some Hindu mystics believe that our lives in the world are nothing more than dreams from which we will awaken at some point with full knowledge of the mysteries of the universe. As writers, we can discover guidance for our stories in our dreams and even "seed" them for helpful information. Seeding simply means to make a suggestion to yourself, just before you go to sleep, that you will dream about something specific: the solution to a problem, greater understanding of the meaning of a previous dream, or validation that you are on track with a relationship, your novel, or anything else you wish to gain knowledge about.

It has been said that we can deceive ourselves all we want when we are awake, but dreams won't lie. We can learn to become attuned and attentive to the sounds and images of our dreams and from the "deep places" inside ourselves. Like writing, it just takes practice.

Inner Power

If you don't yet have a sense of a story, just fragments, find ways to prime the pump. Start with the fragment, begin writing, and see where it leads. Write from inspiration derived from reading the works of others. For example, if you're passionate about the poetry of Mirabai, a 15th century Indian mystic, do what Robert Bly did. He wrote *Mirabai Versions* (Red Ozier Press), a collection of poems that closely resemble the lyricism and evocative language of Mirabai's poetry, which was inspired by her passionate love for God.

It's often easier to be passionate about other people's writing, and less so when it's our own. A lack of confidence, a weak will, and the negative dialogue of the Inner Critic can easily sabotage our work. We need to believe in our stories and have confidence that no one else can hold the vision for them but us. We must follow our passion and write the stories that matter most to us.

Mythologist Joseph Campbell said that if you follow your passion, doors will open that you didn't know existed. Jung, who was fascinated throughout his life with the unknown, said that we must never underestimate the feeling of satisfaction derived from seeking and finding. This seeking and finding, like inner urging and outward expression, runs like a recurring theme through the writer's life.

The inner drive to express ideas is something all creative people experience. Bengali writer and Nobel Laureate Rabindranath Tagore wrote philosophically in *Thought Relics* that the great impulse in humanity is the quest of the unattained, and that impulse in response to the quest brings forth all humankind's best creations. Latin America's foremost living poet, Octavio Paz, said in his acceptance speech for the Nobel Prize in Literature that when he began writing poems, he didn't know why he wrote them, only that he was driven by an inner need to do it.

Your first attempts may be a far cry from poetic genius, but later on, when you've matured as a writer and learned the craft as well as the art, you may discover in your early material a kind of raw power that needs only a little refining. Yet, if you never write these early pieces, you won't have this power to work with later on.

Power from the Places of Darkness

I believe the power and passion of writing originate in the deep places within the writer's heart and psyche and are then propelled into expression by the strength of those passions and the elements and circumstances of life that allow them to spring forth. We may aspire to write from places of light, happiness, and well-being, but often it is from the dark places of fear and unknowing within us that we write most powerfully. Who, among us, hasn't harbored some deep, dark secret? Tried to shrink from our fears? Hidden our insecurities? Avoided confronting the undesirable parts of ourselves?

Most of us learn early on that not everyone sees the world in exactly the same way as we do. To a child, that can be frightening. In fact, it can be the source for what Hal Zina Bennett, Ph.D., and Susan J. Sparrow, authors of *Follow Your Bliss*, call the "essential wound." The authors noted in their book that essential wounds are universal elements of human experience. They come about when our own perceptions lead us into experiences that bring us great pain or cause others we care about to suffer. Thereafter we may question the trustworthiness of not only our perceptions, but ourselves. The memories of these wounds become the source of fear, guilt, self-blame, and even hatred that hover like great shadows over our lives until we heal them.

Remember the story of *The Velveteen Rabbit*? When the little boy becomes ill and his clothing and linens must be burned to keep from reinfecting him, the stuffed rabbit he loves must also be destroyed. The boy sees the rabbit as an object of delight and pleasure, but the adults around him see it as dangerous. They destroy it in a bonfire along with the bedding.

Now suppose that the rabbit were real and had to be destroyed. The boy's despair and pain of loss would be no less great than if he'd lost his best friend. He might grow up always wanting to work with animals, particularly rabbits, but with a sense of dread and doom in his otherwise bright and hopeful dream. Though he might not know why consciously, that feeling of dread could hold him back from pursuing a career with animals. Locked away in a dark place where he'd never have to look at it would lie his essential wound. If one day he were brave enough to explore that wound, he would discover the potential for healing and the power to finally claim and fulfill his dream.

Inner exploration and discovery of our psychological and emotional scars and wounds, regardless of our cultural backgrounds, is empowering on many inner and outer levels. By taking the power hidden in darkness and bringing illumination to it, we enrich our writing through our self-discovery and knowledge.

In another way, we sense the power of darkness in the villains of our stories. While we identify with the hero or heroine, it is nonetheless true that without a worthy adversary pitted against the protagonist, it is doubtful we would want to read the hero's or heroine's story.

These two character types—the monstrous villain who symbolizes the force of evil or the unknown and who lurks around in darkness waiting to do battle with the "good guy," and the "good guy" or warrior who conquers the villain—are universal archetypes. They are found in stories from all cultures. They symbolize inner demons and the warriors within our own selves. As such, they are powerful sources we can tap in our writing.

The Universal and Eternal

Librarian Betsy Levins notes that "novels about Native Americans have wide appeal." *Library Journal* featured her column in its June 1991 issue focusing on overlooked, yet outstanding books referred to as "sleepers." These books have achieved some recognition through the power of word of mouth. Among the featured "sleepers" were *The Indian Lawyer* (Norton) by James Welch, the tale of attorney Sylvester Yellow Calf and his conflict over being trapped between the white establishment (he has political ambitions) and the Blackfeet Reservation. The unexpected success of a "sleeper" like *The Indian Lawyer* may lie in its universality, even though on the surface it is the tale of an Indian. A story that touches readers so deeply that they tell fellow readers who, also touched, tell others, creates its own chain reaction. These readers may not be Native Americans themselves, but something universal within the story "speaks to them" even so.

Stories may be narrowly focused on a specific culture, yet can have elements that lift them into the universal realm. And how much more powerful they are when that happens. Madeleine L'Engle, in her book *Walking On Water, Reflections on Faith and Art* (Harold Shaw Publishers), noted the importance of writing to communicate with as many people as possible. She pointed out that immediately after an author's death, there is a period of "eclipse of his work." She goes on to say that if this work reflects only his or her own culture, the work will live on only in that culture. However, if the work of that author "reflects the eternal and universal," it will endure.

The Energy of the Sacred

"Being in the flow" is an expression I've heard writers use when talking about particular instances when their writing seemed to flow effortlessly from mind to page. The flow typifies peak creative experience. Some refer to this experience as emanating from God or from the Creative Fire, Force of the Universe, Great Spirit, or Divine Mind. By surrendering to this force that we sense is far greater than we are, we may find ourselves "being in the flow." We relinquish the control of the Inner Critic and move outside of ourselves. When we experience the intensity of this state, we forget time and place and are wholly immersed in the energy of creation.

Stories written from such creative energy often need meticulous editing. Others may seem to spring forth nearly perfect. But nearly always, they will communicate our passion and interpretation more compellingly to readers. Stories that address ethnic issues with this level of feeling can lead readers toward a greater understanding of the human issues involved. The ethnic themes of these stories lend added power and levels of meaning to the relationships among people. The sources for these themes and stories are many.

The Power of Love and Hate in Interracial Stories

Depending upon the social perceptions and cultural taboos or prejudices involved, a precious few moments of passion shared by interracial lovers in a forbidden liaison can contain the seeds of hate, love, passion, shame, guilt, religious experience, and cultural or interracial conflict. Forbidden love that transcends cultural boundaries is so filled with power, so explosive, that it is often an essential ingredient of blockbuster novels and miniseries. *Shogun, Noble House*, and *Tanamera—Lion of Singapore*, a miniseries televised in 1991, features just this type of situation. In *Tanamera*, Johnny Dexter and Julie Soong are lovers whose British and Chinese families, respectively, are two of the most powerful in colonial Singapore in 1935. Johnny and Julie fall in love and strive to find a way to become man and wife in spite of family rules forbidding their liaison, separation by war, and connivances of Keow Tak, a villainous communist leader who hates Johnny with as much passion as he loves Julie.

Heat and Dust, a film from Merchant Ivory Productions based on a novel by Ruth Prawer Jhabvala, features a love affair between the beautiful wife of an Englishman (in the service of the Crown in India) prior to India's independence and a nawab (Muslim prince), who has a lot of time, money, and interest in pursuing her. Their passionate liaison breeds more than the seeds of discord within their families. She abandons her marriage, deals with the consequences of a primitive abortion, and forsakes everything for him while he struggles with his past, his mother's prejudices, and India's societal and cultural taboos. In an interesting twist, the niece of the English woman travels to India many years later to discover for herself the exploits of her rebellious aunt and ends up repeating the cycle.

Another recent example of the power of interracial love is Spike Lee's *Jungle Fever*. Striving to establish "that black-Italian thing" by juxtaposing elements of the neighborhoods of Bensonhurst (where Yusef Hawkins was murdered in 1990) and Harlem, Lee has the two interracial lovers struggling against family bonds and ties to friends. The film also deals with the issue of how drugs destroy families, and it explores racial myths and stereotyping.

In none of these stories are the characters named Montague and Capulet, but they illustrate a cultural variation on Shakespeare's *Romeo and Juliet*. The ancient drama with its universal themes still works. And with ethnic updating, it continues to pack quite a punch.

Powerful Stories of the Refugee or Immigrant Experience

Refugees as opposed to immigrants, by the very nature of definition, are people who flee one country for asylum or refuge in another. Often the choice to flee is made hastily because of the threat of danger. The consequences may involve the risk of bodily harm or death in the escape attempt, the loss of finances, the loss of relatives and friends, and the severe pain of separation from one's homeland. These experiences affect the adjustment of a refugee's life in the new chosen country.

Individuals from Cambodia, Laos, Vietnam, Haiti, Nicaragua, Cuba, and other countries of origin share in the refugee or immigrant resettlement experience, which often spans generations. There is a wealth of material to be found in the experiences of these peoples. Salman Rushdie, author of *Satanic Verses*, says in his latest work *Imaginary Homelands*, that his books are "written from the very experience of uprooting, disjuncture, and metamorphosis that is the migrant condition." Rushdie points out that Indian writers living abroad are able to write from a dual perspective because they are both insiders and outsiders in their own society.

The emotions inherent in the refugee or immigrant experience are often reflected in segments of America's subcultures and in many Third World cultures, where life is an uphill battle to eke out a daily existence. Often the privileged life of fortune and power belongs to the elite few, while the rest suffer in poverty. Passions run high. Poverty breeds frustration, anger, and often violence. A writer from those cultures or that substrata of American life can write from those passions, but an outsider will have to capture the passion and honesty by claiming the story emotionally, intellectually, and with every fiber of his or her being.

I once asked my father-in-law, the child of Russian and Austrian Jewish immigrants, to tell me the story of his adventures as a crew member aboard the *Exodus*. From his recruitment by the Haganah on the streets of Brooklyn to the running of the British blockade of Palestine onboard the *Exodus*, a.k.a. *The President Warfield*, his story, I knew, would be interesting. I thought I'd turn it into a quick sale.

What I didn't realize was that while listening to his story, I would find myself choking up with tears more than once, all the while developing a heightened sense of respect and admiration for him, the crew, and the 4,500 Jews from displaced persons camps in Europe who were seeking a Jewish homeland. I realized that for him, the experience must have shaped his life.

That story isn't the kind one writes for a quick sale. It will be written as powerfully as I am able to do it, as powerfully as he told it, with all the emotion and honesty. In essence, this is what we as writers must do with the immigrant or refugee story—make it our own: claim it with our hearts and minds and souls, then write it with respect and a commitment to preserve its integrity.

The Power of Language

For centuries in India, spiritual aspirants have been given mantras to recite in daily devotions and anusthans (spiritual practices toward a specific goal). The mantras contain a secret bija (seed sound and image) that confers its hidden powers on the aspirant once the aspirant unlocks the power through meditation and subsequent realization. At first, however, the seeker may be only subtly aware of the power of the mantra.

In a way, the tone, timbre, style, and language we as writers choose in which to express our stories are like mantras, imparting a secret power to our writing. You can sense that kind of power beneath the language of Chicana poet Lorna Dee Cervantes, *From the Cables of Genocide: Poems of Love and Hunger*; in the essays of Afro-American essayist and novelist James Baldwin, *Go Tell It on the Mountain* and *The Fire Next Time*; and through the writings of Polish-born Issac Bashevis Singer, whose work dealt with the issues of European Jews adjusting to life in America. Their writing resonates with cultural insight and honesty and, above all, entices the reader to participate in a highly charged, potentially transformative experience.

Passion's Power in Story

Passion reflects a deep, overwhelming feeling of emotion: love, hatred, anger, greed. Passion calls forth physical and mental resources we may not know we have. Passion can drive a writer to create, just as it drives conflict in story. Whether it's a biblical tale, an Indian ballad, a Greek myth, or a modern work of fiction, passion will set the stage for conflict.

Remember Esau, first-born son of Issac and grandson of Abraham, who thoughtlessly traded his father's fortune and all the blessings God had promised Abraham to his twin brother Jacob for a bowl of lentils? At first Esau lamented and begged Jacob to let him out of the promise. When Jacob refused, Esau's sadness turned to anger and then to rage, with disastrous consequences.

Sadness, outrage, and betrayal are what the Greek goddess Demeter felt upon learning that her daughter Persephone had been abducted, raped, and taken to the underworld by Hades to be his unwilling bride.

Forbidden love between India's rebel poet priest Chandidas, a high-caste Brahmin, and the low-born washer maid Rami in the mediaeval Bengali village of Nannur resulted in violence, yet provided the basis for a legacy of great love poems and gave birth to the Indian Sahaja movement—the worship of love-making as a path to union with God.

In the novel *Dr. Zhivago*, by Russian author Boris Pasternak, the passions of love and lust drive the conflict within Yurii Andreievich Zhivago as he is torn between his need to support and protect his wife and children in war-torn Russia and his desire to act on his passion for nurse Lara Antipova, whom he loves beyond reason.

No passion, no conflict. The universality of passion and conflict increases the marketability of a story and its chances to endure. For such stories, great writers draw upon life. By studying the tales from many different communities of the world, we'll find interesting and varied stories that tell of universal human experience.

The Transforming Power of Writing

When driven by passion into conflict, characters within stories emerge on the other side of the "fire" in some way transformed. I believe that we who write such stories are also transformed. This transformation means growth. As a knowledgeable soul somewhere once said, to some degree you become what you write. Indeed, writing can be a transformative endeavor if you honor the inner urging to explore the unknown, to travel the path outward from the self in order to turn inward to the deep places within, or vice versa.

When you are writing from your passions, as Madeleine L'Engle observed in *Walking on Water, Reflections on Faith and Art*, your heart and mind stop fighting and are united in the creative process. It's as though two lovers are yoked in the same harness, pulling together. With heart and mind united, you write from a place of exalted creativity.

Alice Walker, author of *The Color Purple* and *Her Blue Body Everything We Know* (Harcourt Brace Jovanovich), shares with her readers that she would have been a suicide victim by the age of 30 had she not been saved by poetry. Her admission speaks profoundly for the transformative power of writing.

Our challenge as writers is to acknowledge rather than to bury our passions and obsessions. By being a willing participant in the transformative process in life and in our stories, we dare to go beyond the information provided. We learn to dream and fantasize. We throw off preconceived notions about the limits of our capacity to create, and we learn how to utilize to the fullest our imagination, our intellect, our experience, and our senses to participate in the creative process. We persevere in our endeavors, embrace the idea that our stories are our most sacred gifts, and risk exposing the most personal sides of ourselves in order to look into cultural mirrors and see reflected there parts of ourselves, not all of them attractive. Through it all, we become empowered as creators—of art, of emotion, of change.

CHAPTER FOUR
Writing Short, Ethnic-Oriented Nonfiction

People of many ancient civilizations, including the Babylonians, Greeks, Chinese, and Egyptians, believed that writing was a glorious and valuable gift from their gods. They discovered that through writing they could record information, pass it on, and acquire and expand knowledge. Writers have been doing that ever since.

Today, those of us who write nonfiction have a variety of formats in which to work—book reviews, first-person essays and op-ed pieces, how-to articles, profiles, inspirational/religious essays, well-researched pieces on specific topics that aim to educate and inform, question and answer interviews, and travel articles.

Many magazines and newspapers accept work from freelance writers. Magazines often have regular columns, departments, and sections open to freelancers. The special sections (food, travel, home and garden, book review section, etc.) are often the easiest places for freelancers to break in with newspaper sales. Consider also the Sunday magazines that most metropolitan newspapers publish for inclusion in their hefty Sunday editions.

Newsletters of organizations, associations, and corporations need material, too. Explore the possibility that ethnicity represents a hot topic within the corporate environment, especially in its relevance to corporate culture, management, and ethics issues as well as the selling of American products to Asian and Eastern European countries in the global market.

Professional resources for cross-cultural counseling in the fields of psychotherapy and social services are also more in demand today than ever before. With the numbers of immigrants and their children in the United States swelling, the need for therapists who can work with individuals and families of varying ethnic origins is increasing. Newsletters in these fields, as well as in the areas of education and health care, represent fertile territory for articles targeting ethnicity as it pertains to these subject areas and issues.

Each type of nonfiction article can incorporate ethnic research, cultural elements, or contemporary issues on a variety of topics to impart information to a targeted ethnic group or readership. The following constitutes a brief description of the various article forms.

Book Reviews

Reviewing ethnic books or books with strong ethnic components is a good way to begin building a portfolio of work with ethnic tie-ins. You won't get rich reviewing books (one reviewer told me she would have to review over 200 books a year just to scrape by). Pay varies from no monetary compensation (though usually you get to keep the book) to $100 and up. Longer reviews tend to command more money, and established writers can sometimes negotiate for higher rates. Most of the ethnic publications for which I've written pay in the $35 to $100 range.

Because I've stated in my query letters and author bio that I'm a freelance writer and reviewer interested in Indian history, religion, and culture, those types of books are sent to me by publishers and editors. I also request these kinds of books whenever I see pre-publication announcements or reviews in *Publishers Weekly*, *Kirkus*, or *Library Journal*.

When you see a book announced and it's one you'd like to review, you can begin querying editors of publications that target specific ethnic readerships. In your query, indicate any information you have on the book, including the publication date, which may be several months away. Discuss with the editor how you will get the book—will the editor request it or will you? If you are to request it, contact the publicity department of the publishing house and say that you've been assigned a review of the book. Ask that the book be sent as soon as it is available, along with any supporting publicity materials. Offer to send a tear sheet of the published review when it is available. Always deliver what you have promised, and do it in a timely manner.

Book reviews are a kind of consumer product report to potential book buyers to help them decide which books to buy or not buy. The reviews should be fair, honest, and interesting. They should not be book reports, puff pieces, or vendettas. If you feel passionately about the subject and the author's treatment of it, that information is certainly appropriate in the review. In fact, one editor told me he looks for the reviewer's passion in the book reviews he assigns.

If the publication you're writing for targets a specific audience, remember to include information on the ethnic elements of the book as well as its author's cultural background and/or interests. A good way to prime the pump before beginning to write book reviews is to read them regularly in newspapers and magazines. *Book Review Digest*, found in the reference section of the public library, lists encapsulated reviews from the various media where reviews of a particular book have appeared. These one- to two-sentence summaries allow you to see what reviewers thought was important about the book. Look up the reviews for any book under the book author's name.

For some newspapers and ethnic publications, faxed queries are acceptable. Information about two forthcoming books that I faxed in a query to the editor of a West Coast Indo-American newspaper resulted in an immediate assignment for a review of *Net of Magic, Wonders and Deceptions in India* (University of Chicago Press, 1991) by Lee Siegel, professor of religion at the University of Hawaii. Consult the periodical section in Part Two of this book for information on how to contact specific editors.

Opinion Pieces

One of the easiest articles to write involves stating your view about some issue and then supporting your view with anecdotes from your personal experiences and/or those of others. Issues, mundane to controversial, can be examined and written about. From within your own ethnic community, find a subject area that you feel strongly about, establish your position on it (are you for or against it), and support your argument with specific examples and anecdotes.

These pieces can be sold to newspapers or magazines as first-person essays or op-eds, short for "opposite the editorial page." Most publications for ethnic communities and many major national magazines have columns or pages devoted to airing the opinions of readers.

Letters to the Editor

These pieces are usually your response to a specific article you've read in newspapers or magazines. They don't actually qualify as articles, but they do constitute publication clips and can be important if you're trying to acquire publication credits. One of my own such experiences revolved around the passing of one of India's well-known freedom fighters, which was noted on the religion page of my local newspaper. I took exception to the article's statement that this man's death meant that the last of India's great freedom fighters was gone.

In fact, I knew of several who were still alive and might even be offended by such a statement. I offered my view in a letter that the editors accepted and published.

The trick to writing a letter to the editor is to keep it succinct, well-written, to the point, and short. Editors almost always publish a statement at the end of the letters section noting that long letters may be edited for space considerations. You can increase your chances at getting published if you keep the pieces short and to the point. You must also mention the author's name, the title, and the date of the article you are responding to.

How-To Articles

Everyone has knowledge about how to create or do something. You may know how to make piñatas used in festival celebrations in certain Latin America countries, or you may be adept at performing certain Middle Eastern dances. You may understand the intricacies of cooking authentic Gujarati vegetarian meals or have mastered the art of Chinese brush painting. The how-to article draws on personal experience to teach someone else how to perform a new skill, technique, or activity.

How-to articles usually follow sequential steps from start to finish, each step building upon the preceding step. There are many different variations on the how-to theme and several ways to write the how-to piece. Helene Schellenberg Barnhart in her book *How to Write and Sell the 8 Easiest Article Types* (Writer's Digest Books) lists three: how to make and do, psychological self-help, and informational. This and other guides for writing nonfiction can provide help for crafting how-to articles.

Profile Pieces

Most local community newspapers and some major metropolitan dailies have sections devoted to profiles of citizens and leaders of the community. A profile is not the whole life story of an individual, but rather a noteworthy or interesting portion (profile) of his or her life. For example, pieces that explore interesting aspects of the life of a Native American Indian lawyer, a Hispanic activist, a Portuguese politician, a Chinese businessman, or a Filipino educator will be marketable to the respective ethnic community newspapers and perhaps to your own. Community magazines, especially those catering to the interests of a particular cultural group in your community or country, are typically good markets for appropriate profile pieces.

Celebrity profiles are always marketable, provided they offer a new perspective, a fresh slant, or new information. Like all types of profiles, they require research and interviews—and often a picture or two. However, setting up an interview with a celebrity (whether author, musician, artist, or performer) can sometimes require considerable time, several long distance phone calls, and a great amount of diplomacy, perseverance, and patience. As an editor, I spent three weeks arranging a Linda Rondstadt interview that nearly didn't happen. Communication between her agents and my client proved ineffective, and it took a third party to finally pull the arrangements together. When the piece finally ran, it provided insights into how the singer's ancestral traditions and cultural roots have influenced her and her music.

Inspirational, Religious, and Theological Articles

Some writers lump inspirational and religious articles together, and some consider them very different article types. We'll explore both here in the context of ethnicity.

The inspirational piece is often an uplifting story about the triumph of good over evil, positive over negative. It will always tug at the heart and point to a higher power beyond human effort that is silently helping the protagonist overcome his or her seemingly insurmountable problem(s) in life. Inspirational pieces do not have to mention God or prayer as elements of the solution. The spirituality and faith inherent in the experience can shine through in words that communicate an understanding of the human condition. The hope and courage the reader gains from reading the inspirational story is the payoff for reading—and writing—the article. You should, however, avoid dramatizing your own spirituality. Self-aggrandizement in any form turns off both editors and readers.

The religious article focuses on the power of God to offer solutions to problems. It often emphasizes some tenet of the religion that is the basis of the article. In this type of piece, it is not only acceptable, but advisable to include religious scriptural quotes, examples, or passages.

Theological articles are often written by (but not limited to) theologians and scholars. These types of articles must be factual, logical, and accurate. Subject matter is as diverse and opulent as the many and diverse sacred texts of the religions of the world, but payment is often nominal.

A good reference book for writers interested in inspirational or religious writing is *Writing to Inspire, A Guide to Writing and Publishing for the Expanding Religious Market* (Writer's Digest Books) by William Gentz, Lee Roddy, et al.

Round-up Pieces

In this type of article, the writer focuses on a specific topic and then "rounds up" a number of different quotes, opinions, or anecdotes on the subject. For example, the subject might be a single question such as, "What special traditions prevail in your home during the celebration of Chanukah?"—or any holiday or festival celebrated in a particular religion. Another question might be, "What special celebrations take place around the birth of a baby in your culture?"

The second step in writing this type of article is to make a list of all those individuals you wish to interview. You can either call them or send a self-addressed card on which they can write their responses. After the cards are returned, you can craft your round-up piece. A general interest piece targeting writers might ask, "What was your first published piece and where did it appear?" To give an article an ethnic focus, you might target Chinese-American authors or Hispanic authors. By selecting different quotes from authors who come from a wide variety of ethnic backgrounds, you can craft an article that might sell to publications targeting both a general audience and the Chinese-American or Hispanic community.

Researched, Informational Articles

I find these articles the most interesting and the most time-consuming to do. The research involved in crafting a quality article can add greatly to the time investment required. While the pay from major magazines often reflects this larger time investment, that is often not the case for smaller ethnic publications. However, if your subject is one you have already researched in another context, you should find that the additional time needed to collect information specific to your article will be more easily managed.

This type of article can be found in almost every type of newspaper and magazine—from general interest to specific trade magazines dealing with narrowly defined subject areas for specific audiences. The word length may vary greatly from publication to publication, but the purpose is always to increase the reader's understanding of a particular subject. The article must have a strong lead or hook, the main body of information, and a conclusion. It will answer the standard reporter's questions of who, what, when, where, why, and how.

You may be expected to include in the article appropriate research data and quotes from experts in the field. Always request the publication's writer's guidelines before undertaking this type of article so that you'll know exactly what to include before you begin.

An example of an ethnic-oriented piece that might fit this type of article form would be an article on cross-cultural marriages. The article might explore issues inherent in marriages that bridge two cultures. Or it could explore the issues faced by mixed-race children. It could explore the problems arising in the home, in the community, in the schools, or in religious institutions. You might look at religion in a home where one spouse practices one religion and the other practices a different religion. In which faith are the children being raised? What problems might result? You could interview psychologists, religious clerics, and couples from different cultural backgrounds or races. Statistics from the U. S. Census Bureau or from other sources can lend credibility to the piece once the slant is determined.

Question and Answer Interviews

The success of an interview article will depend a great deal on the specific questions you ask and how you ask them, the interviewee's responses, and the overall focus of the interview. The magazine or newspaper editor may give you a few questions to ask, but it is up to you to follow through on new or interesting issues that may surface from those questions.

For a celebrity interview, read numerous interviews and articles on that individual before you proceed to set up your own. Then read up on the cultural background of the individual. By doing your "homework" in this way, you will (1) come across as someone who is both prepared and professional; (2) be in a better position to find new subject areas to explore with the interviewee because you won't be asking redundant questions or questions that have no bearing; (3) be able to use the time more productively, focusing on one or two new areas; and (4) find the interview process less intimidating. When you appear knowledgeable about the interviewee's life and accomplishments, the interviewee, in turn, will see that you've invested time and energy in your work. That alone will often ensure having him or her give you more consideration and cooperation than someone who comes in with a long list of questions that have all been asked before.

Many interview pieces open with a set-up (a touch of background information that establishes the direction of the piece) and occasionally with information about the interviewer.

Travel Articles

Travel articles are fairly easy to research and write provided you write them in accordance with the guidelines of the publication buying them. If it's for a newspaper, ascertain the article's appropriateness for an upcoming issue. Newspapers frequently create a yearly theme list of the travel subjects they plan to buy for each issue. The paper's schedule might be something like this: June—exploring California; July—Orient and South Pacific; August—Alaska; etc. Write and request any information or guidelines available.

Often newspaper travel editors will prefer the complete manuscript to a query, at least until they get to know you and your writing. Multiple submissions to newspapers are acceptable as long as the papers' circulation areas do not overlap. Veteran travel writer Elaine O'Gara notes in her book *Travel Writer's Markets* (Winterbourne Press) that some writers use a hundred miles as a general rule of thumb for judging circulation distance. They won't submit to two papers within a hundred miles of each other.

For travel article ideas, you might start by looking at day trips to locales in your area. Try tailoring your piece for parents of small children and selling it to a different market—parenting magazines. Then tailor it toward an ethnic group and place it with a periodical targeting that ethnic audience.

Within the field of travel writing there are a number of different types of articles. The most common are the destination piece, the round-up piece, the unique angle piece, the historical piece, and the piece that focuses on a locale currently in the news.

In-flight magazines such as *Latitudes South*, a bimonthly publication tucked into the seat pockets of American Eagle flights serving Miami and San Juan, Puerto Rico, publishes destination articles, particularly Florida destination pieces that include history and culture. The publication's editor does not want the pieces to be rehashes of guidebook material.

India Currents magazine, a monthly publication based in San Jose, California, offers its readers travel articles from writers who've returned from trips to India. The pieces incorporate the perspective of the writer based on firsthand experiences. Ethnic elements such as Indian history, culture, religion, architecture, art, music, food, politics, health, and transportation often figure in the material.

Poetry

Publishers (that we surveyed) who accept poetry with multicultural themes, issues, and elements are listed in the back of this book. There are many literary magazines affiliated and subsidized by universities in America that accept poetry. Independent small presses that publish either magazines, newspapers, newsletters, or chapbooks are often good markets as well. Writers of poetry may find it helpful to peruse a copy of *The Poet's Handbook* (Writer's Digest Books) by Judson Jerome.

CHAPTER FIVE
Ethnicity in Film

Writing for film is unlike any other writing. It's an exacting form that demands control and focus. Script structure is much more confining than a novel. It plays to only two of our five senses: hearing and sight. According to the late Niven Busch (*The Postman Always Rings Twice*, among others), the screenwriter turns his soul into an eye, "borrowing for a time the relentless optic nerve of the camera," which can only record what it sees and nothing more.

While there are many excellent books on writing scripts for TV and feature film—books with extensive information on plot, characterization, dialogue, climax, the acts, scenes, hooks, beginnings and endings, etc.—there are far fewer books on marketing scripts. To my knowledge, no one has yet written a book telling writers how to write and market ethnic-oriented material for the film industry. The assumption has been that a great story is a great story, whether it contains ethnic elements or not, and if it's a great story, everyone will want it.

The truth is, however, that a growing portion of the audience for films and of the actors and actresses who perform in them is made up of people of various ethnic groups and backgrounds. These individuals want to see stories coming out of Hollywood that speak to their own lives and issues and to the realities they face every day. They want to play roles that transcend the stereotypes of black drug dealer or street bum, illiterate Mexican field hand, or savage American Indian warrior. Physically limited individuals also hope for stories or acting opportunities that help them transcend their limitations through stories and roles that make them contributors to the general human condition. Traditional films directed at mainstream America, while still valuable, can no longer fulfill the desires of the entire acting and viewing public. New directions are appearing and proving their value.

The Growing Force of Ethnicity in Film

For years, mainstream Hollywood has relied upon a tradition of films that target a general market. Sometimes these films have cast Afro-Americans, Hispanics, or Americans from ethnic origins other than white Anglo-Saxon in roles that drive certain aspects of the story. However, seldom has the industry set out to make a film that singles out a particular ethnic group. According to Charles Slocum, director of industry analysis for the Writers Guild of America, West, "Ethnic films aimed at the ethnic market kind of go against the grain of what Hollywood is there to do—to make movies with broad appeal." On the other hand, he also indicated that the work of black filmmakers on black subjects reflected one angle on ethnicity in film. He said, "There are producers who believe scripts with ethnic themes or ethnic characters should be made, that those communities should be put in films and shown on the screen. There's a growing sensitivity to that."

The unprecedented offering of Afro-American films from young minority filmmakers in 1991—John Singleton (*Boyz N the Hood*), Matty Rich (*Straight Out of Brooklyn*), Spike Lee (*Jungle Fever*), Joseph Vasquez (*Hangin' with the Homeboys*), and others—may signal a new era in filmmaking where the offerings will focus on ethnic issues, elements, and themes. In *Boyz N the Hood*, for example, the overriding theme was the role family and friends played in helping young Afro-Americans survive in an urban world of violence, drugs, and gangs. Filmmaker John Singleton, whose next writing and directing project was *Poetic Justice*, to be shot in Oakland and Los Angeles, opened *Boyz N the Hood* with the grim statistic that one in every 21 black males will be murdered before he is 25 and that most will die at the hands of other black men. The filmmaker offered solutions, both simplistic and realistic: Don't make babies and abandon them; be responsible for yourself.

Yet no one community holds the monopoly on violence, drugs, and gangs. So while *Boyz N the Hood*, for example, is considered a "black" film dealing with the role family and friends play in helping young Afro-Americans survive, its theme is truly a universal one applicable to many cultures of the world. Universality lifts a story from a specific, narrowly targeted community of viewers to a more mainstream audience. Conflict that erupts in violence is something that most communities can relate to.

Yet on-screen violence that in some way seems to trigger off-screen violence may jeopardize the making of certain kinds of films. Peter Dekom, an entertainment lawyer whose Los Angeles law firm represents black filmmakers, suggested that violence at theaters or as a result of viewers seeing certain films may make it more difficult to persuade studios to make movies about inner city life.

On the other hand, the so-called black films released over the summer of 1991 made money, and making money is what the Hollywood film industry is all about. According to the *San Francisco Chronicle* (August 29, 1991), "*Boyz N the Hood* is on its way to becoming the most acclaimed, highest-grossing black genre film ever made." That these films can make money challenges the prevailing notions that films with strong ethnic elements won't play well across middle America, that theater turn-out is destined to be low for such films, and that casting the film with non-Caucasian actors and actresses in starring as well as supporting roles is a mistake that ultimately affects the bottom line.

Larry Fishburne, star of *Boyz N the Hood*, pointed out in an interview that ran in the *San Jose Mercury News* (July 17, 1991) that "black sells right now." He also expressed hope that "some people will be smart enough to make more films like this one [*Boyz N the Hood*], films that are more than an excuse to put a rapper in a movie."

Independent Afro-American filmmakers aspiring to bring about change through their films are making a conscious choice to deal with issues on screen—issues such as changing the context of how Afro-Americans define themselves, dispelling gender biases and myths within and outside their race, or breaking down the barriers of invisibility and discrimination that exist for ethnic men and women in a "white world." Sometimes there just aren't any answers, but according to Slocum, "The tremendous strength in a film like *Do the Right Thing* is its challenge to the audience to think. In that film there's no exactly right answer," he said.

While the issues depicted in many of these films may be viewed by some as cultural, others see them as universal concerns that we all have. Universality of theme or universal elements in a story can make it appealing to a wider audience. In addition, the universal appeal of a story can lift it out of mediocrity to higher levels of recognition.

Filmmakers like Luis Valdez (*La Bamba, Zoot Suit*, and an adaptation of *Corridos! Tales of Passion and Revolution*), Keith Merrill (*Windwalker*), Spike Lee (five feature films including *Do the Right Thing, Jungle Fever*, and the forthcoming *Malcolm X*), William Morse (*House Made of Dawn*), Robert Redford (*Milagro Bean Field Wars*), and Kevin Costner (*Dances with Wolves*) all chose not to diminish or devalue the ethnic elements in their projects. Had any one of them looked upon the ethnic and cultural elements of their film stories as impediments, those stories might never have been produced, and America would be the poorer.

Greater Recognition for Ethnic Films

At least two films dealing with cultural stories won major film awards in 1991. The Academy Award for best foreign language film was given to *Journey of Hope*, a story about a Turkish family and their harrowing journey over the Swiss Alps in search of a better life. The winner of the 1991 Sundance Award (sponsored by Sundance Institute) honored *Daughters of the Dust*. The story, set in 1902 on remote islands off the coast of South Carolina and Georgia, focused on the women of the Peazant family. Their ancient lineage to Ibo Landing ancestors and the legend that the ancestors, refusing to live in slavery, walked on the water in an attempt to return to Africa provided a theme that addressed the difficulty of holding on to ancient African traditions in the face of a people's need for a better life. The film was featured in Oakland, California's Black Filmworks Festival early in 1991, along with Charles Burnett's *Killer of Sheep* (honored by the Library of Congress) and several other films.

Hollywood Reporter and other newspapers and trade magazines have noted more multicultural films in the offing from Hollywood, among them, the life story of the legendary Mexican artist Frida Kahlo. The project will be brought to the big screen by New Line Cinema and producers Donald Zuckerman and Eduardo Russoff. Writer and director is Luis Valdez, co-writing the script with his wife Lupe. Another film, *Blood In . . . Blood Out*, the story of three Latino youths from East Los Angeles, was scheduled for production in 1991. Jimmy Santiago Baca, who taught himself to read and write while in prison and is now the author of six books of poetry, co-wrote this script.

Beyond the confines of Hollywood are many independent film-makers—people like Northern California's Gary Soto, poet and writer of stories and novels for young Chicanos. Soto plans to do educational films like *The Bike* (his new short subject film) because he believes there is a need for bilingual films for Mexican children to help them feel that their stories are just as important as everyone else's.

In network television, TV movies or miniseries are often targeted by scriptwriters as markets for stories with ethnic components. Carrie Stein, vice president of development for Cosgrove-Meurer Productions, said, "In TV movies today, a variety of stories are being explored, and I think ethnicity can be one element of these stories." She pointed out that the Afro-American and Hispanic communities represent a large market. "An unusual ethnic element, in and of itself, does not make a story interesting. Ethnicity should be explored as a backdrop for a bigger story."

Charles Slocum said that he expects black ethnic components to be integrated into mainstream entertainment much more quickly than Spanish, Asian, and other ethnic groups. "Spike Lee's films have a black attitude. That's going to keep some of the white and other non-black viewers away from his films." Slocum said that there are other filmmakers making films in which viewers cannot tell what race or ethnic group the writer or producer belongs to. He asked, "Is it the goal of the industry to be colorblind, or is it to make a point that the film is for a specific ethnic audience?"

Slocum suggested that while some film industry professionals may be responsive to scripts with strong ethnic components, others may not. He pointed out that in some cases, "Ethnic components can put up barriers to even an attractive story. Individual producers will look at such a story with different perspectives. And distributors want to know who does this story appeal to, why, and how do we get them in the [theater] door. Eventually," said Slocum, "everything is going to gravitate toward the mainstream, mass audience."

Maura Dunbar, executive director for ABC Network TV, said TV programming is influenced by advertising revenue, and that, in turn, affects the kinds of stories that networks do. "Interracial love stories are incredibly controversial," she said, adding that at ABC, "we'd love to find something to do which would have a positive, pro-social value and deal with the love between a black and white interracial couple. When people think of interracial, they mostly picture black and white relationships. However, they forget that 'interracial' can be Anglo-Saxon and Asian, Hispanic, or any other divergent races. It's a sad commentary on our marketplace, but it is the nature of our industry that the bottom line is always a matter of economics. While we are in the entertainment business, we are a 'business,' and the only way TV movies can earn a profit is when the advertisers buy spot time in our TV programs. Unfortunately, there is a heightened sensitivity to subject matters and issues which might be deemed by an increasingly conservative majority as aberrant and socially unacceptable behavior. When advertisers see programming that involves such, as in the case of 'interracial relationships,' they are more apt to pull out their advertising dollars in an effort to avoid a backlash from special interest groups which might threaten to boycott their products. It is getting tougher and tougher to make the kinds of socially responsible and challenging films that we would like to. But this doesn't mean we are steering away from issues that deal with the relevancy of race in America. The preconceptions, prejudgments, and biases we often have of one another simply can't hold water any longer. We are truly a global community, and to pander to the lowest common denominator of fear and prejudice would only be 'socially unacceptable'."

According to Dunbar, ABC, which offered viewers *Separate But Equal*, has been a forerunner of pursuing projects that "talk about more than just a white experience—more of the multiracial and multinational experiences because that's what America is. The people watching network TV are a mainstream audience, and they are more multicultural than ever before. Preliminary studies are beginning to show an ethnic, cross-cultural demographic. In our department at ABC, we are certainly seeking out material that would speak to these multicultural viewers."

The TV miniseries format, according to Stein of Cosgrove-Meurer, allows a writer to explore not only "the interrelationship between cross-cultural and/or interracial lovers, but also their families, the historic, cultural background, and political backdrop." She noted that "you don't sell miniseries based on a pitch or a fictional idea. Ideas for miniseries tend to come from true life stories or from books." She suggested writers look to such interracial and cross-cultural stories as those emerging from China, South Africa, and the Soviet Union. Miniseries differ from TV movies in that they are longer, more complex, and are packed with information that educates and inspires. But first and foremost, she said, they have to entertain.

Script Markets

Currently, markets for scripts abound. Eric Witt, director of finance for Dino De Laurentiis Communications, said the changes in Eastern Europe have had a profound effect on the need for new material in those markets. "The privatization of previously government-controlled TV stations in Italy and other countries in Europe will create new markets for scriptwriters," he pointed out.

WGA's Slocum suggested writers also think about info-films, educational films, and corporate videos as markets for their work. His advice to writers is to write the stories they want most to write. "There are a lot of options in the TV movie market. If you write a horror movie, you could send it to USA, a woman's story to Lifetime, and a family story to The Family Channel, and all kinds of stories to Basic Cable."

Carl Sautter, author of *How to Sell Your Screenplay: The Real Rules of Film and Television* (New Chapter Press), suggested scriptwriters look to writing for the TV video market because movies made for TV can sell directly to theaters in Europe. He noted that English is rapidly becoming the world language for film.

Ethnically aware writers, filmmakers, and education professionals may one day soon produce multicultural TV shorts for cable, accomplishing for TV short subjects what VH1 and MTV did for music videos. Naturally, scripts will be needed for such endeavors, and that translates into new markets for writers.

Cable TV stations and companies, an insatiable market according to some scriptwriters, are aware that a huge multicultural viewing audience exists, and they are doing something about it. An international cable channel, the nation's first multilingual network operating seven days a week for 24 hours daily through United Artists Cable, features programming that includes first-run dramas, news, and motion pictures in Armenian, Arabic, Cambodian, Chinese, Filipino, Hindi, Hebrew, Italian, Korean, Japanese, Persian, Russian, and Vietnamese. It, along with other cable TV stations and the major TV networks, represents market possibilities for scriptwriters of ethnic material.

While competition and revenue problems may send some public television stations into receivership, KMTP (MTP stands for Minority Television Project) out of San Francisco introduced a new offering in 1991. KMTP broadcast plans included programming that targeted minority interests, including the acquisition of programs from national programming consortiums of shows for and by Afro-Americans, Asian-Americans, Native American Indians, and Latinos. Film industry professionals including Catherine Tarr (story department head at Creative Artists Agency) noted that there exists a real need in the film industry for talented Afro-American and Hispanic writers to create scripts to accommodate the interest in the marketplace.

The foreign market and its fast-growing demand for U. S. movies motivated at least one well-known company—Carolco (*Rambo, Terminator, Terminator 2: Judgment Day, Air America, The Doors*, etc.)—to position itself to distribute and make money on films that play well in other countries and languages. Compared with major studio releases of anywhere from 15 to 20 per year, Carolco makes four or five big-budget pictures each year and about the same number of smaller-budget films destined for the home video market.

Changes in the foreign market mean changes for U. S. scriptwriters, according to James Ulmer, the international editor for *The Hollywood Reporter*. His article, "Who the World Loves Now" (*Premiere*, July 1991), featured the results of an updated and expanded *Hollywood Reporter* poll that assessed the "bankability of America's top stars on foreign shores." Ulmer wrote, "The action-adventure film interest is waning overseas (except in the Far East), while interest in the romantic film is on the rise. Bad scripts, even those that are star-driven, won't be tolerated as movie goers become extremely discriminating about the movies they will spend discretionary income on.

They're more inclined to see a good film several times over than a bad film once."

Ulmer pointed out that films that have the greater chance for success in the foreign market will be those that are story-driven rather than those that are star-driven.

While the boundaries of our world are shrinking, the film industry is growing globally. It's good news for scriptwriters, particularly those interested in writing material that deals with multicultural, cross-cultural, multinational, or interracial issues, themes, or elements. The need for good scripts is increasing at a time when multicultural awareness is reaching unprecedented heights. In the words of television scriptwriter Madeline DiMaggio, author of the book *How to Write for Television* and the screenplays *Belly Up* and *If the Shoe Fits*, "With all the changes taking place in the world, there's never been a more exciting time to be a writer than now."

PART TWO

Book Publishers

The information listed within each publisher's entry will enable you to quickly pinpoint potential markets for your book-length manuscripts.

How to Use the Information in This Section

The first paragraph of each entry identifies the publishing company, lists its location, and describes its publishing history. Subsequent information reveals where to send your submission, what to include in and on the envelope, when you can expect an initial response, and in general, what to expect in terms of payment if you are offered a publishing contract. Some publishers hire editors to work in specific ethnic subject areas. When that is the case, each editor is listed with his or her area of ethnic interest.

Subjects of Interest

This section is divided into two fields: fiction and nonfiction (which includes poetry). We have listed the ethnic area of interest for each and included recent titles representative of the types of books published by that press in that field. Some publishers are explicit about what they don't want. Read the entries carefully, and don't waste your time trying to force through an exception.

Initial Contact

This section explains how publishers want you to initially contact their press or publishing house. The information in this area is so specific that you can send editors exactly what they want. Always include any additional material requested. When sending a requested resumé, biography, or curriculum vitae, include only those details of your life that are relevant to your authority to write the book. If the book is about a specific ethnic culture or targets a specific ethnic audience, be sure to include your qualifications for writing about that culture and for that audience. Always include a self-addressed, stamped envelope (SASE) for the editor's response or return of your materials.

Acceptance Policies

Unagented manuscripts: Many larger publishing houses will look only at manuscripts submitted by an agent. Smaller presses are more often willing to consider unagented manuscripts submitted by the author directly. There are many such presses in the United States as well as in other parts of the world.

First novels: This category is included only if the publisher has indicated an interest in publishing an author's first novel.

Simultaneous submissions: If the publisher's response was "yes" to simultaneous submissions, you may submit your manuscript to several different publishers at the same time, but you should inform each publisher that the manuscript is being simultaneously submitted.

Response time to initial inquiry: Response time varies greatly. A week or two after the specified response time (listed in the publisher's entry), it is appropriate to send a written request for information concerning the status of your submission. It's best to avoid phoning unless you've been instructed to do so by the publisher.

Average time until publication: This information (always dependent upon a number of factors) gives you an approximate idea of how long the process takes after the publisher has accepted and received the completed manuscript.

Subsidy or co-publishing: In general, this means the author pays some portion of the production and promotion costs and potentially stands to earn more than a basic royalty if the book sells well. Many legitimate small publishing houses simply do not have the money to finance all costs and, for that reason, encourage author investment.

Co-publishing with responsible small presses can be a viable option for authors with specialty books that target specific markets. Co-publishing deals take many forms, so obtain all the facts, get the terms in writing, and seek legal advice before signing. Avoid so-called vanity publishers who do little more than collect your money.

Advance: This is often negotiable. Small or mid-size presses tend to offer smaller advances than the larger, established publishing houses. A small press's money goes primarily into production and promotion. An advantage of working with a small press is that your book may be one of only a few the press is publishing, or it may be the only title for a given season. Thus, your book will conceivably receive more attention than it would on a list of dozens of offerings from a larger publishing house.

Royalty: Some royalties are computed on the retail cover price, but most are based on the publisher's net receipts, which are the monies a publisher actually receives for the book. Some publishers may deduct expenses from their net receipts before computing royalties. If your personal negotiations with a publisher have reached the contract stage, seriously consider paying an agent or a publishing attorney to review and evaluate the contract before you sign.

Marketing Channels

Publishers market books primarily through direct sales to individuals and libraries and sales to distributors (who stock, sell, and distribute books to bookstores and libraries). Other marketing avenues include catalog, conference, independent, and special sales (book clubs, professional and social organizations, and special interest groups). If your book has such special sales potential, be sure to mention that fact in your initial contact with the publisher.

Subsidiary rights: If the publisher lists "all," that means he or she is buying and handling all subsidiary rights to ensure that the publishing house realizes as much profit from the book as possible. An experienced agent or publishing attorney can advise you if you are unsure whether or not to sell all these rights.

Additional Information

This is the publisher's opportunity to supply any supplemental information not covered in the preceding sections. Tips are specific reommendations from the publisher to the author and should be seriously considered.

Writers guidelines: Whenever guidelines are offered, request them before you write or submit anything targeted for a particular publishing house. If no entry is listed, the publisher does not have printed guidelines available.

Catalog: Your first step toward any publishing company should be to send for the catalog of books that the press has published. This will enable you to see the ethnic interest of that press and get a sense of the types of books it focuses on.

Abbreviations

n/i means no information was given to us by the publisher
n/a means that this information does not apply to the publisher

---

AEGINA PRESS, INC. (Imprint: University Editions). 59 Oak Lane. Spring Valley. Huntington, WV 25704. (304) 429-7204. Submissions Editor: Ira Herman. Founded: 1983. Number of titles published: cumulative 100+, 1992—40. Hardback 5%, softback 95%.

Subjects of Interest. Fiction—all subjects for all ethnic groups. Recent publications: *Water Dancing* (a short story collection by black author Pearl Duncan). **Nonfiction**—all subjects for all ethnic groups; translations. Recent publications: *A Tough Row to Hoe*, by Ray Pryor, Jr. (black autobiography).

Initial Contact. Query letter with synopsis/outline, or book proposal with sample chapters, or entire manuscript (preferred). SASE required.

Acceptance Policies. Unagented manuscripts: yes. First novels: yes. Simultaneous submissions: yes. Response time to initial inquiry: 2 months (query us if we take longer). Average time until publication: 6-9 months. **Advance:** not offered. **Royalty:** negotiable.

Marketing Channels. Distribution houses; direct mail. Subsidiary rights: Subsidiary rights remain the property of the author; however, we will contact agents and other publishers to market subsidiary rights.

Additional Information. Tips: Send a query or full manuscript with a cover letter and a SASE with sufficient postage for return of manuscript. Writer's guidelines: #10 SASE, 1 first class stamp. Catalog: $2, 9x12 SASE with $1.25 postage affixed.

AFRICAN AMERICAN IMAGES. 9204 Commercial, Ste. 308. Chicago, IL 60617. (312) 375-9682. Submissions Editor: Kimberly Vann. Founded: 1980. Number of titles published: 4-8 books per year. Softback 100%.

Subjects of Interest. Nonfiction—African-American issues in the areas of biography, education, children's books, human potential, minority issues, family life, film/television/video, history, sociology. Recent publications: *The Mugging of Black America; The Best Face of All* (positive black images for children); *Critical Issues in Educating African American Youth.* Do not want: fiction; poetry; autobiographies; religion.

Initial Contact. Overview, table of contents, and first chapter. SASE required.

Acceptance Policies. Unagented manuscripts: yes. Simultaneous submissions: yes. Response time to initial inquiry: n/i. Average time until publication: n/i. **Advance:** negotiable up to $500. **Royalty:** 10%; based on wholesale, paid semiannually.

Marketing Channels. Distributors. Subsidiary rights: all.

Additional Information. We publish books from an African frame of reference that promote self-esteem, collective values, liberation, and skill development. Tips: If manuscript is accepted for publication, a rough draft should be submitted on diskette, preferably WordPerfect.

AHSAHTA PRESS. Boise State University. 1910 University Dr. Boise, ID 83725. (203) 385-1246. Submissions Editor: Tom Trusky. Founded: 1974. Number of titles published: cumulative—45, 1992—3. Softback 100%.

Subjects of Interest. Nonfiction—Western-American poetry (Native Americans, Hispanics, Basques, Japanese, Chinese). Recent publications: *Going Home Away Indian* (Hispanic). Do not want: conventional poetry.

Initial Contact. Query with poetry sampler sent between January and March only. SASE required.

Acceptance Policies. Unagented manuscripts: yes. Simultaneous submissions: yes. Response time to initial inquiry: 6-8 weeks (January-March). Average time until publication: 1 year. **Advance:** not offered. **Royalty:** 25%; commences with third printing.

Marketing Channels. Distribution houses; direct mail. Subsidiary rights: reprint rights.

Additional Information. Tips: Be familiar with our material. Writer's guidelines: upon request. Catalog: upon request.

ALASKA NATIVE LANGUAGE CENTER. University of Alaska. PO Box 900111. Fairbanks, AK 99775-0120. (907) 474-7874. Fax: (907) 474-6586. Submissions Editor: Tom Alton. Founded: 1967. Number of titles published: cumulative—270, 1992—5. Hardback .5%, softback 99.5%.

Subjects of Interest. Fiction—Alaska Native folklore; children's and young adult. Recent publications: first novel entirely in Yup'ik Eskimo. **Nonfiction**—Alaska Native language texts, dictionaries, grammars, schoolbooks; linguistic research papers. Recent publications: *Ahtna Dictionary; K'etetaalkkaanee,* (Aleut tales and narratives, collected 1909-1910). Do not want: books by any authors except Alaska Natives themselves or scholars on Alaska Native languages.

Initial Contact. Phone us at (907) 474-7874.

Acceptance Policies. Unagented manuscripts: yes. Simultaneous submissions: n/a. Response time to initial inquiry: immediate. Average time until publication: by arrangement. **Advance:** not offered. **Royalty:** none; specialized situation.

Marketing Channels. Direct mail. Subsidiary rights: none.

Additional Information. We have a brochure available describing our work with Alaska Native languages. Catalog: write or phone.

Anand Paperbacks *see* **ORIENT PAPERBACKS.**

ARTE PUBLICO PRESS. University of Houston. Houston, TX 77204-2090. (713) 749-4768. Submissions Editor: Nicolas Kanellos. Founded: 1979. Number of titles published: cumulative—100, 1992—25. Softback 100%.

Subjects of Interest. Fiction—contemporary prose and drama by U.S. Hispanics. Recent publications: *The Harvest/La Cosecha* (bilingual edition, stories of Mexican-Americans set within the migrant labor cycle); *The Wedding* (the Mexican-American blue-collar subculture); *Necessary Theater: Six Plays about the Chicano Experience; Nuevos Pasos: Chicano and Puerto Rican Drama; The Rag Doll Plagues; Only Sons; Macho!.* **Nonfiction**—poetry by U.S. Hispanics; autobiography and biography about U.S. Hispanics; literary. Recent publications: *Silent Dancing: A Partial Remembrance of a Puerto Rican Childhood; Diary of an Undocumented Immigrant; Rain of Gold; Paradise Lost or Gained: The Literature of Hispanic Exile.* Do not want: other nonfiction.

Initial Contact. Query letter with synopsis/outline; or send manuscript with query letter.

Acceptance Policies. Unagented manuscripts: yes. Simultaneous submissions: no. Response time to initial inquiry: immediate acknowledgement of receipt; thereafter 3-6 months. Average time until publication: 12-18 months. **Advance:** none. **Royalty:** 10% of sales.

Marketing Channels. Distribution houses; cooperative distribution; direct mail; independent reps. Subsidiary rights: all.

Additional Information. Catalog: call or write for free catalog. Writer's guidelines: call or write.

ASIAN HUMANITIES PRESS. PO Box 3523. Fremont, CA 94539. (510) 659-8272. Fax: (510) 659-8272. Submissions Editor: M. K. Jain. Founded: 1976. Number of titles published: cumulative—100, 1992—12. Hardback 50%, softback 50%.

Subjects of Interest. Nonfiction—Asian literature, religions, philosophies, cultures, art; translations. Recent publications: *Why Does God Allow Suffering?* (essay on a spiritual quest); *New Mahayana: Buddhism for a Post Modern World.* Do not want: books without some Asian element.

Initial Contact. Query letter with synopsis/outline. Include author bio, prior publications, and author's view on potential market. SASE required.

Acceptance Policies. Unagented manuscripts: yes. Simultaneous submissions: no. Response time to initial inquiry: 6 weeks. Average time until publication: 9-12 months. **Advance:** occasionally, $1000-$2000. **Royalty:** 5-8%; based on retail price.

Marketing Channels. Distribution houses; direct mail. Subsidiary rights: all.

Additional Information. Writer's guidelines: upon request. Catalog: upon request.

ASSOCIATED PUBLISHERS, INC., THE. 1407 14th St., NW. Washington, DC, 20005. (202) 265-1441. Fax: (202) 328-8677. Submissions Editor: Willie Leanna Miles. Founded: 1920. Number of titles published: cumulative—100, 1992—2. Hardback 75%, softback 25%.

Subjects of Interest. Nonfiction—Afro-American history. Do not want: anything other than historical materials on Afro-Americans.

Initial Contact. Query letter with synopsis/outline. Include background of the author.

Acceptance Policies. Unagented manuscripts: yes. Simultaneous submissions: no. Response time to initial inquiry: 10-15 days. Average time until publication: 1 year. Subsidy or co-publishing basis: 40-50%. **Advance:** not offered. **Royalty:** 10-20%; more if author contributes to cost of publication.

Marketing Channels. Direct mail; independent reps; in-house staff; special sales. Subsidiary rights: all.

Additional Information. We are the oldest Afro-American publishing company in America. Tips: Be sure your information on Afro-Americans is authentic. Writer's guidelines: use standard manuscript form. Catalog: upon request.

AVALON BOOKS. (Imprint of Thomas Bouregy & Co., Inc.). 401 Lafayette St. New York, NY 10003. (212) 598-0222. Submissions Editor: Barbara J. Brett. Founded: 1946. Number of titles published: cumulative—60 per year since 1946, 1992—60. Hardback 100%.

Subjects of Interest. Fiction—ethnic characters in the genres of romance, career romance, mystery romance, Westerns. Recent publications: *On the Terror Trail* (Western with black marshall as hero).

Initial Contact. Query letter with synopsis and first chapter. SASE required.

Acceptance Policies. Unagented manuscripts: yes. First novels: yes. Simultaneous submissions: no. Response time to initial inquiry: 3 months. Average time until publication: 3-6 months. **Advance:** $600 for the first book, $800 for the second, and $1000 for subsequent books. **Royalty:** paid against the first 3500 copies sold; 10% is paid on additional sales.

Marketing Channels. Books are sold to libraries only. Subsidiary rights: all; sub rights shared with author, 50%.

Additional Information. Our books are wholesome adult fiction, suitable for family reading. There is no graphic or premarital sex and no profanity. Tips: Our characters, plots, and story lines should be contemporary. Writer's guidelines: SASE. Catalog: none available.

AVANYU PUBLISHING, INC. PO Box 27134. Albuquerque, NM 87125. (505) 266-6128, 243-8485. Fax: (505) 821-8864. Submissions Editor: J. Brent Ricks. Founded: 1985. Number of titles published: cumulative—15, 1992—7. Hardback 10%, softback 90%.

Subjects of Interest. Fiction—Native American Indians; Southwest Americana. **Nonfiction**—Native American Indians; Southwest Americana. Recent publications: *Petroglyphs and Pueblo Myths of the Rio Grande*; *Tonita Pena* (biography of first female Pueblo artist); *The Navajo* (reprint of 1911 mail order catalog).

Initial Contact. Query letter with synopsis/outline.

Acceptance Policies. Unagented manuscripts: yes. Simultaneous submissions: yes. Response time to initial inquiry: 4 weeks. Average time until publication: 1 year. **Advance:** subject to negotiation. **Royalty:** yes.

Marketing Channels. Distribution houses; independent reps. Subsidiary rights: reprint rights; translation and foreign rights; English language publication outside the United States and Canada.

Additional Information. Catalog: upon request.

AVON BOOKS. (Subsidiary of The Hearst Corporation). 1350 Avenue of The Americas. New York, NY 10019. (212) 261-6800. Fax: (212) 261-6895. Submissions Editors: Ellen E. Krieger (editorial director for Books for Young Readers); Mark Gompertz (associate publisher for trade books). Founded: 1941. Number of titles published: 1992—500. Softback 100%.

Subjects of Interest. Fiction—children's and young adult books; quality adult fiction. Recent publications: *Have a Happy . . .* (children's novel). **Nonfiction**—adult trade. Recent publications: *Bullwhip Days* (adult trade).

Initial Contact. Book proposal with 3 sample chapters or entire manuscript. SASE required.

Acceptance Policies. Unagented manuscripts: yes. First novels: yes. Simultaneous submissions: yes. Response time to initial inquiry: 3-5 months. Average time until publication: 18-24 months. **Advance:** n/i. **Royalty:** based on cover price.

Marketing Channels. Distribution houses; direct mail; independent reps; in-house staff; special sales. Subsidiary rights: first serialization; second serialization; dramatization, motion picture, and broadcast; video distribution; sound reproduction and recording; direct mail or direct sales; book club; translation and foreign; computer and other magnetic and electronic media; English language publication outside the United States and Canada.

Additional Information. Writer's guidelines: upon request, specify adult or juvenile.

BEACON PRESS. 25 Beacon St. Boston, MA 02108. (607) 742-2110. Fax: (617) 723-3097. Submissions Editors: Lauren Bryant (anthropology, women's studies, religion, education); Deanne Urmy (environment, nature writing); Deborah Chasman (blacks, Africans, Native Americans, Jewish studies); Marya Van't Hul (Asian studies); Andrew Hrycyna (Russian studies, politics, philosophy). Founded: 1854. Number of titles published: cumulative—400, 1992—60. Hardback 40%, softback 60%.

Subjects of Interest. Fiction—Mostly reprints and some original African-American, Asian-American, Native American, Hispanic, and Jewish books; children's. Recent publications: *Spider Woman's Granddaughters: Traditional Tales and Contemporary Writing* (Native American studies); *Plum Bun: A Novel Without a Moral* (Black Women Writers Series); *The Butcher's Wife* (translated from the Chinese). **Nonfiction**—ethnic groups (African-Americanss, Asian-Americans, Native Americans, Hispanics, Jews); gay/lesbian issues; educational issues. Recent publications: *A Season of Our Joy: A Celebration of Modern Jewish Renewal*; *Shouting at the Crocodile* (freeing of South Africa); *The Spirit and the Flesh: Sexual Diversity in American Indian Culture*. Do not want: poetry.

Initial Contact. Query letter with synopsis/outline. Include curriculum vitae. SASE required.

Acceptance Policies. Unagented manuscripts: yes. Simultaneous submissions: yes. Response time to initial inquiry: 6-8 weeks. Average time until publication: 9 months. **Advance:** varies. **Royalty:** varies.

Marketing Channels. Distribution houses; cooperative distribution; direct mail; special sales. Subsidiary rights: all.

Additional Information. Beacon is an independent house dedicated to appreciating the diversity of life and opinions on Earth. Tips: We are a scholarly publisher and seek manuscripts with potential for college course adoption as well as a bookstore market. Writer's guidelines: SASE. Catalog: 8x11 SASE.

BEAR AND COMPANY, INC. PO Drawer 2860. Santa Fe, NM 87504-2860. (505) 983-5968. Submissions Editor: Barbara Clow. Founded: 1983. Number of titles published: cumulative—70, 1992—12. Hardback 10%, softback 90%.

Subjects of Interest. Nonfiction—Native American issues; holistic practices; metaphysics/new age; environment/ecology; emphasis on Native American spirituality; wildlife; women's issues. Recent publications: *Medicine Cards*; *Profiles in Wisdom*. Do not want: channeling; poetry; fiction.

Initial Contact. Query letter with synopsis/outine with 3 sample chapters. Include author bio, color art, and SASE.

Acceptance Policies. Unagented manuscripts: yes. Simultaneous submissions: yes. Response time to initial inquiry: 3 months. Average time until publication: 8 months. **Advance:** yes. **Royalty:** negotiable.

Marketing Channels. Distribution houses; direct mail; independent reps; in-house staff; special sales. Subsidiary rights: all.

Additional Information. We are interested in books dealing with celebrating the earth and healing its problems. Our audience is interested in new age ideas. Tips: Do not call for information. No reply without SASE. Catalog: SASE.

BEAR FLAG BOOKS. (Subsidiary of Padre Productions). PO Box 840. Arroyo Grande, CA 93421-0840. (805) 473-1947. Submissions Editor: Lachlan P. MacDonald. Founded: 1974. Number of titles published: cumulative—30, 1992—8. Hardback 10%, softback 90%.

Subjects of Interest. Fiction—only with California settings. **Nonfiction**—any Western states subject; guide books to ethnic points of interest in the West. Recent publications: *Cuentos: Authentic Folk Tales; California the Curious*. Do not want: poetry; picture books for juveniles.

Initial Contact. Query letter with synopsis/outline, book proposal, and sample chapters. Include publication credits, sales prospects, or promotional opportunities. SASE required.

Acceptance Policies. Unagented manuscripts: yes. First novels: yes, but rarely. Simultaneous submissions: yes. Response time to initial inquiry: 2-8 weeks. Average time until publication: 1-2 years. **Advance:** negotiable. **Royalty:** yes.

Marketing Channels. Distribution houses; direct mail; independent sales; in-house staff. Subsidiary rights: all.

Additional Information. We want nonfiction for specific California ethnic groups. Tips: Master the basics. Include photography and art skills for nonfiction. Writer's guidelines: #10 SASE, 1 first class stamp. Catalog: 9x12 SASE, 2 ounces, first class postage.

BEAR WALLOW PUBLISHING COMPANY, THE. PO Box 370. Union, OR 97883. (503) 562-5687. Submissions Editor: Jerry Gildemeister. Founded: 1976. Number of titles published: cumulative—7, 1992—1. Hardback 100%.

Subjects of Interest. Nonfiction—Native Americans; illustrated historical works; Western history. Recent publications: *An American Vignette; A Letter Home.*

Initial Contact. Query letter only. Most productions are in-house projects. We do assist self-publishers. SASE not required.

Acceptance Policies. Unagented manuscripts: yes. Simultaneous submissions: n/a. Response time to initial inquiry: promptly. Average time until publication: varies. Subsidy or co-publishing basis: stage payments for production services, design, camera-ready, printing and binding. **Advance:** not offered. **Royalty:** yes.

Marketing Channels. Direct mail; independent reps. Subsidiary rights: n/a.

Additional Information. We provide complete services to self-publishers.

BERGLI BOOKS, LTD. Chriesistrasse 1. CH-6353 Weggis/LU, Switzerland. (00114) 1 41 93 28 20. Fax: (00114) 1 41 93 28 76. Submissions Editor: Dianne Kiefer-Dicks. Founded: 1990. Number of titles published: cumulative—1, 1992—1. Softback 100%.

Subjects of Interest. Fiction—European setting. **Nonfiction**—personal experiences and humorous, informative, entertaining stories by writers of various nationalities about crossing cultures, intercultural marriage. Recent publications: *Ticking Along with the Swiss; Ticking Along Too.* Do not want: brutality.

Initial Contact. Query letter with synopsis/outline. SASE with IRC (international reply coupon) required.

Acceptance Policies. Unagented manuscripts: yes. First novels: yes. Simultaneous submissions: yes. Response time to initial inquiry: 2 weeks. Average time until publication: 6-12 months. **Advance:** not offered. **Royalty:** on novels, but not on short stories.

Marketing Channels. Cooperative distribution; direct mail. Subsidiary rights: all.

Additional Information. We are most interested in short stories about crossing cultures in Europe. Tips: Your story should be of interest to an English-speaking resident of a European country. Writer's guidelines: upon request with IRC. Catalog: not available.

BILINGUAL PRESS/EDITORIAL BILINGUE. (Bilingual Review/Press). Hispanic Research Center. Arizona State University. Tempe, AZ 85287-2702. (602) 965-3867. Fax: (602) 965-8309. Submissions Editor: Gary D. Keller. Founded: 1973. Number of titles published: cumulative—108, 1992—12. Hardback 20%, softback 80%; some published in cloth and paper.

Subjects of Interest. Fiction—U.S. Hispanic (Latino) novels, short stories, theater; translations. Recent publications: *The Devil in Texas/El diablo en Texas* (bilingual edition); Nonfiction—U.S. Hispanic literary criticism; scholarly works; poetry. Recent publications: *Sociolinguistics of the Spanish-Speaking World; Hogueras/Bonfires* (poetry). Do not want: books about the experiences of Americans in Latin America; genre fiction; children's literature.

Initial Contact. Query letter with synopsis/outline. Include resumé and other publications, if any. SASE required.

Acceptance Policies. Unagented manuscripts: yes. First novels: yes. Simultaneous submissions: no. Response time to initial inquiry: 2-3 weeks. Average time until publication: 12-18 months. Subsidy or co-publishing basis: only on scholarly works. **Advance**: $200-$1000, varies by genre. **Royalty**: 10%.

Marketing Channels. Distribution houses; direct mail; independent reps; conferences. Subsidiary rights: all.

Additional Information. We are a publisher of serious creative literature by and/or focusing on U.S. Hispanics. Writer's guidelines: SASE. Catalog: upon request.

Bison Books *see* **UNIVERSITY OF NEBRASKA PRESS.**

BLACK ANGELS PRESS. PO Box 50892. Palo Alto, CA 94303. (415) 321-2489. Submissions Editor: Abimbola Adama. Founded: 1991. Number of titles published: cumulative—2, 1992—6. Softback 100%.

Subjects of Interest. Fiction—African-American interests; self-help; new age (possibly). Nonfiction—poetry by and about the African-American experience. Recent publications: directory of African-American writers (due out 12/91). Do not want: rhyming, greeting card verse.

Initial Contact. Query letter with poetry. Include biography and credits, if any. SASE required.

Acceptance Policies. Unagented manuscripts: yes. Simultaneous submissions: yes. Response time to initial inquiry: 4-6 weeks. Average time until publication: 3-6 months. **Advance**: not offered. **Royalty**: paid in books.

Marketing Channels. Direct mail; wholesalers; special sales. Subsidiary rights: none.

Additional Information. We encourage strong poets, particularly unpublished ones. Tips: Send us the quality and kind of book you would like to read. Writer's guidelines: not available. Catalog: not available.

BLAIR, PUBLISHER, JOHN F. 1406 Plaza Dr. Winston-Salem, NC 27103. (919) 768-1374. Fax: (919) 768-9194. Submissions Editor: Steve Kirk. Founded: 1954. Number of titles published: cumulative—65, 1992—8. Hardback 50%, softback 50%.

Subjects of Interest. Fiction—folklore and literary novels focused on the Southeastern United States. **Nonfiction**—biography, cooking, folklore, recreation, travel, Civil War material focused on the Southeastern United States. Recent publications: *My Folks Don't Want Me to Talk about Slavery; Before Freedom When I Just Can Remember* (oral histories about slavery); *The American Indian in North Carolina; Tales from the Cherokee Hills* (folklore).

Initial Contact. Query letter with synopsis/outline. Include information about author's background and qualifications. SASE required.

Acceptance Policies. Unagented manuscripts: yes. First novels: yes. Simultaneous submissions: yes. Response time to initial inquiry: 8 weeks. Average time until publication: 1 year. **Advance:** negotiable. **Royalty:** negotiable

Marketing Channels. Direct mail; in-house staff; special sales. Subsidiary rights: all.

Additional Information. We are interested in expanding the ethnicity of our line if it relates to the Southeast. Tips: Order our catalog and editorial guidelines. Writer's guidelines: call (800) 222-9796. Catalog: call (800) 222-9796.

BUDDHA ROSE PUBLICATIONS. PO Box 902. Hermosa Beach, CA 90254. (213) 543-3809. Submissions Editor: Eliot Sebastian. Founded: 1989. Number of titles published: cumulative—32, 1992—15. Hardback 25%, softback 75%.

Subjects of Interest. Fiction—adventure, avant-garde, contemporary, erotica, metaphysics/new age, all with a focus on Asian cultures. Recent publications: *Bangkok and the Nights of Drunken Stupor; Shanghai Whispers, Shanghai Screams; Shyama Baba, The Back Streets of Bangkok.* **Nonfiction**—adventure, anthropology, archaeology, art, philosophy, politics/world affairs, religion (Buddhism, Hinduism, Taoism, Zen), metaphysics, cultural studies, poetry, sociology, yoga, all with an Asian focus. Recent publications: *Cambodian Refugees in Long Beach, California; The Definitive Study, Los Angeles Koreatown: An Urban Geographical View of Its Inception and Current Urbanization; Southeast Asian Immigration into Los Angeles and Orange Counties: A Populative and Demographic View.*

Initial Contact. Entire manuscript.

Acceptance Policies. Unagented manuscripts: yes. First novels: yes. Simultaneous submissions: yes. Response time to initial inquiry: 3 months. Average time until publication: 6 months. Subsidy or co-publishing basis: with new authors. **Advance:** none. **Royalty:** 15% of total sales.

Marketing Channels. Distribution houses; direct mail; in-house staff. Subsidiary rights: all.

Additional Information. Catalog: upon request.

CALYX BOOKS. PO Box B. Corvallis, OR 97339. (503) 753-9384. Submissions Editor: address to Editor. Founded: 1986. Number of titles published: cumulative—13, 1992—3. Hardback and softback published concurrently.

Subjects of Interest. Fiction—short stories and literature written by women in the following areas: all ethnic groups, avant-garde, contemporary, fantasy, folklore, women's issues. Recent publications: *Ginseng and Other Tales from Manila; The Forbidden Witch: An Asian American Women's Anthology* (1990 American Book Award winner). **Nonfiction**—poetry, essays, translations of works written by women of any ethnic group. Recent publications: *Idleness is the Root of All Love* (German translation); *Indian Singing in 20th Century America* (American-Indian poetry).

Initial Contact. We will next look at book manuscripts from January 1993 though March 15, 1993. Query letter with synopsis/outline. Include 3 sample chapters. Send 15 poems. SASE required.

Acceptance Policies. Unagented manuscripts: yes. First novels: yes. Simultaneous submissions: yes. Response time to initial inquiry: 2 weeks. Average time until publication: 2-3 years. **Advance:** not offered. **Royalty:** 10%; based on net receipts.

Marketing Channels. Distribution houses; independent sales. Subsidiary rights: all.

Additional Information. We are a feminist, nonprofit press that publishes art and fine literature by women. We only publish 3 books per year. We also publish two issues per year of

Calyx, A Journal of Art and Literature by Women (accepts submisions of poetry, fiction, art, essays between 10/1-11/15 and 3/1-4/15. Send SASE for guidelines. Tips: We are not open for book submissions until January 1993. Writer's guidelines: SASE. Catalog: write and ask to be put on our mailing list.

CAROLINA WREN PRESS. (Imprints: Lollipop Power Books). PO Box 277. Carrboro, NC 27510. (919) 560-2738. Submissions Editors: Katherine Lovatt (fiction); Ruth Smollin (children's books); Marily Bulman (poetry); Elaine Goolsby (editor in chief). Founded: 1976. Number of titles published: cumulative—32, 1992—2. Hardback 1%, softback 99%.

Subjects of Interest. Fiction—all genres; children's; ethnic groups (Afro-Americans, Hispanics, Native Americans). Recent publications: *Love, Or a Reasonable Facsimile* (semi-autobiographical story of handicapped black girl growing up in the South).
Nonfiction—ethnic groups (Afro-Americans, Hispanics, Native Americans); women's autobiographical writings; translations; poetry. Recent publications: *This Road Since Freedom* (poetry). Do not want: romance novels.

Initial Contact. Book proposal with sample chapters. SASE required.

Acceptance Policies. Unagented manuscripts: yes. First novels: yes. Simultaneous submissions: yes. Response time to initial inquiry: 3 months. Average time until publication: 18 months. **Advance:** not offered. **Royalty:** 10%; based on print run.

Marketing Channels. Distribution houses; direct mail. Subsidiary rights: none.

Additional Information. All other things being equal, we give priority to new writers, women writers, minority writers. Tips: Be patient. Find some of our books to see if your book fits in with our current backlist. Writer's guidelines: large SASE, specify children's or adult. Catalog: large SASE, 2 ounces postage.

CAROLRHODA BOOKS, INC. (Subsidiary of Lerner Publications. Imprints: First Avenue Editions). 241 1st Ave., N. Minneapolis, MN 55401. (612) 332-3344. Fax: (612) 332-7615. Submissions Editor: Rebecca Poole. Founded: 1969. Number of titles published: cumulative—600, 1992—61. Hardback 70%, softback 30%.

Subjects of Interest. Fiction—folktales and historical fiction for children. Recent publications: *Everybody Cooks Rice; Song of the Chirimia* (translation). **Nonfiction**—science, biographies, photo books for children. Recent publications: *The Children of Egypt; Arctic Explorer: The Story of Matthew Henson*. Do not want: textbooks; workbooks; songbooks; puzzles; plays; religious material.

Initial Contact. Entire manuscript with cover letter. SASE required.

Acceptance Policies. Unagented manuscripts: yes. First time author: yes. Simultaneous submissions: yes, inform us. Response time to initial inquiry: up to 3 months. Average time until publication: varies. **Advance:** varies. **Royalty:** varies.

Marketing Channels. Distribution houses; direct mail; independent reps; in-house staff; special sales. Subsidiary rights: all.

Additional Information. Tips: Steer clear of alphabet books, preachy stories, and stories featuring anthropomorphic protagonists. Writer's guidelines: #10 SASE. Catalog: 9x12 SASE, third class postage.

CENTER FOR EAST ASIAN STUDIES. Western Washington University. Bellingham, WA 98225. (206) 676-3041. Fax: (206) 676-3044. Submissions Editor: n/i. Founded: 1971. Number of titles published: cumulative—19, 1992—2. Hardback 50%, softback 50%.

Subjects of Interest. Nonfiction—scholarly books on East Asian topics including China, Tibet, Japan, Korea, and Mongolia. Recent publications: *The Minorities of Northern China; The Korean Peasant at the Crossroads: A Study in Attitudes.* Do not want: non-scholarly manuscripts.

Initial Contact. Query letter with synopsis/outline.

Acceptance Policies. Unagented manuscripts: yes. Simultaneous submissions: no. Response time to initial inquiry: 2 weeks. Average time until publication: 1 year. **Advance:** not offered. **Royalty:** not offered.

Marketing Channels. Distribution houses; direct mail; special sales; conferences. Subsidiary rights: reprint; sound reproduction and recording; translation and foreign; computer and other magnetic and electronic media; commercial; English language publication outside the United States and Canada.

CENTER FOR MIGRATION STUDIES OF NEW YORK, INC. 209 Flagg Pl. Staten Island, NY, 10304. (718) 351-8800. Fax: (718) 667-4598. Submissions Editor: Lydio F. Tomasi, Ph.D. Founded: 1964. Number of titles published: cumulative—401, 1992—14. Hardback 50%, softback 50%.

Subjects of Interest. Nonfiction—migration; refugees; ethnic group relations. Recent publications: *The Politics of Immigration Policy; Chinese American Intermarriage.*

Initial Contact. Entire manuscript.

Acceptance Policies. Unagented manuscripts: yes. Simultaneous submissions: no. Response time to initial inquiry: 3 months. Average time until publication: n/i. **Advance:** not offered. **Royalty:** varies.

Marketing Channels. Direct mail; independent sales. Subsidiary rights: all.

Additional Information. Writer's guidelines: upon request. Catalog: upon request.

CHILDREN'S BOOK PRESS. 1461 Ninth Ave. San Francisco, CA 94122. Submissions Editor: Harriet Rohmer. Founded: 1975. Number of titles published: cumulative—26, 1992—6.

Subjects of Interest. Fiction—multicultural literature for children; picture books only. Recent publications: *The Woman Who Outshone the Sun* (legend from Oaxaca, Mexico); *Baby Rattlesnake* (Native American); *Uncle Nacho's Hat* (Nicaragua); *Nine-in-One* (Laos); *Family Pictures* (Mexican-American). Nonfiction—children's biography. Recent publications: *I Remember 121* (memoirs of an African-American childhood).

Initial Contact. Entire manuscript; explain why you feel it is important to publish the story at this time.

Acceptance Policies. Unagented manuscripts: yes. Simultaneous submissions: yes. Response time to initial inquiry: 4 months. Average time until publication: 1 year. **Advance:** varies. **Royalty:** 5% author; 5% artist.

Marketing Channels. Distribution houses; direct mail; independent reps; special sales. Subsidiary rights: all.

Additional Information. We publish bilingual and multicultural folktales and contemporary stories reflecting the traditions and culture of Third World communities both in the United

States and in the Third World. Tips: Writers should be from the community they are writing about. Send for editorial guidelines. Catalog: upon request.

CHINA BOOKS & PERIODICALS, INC. 2929 Twenty-fourth St. San Francisco, CA 94110. (415) 282-2994. Fax: (415) 282-0994. Submissions Editor: Bob Schildgen. Founded: 1960. Number of titles published: cumulative—40, 1992—10. Hardback 30%, softback 70%.

Subjects of Interest. Fiction—novels and short story collections by Chinese and Chinese-Americans. Recent publications: *Old Well* (novel about the Chinese countryside in 1980s). Nonfiction—history, politics, art, culture of Chinese and Chinese-Americans; translations of any material originally written in Chinese; translations of material about China written in any language. Recent publications: *Grandmother Had No Name* (autobiography by Chinese-American woman); *The Piano Tuner* (translation). Do not want: work that doesn't have a Chinese, East-Asian, or Chinese-American theme.

Initial Contact. Query letter with synopsis/outline, book proposal, and sample chapters. Include author's concept of potential market and published writing samples, if available. SASE required.

Acceptance Policies. Unagented manuscripts: yes. First novels: yes. Simultaneous submissions: yes. Response time to initial inquiry: 1 month. Average time until publication: 1 year. Subsidy or co-operative publishing: payment from authors. **Advance: $1000. Royalty:** based on net receipts.

Marketing Channels. Distribution houses; direct mail; independent sales; in-house staff; special sales; overseas retail sales and distribution. Subsidiary rights: all.

Additional Information. We are dedicated to China, and have been for over 30 years. Tips: Take a look at the kind of books we publish and distribute in order to see if your work fits our list. Make a pitch for the book's marketability. Writer's guidelines: SASE, 1 first class stamp. Catalog: SASE, $.72 postage.

CHRONICLE BOOKS. 275 Fifth St. San Francisco, CA 94103. (415) 777-7240. Submissions Editor: Kristen Breck, editorial assistant. Founded: 1966. Number of titles published: 1992—20 children's books. Hardback 95%, softback 5%.

Subjects of Interest. Fiction—children's picture books, visual books (ages 2-13), and stories with a United States setting that depict our ethnically diverse culture; translations from Mexico, the Caribbean, Central America. Recent publications: *Ten Little Rabbits* (picture book); *Mama Do You Love Me?* Do not want: fiction for older readers at this time.

Initial Contact. Query letter with synopsis/outline for stories for older children; entire manuscript for picture books. Include any previous publishing experience and author's particular interest in/or relevance to writing ethnic materials. SASE required.

Acceptance Policies. Unagented manuscripts: yes. Simultaneous submissions: yes. Response time to initial inquiry: 1-8 weeks. Average time until publication: 1-3 months. **Advance**: varies; sometimes we pay flat fees. **Royalty**: varies; based on retail price.

Marketing Channels. Distribution houses; independent reps; in-house staff; special sales; library binders; mail order catalogs. Subsidiary rights: all.

Additional Information. Writer's guidelines: SASE. Catalog: SASE.

CLARITY PRESS, INC. 3277 Roswell Rd., NE, Ste. 469. Atlanta, GA 30305. (404) 231-0649. Fax: (404) 231-3899. Submissions Editor: editorial committee. Founded: 1984. Number of titles published: cumulative—10, 1992—3. Softback 100%.

Subjects of Interest. Nonfiction—quality trade originals and translations in the areas of Afro-American political, social, minority, and human rights issues. Recent publications: *International Law and the Black Minority in the United States; Dalit: The Black Untouchables of India; The End of Zionism.*

Initial Contact. Query letter only. We will respond if interested.

Acceptance Policies. Unagented manuscripts: yes. Simultaneous submissions: yes. Response time to initial inquiry: within 3 months if we are interested. Average time until publication: varies. **Advance:** not offered. **Royalty:** yes.

Marketing Channels. Distribution houses; direct mail; independent sales. Subsidiary rights: all.

Additional Information. We are nonsectarian, nonaligned. Writer's guidelines: We will send if query letter is pursued by us. Catalog: upon request.

Classic Reprint Series *see* **UNIVERSITY OF ALASKA PRESS.**

CLEIS PRESS. PO Box 14684. San Francisco, CA 94114. Submissions Editor: Frederique Delacoste. Founded: 1980. Number of titles published: cumulative—16, 1992—7. Softback 100%.

Subjects of Interest. Fiction—feminist; gay/lesbian; literary; translations. Recent publications: *Another Love; The Wall.* Do not want: romance. **Nonfiction**—ethnic groups (all cultures with an emphasis on Arabs, Latin Americans, Russians); history; human rights; immigration; feminist; gay/lesbian (major focus); minority issues; women's issues; books by and about Latin American women; politics/world affairs (major focus); sociology; translations (major focus). Recent publications: *Good Sex* (anthology of essays). Do not want: religious or spiritual works; topics that have been overworked.

Initial Contact. Query letter or outline and sample chapters or complete manuscript. Send complete manuscript for fiction.

Acceptance Policies. Unagented manuscripts: yes. Simultaneous submissions: yes; inform us as to who and when. Response time to initial inquiry: 1 month. Average time until publication: 6 months. **Advance:** n/i. **Royalty:** varies.

Marketing Channels. n/i. Subsidiary rights: n/i.

Additional Information. We are interested in books which will sell in feminist and progressive bookstores and will sell in Europe for translation rights. Tips: Author should spend time in a bookstore whose clientele resembles her audience. Know your market. Catalog: #10 SASE and 2 first class stamps.

COUNCIL FOR INDIAN EDUCATION. 517 Rimrock Rd. Billings, MT 59102. (406) 252-74545. Submissions Editor: Hap Gilliland. Founded: 1963. Number of titles published: cumulative—114, 1992—8. Hardback 25%, softback 75%.

Subjects of Interest. Fiction—Native American adventure, children's/young adult, contemporary, folklore, historical fiction, humor. Recent publications: *Search for Identity.* Nonfiction—Native American adventure, anthropology, archaeology, art, biography, children's, comedy, crafts, education, folklore, history, nature, self-help, tribal issues. Recent publications: *The Handsome People: History of the Crow Indians*. Do not want: sex and vulgarity.

Initial Contact. Query letter with synopsis/outline or book proposal with sample chapters or entire manuscript. SASE required.

Acceptance Policies. Unagented manuscripts: yes. First novels: yes. Simultaneous submissions: yes. Response time to initial inquiry: 3 months. Average time until publication: 1 year. **Advance:** not offered. **Royalty:** 10%; based on wholesale price of book.

Marketing Channels. Direct mail; independent sales. Subsidiary rights: none.

Additional Information. More than 50% of our sales are to schools with Indian students. Tips: Be sure a particular identified Indian culture at a particular time is portrayed accurately and positively. Writer's guidelines: #10 SASE. Catalog: #10 SASE, 1 first class stamp.

COUNTRYWOMAN'S PRESS, THE. (Subsidiary of Padre Productions).
PO Box 840. Arroyo Grande, CA 93421-0840. (805) 473-1947. Submissions Editor: Karen L. Reinecke. Founded: 1984. Number of titles published: cumulative—6, 1992—6. Softback 100%.

Subjects of Interest. Nonfiction—cookbooks, ethnicity in America is our area of interest. Do not want: books based on overseas diets.

Initial Contact. Query letter with synopsis/outline and book proposal. Emphasize author's skills and resources for promoting book sales. SASE required.

Acceptance Policies. Unagented manuscripts: yes. Simultaneous submissions: yes. Response time to initial inquiry: 2 weeks. Average time until publication: 1-2 years. **Advance:** not offered. **Royalty:** negotiable.

Marketing Channels. Distribution houses; direct mail; independent reps; in-house staff. Subsidiary rights: all.

Additional Information. We do not consider unhealthful diets; natural foods are preferred. Tips: We prefer specialized topics rather than general cookbooks. Writer's guidelines: #10 SASE, 1 first class stamp. Catalog: 9x12 SASE, 2 ounces, first class postage.

Crime and Social Justice Associates *see* **SOCIAL JUSTICE.**

CROSS CULTURAL PUBLICATIONS, INC. PO Box 506. Notre Dame, IN
46556. (219) 272-0889. Submissions Editor: C. Pullapilly. Founded: 1980. Number of titles published: cumulative—18, 1992—6. Hardback 100%.

Subjects of Interest. Nonfiction—ethnic groups (Indians from India, Chinese, Japanese); religions (Christianity, Islam, Hinduism); history; intercultural topics. Recent publications: *Christian Missions in China*.

Initial Contact. Query letter with synopsis/outline. Include resumé. SASE required.

Acceptance Policies. Unagented manuscripts: yes. Simultaneous submissions: no. Response time to initial inquiry: 1-2 months. Average time until publication: 6 months. **Advance:** not offered. **Royalty:** based on sales.

Marketing Channels. Direct mail; journal reviews. Subsidiary rights: all.

CROSSING PRESS, THE. PO Box 1048. Freedom, CA 95019. (408) 722-
0711. Submissions Editors: John or Elaine G. Gill. Founded: 1972. Number of titles published: cumulative—350, 1992—28. Hardback 10%, softback 90%.

Subjects of Interest. Fiction—literary; feminist; general interest; mysteries; sci-fi feminist; women's books. Recent publications: *Married Life and Other Adventures; Trespassing.* **Nonfiction**—cookbook series; gay/lesbian issues; helath/fitness; holistic practices; men's issues; self-help; women's issues; women's health series; parenting series; women's spirituality series. Recent publications: *Island Cooking: Recipes from the Caribbean; Sun-Dried Tomatoes; Men and Intimacy; All Women Are Healers.* Do not want: romance novels; historical fiction; children's stories.

Initial Contact. Query letter with synopsis/outline. Include sample chapters.

Acceptance Policies. Unagented manuscripts: yes. First novels: yes. Simultaneous submissions: yes. Response time to initial inquiry: 3-4 weeks. Average time until publication: 6-12 months. Subsidy basis: negotiable. **Advance:** negotiable. **Royalty:** 7-10% of net.

Marketing Channels. Distribution houses; direct mail; independent reps; in-house staff; special sales. Subsidiary rights: all.

Additional Information. We recently moved to new offices, expanded our production facility, and expanded our seasonal releases. Tips: Study our catalog and contact us one year prior to desired release. Writer's guidelines and catalog: call (800) 777-1048.

CRUMB ELBOW PUBLISHING.
(Imprints: Tyee Press, Oregon Fever Books, Trillium Art Productions, Research Centrex, Silhouette Imprints). PO Box 294. Rhododendron, OR 97049. (503) 622-4798. Submissions Editor: Michael P. Jones. Founded: 1975. Number of titles published: cumulative—50, 1992—20. Hardback 50%, softback 50%.

Subjects of Interest. Fiction—ethnic groups (Native Americans, Gypsies, Asians, Afro-Americans, Europeans, etc.). **Nonfiction**—ethnic (Native Americans, Gypsies, Asians, Afro-Americans, Europeans, etc.); translations. Recent publications: *Between Two Worlds* (a Tlingit Indian story). Do not want: racist-oriented manuscripts.

Initial Contact. Query letter with synopsis outline, book proposal, and sample chapters. SASE must be included.

Acceptance Policies. Unagented manuscripts: yes. First novels: yes. Simultaneous submissions: yes. Response time to initial inquiry: 1-2 months. Average time until publication: 8-12 months. Subsidy or co-publishing basis: cooperative publishing venture. **Advance:** not offered. **Royalty:** payment in published copies.

Marketing Channels. Direct mail; independent sales; in-house staff; special sales; catalogs. Subsidiary rights: all rights are split fifty-fifty with author.

Additional Information. We have a strong leaning towards Native Americans, but we are open to all. Tips: Patience, we are incredibly busy. Don't be pushy. No prima donnas, please. No racists. Writer's guidelines: SASE. Catalog: $3.

DANTE UNIVERSITY PRESS.
17 Station St., Box 843. Brookline, MA 92147. (617) 734-2045. Fax: (617) 734-2046. Submissions Editor: address to editor. Founded: 1975. Number of titles published: cumulative—10, 1992—2. Hardback 80%, softback 10%.

Subjects of Interest. Fiction—literary (Italian or Italian-American). Recent publications: *Tales of Suicide* (Pirandello). **Nonfiction**—Italian culture; biography; translations from the Italian. Recent publications: *Dante in the 20th Century; Dante's Inferno* (translation). Do not want: trash.

Initial Contact. Query letter only. SASE required.

Acceptance Policies. Unagented manuscripts: yes. Simultaneous submissions: no. Response time to initial inquiry: 10 days. Average time until publication: 6 months. **Advance:** not offered. **Royalty:** yes.

Marketing Channels. Distribution houses. Subsidiary rights: all.

Additional Information. We emphasize Italian-Americana. Tips: Follow submission requirements. Writer's guidelines: none. Catalog: not available.

DENALI PRESS, THE. PO Box 021535. Juneau, AK 99802. (907) 586-6014.
Fax: (907) 463-6780. Submissions Editor: Sally Silvas-Ottumwa. Founded: 1986. Number of titles published: cumulative—17, 1992—4. Softback 100%.

Subjects of Interest. Nonfiction—ethnic groups (Hispanics, Native Americans, Alaska Natives); refugees; cultural diversity. Recent publications: *Native American Reader; Hispanic Resource Directory 1992-1994.*

Initial Contact. Query letter only. SASE required.

Acceptance Policies. Unagented manuscripts: yes. Simultaneous submissions: yes. Response time to initial inquiry: 4 weeks. Average time until publication: 9 months. **Advance:** not offered. **Royalty:** yes; based on 10% of net price.

Marketing Channels. Cooperative distribution; direct mail; space ads. Subsidiary rights: all.

Additional Information. We publish principally reference books. Catalog: upon request.

Destiny Books *see* **INNER TRADITIONS INTERNATIONAL.**

DIAL BOOKS FOR YOUNG READERS. (Subsidiary of Penguin USA.
Imprints: Dial Easy-to-Read, Puffin, Pied Piper). 375 Hudson St. New York, NY 10014. (212) 366-2800. Fax: (212) 366-2040, 366-2020. Submissions Editor: address all correspondence to Submissions Editor. Founded: 1961. Number of titles published: cumulative—609 in print, 1992—80. Hardback 50%, softback 50%.

Subjects of Interest. Fiction—children's and young adult only (all ethnic cultures). Recent publications: *Roll of Thunder, Hear My Cry* (Mildred Taylor); *Brother Eagle, Sister Sky* (Chief Seattle); *Journey of Meng.* Nonfiction—non-textbook biographies. Recent publications: biography on Rosa Parks due out. Do not want: genre fiction; mass-market; puzzles; coloring books.

Initial Contact. Complete manuscript for picture books. Query letter with synopsis/outline and sample chapters for longer fiction and nonfiction. SASE required.

Acceptance Policies. Unagented manuscripts: yes. First novels: yes. Simultaneous submissions: yes, inform us. Response time to initial inquiry: 3 months. Average time until publication: n/i. **Advance:** varies with circumstances. **Royalty:** yes.

Marketing Channels. Distribution houses; cooperative distribution; independent reps; in-house staff; special sales. Subsidiary rights: all.

Additional Information. Tips: Make sure your story avoids overworked themes, moralizing, religious proselytizing, and racial or sexual stereotypes. Writer's guidelines: #10 SASE, 1 first class stamp. Catalog: 9x12 SASE, $1.10 postage.

EASTERN CARIBBEAN INSTITUTE. PO Box 1338. Frederiksted, St. Croix. Virgin Islands 00841. (809) 772-1011. Fax: (809) 772-3665. Submissions Editor: S. B. Jones-Hendrickson, Ph. D. Founded: 1982. Number of titles published: cumulative—8, 1992—5. Hardback 40%, softback 60%.

Subjects of Interest. Fiction—Afro-Caribbean. Recent publications: *Sonny Jim of Sand Point.* Nonfiction—Afro-Caribbean; poetry; economics. Recent publications: *Caribbean Visions.* Do not want: religious works.

Initial Contact. Query letter only. SASE required.

Acceptance Policies. Unagented manuscripts: yes. First novels: yes. Simultaneous submissions: yes. Response time to initial inquiry: 1 month. Average time until publication: 6-9 months. Subsidy or co-publishing basis: negotiable. **Advance:** 25%. **Royalty:** not offered.

Marketing Channels. Distribution houses; direct mail; independent reps. Subsidiary rights: first serialization; book club.

Additional Information. We are a small press with a Caribbean orientation looking for quality work. Tips: Understand the texture of the Caribbean. Catalog: upon request.

EDICIONES UNIVERSAL. PO Box 450353. Miami, FL 33245-0353. (305) 642-3355. Fax: (305) 642-7978. Submissions Editor: Juan M. Salvat. Founded: 1965. Number of titles published: cumulative—800, 1992—50. Hardback 2%, softback 98%.

Subjects of Interest. Fiction—Cuban topics written in Spanish. Recent publications: *El Circulo del Alacran.* Nonfiction—Cuban topics written in Spanish. Recent publications: *Reflexiones Sobre Cuba y Su Futuro.*

Initial Contact. Query letter with synopsis/outline. SASE required.

Acceptance Policies. Unagented manuscripts: yes. First novels: yes. Simultaneous submissions: yes. Response time to initial inquiry: 3 weeks. Average time until publication: 6 months. Subsidy or co-publishing basis: depends. **Advance:** varies. **Royalty:** varies.

Marketing Channels. Distribution houses; direct mail. Subsidiary rights:varies.

Additional Information. We are a small press. Writer's guidelines: none available. Catalog: upon request.

EIGHTH MOUNTAIN PRESS, THE. 624 SE 29th. Portland, OR 97214. (503) 233-3936. Submissions Editor: Ruth Gundle. Founded: 1985. Number of titles published: cumulative—11, 1992—3. All books are published in both hardback and softback.

Subjects of Interest. Fiction—literary; women's issues; all ethnic groups. Nonfiction—essays; poetry; gay/lesbian issues; all ethnic groups. Recent publications: *The Eating Hill* (poetry).

Initial Contact. Query letter only. SASE required.

Acceptance Policies. Unagented manuscripts: yes. First novels: yes. Simultaneous submissions: no. Response time to initial inquiry: 1 month. Average time until publication: 18 months. **Advance:** yes. **Royalty:** yes.

Marketing Channels. Distribution houses; direct mail; independent reps; special sales. Subsidiary rights: all.

Additional Information. We are a feminist literary press and publish only women writers. Writer's guidelines: SASE. Catalog: send $.52 postage.

ENSLOW PUBLICATION, INC. Box 777, Bloy St. and Ramsey Ave. Hillside, NJ 07205. (908) 964-4116. Fax: (908) 687-3829. Submissions Editor: Brian Enslow. Founded: 1976. Number of titles published: cumulative—n/i, 1992—n/i. Hardback 98%, softback 2%.

Subjects of Interest. Nonfiction—Hispanic, Asian, and African-American topics in the school curriculum. Recent publications: biographies of African-Americans written for second graders. Do not want: picture books; fiction.

Initial Contact. Query letter with synopsis/outline. Include any experience in writing children's books. SASE required.

Acceptance Policies. Unagented manuscripts: yes. Simultaneous submissions: yes. Response time to initial inquiry: 6 weeks. Average time until publication: n/i. **Advance:** n/i. Royalty: n/i.

ESOTERICA PRESS. (Imprints: *Notebook/Cuaderno: a Literary Journal*). PO Box 15607. Rio Rancho, NM 87174. Submissions Editor: Y. Zentella. Founded: 1985. Number of titles published: cumulative—4, 1992—3. Softback 100%.

Subjects of Interest. Fiction—avant-garde; children's bilingual; erotica; ethnic groups (Afro-Americans, Arabs, Hispanics, Indians, Italians, Latin Americans, Native Americans); folklore; historical fiction; literary; short stories; women's issues. Nonfiction—ethnic groups (Afro-Americans, Arabs, Hispanics, Indians, Italians, Latin Americans, Native Americans); cooking; culture; dance; education; erotica; folklore; gay/lesbian issues; holistic practices; religion (Islam); self-help; women's issues. Do not want: trash; explicit sex; love stories.

Initial Contact. Query letter with synopsis/outline. Include author's bio. SASE required.

Acceptance Policies. Unagented manuscripts: yes. First novels: yes. Simultaneous submissions: yes. Response time to initial inquiry: 12-20 weeks. Average time until publication: 1 year. **Advance:** not offered. **Royalty:** Our expenses are paid first. The profits are then split 40% to the publisher, 60% to the author.

Marketing Channels. Distribution houses; direct mail. Subsidiary rights: specified in contract.

Additional Information. Writer's guidelines: legal-size SASE. Catalog: legal-size SASE.

FAIRLEIGH DICKINSON UNIVERSITY PRESS. 285 Madison Ave. Madison, NJ 07940. (201) 593-8564. Submissions Editor: Harry Keyishian. Founded: 1966. Number of titles published: cumulative—700, 1992—30. Hardback 99.5%, softback .05%.

Subjects of Interest. Nonfiction—scholarly works for the academic market. Recent publications: *The Irish Relations: Trials of an Immigrant Tradition*. Do not want: fiction; poetry; nonfiction for general audience.

Initial Contact. Query letter with synopsis/outline. Include curriculum vitae and previous publications. SASE not required.

Acceptance Policies. Unagented manuscripts: yes. Simultaneous submissions: no. Response time to initial inquiry: 2 weeks. Average time until publication: 12-18 months. Advance: not offered. **Royalty:** negotiable.

Marketing Channels. Direct mail; ads in appropriate journals; conferences. Subsidiary rights: negotiable.

Additional Information. Contracts are between authors and Associated University Presses. Tips: Be sure documentation is in accordance with scholarly standards. Use *Chicago Manual of Style* rather than MLA format. Writer's guidelines: upon request. Catalog: upon request.

FARRAR, STRAUS & GIROUX, INC. (Young Readers Division). 19 Union Square West. New York, NY 10003. (212) 741-6900. Submissions Editor: Books for Young Readers. Founded: 1946. Number of titles published: cumulative—450 books in print, 1992—75. Hardback 85%, softback 15%.

Subjects of Interest. Fiction—picture book to young adult with ethnic themes; translations for middle readers to young adult. Nonfiction—picture book to young adult with ethnic themes; translations for middle readers to young adult.

Initial Contact. Query letter only. SASE required.

Acceptance Policies. Unagented manuscripts: yes. First novels: yes. Simultaneous submissions: no. Response time to initial inquiry: 1-2 months. Average time until publication: 18-24 months. **Advance:** yes. **Royalty:** yes.

Marketing Channels. Independent reps; in-house staff; special sales. Subsidiary rights: all.

Additional Information. Writer's guidelines: SASE. Catalog: 6 1/2 x 9 1/2 SASE.

First Avenue Editions *see* **CAROLRHODA BOOKS, INC.**

FOLKLORE INSTITUTE. PO Box 1142. Berkeley, CA 94701. (510) 547-3219. Submissions Editor: Ved Prakash Vatuk. Founded: 1978. Number of titles published: cumulative—19, 1992—4. Hardback 100%.

Subjects of Interest. Fiction—children's books on India. Nonfiction—sociology, anthropology, folklore of India; poetry, creative literature in Hindi. Recent publications: *Political Economy in Vietnam; Transforming the Soul Wound: A Theoretical, Clinical Approach to American Indian Psychology.* Do not want: sectarian religion.

Initial Contact. Query letter only. Include information about the author. SASE requested.

Acceptance Policies. Unagented manuscripts: yes. Simultaneous submissions: yes. Response time to initial inquiry: 2 weeks. Average time until publication: 3-6 months. Subsidy or co-publishing basis: negotiable as co-publishers. **Advance:** not offered. **Royalty:** 10%; based on net sales.

Marketing Channels. Direct mail. Subsidiary rights: none.

Additional Information. We publish well-researched scholarly books, mostly on India. Catalog: upon request.

FORTRESS PRESS. (Subsidiary of Augsburg Fortress Publishers). 426 S. Fifth St. PO Box 1209. Minneapolis, MN 55440. (612) 330-3300. Fax: (612) 330-3455. Submissions Editors: Dr. Marshall D. Johnson, editorial director; J. Michael West, senior editor. Founded: n/i. Number of titles published: cumulative—600, 1992—60. Hardback 25%, softback 75%.

Subjects of Interest. Nonfiction—contextual theology from black, Hispanic, or Asian-American theologians; translations of liberation theology from Latin America or Africa. Recent publications: *Protest and Praise* (black religious music); *Liberating Visions* (black moral philosophers; *We Are a People* (Hispanic-American theology); *Luther and Liberation* (translation). Do not want: fiction; poetry; inspiration; devotional works.

Initial Contact. Query letter with synopsis/outline. Include curriculum vitae. SASE not required.

Acceptance Policies. Unagented manuscripts: yes. Simultaneous submissions: no. Response time to initial inquiry: 60-90 days. Average time until publication: 1 year. **Advance:** $300. **Royalty:** 7 1/2-10%; based on retail cover price.

Marketing Channels. Distribution houses; independent reps. Subsidiary rights: all.

Additional Information. We publish academic books on religion, biblical studies, theology, and ethics. Tips: Guidelines are not needed; simply send proposal and curriculum vitae. Catalog: upon request.

Gold Eagle *see* **HARLEQUIN ENTERPRISES LIMITED.**

GOLDEN WEST PUBLISHERS. 4113 N. Longview Ave. Phoenix, AZ 85014. (602) 265-4392. Submissions Editor: Hal Mitchell. Founded: 1972. Number of titles published: cumulative—45, 1992—5. Softback 100%.

Subjects of Interest. Nonfiction—cookbooks; Mexican cookbooks; Arizona books; Southwest. Recent publications: *Best Barbeque Recipes; Arizona Legends and Lore; Verde River Recreation Guide.* Do not want: children's books; poetry; religion.

Initial Contact. Query letter only. Include table of contents and author's background.

Acceptance Policies. Unagented manuscripts: yes. Simultaneous submissions: yes. Response time to initial inquiry: 2-3 weeks. Average time until publication: 1 year. **Advance:** none. **Royalty:** based on sales.

Marketing Channels. Distribution houses; direct mail; independent reps. Subsidiary rights: all.

Additional Information. We've been particularly successful with Southwestern cookbooks. Catalog: upon request.

GREENHAVEN PRESS, INC. PO Box 289009. San Diego, CA 92198-0009. (619) 485-7424. Submissions Editor: Bruno Leone. Founded: 1970. Number of titles published: cumulative—440, 1992—35. Softback 100%.

Subjects of Interest. Nonfiction—children's and young adult. Adult *Opposing Viewpoint Series* in the field of crime; contemporary social issues; controversial topics; environment/ecology; politics/world affairs; science; sociology. Recent publications: *Opposing Viewpoint Series: American Values; America's Future; Crime and Criminals; The Elderly; Euthanasia; The Homeless; Genetic Engineering; Japan; Male/Female Roles; Sexual Values; Third World; Immigration; Racism in America; Latin American and U.S. Foreign Policy.*

Initial Contact. Query letter with sample chapter.

Acceptance Policies. Unagented manuscripts: yes. Simultaneous submissions: yes, inform us. Disk submissions: no. Response time to initial inquiry: 1 month. Average time until publication: 1 year. **Advance:** none. **Royalty:** flat fee. First run: varies.

Marketing Channels. Distribution houses; direct mail. Subsidiary rights: English language publication outside the United States and Canada.

Additional Information. Catalog: write or call. Writer's guidelines: write or call.

GUERNICA EDITIONS. PO Box 633, Station NDG. Montreal, Canada H4A 3R1. (514) 987-7411. Fax: (514) 982-9793. Submissions Editor: Antonio D'Alfonoso. Founded: 1978. Number of titles published: cumulative—110, 1992—20. Softback 100%.

Subjects of Interest. Fiction—all subjects. Recent publications: *Infertility Rites; Bittersweet Pieces* (Dutch short stories). Nonfiction—biography; poetry; subjects dealing with Italian culture; translations. Recent publications: *Comparative Essays on Italian-Canadian*

Writing; Conceptions (poetry); *Arrangiarsi: The Italian Immigration Experience in Canada.* Do not want: nostalgic writings.

Initial Contact. Query letter only. SASE with Canadian postage required.

Acceptance Policies. Unagented manuscripts: yes. First novels: yes. Simultaneous submissions: no. Response time to initial inquiry: 1-3 months. Average time until publication: 18 months. **Advance:** $1000. **Royalty:** 8-10%; based on sales.

Marketing Channels. Distribution houses; direct mail. Subsidiary rights: all.

Additional Information. Our concentration is on Italian culture. Catalog: upon request.

HARLEQUIN ENTERPRISES LIMITED. (Imprints: Harlequin, Silhouette, Worldwide, Gold Eagle). 225 Duncan Mills Rd. Don Mills, Ontario, Canada M3B 3K9. (416) 445-5860. Submissions Editor: send for guidelines as each division has its own editor. Founded: 1949. Number of titles published: cumulative—5000+, 1992—750. Softback 100%.

Subjects of Interest. Fiction—romance, historical romance, romantic suspense often with ethnic characters. Recent publications: *Rites of Love* (Native American heroine); *Yes Is Forever* (Eurasian heroine); *For All the Right Reasons* (Hispanic hero); *A Woman's Prerogative* (Puerto Rican protagonists); *Adam and Eva* (black hero and heroine).

Initial Contact. Query letter only. Include length of your manuscript, a brief synopsis, any pertinent information about yourself, including publishing credits and professional affiliations. Our guidelines give specific information as to the requirements of each separate line. Send for them first. SASE required.

Acceptance Policies. Unagented manuscripts: yes. Simultaneous submissions: no. Response time to initial inquiry: 3 weeks for query letter; 12 weeks for complete submissions. Average time until publication: 1-2 years. **Advance:** yes; amount confidential. **Royalty:** yes; based on net sales.

Marketing Channels. Distribution houses; direct mail. Subsidiary rights: all.

Additional Information. We have distribution in more than 100 international markets and translations into 20 languages. We are proud of the wide variety of romance fiction we publish, and this variety includes characters of varying ethnic backgrounds. Tips: We look for well-written, entertaining romances featuring convincing characters with believable emotions in the context of a well-developed romantic relationship. Writer's guidelines: SASE.

Healing Arts Press *see* **INNER TRADITIONS INTERNATIONAL.**

HEMINGWAY WESTERN STUDIES SERIES. Boise State University. 1910 University Dr. Boise, ID 83725. (208) 385-1999. Submissions Editor: Tom Trusky. Founded: 1985. Number of titles published: cumulative—7, 1992—1. Hardback 20%, softback 80%.

Subjects of Interest. Nonfiction—ethnic groups (Chinese, Hispanics, Indians of Central/South America, Basques) relating to intermountain West in areas of popular scholarship (anthropology, contemporary and social issues, and ethnic groups). Recent publications: *Preserving the Game* (essays on gambling, mining, and hunting in the West). Do not want: local history.

Initial Contact. Query letter with synopsis/outline.

Acceptance Policies. Unagented manuscripts: yes. Simultaneous submissions: yes. Response time to initial inquiry: 2-3 months. Average time until publication: 1 year. **Advance:** not offered. **Royalty:** 12% average; based on wholesale.

Marketing Channels. Distribution houses; direct mail; independent reps. Subsidiary rights: none.

Additional Information. Not interested in jargon-laden academic works or Utah's Bermuda Triangle (i.e., footnote heaven or regional voodoo). Tips: We want reliable, authoritative, lively nonfiction studies relating to Rocky Mountain art, history, environment, politics, religions, sociology, anthropology (any "ology"). Writer's guidelines: upon request. Catalog: upon request.

HERALD PRESS. (Subsidiary of Mennonite Publishing House). 616 Walnut Ave. Scottsdale, PA 15683-1999. (412) 887-8500. Fax: (412) 887-3111. Submissions Editor: S. David Garber. Founded: 1908. Number of titles published: cumulative—1000, 1992—30. Hardback 10%, softback 90%.

Subjects of Interest. Fiction—children's/young adult; mystery (juvenile); historical fiction; women's issues; short story collections. All forms often have a Mennonite or Amish focus. Recent publications: *Sara's Summer* (teen visits the Hutterites). **Nonfiction**—Mennonite and Amish history and experience; current issues; peace and justice; missions and evangelism; family life; personal experience; Bible study; translations on radical reformation, Anabaptist sources. Recent publications: *Copper Moons* (a Mennonite's first year of marriage is spent doing service work in Africa); *Classics of the Radical Reformation* (translation). Do not want: war; drugs; cops and robbers; explicit sex.

Initial Contact. Query letter with 1-page book summary, chapter synopsis, and 2 sample chapters. Include bio and qualifications, target audience, and significance of book. SASE required.

Acceptance Policies. Unagented manuscripts: yes. First novels: yes. Simultaneous submissions: prefer not to. Response time to initial inquiry: 2 months. Average time until publication: 10 months. **Advance:** not offered. **Royalty:** 10%; based on retail sales.

Marketing Channels. Distribution houses; direct mail; in-house staff; special sales; ads; book clubs. Subsidiary rights: all.

Additional Information. We publish books which are consitent with Scripture as interpreted in the Anabaptist/Mennonite tradition. Tips: Your submission should be honest in presentation, clear in thought, stimulating in content, and conducive to the spritual growth and welfare of the reader. Know your subject and polish and revise your manuscript. Writer's guidelines: write or call. Catalog: $.60

HEYDAY BOOKS. PO Box 9145. Berkeley, CA 94709. (510) 549-3564. Fax: (510) 549-1889. Submissions Editor: Tracey Broderick. Founded: 1974. Number of titles published: cumulative—28, 1992—35. Hardback 5%, softback 95%.

Subjects of Interest. Fiction—ethnic stories, folklore, historical novels, literary, Western, women's issues with a Native American, California focus; California literature. Recent publications: *The Maidu Indian Myths and Stories of Hanc'ibyjim.* Nonfiction—California Indians; California history titles, guidebooks based on natural history; translations of California Indian tales. Recent publications: *To the American Indian: Reminiscences of a Yurok Woman.* Do not want: books without a strong California focus.

Initial Contact. Book proposal. SASE required.

Acceptance Policies. Unagented manuscripts: yes. First novels: yes. Simultaneous submissions: no. Response time to initial inquiry: 1 week. Average time until publication: 1-2 years. **Advance:** not offered. **Royalty:** 8%; based on list price.

Marketing Channels. Distribution houses; in-house staff. Subsidiary rights: all.

Additional Information. Catalog: manila envelope, 2 ounces first class postage.

HILL BOOKS, LAWRENCE. (Subsidiary of Chicago Review Press). 230 Park Pl., Ste. 6A. Brooklyn, NY 11238. (718) 857-1015. Submissions Editor: Shirley A. Cloyes, director. Founded: 1972. Number of titles published: cumulative—60, 1992—8. Hardback 1%, softback 99%.

Subjects of Interest. Nonfiction—ethnic groups (blacks, Middle Eastern cultures, Native Americans, Latin Americans, Third World cultures); contemporary politics, minority issues; biography; translations; women's issues. Recent publications: *Civilization or Barbarism* (translated from the French); *Assata: An Autobiography by Assata Shakur*. Do not want: fiction.

Initial Contact. Query letter only. Include author bio. SASE required.

Acceptance Policies. Unagented manuscripts: yes. Simultaneous submissions: yes. Response time to initial inquiry: 1 week. Average time until publication: 9 months. **Advance:** yes. **Royalty:** 8-15% sliding scale determined by number of copies sold; based on gross sales except where discount exceeds 50%.

Marketing Channels. Distribution houses; direct mail; independent reps; special sales. Subsidiary rights: all.

Additional Information. Although we are not sectarian, all of our books are politically progressive. Writer's guidelines: call or write. Catalog: call or write.

HIPPOCRENE BOOKS, INC. 171 Madison Ave. New York, NY 10016. (212) 685-4371. Fax: (212) 779-9338. Submissions Editor: George Blagowidow. Founded: 1971. Number of titles published: cumulative—1000, 1992—80. Hardback 50%, softback 50%.

Subjects of Interest. Nonfiction—travel, military history, foreign language dictionaries. Do not want: fiction.

Initial Contact. Query letter only or query letter with synopsis/outline. SASE required.

Acceptance Policies. Unagented manuscripts: yes. Simultaneous submissions: yes. Response time to initial inquiry: 6 weeks. Average time until publication: 1 year. **Advance:** $2500 (average). **Royalty:** 10% cloth, 6% paper; based on retail price.

Marketing Channels. In-house staff. Subsidiary rights: standard publishing terms.

Additional Information. Writer's guidelines: SASE. Catalog: upon request.

HOLIDAY HOUSE. 425 Madison Ave. New York, NY 10017. (212) 688-0085. Submissions Editors: Margery Cuyler, editor in chief; Alyssa Chase, assistant editor. Founded: n/i. Number of titles published: cumulative—n/i, 1992—n/i. Hardback n/i, softback n/i.

Subjects of Interest. Fiction—multicultural picture books to short-chapter books for middle-grade readers in the areas of adventure, historical fiction, humor, fantasy. Recent publications: *The Dog Who Had Kittens; Ghosts in the Fourth Grade*.
Nonfiction—multicultural poetry, tales, biography; science. Recent publications: *Pueblo*

Storyteller; Where Food Comes From; Dancing Teepees: Poems of American Indian Youth; The Fourth Question: A Chinese Folktale.

Initial Contact. Complete manuscript for picture books. Outline and three sample chapters for novels and nonfiction. SASE required.

Acceptance Policies. Unagented manuscripts: yes. Simultaneous submissions: yes, inform us. Response time to initial inquiry: 6-8 weeks. Average time until publication: n/i. **Advance:** not offered. **Royalty:** n/i; based on .

Marketing Channels. n/i. Subsidiary rights: n/i.

Additional Information. Tips: Writer's guidelines: upon request. Catalog: upon request.

HOWARD UNIVERSITY PRESS. 2900 Van Ness St., NW. Washington, DC 20008. (202) 806-8450. Fax: (202) 806-8474. Submissions Editors: Edwin J. Gordon (Hispanics, Native Americans); Renee Mayfield (African-Americans). Founded: 1972. Number of titles published: cumulative—204, 1992—10. Hardback 30%, softback 70%.

Subjects of Interest. Nonfiction—ethnic groups (Hispanics, Native Americans, African-Americans, Latin Americans); diaspora; political science; history; biography; literary criticism; translations. Recent publications: *Split Image* (study of the portrayal of blacks in all areas of mass media); *Black Writers in French* (translation of Keteloot's history of negritude).

Initial Contact. Query letter with synopsis/outline or book proposal with sample chapters. SASE required.

Acceptance Policies. Unagented manuscripts: yes. Simultaneous submissions: yes. Response time to initial inquiry: 30-day acknowledgement; 60-90 days for acceptance/rejection. Average time until publication: 9 months. **Advance:** rarely given. **Royalty:** varies.

Marketing Channels. Distribution houses; direct mail; in-house staff; space advertising. Subsidiary rights: open.

Additional Information. Tips: Have your market thoroughly analyzed and be prepared to show product uniqueness and audience needs. Writer's guidelines: upon request. Catalog: upon request.

Illini Books *see* **UNIVERSITY OF ILLINOIS PRESS.**

ILLUMINATIONS PRESS. 2110-B 9th St. Berkeley, CA 94710. (510) 849-2102. Submissions Editors: Norman Moser (poetry); Randy Fingland (prose). Founded: 1965. Number of titles published: cumulative—9, 1992—1. Softback 100%.

Subjects of Interest. Fiction—all ethnic groups; avant-garde; contemporary; folklore; general interest; humor; literary; mainstream; metaphysics/new age; plays/drama; short story collections. Recent publications: *Illuminations Reader: Anthology of Contemporary Literature.* Nonfiction—all ethnic groups with concentration on Afro-Americans, Asians, Hispanics, Indians of Central/South America, Latin Americans, Mexicans, Native Americans; art; comedy/humor; cooking; crafts; dance; family issues; folklore; general interest; immigrants/immigration; literary; metaphysics/new age; music; mythology; nature; philosophy; poetry; religion (Buddhism, Zen). Recent publications: *El Grito del Norte* (stories and tales); *The Illuminations Reader: Anthology of Writing and Art* (limited run of cloth copies); *Cleft Between Heaven and Earth* (poetry). Do not want: Christian verse.

Initial Contact. Query letter; book proposal with 10-15 pages of prose; 5-10 pages of poetry. Include subscription to anthology; author bio; credits. We can be contacted by phone. We do charge a reading fee for unsolicited mansucripts, payable in advance or with manuscript.

Acceptance Policies. Unagented manuscripts: yes. Simultaneous submissions: yes. Response time to initial inquiry: 2-3 months. Average time until publication: 12-18 months. Subsidy basis: 50% or less of costs plus $43 subscription fee to new '80s-'90s book series. **Advance:** none. **Royalty:** percent of profits based on investment.

Marketing Channels. Distribution houses; direct mail; special sales; subscription. Subsidiary rights: all.

Additional Information. We'll stick with quality even in these hard times called the '90s. Many of our writers are of ethnic backgrounds and address themselves to ethnic issues. Tips: Fiction needs convincing specificity; nonfiction needs authenticity. Writer's guidelines: SASE. Catalog: SASE.

INDIAN COUNTRY COMMUNICATIONS, INC. Rt. 2, Box 2900-A.
Hayward, WI 54843. (715) 634-5226. Fax: (715) 634-3243. Submissions Editor: Paul DeMain. Founded: 1987. Number of titles published: cumulative—2, 1992—n/i. Softback 100%.

Subjects of Interest. Fiction—Ojibway American-Indian ethnic works, short story collections, and translations. Recent publications: *Generation to Generation.* **Nonfiction**—Native American; Ojibway to English translations. Recent publications: Mishomis traditional teachings (translation).

Initial Contact. Query letter only.

Acceptance Policies. Unagented manuscripts: yes. First novels: yes. Simultaneous submissions: yes. Response time to initial inquiry: 2 months. Average time until publication: 9 months. **Advance:** not offered. **Royalty:** yes.

Marketing Channels. Direct mail; independent reps; special sales. Subsidiary rights: none.

INNER TRADITIONS INTERNATIONAL. (Imprints: Destiny Books, Healing
Arts Press, Park Street Press). One Park St. Rochester, VT 05767. (802) 767-3174. Fax: (802) 767-3726. Submissions Editor: Lee Wood. Founded: 1975. Number of titles published: cumulative—300, 1992—40. Hardback 5%, softback 95%.

Subjects of Interest. Nonfiction—ethnic groups (Afro-Americans, Indians from India, Indians of Central/South American, Native Americans); cooking; erotica; human potential; magic; martial arts; alternative medicine; men's issues; metaphysical/new age; esoteric music; mythology; nature/environment; philosophy; psycho-spiritual; religion (Buddhism, Islam, Tao, Zen); self-help; tribal issues; women's issues; yoga. Recent publications: *The Healing Drum* (African); *The Drummer's Path* (African); *Voices of the First Day* (Australian Aboriginal); *Sacred Earth: The Spiritual Landscape of Native America.*

Initial Contact. Book proposal with sample chapters. Include chapter-by-chapter summary, author's background, and experience in subject area. SASE required.

Acceptance Policies. Unagented manuscripts: yes. Simultaneous submissions: yes. Response time to initial inquiry: 3 months. Average time until publication: 1 year. **Advance:** $1000. **Royalty:** 8-10%; based on net.

Marketing Channels. Distribution houses; cooperative distribution; direct mail; independent reps; in-house staff; special sales. Subsidiary rights: all.

Additional Information. Especially interested in the wisdom contained in the teachings of indigenous cultures and what this has to offer to our spiritual awareness and overall health today, with awareness of the total environment. Writer's guidelines: SASE. Catalog: upon request.

IN ONE EAR PRESS. 3527 Voltaire St. San Diego, CA 92106. (619) 223-1871. Submissions Editor: Elizabeth Reid. Founded: 1989. Number of titles published: cumulative—2, 1992—4. Softback 100%.

Subjects of Interest. Fiction—Hispanic focus on folkore, general interest, historical fiction, holiday stories, translations. Nonfiction—ethnic groups (Hispanics, Indians of Central/South America, Latin Americans, Mexicans, Native Americans); children's; education; family isues; folklore; general interest; immigrants/immigration; reference books; self-help; translations; travel; language books (Spanish, English). Recent publications: *Bilingual Cooking: La Corina Bilingue; Bilingual Recipes: Recetas Bilingues; Moms and Dads: Mamis y Papis; Spanish Lingo for the Savvy Gringo.* Do not want: epic poetry.

Initial Contact. Query letter only. Include author's bio and qualifications.

Acceptance Policies. Unagented manuscripts: yes. Simultaneous submissions: yes. Response time to initial inquiry: 1 month. Average time until publication: 6 months. Subsidy basis: negotiated. **Advance:** none. **Royalty:** buy either all rights or publishing rights.

Marketing Channels. Cooperative distribution; direct mail; special sales. Subsidiary rights: reprint; book club.

Additional Information. We will consider short how-to books (75-100 pages) on topics of general interest. Tips: We like a light, humorous approach where appropriate, with simple to understand language. Catalog: SASE.

ISM PRESS. PO Box 12447. San Francisco, CA 94112. (415) 333-7641. Submissions Editor: Daniel Fogel. Founded: 1982. Number of titles published: cumulative—8, 1992—0. Hardback 33%, softback 67%.

Subjects of Interest. Nonfiction—all ethnic groups; anthropology; gay/lesbian issues; history; minority issues; multicultural/multilingual education; women's studies; people's freedom movements; translations. Recent publications: *Junipero Serra, The Vatican, and Enslavement Theology* (deals with the Spanish mission system and how it impacted California's Indians); *Esta Puente, Mi Espalda: Voces de Mujeres Tercermudnistas en los EEUU* (Spanish translation of *This Bridge Called My Back: Writings by Radical Women of Color*). Do not want: "new age" metaphysics; manuscripts containing only poetry.

Initial Contact. Query letter with synopsis/outline.

Acceptance Policies. Unagented manuscripts: yes. Simultaneous submissions: yes; if we contract to publish the book, we'll want an exclusive deal. Response time to initial inquiry: 1 month. Average time until publication: 18 months. **Advance:** yes. **Royalty:** yes, based on net income.

Marketing Channels. Distribution houses; direct mail or direct sales. Subsidiary rights: book club; translation and foreign; English language publication outside the United States and Canada.

Additional Information. We publish some books in Spanish and some bilingual. Tips: We favor broad but rigorous coverage of a field of nonfiction. Catalog: upon request.

ITALICA PRESS. 595 Main St., Ste. 605. New York, NY 10044. (212) 935-4230. Fax: (212)838-7812. Submissions Editors: Eileen Gardiner, Ronald G. Musto. Founded: 1985. Number of titles published: cumulative—19, 1992—6. Hardback 15%, softback 85%.

Subjects of Interest. Fiction—translations of contemporary Italian fiction. Recent publications: *Dolcissimo*. **Nonfiction**—medieval and Renaissance Latin text. Recent publications: *Naples: An Early Guide.*

Initial Contact. Cover letter with synopsis/outline. SASE required.

Acceptance Policies. Unagented manuscripts: yes. Simultaneous submissions: yes. Response time to initial inquiry: 1 month. Average time until publication: 6-12 months. **Advance:** not offered. **Royalty:** varies; based on net.

Marketing Channels. Distribution houses; direct mail; in-house staff; catalogs; book clubs. Subsidiary rights: translation and foreign rights.

Additional Information. Tips: Use *Chicago Manual of Style*. Catalog: write or phone.

JONATHAN DAVID PUBLISHERS, INC. 68-22 Eliot Ave. Middle Village, NY 11379. (718) 456-8611. Fax: (718) 894-2818. Submissions Editor: Alfred J. Kolatch. Founded: 1948. Number of titles published: cumulative—10,000, 1992—22. Hardback 80%, softback 20%.

Subjects of Interest. Nonfiction—emphasis on Judaica. Recent publications: *The Jewish Home Advisor; Chinese Kosher Cooking; The Christian Book of Why.* Do not want: fiction; poetry.

Initial Contact. Query letter with synopsis/outline. Include author bio. SASE required.

Acceptance Policies. Unagented manuscripts: yes. Simultaneous submissions: no. Response time to initial inquiry: 10 days maximum. Average time until publication: 12-18 months. **Advance:** varies. **Royalty:** yes.

Additional Information. Writer's guidelines: not available. Catalog: upon request.

JORDAN ENTERPRISES PUBLISHING COMPANY. (Subsidiary of Scojtia). 6457 Wilcox Station. PO Box 38002. Los Angeles, CA 90038. Submissions Editor: (Mr.) Patrique Quintahlen. Founded: 1989. Number of titles published: cumulative—5, 1992—3. Hardback 10%, softback 90%.

Subjects of Interest. Fiction—all subjects, including all ethnic groups, which have an affect on black thinking. Recent publications: *The Strawberry Fox* (fantasy art for ages 8-14); *Reuben, The Boy Who Opened Doors* (international art, black hero). **Nonfiction**—all subjects, including all ethnic groups, which have an affect on black thinking; translations (Spanish, French, Afrikaans, German, Japanese). Do not want: racial subjects.

Initial Contact. Query letter with synopsis/outline. Include publishing credits. SASE required.

Acceptance Policies. Unagented manuscripts: yes. First novels: yes. Simultaneous submissions: yes. Response time to initial inquiry: 2-4 months on query; 6-12 months on manuscript. Average time until publication: 12-18 months. Subsidy or co-publishing basis: small subsidy for poetry only. **Advance:** $500-$5000. **Royalty:** 8-10%; based on retail price.

Marketing Channels. Distribution houses; cooperative distribution; direct mail; independent reps; in-house staff; special sales. Subsidiary rights: all.

Additional Information. Our interests are in enlightened black thinking, art, and philosophy. Tips: Know the four stages of writing and transcend them. Know the editor's importance, skill requirements, and the difference between an editor and a critic. Know the business of publishing. Writer's guidelines: SASE. Catalog: not available.

KAR-BEN COPIES, INC. 6800 Tildenwood Lane. Rockville, MD 20852. (301) 984-8733. Fax: (301) 881-9195. Submissions Editor: Judye Groner. Founded: 1975. Number of titles published: cumulative—85, 1992—10. Hardback 30%, softback 70%.

Subjects of Interest. Fiction—Jewish themes for young children. **Nonfiction**—Jewish themes for young children. Recent publications: *Hanukkah Fun; Benjy's Bible Trails; Family Services for High Holidays.* Do not want: adult manuscripts; anything without Jewish content.

Initial Contact. Cover letter with entire manuscript. SASE required.

Acceptance Policies. Unagented manuscripts: yes. First novels: yes. Simultaneous submissions: yes. Response time to initial inquiry: 3-6 weeks. Average time until publication: 6-12 months. **Advance:** $500-$1000. **Royalty:** 6% author, 6% artist; based on net sales.

Marketing Channels. Distribution houses; direct mail; independent reps; special sales; trade and Jewish conferences. Subsidiary rights: all.

Additional Information. We publish books, tapes, and calendars on Jewish themes for young children. Writer's guidelines: SASE. Catalog: upon request.

KARNAK HOUSE. 300 Westbourne Park Rd. London, England W11 1EH. (071) 221-6490. Fax: (071) 221-6490. Submissions Editor: Mr. A. S. Saakana. Founded: 1979. Number of titles published: cumulative—44, 1992—9. Hardback 30%, softback 70%.

Subjects of Interest. Fiction—African children's/young adult, folklore, historical novels, literary, and short story collections. Recent publications: *House of Bondage* (issue of collaboration in South Africa). **Nonfiction**—African anthropology, archaeology, biography, crafts, dance, education, essays; translations from French to English. Recent publications: *African Background to Medical Science: Essays on Ancient Egypt; Ancient Egypt and Black Africa: Philosophy, Linguistics, Gender Relations.* Do not want: poetry; humor.

Initial Contact. Book proposal with sample chapters. SASE required.

Acceptance Policies. Unagented manuscripts: yes. First novels: yes. Simultaneous submissions: n/i. Response time to initial inquiry: 3-6 months. Average time until publication: 12-18 months. **Advance:** not offered. **Royalty:** 8% for paperback; 10% for hardback.

Marketing Channels. Distribution houses; direct mail; special sales. Subsidiary rights: all.

Additional Information. We are oriented to articulating the global condition of Africans. Tips: All manuscripts must be typed, double spaced, and clearly and coherently articulated. Writer's guidelines: not available. Catalog: upon request.

Kazan Books *see* **VOLCANO PRESS, INC.**

KODANSHA INTERNATIONAL. New York Editorial Office. 114 Fifth Ave. New York, NY 10011. (212) 727-6960. Fax: (212) 727-9117. Submissions Editors: Paul De Angelis, Helena Franklin, Tina Isaac. Founded: 1989. Number of titles published: cumulative—10, 1992—10-15. Hardback 80%, softback 20%.

Subjects of Interest. Nonfiction—Asia or Asian-Americans; international and cross-cultural subjects; translations on the above topics. Do not want: books which are not serious and of high quality.

Initial Contact. Query letter with synopsis/outline. SASE required.

Acceptance Policies. Unagented manuscripts: yes. Simultaneous submissions: yes. Response time to initial inquiry: n/i. Average time until publication: n/i. **Advance:** n/i. **Royalty:** n/i; based on .

Marketing Channels. Distributed by Farrar, Straus & Giroux and our own representatives. Subsidiary rights: all.

Additional Information. Catalog: upon request.

LION BOOKS PUBLISHER. (Subsidiary of Sayre Publishing, Inc.). 210 Nelson Rd., Ste. B. Scarsdale, NY 10583. (914) 725-3572. Submissions Editor: Harriet K. Ross. Founded: 1968. Number of titles published: cumulative—160, 1992—10. Hardback 85%, softback 15%.

Subjects of Interest. Fiction—ethnic groups; folklore; historical fiction; horror; sports; young adult. Nonfiction—ethnic groups (blacks, Asians, Chinese). Recent publications: *African Crafts; Phyllis Wheatly, Negro Slave; Asian Crafts.* Do not want: picture books for children.

Initial Contact. Entire manuscript. Include where author has been previously published. SASE required.

Acceptance Policies. Unagented manuscripts: yes. Simultaneous submissions: no. Response time to initial inquiry: 10 days. Average time until publication: 6 months. **Advance:** negotiable. **Royalty:** yes; or work-for-hire.

Marketing Channels. Schools; wholesalers to schools and libraries. Subsidiary rights: negotiable.

Additional Information. Writer's guidelines: not available. Catalog: upon request.

LITTLE, BROWN AND COMPANY. (Subsidiary of Time Warner, Inc. Imprint: Little, Brown Children's Books). 34 Beacon St. Boston, MA 02108. (617) 227-0730. Fax: (617) 227-8344. Submissions Editors: Maria Modugno (editor in chief); Stephanie O. Lurie (senior editor); Hilary M. Breed (associate editor). Founded: 1837. Number of titles published: 1992—80. Hardback 90%, softback 10%.

Subjects of Interest. Fiction—holiday tales (Jewish); picture books with ethnic characters; native tales to specific areas; novels of ethnic experience; picture books translated from French to English. Recent publications: *Irene and the Big, Fine Nickel; Anancy and Mr. Dry-Bone; Osa's Pride.* Nonfiction—dual language song books, word books (Spanish/English); Native American tales.

Initial Contact. Book proposal with sample chapters or entire manuscript. Inform if work is a multiple submission, and include author's publishing history. SASE required.

Acceptance Policies. Unagented manuscripts: yes. First novels: yes. Simultaneous submissions: yes, inform us. Response time to initial inquiry: up to 3 months. Average time until publication: 1-2 years. **Advance:** varies. **Royalty:** up to 10%.

Marketing Channels. Distribution houses; direct mail; independent reps; in-house staff; special sales. Subsidiary rights: all.

Additional Information. Little, Brown is a trade publisher that produces very high quality books for children. We do not do mass market projects. We are open to anything as long as it is appropriate for children. Tips: Be patient. Writer's guidelines: SASE. Catalog: 10x13 SASE.

LODESTAR BOOKS. (Affiliate of Dutton Children's Books, a division of Penguin USA). 375 Hudson St. New York, NY 10014. (212) 366-2627. Submissions Editor: Rosemary Brosnan. Founded: 1860 (Dutton). Number of titles published: 1992—30. Hardback 100%.

Subjects of Interest. Fiction—picture book through young adult with a special interest in books about Hispanic, African-American, Asian-American, and Native American young people. Recent publications: *Fast Talk on a Slow Track; The Honorable Prison.* Nonfiction—children's and young adult. Recent publications: *Getting Elected.*

Initial Contact. Query letter only. Include short biographical sketch and whether or not you have published previously. SASE required.

Acceptance Policies. Unagented manuscripts: yes. First novels: yes. Simultaneous submissions: prefer not to. Response time to initial inquiry: 2 months. Average time until publication: varies. **Advance:** varies. **Royalty:** novel, 10%; picture book, 5% author, 5% illustrator.

Marketing Channels. In-house staff; special sales. Subsidiary rights: all.

Additional Information. We publish high-quality hardcover books for children and young adults. Tips: Spend time in bookstores and libraries studying what young people are reading. Writer's guidelines: none available. Catalog: 9x12 SASE, $1.90 postage.

Lollipop Power Books *see* **CAROLINA WREN PRESS.**

LOS HOMBRES PRESS. PO Box 63279. San Diego, CA 92163-2729. (619) 298-4804. Submissions Editors: send to either Marsh Cassady or Jim Kitchen, co-publishers and editors. Founded: 1989. Number of titles published: cumulative—8, 1992—5. Softback 100%.

Subjects of Interest. Fiction—gay/lesbian writings and short story collections with any ethnic background. Nonfiction—Haiku poetry only. Do not want: romances; Westerns; non-Haiku poetry.

Initial Contact. Query letter with synopsis outline. SASE required.

Acceptance Policies. Unagented manuscripts: yes. First novels: yes. Simultaneous submissions: yes. Response time to initial inquiry: 2 weeks. Average time until publication: 1 year. **Advance:** not offered. **Royalty:** 10%; based on retail price of book.

Marketing Channels. Distribution houses; direct mail. Subsidiary rights: all.

Additional Information. We are not interested in porno or extensive explicit sex scenes. Tips: We look for good writing, with gay/lesbian protagonists presented in a positive way. Any ethnic background is okay. Writer's guidelines: upon request. Catalog: upon request.

LOTUS PRESS, INC. (Imprints: Penway Books). PO Box 21607. Detroit, MI 48221. (313) 861-1280. Submissions Editor: Naomi Long Madgett. Founded: 1972. Number of titles published: cumulative—74, 1992—2. Hardback 5%, softback 95%.

Subjects of Interest. Nonfiction—poetry. Recent publications: *Whole Grain: Collected Poems, 1958-1989* (James Emanuel). Do not want: anything other than poetry.

Initial Contact. Query letter only. We are not accepting unsolicited material at this time. SASE required.

Acceptance Policies. Unagented manuscripts: yes. Simultaneous submissions: no. Response time to initial inquiry: 6 weeks. Average time until publication: 10 months. **Advance:** not offered. **Royalty:** payment in copies.

Marketing Channels. Distribution houses; direct mail. Subsidiary rights: first serialization.

Additional Information. Most of our authors are African-Americans. Their work is of high literary quality. Tips: Study your craft. Poetry is an art form. We are interested in seeing material that is polished, not the result of emotional catharsis. We do not accept the typical work of amateurs. Writer's guidelines: SASE. Catalog: SASE.

LOUISIANA UNIVERSITY PRESS. Baton Rouge, LA 70893. (504) 388-6618. Fax: (504) 388-6461. Submissions Editors: Margaret Dalrymple (nonfiction); Martha Hall (fiction). Founded: 1935. Number of titles published: cumulative—940 in print, 1992—65-70. Hardback 95%, softback 5%.

Subjects of Interest. **Fiction**—African-American authors or subjects; any ethnic group in the South. Recent publications: *Leechtime*; *Turbulence* (translation). **Nonfiction**—African-American history, literature, culture, politics, etc.; any ethnic group in the South; poetry by or about African-Americans; translations. Recent publications: *Africans in Colonial Louisiana: The Development of Afro-Creole Culture in the Eighteenth Century*.

Initial Contact. Book proposal with sample chapters. SASE not required.

Acceptance Policies. Unagented manuscripts: yes. First novels: yes. Simultaneous submissions: yes. Response time to initial inquiry: 2-3 weeks. Average time until publication: 12-18 months. **Advance:** not offered. **Royalty:** yes.

Marketing Channels. Distribution houses; direct mail; independent reps; in-house staff; special sales. Subsidiary rights: all.

Additional Information. The focus of our program is the U.S. South. We would be interested in any materials pertaining to ethnicity in this region. Tips: This is a university press catering to an academic audience and to literate and discriminating general readers. Writer's guidelines: upon request. Catalog: upon request.

MAGE PUBLISHERS. 1032 29th St., NW. Washington, DC 20007. (202) 342-1642. Submissions Editor: A. Seperi. Founded: 1985. Number of titles published: cumulative—27, 1992—3. Hardback 100%.

Subjects of Interest. **Fiction**—folklore, historical novels, humor, literary, short story collections, women's issues with a focus on Iran. **Nonfiction**—architecture, art, literary, religion (Islam) with a focus on Iran and its culture. Recent publications: *Art of Persian Music; Stories from Iran: 1921-1991*. Do not want: anything not dealing with Iran or its culture.

Initial Contact. Query letter with synopsis/outline. Include 2 sample chapters and possible markets. SASE required.

Acceptance Policies. Unagented manuscripts: yes. First novels: yes. Simultaneous submissions: yes. Response time to initial inquiry: 3 months. Average time until publication: 18 months. **Advance:** not offered. **Royalty:** yes.

Marketing Channels. Distribution houses; direct mail; in-house staff. Subsidiary rights: n/i.

Additional Information. Writer's guidelines: upon request.

MaggPie Productions *see* **WINSTON-DEREK PUBLISHERS, INC.**

Monograph Series *see* **UNIVERSITY OF ALASKA PRESS.**

MOON PUBLICATIONS, INC. 722 Wall St. Chico, CA 95928. (916) 345-5473. Fax: (916) 345-6751. Submissions Editor: Taran March. Founded: 1976. Number of titles published: cumulative—41, 1992—14. Softback 100%.

Subjects of Interest. Nonfiction—comprehensive travel handbooks to Asia, the Pacific rim, Caribbean countries, and the United States and Canada. Recent publications: travel handbooks to Nepal, Jamaica, Bangkok, and Baja.

Initial Contact. Query letter with synopsis/outline. SASE not required.

Acceptance Policies. Unagented manuscripts: yes. Simultaneous submissions: yes. Response time to initial inquiry: 2-4 weeks. Average time until publication: 1-2 years. **Advance:** $4000-$7000. **Royalty:** 12%; based on net sales.

Marketing Channels. Distribution houses; cooperative distribution; direct mail; in-house staff. Subsidiary rights: reprint rights; direct mail or direct sales; translation and foreign; English language publication outside the United States and Canada.

Additional Information. We support cultural and geopolitical awareness through responsible tourism and travel. Tips: Familiarize yourself with our handbooks; demonstrate a sensitivity to ethnic and global issues and a comprehensive expertise on travel destination covered in mansucript. Writer's guidelines: upon written request. Catalog: call or write.

MR. COGITO PRESS. Pacific University. Humanities Department. Forest Grove, OR 97116. (503) 226-4135. Submissions Editors: Robert Davies, John Gogol. Founded: 1978. Number of titles published: cumulative—11, 1992—12. Softback 100%.

Subjects of Interest. Nonfiction—poetry; poetry translations (some). Recent publications: *Canoeing in the Rain* (poems regarding an adopted Indian child); *To Recognize This Dying* (on Central America); *The Arab/Muslim World* (poetry); forthcoming: Eastern European poetry of the '90s. Do not want: any unsolicited books or inquiries regarding same. All submissions (4-5) should go to the magazine *Mr. Cogito.*

Initial Contact. Submission first to magazine. SASE required.

Acceptance Policies. Unagented manuscripts: n/a. Simultaneous submissions: n/a. Response time to initial inquiry: up to 2 months. Average time until publication: up to 6 months. Subsidy or co-publishing: possible negotiation in future. **Advance:** not offered. **Royalty:** 10% of copies.

Marketing Channels. Distribution houses; direct mail; special sales. Subsidiary rights: none.

Additional Information. We are open to quality poetry and translations of most schools. Theme-oriented contests are often held, some of them with an ethnic focus. We accept line graphics and poetry only. We like moving poems (political and social context welcome) and are human-rights oriented. Tips: Send 4-5 poems to *Mr. Cogito* magazine with SASE. Writer's guidelines: SASE. Catalog: upon request.

MUIR PUBLICATIONS, JOHN. PO Box 613. Santa Fe, NM 87504. (505) 982-4078. Submissions Editor: Ken Luboff. Founded: 1969. Number of titles published: cumulative—70, 1992—30. Softback 100%.

Subjects of Interest. Nonfiction—ethnic groups (Native Americans, Hispanics); art; children's; contemporary issues; travel; environment; family; women's issues. Recent publications: *The Indian Way: Learning to Communicate with Mother Nature; Indian America: A Traveler's Companion; Kids Explore America's Hispanic Heritage.* Do not want: fiction; cookbooks; poetry.

Initial Contact. Query letter; or query letter with synopsis/outline.

Acceptance Policies. Unagented manuscripts: yes. Simultaneous submissions: yes. Response time to initial inquiry: 8 weeks. Average time until publication: varies. **Advance:** n/a. **Royalty:** n/a.

Marketing Channels. Cooperative distribution. Subsidiary rights: all.

NATUREGRAPH PUBLISHERS, INC. (Imprints: Prism Editions).
3543 Indian Creek Rd. PO Box 1075. Happy Camp, CA 96039. (916) 493-5353. Submissions Editor: Barbara Brown. Founded: 1946. Number of titles published: cumulative—100+, 1992—6. Hardback 5%, softback 95%.

Subjects of Interest. Nonfiction—natural history; Native Americans; health; crafts dealing with natural history or Native Americans. Recent publications: *Apache Legends; Health Unlimited—Unleash Your Healing Power; Mystery Tracks in the Snow Karuk, the Upriver People.* Do not want: anything outside our category.

Initial Contact. Query letter; give reasons why book would sell, places to market it, a good sales pitch, and how this book differs from other books on the subject.

Acceptance Policies. Unagented manuscripts: yes. Simultaneous submissions: yes; alert us; encourages quick publisher response. Response time to initial inquiry: 1 week if not interested; 2 months if interested. Average time until publication: 18 months after contract. Subsidy basis: rarely; maybe 3-5%, and then we repay the investment at a rate of so much per book sold. Occurs when we want a book and can't afford to produce it without outside help. **Advance:** none. **Royalty:** 10% of net amount invoiced.

Marketing Channels. Distribution houses; direct mail; independent reps; special sales. Subsidiary rights: reprint; dramatization, motion picture, and broadcast; direct mail or direct sales; book club; translation and foreign; commercial; English language publication outside United States and Canada.

Additional Information. We are both publishers and printers. Predominantly we print only our own publications, but we also produce books commercially. Tips: We appreciate neatly typed, double-spaced, properly margined pages with a black typewriter ribbon. Catalog: upon request.

NEW DAY PRESS, INC. 2355 E. 89th St. Cleveland, OH 44106. (216) 795-7070. Submissions Editor: Carolyn Gordon, chair, editorial committee. Founded: 1972. Number of titles published: cumulative—15, 1992—1. Softback 100%.

Subjects of Interest. Fiction—Afro-American children's works in the areas of folklore and history; short stories. Recent publications: *Fireside Tales.* Nonfiction—Afro-American children's works in the areas of culture, education, human potential, minority issues. Recent publications: *Freedom Light: Stories of the Underground Railroad in Ripley, Ohio.*

Initial Contact. Query letter only or query letter with synopsis/outline or book proposal with sample chapters or entire manuscript.

Acceptance Policies. Unagented manuscripts: yes. First novels: yes. Simultaneous submissions: yes. Response time to initial inquiry: up to 3 months. Average time until publication: 6-12 months. **Advance:** varies. **Royalty:** yes.

Marketing Channels. Cooperative distribution; direct mail; independent reps; in-house staff; special sales. Subsidiary rights: all.

Additional Information. We look for Afro-American oriented children's stories, ages 5-12. Tips: Acquire our guidelines as we only consider materials which meet goals stated in our mission statement. Writer's guidelines: upon request. Catalog: upon request.

NEW SEED PRESS. PO Box 9488. Berkeley, CA 94709. (510) 540-7576. Submissions Editor: Helen Chetin. Founded: 1971. Number of titles published: 1992—12. Softback 100%.

Subjects of Interest. Fiction—feminist press looking for nonsexist, nonracist stories for children which actively confront bigotry issues. Recent Publications: *The Girls of Summer* (written and illustrated by black women); *The Good Bad Wolf; My Mother and I Are Growing Strong* (Spanish/English); *Angel Island Prisoner 1922* (Chinese/English); *Red Ribbons for Emma* (Navajo grandmother and sheepherder fights the polluting of reservation lands).

Initial Contact. Query letter; brief summary; SASE.

Acceptance Policies. Unagented manuscripts: yes. First novels: yes. Simultaneous submissions: yes. Response time to initial inquiry: 2 weeks. Average time until publication: 1 year. **Advance:** percent of royalty. **Royalty:** 10%.

Marketing Channels. Distribution houses; direct mail. Subsidiary rights: none.

Additional Information. We are not looking at manuscripts until 1993. Catalog: SASE.

NOBLE PRESS, THE. 213 W. Institute Pl., Ste. 508. Chicago, IL 60615. (312) 642-1168. Submissions Editors: Mark Harris, Suzanne Roe. Founded: 1988. Number of titles published: cumulative—11, 1992—15. Softback 100%.

Subjects of Interest. Nonfiction—all aspects of minority issues. Recent publications: *Joyce Ann Brown: Justice Denied* (biography of black woman jailed nine years for crime she did not commit). Do not want: fiction.

Initial Contact. Book proposal with 2 sample chapters. Include author's credentials. SASE required.

Acceptance Policies. Unagented manuscripts: yes. Simultaneous submissions: yes. Response time to initial inquiry: 6-8 weeks. Average time until publication: 9-12 months. **Advance:** varies. **Royalty:** varies.

Marketing Channels. Distribution houses; direct mail; in-house staff; special sales. Subsidiary rights: all.

Additional Information. We are interested in minority issues as they pertain to larger social issues. Tips: Try to consider why a large group of people would be interested enough in your manuscript to pay $10-$15 for it. It must appeal to a large audience for it to interest us. Writer's guidelines: SASE. Catalog: #10 SASE, 2 first class stamps.

NORTHLAND PUBLISHING COMPANY, INC. PO Box 1389. Flagstaff, AZ 86002. Submissions Editor: Susan McDonald. Founded: 1958. Number of titles published: cumulative—200+, 1992—18. Hardback 30%, softback 70%.

Subjects of Interest. Fiction—multicultural children's picture books and stories; folkore; translations. Recent publications: *At the Singapore Zoo* (translation of Singapore children's story); *The Mouse Bride* (Chinese translation); *Flute Player* (Apache folktale); *Monster Slayer* (Navajo folktale). **Nonfiction**—ethnic groups (Asians, Chinese, Indians of Central/South America, Native Americans, Scandinavians, Slavic peoples); regional (American West,

Southwest); art; illustrated books; cookbooks; environment/ecology; folklore; mythology; nature. Recent publications: *Sisters of the Dream* (Native American and Anglo characters, regional, feminist); *Changing Woman: The Life and Art of Helen Hardin* (fine art); *A Celebration of Being* (photography of Navajo and Hopi). Do not want: "How to kill cockroaches in New York."

Initial Contact. Query letter with synopsis/outline and sample chapters.

Acceptance Policies. Unagented manuscripts: yes. Simultaneous submissions: yes. Response time to initial inquiry: 1-2 months. Average time until publication: 10 months. **Advance:** $1000. **Royalty:** varies, but based on net receipts.

Marketing Channels. Distribution houses; direct mail; independent reps; in-house staff; special sales; telemarketing. Subsidiary rights: all.

Additional Information. Our current ethnic orientation has us acquiring children's stories and cookbooks primarily, with an emphasis on children's and ethnic folktales. Catalog: upon request. Writer's guidelines: upon request.

One Horn Press *see* **WINSTON-DEREK PUBLISHERS, INC.**

OPEN HAND PUBLISHING, INC. PO Box 22048. Seattle, WA 98122. (206) 323-3868. Submissions Editor: Pat Andrus. Founded: 1981. Number of titles published: cumulative—25, 1992—4. Hardback 40%, softback 60%.

Subjects of Interest. Fiction—ethnic groups (emphasis on African-Americans); historical fiction; children's/young adult. Recent publications: *The Little Bitty Snake* (3 bilingual editions: English/Spanish, English/French, English/Japanese). **Nonfiction**—autobiography; ethnic groups (African-American emphasis); social history; poetry. Recent publications: *Black Heroes of the Wild West* (children's); *Puerto Rican Writers at Home in the USA* (anthology); *The Black West: A Pictorial History*. Do not want: unsolicited poetry.

Initial Contact. Cover letter with a 2-paragraph (minimum) synopsis. Include author's bio. SASE required.

Acceptance Policies. Unagented manuscripts: yes. Simultaneous submissions: yes. Response time to initial inquiry: 3 weeks. Average time until publication: 12-18 months. **Advance:** not offered. **Royalty:** yes.

Marketing Channels. Distribution houses; direct mail. Subsidiary rights: all.

Additional Information. Our primary focus is on African-American issues. Tips: Request guidelines and follow them closely. Writer's guidelines: SASE. Catalog: SASE.

Oral Biography Series *see* **UNIVERSITY OF ALASKA PRESS.**

Oregon Fever Books *see* **CRUMB ELBOW PUBLISHING.**

OREGON STATE UNIVERSITY PRESS. 101 Waldo Hall. Corvallis, OR 97331-6407. (503) 737-3166. Submissions Editor: Jo Alexander. Founded: 1961. Number of titles published: cumulative—150+\-, 1992—6. Hardback 50%, softback 50%.

Subjects of Interest. Nonfiction—ethnic groups in the Northwest (Chinese, Hispanics, Indians of Central/South America, Mexicans, Native Americans); history (environmental or regional); biography (regional); Pacific Northwest studies; natural resource management; contemporary and social issues; scholarly. Recent publications: *Following the Nez Perce*

Trail, A Historical Travel Guide (guide to following the trail with history and eyewitness acounts); *Birds of Malheur National Wildlife Refuge*; *Nehalem Tillamook Tales* (reprint of Native American oral literature). Do not want: poetry; fiction; any subjects not listed above.

Initial Contact. Query letter with synopsis/outline or book proposal. Include sample chapters. SASE required.

Acceptance Policies. Unagented manuscripts: yes. Simultaneous submissions: no. Response time to initial inquiry: 2-4 weeks. Average time until publication: 1 year. Subsidy or co-publishing: subventions sometimes necessary; not from author personally. **Advance:** not offered. **Royalty:** 10-15% average; based on net receipts.

Marketing Channels. Distribution houses; direct mail; independent reps. Subsidiary rights: those appropriate to regional and scholarly books.

Additional Information. We are interested in ethnic materials from or about the Pacific Northwest. Given the shamefully racist history of the region, this is realistically going to limit the ethnic subject areas of interest to us. Catalog: upon request.

ORIENT PAPERBACKS. (Subsidiary of Vision Books PVT, LTD. Imprints: Orient Paperbacks, Anand Paperbacks). 1590 Madarsa Rd. Kashmere Gate. Delhi, India 110054. (011) 251-2267, 251-7001. Submissions Editor: Sudhir Malhotra. Founded: 1977. Number of titles published: cumulative—400, 1992—50. Hardback 10%, softback 90%.

Subjects of Interest. Fiction—erotica; humor; literary. **Nonfiction**—ethnic groups (Indians from India, Eastern cultures); astrology; business/economics; computers; cooking; games and puzzles; gay/lesbian issues; health; holistic practices; philosophy; religion (Buddhism); self-help; trade publications; yoga.

Initial Contact. Book proposal. Include bio or curriculum vitae.

Acceptance Policies. Unagented manuscripts: yes. First novels: yes. Simultaneous submissions: yes. Response time to initial inquiry: 6-8 weeks. Average time until publication: 6 months. **Advance:** not offered. **Royalty:** yes; based on percentage of sales.

Marketing Channels. Cooperative distribution. Subsidiary rights: first serialization; second serialization; reprint; book club; translation and foreign; English language publication outside the United States and Canada.

Park Street Press *see* **INNER TRADITIONS INTERNATIONAL.**

PELICAN PUBLISHING COMPANY, INC. 1101 Monroe St. Gretna, LA 70053. (504) 368-1175. (504) 368-1175. Fax: (504) 368-1195. Submissions Editor: Nina Kooij. Founded: 1926. Number of titles published: cumulative—600, 1992—45. Hardback 65%, softback 35%.

Subjects of Interest. Fiction—stories with ethnic characters and/or themes (blacks, Hispanics, Native Americans, Orientals, etc.) Recent publications: *Wolf Dog of the Woodland Indians* (children's story). **Nonfiction**—topics concerned with ethnic history (blacks, Native Americans, etc.). Recent publications: *Quanah Parker: Comanche Chief* (children's biography).

Initial Contact. Query letter only. Include writing and professional background, promotional contacts and ideas. SASE required.

Acceptance Policies. Unagented manuscripts: yes. First novels: yes. Simultaneous submissions: no. Response time to initial inquiry: 1 month. Average time until publication: 9-18 months. **Advance:** not offered. **Royalty:** 10%; based on actual receipts.

Marketing Channels. Distribution houses; direct mail. Subsidiary rights: all.

Additional Information. We are building a strong list based on Native Americans and African-Americanss. We are also looking for stories of famous people from Florida, for example, with various backgrounds. We also have a branch office in the Southwest and are looking for appropriate materials. Tips: The author should plan to write several books with us in his or her genre and should be available and willing to promote those works. Writer's guidelines: SASE. Catalog: upon request.

Penway Books *see* **LOTUS PRESS, INC.**

PHILOMEL BOOKS. (Subsidiary of The Putnam Publishing Group). 200 Madison Ave. New York, NY 10016. (212) 951-8700. Fax: (212) 532-3693. Submissions Editor: Paula Wiseman. Founded: 19n/i. Number of titles published: 1992—50. Hardback n/i, softback n/i.

Subjects of Interest. Fiction—children's through young adult regional and ethnic stories with a strong, believable voice and original premise. Recent publications: *Sweetgrass.* **Nonfiction**—children's through young adult regional and ethnic material with a strong, believable voice and original premise; translations. Recent publications: *A Tree Still Stands; Ho Lim Lim* (translation).

Initial Contact. Query letter with synopsis outline or book proposal with 3 sample chapters. Include origin of story. SASE required.

Acceptance Policies. Unagented manuscripts: yes. First novels: yes. Simultaneous submissions: yes. Response time to initial inquiry: 2-3 months. Average time until publication: 1-2 years. **Advance:** varies with experience. **Royalty:** varies with experience; based on past success.

Marketing Channels. Distribution houses; cooperative distribution; direct mail; independent reps; in-house staff; special sales. Subsidiary rights: all.

Additional Information. Writer's guidelines: SASE. Catalog: SASE, $1 postage.

Prairie State Books *see* **UNIVERSITY OF ILLINOIS PRESS.**

PRESS OF MACDONALD & REINECKE, THE. (Subsidiary of Padre Productions). PO Box 840. Arroyo Grande, CA 93421-0840. (805) 473-1947. Submissions Editor: Mack Sullivan (fiction). Founded: 1974. Number of titles published: cumulative—11, 1992—4. Hardback 20%, softback 80%.

Subjects of Interest. Fiction—children's/young adult; literary; short stories; women's issues. Recent publications: *Flower Tumbles* (children's story about California Indian life); *Contemporary Insanities* (short fiction). **Nonfiction**—literary criticism; biography; history; photography; poetry. Do not want: felon autobiographies.

Initial Contact. Query letter with synopsis/outline. Include sample chapters. SASE required.

Acceptance Policies. Unagented manuscripts: yes. First novels: yes. Simultaneous submissions: yes. Response time to initial inquiry: 2-8 weeks. Average time until publication: 1-2 years. **Advance:** not offered. **Royalty:** yes.

Marketing Channels. Distribution houses; direct mail; in-house staff. Subsidiary rights: all.

Additional Information. We are open to all literary forms and material. Tips: Avoid common errors of grammar and spelling, as we can't be your teacher of basics. Be professional. Writer's guidelines: #10 SASE, 1 first class stamp. Catalog: 9x12 SASE, 2 ounces, first class postage.

PUBLISHERS ASSOCIATES. (Members of the consortium: Ide House; Liberal Arts Press; The Liberal Press; Minuteman Press; Monument Press; Nichole Graphics; Scholars Books; Tangelwuld Press). PO Box 140361. Las Colinas, TX 75014-0361. (214) 686-5332. Submissions Editor: Jeff Stryker. Founded: 1974. Number of titles published: cumulative—150, 1992—30. Hardback 1%, softback 99%.

Subjects of Interest. Nonfiction—ethnic groups (all groups, with an emphasis on Arabs, Afro-Americans, Greeks, Hispanics, Native Americans, Russians, Slavic peoples, Scandinavians); scholarly works in the areas of biography, gay/lesbian issues, history, law, men's issues, minority issues, politics/world affairs, women's issues. Recent publications: *Chinese Women: Past and Present; Black Woman in Contemporary Business; The Blood Tattoo* (life in a Nazi concentration camp). Do not want: fiction; poetry; religious right.

Initial Contact. Query letter with synopsis.

Acceptance Policies. Unagented manuscripts: yes. Simultaneous submissions: no. Response time to initial inquiry: 3 months. Average time until publication: 4 months. Advance: none. **Royalty:** based on sales.

Marketing Channels. Distribution houses; direct mail; in-house staff; special sales. Subsidiary rights: all.

Additional Information. We are a minority-owned press, sensitive to liberal/feminist and gay/lesbian issues. We don't publish evangelical/fundamental theology or the political right. Tips: Works must be nonfiction, nonsexist. We are seeking liberal material only. Will publish biographies (no autobiographies) if documentation is included. Catalog: write the consortium.

Prism Editions *see* **NATUREGRAPH PUBLISHERS, INC.**

R&M PUBLISHING COMPANY. PO Box 1276. Holly Hill, SC 29059. (804) 732-4094. Submissions Editor: address to editor. Founded: 1978. Number of titles published: cumulative—18, 1992—2. Softback 100%.

Subjects of Interest. Nonfiction—African American topics.

Initial Contact. Book proposal with sample chapters. SASE required.

Acceptance Policies. Unagented manuscripts: yes. Simultaneous submissions: yes. Response time to initial inquiry: 6-8 weeks. Average time until publication: 6-8 months. Subsidy or co-publishing basis: will consider cooperative publishing. **Advance:** not offered. **Royalty:** 15%; based on net.

Marketing Channels. Distribution houses; cooperative distribution; direct mail; independent reps; special sales. Subsidiary rights: all.

Additional Information. We will review any information concerning African-Americans and others of color. Tips: Submit your manuscript in the most professional form and as complete as possible.

Rasmuson Historical Translation Series *see* **UNIVERSITY OF ALASKA PRESS.**

RED CRANE BOOKS. (Subsidiary of O'Shaughnessy, Mafchir and Mayans). 826 Camino de Monte Rey. Santa Fe, NM 87501. (505) 988-7070. Fax: (505) 989-7476. Submissions Editor: Michael O'Shaughnessy. Founded: 1989. Number of titles published: cumulative—11, 1992—6. Hardback 10%, softback 90%.

Subjects of Interest. Fiction—literary; foreign translations. **Nonfiction**—Native Americans; history; art; children's nonfiction; biography; natural history; Southwest; Americana. Recent publications: *The Taos Indians and the Battle for Blue Lake; El Norte, The Cuisine of Northern Mexico; A Painter's Kitchen, Recipes from the Kitchen of Georgia O'Keefe; Working in the Dark.* Do not want: how-to books.

Initial Contact. Book proposal. Include outline, sample chapters, and author's resumé and credentials.

Acceptance Policies. Unagented manuscripts: yes. Simultaneous submissions: yes; inform us. Response time to initial inquiry: 2 months. Average time until publication: 1 year. **Advance:** rare/small. **Royalty:** negotiable.

Marketing Channels. Distribution houses; independent reps. Subsidiary rights: all.

Additional Information. Catalog: by phone or mail. Writer's guidelines: by phone or mail.

Research Centrex *see* **CRUMB ELBOW PUBLISHING.**

SCHOLASTIC, INC. 730 Broadway. New York, NY 10024. (212) 505-3244. Fax: (212) 505-3277. Submissions Editor: Ann Reit. Founded: 1920. Number of titles published: cumulative—n/i, 1992—200. Hardback 10%, softback 90%.

Subjects of Interest. Fiction—ethnic groups (African-Americans, Hispanics, Native Americans, Asians); adventure; historical fiction; horror; literary; mystery; middle grades to Y/A only. Recent publications: *Oh Brother*. **Nonfiction**—biography; ethnic groups (African-Americans, Indians from India, Chinese, Filipinos, Hispanics, Native Americans, Vietnamese); middle grades to Y/A only. Recent publications: *Undying Glory* (Massachusetts 54th regiment); *Jessie Jackson.*

Initial Contact. Query letter with synopsis/outline or book proposal with sample chapters. SASE required.

Acceptance Policies. Unagented manuscripts: yes. First novels: yes. Simultaneous submissions: yes, inform us. Response time to initial inquiry: 3 months. Average time until publication: 18 months. **Advance:** depends on author. **Royalty:** depends on author.

Marketing Channels. Distribution houses; direct mail; independent reps; special sales; book fairs. Subsidiary rights: depends on writer and subject.

Additional Information. We are interested in quality books only. Tips: Get a sense of the kinds of things we do. Catalog: upon request.

Scythe Books *see* **WINSTON-DEREK PUBLISHERS, INC.**

SEAL PRESS. 3131 Western Ave., Ste. 410. Seattle, WA 98121. (206) 283-7844. Fax: (206) 285-9410. Submissions Editors: Faith Contor, Barbara Wilson. Founded: n/i. Number of titles published: cumulative—80, 1992—12. Hardback 5-10%, softback 90-95%.

Subjects of Interest. Fiction—ethnic groups (African-Americans, Asian-Americans, Latinas; Native Americans, Jews); literary; mystery; short story collections; women's issues; children's/young adult. Recent publications: short story collections and novels by women writers of the above ethnicities. **Nonfiction**—issues affecting women of ethnic bakcgrounds, written by women of ethnic backgrounds. Recent publications: *Black Women's Health Book; Chain Chain Change: For Black Women Dealing with Abusive Relationships* (similar book for Latinas). Do not want: books by men.

Initial Contact. Query letter only. Include published works and areas of expertise if a nonfiction project. SASE required.

Acceptance Policies. Unagented manuscripts: yes. First novels: yes. Simultaneous submissions: prefer not to. Response time to initial inquiry: 4-8 weeks. Average time until publication: 1-3 years; depends greatly on project. **Advance:** rarely. **Royalty:** 7-8%; based on retail price of trade paperback.

Marketing Channels. Distribution houses; direct mail; independent reps; in-house staff; special sales. Subsidiary rights: all.

Additional Information. We are a feminist press specializing in women writers and very interested in books by women of color. Tips: Research our press to see if we are a suitable publisher for your particular project. Writer's guidelines: SASE. Catalog: SASE.

Signal Editions *see* **VÉHICULE PRESS.**

Silhouette Imprints *see* **CRUMB ELBOW PUBLISHING.**

Silhouette *see* **HARLEQUIN ENTERPRISES LIMITED.**

SOCIAL JUSTICE. (Subsidiary of Global Options. Imprint: Crime and Social Justice Associates). PO Box 40601. San Francisco, CA 94140. (415) 550-1703. Submissions Editor: Gregory Shank. Founded: 1974. Number of titles published: cumulative—44, 1992—4. Softback 100%.

Subjects of Interest. Nonfiction—all ethnic groups; racism; powerlessness; justice; contemporary issues; immigrants/immigration; law; sociology; women's issues. Recent publications: *Racism, Powerlessness and Justice; Attica, 20 Years Later; The War of Drugs.* Do not want: fiction; short stories.

Initial Contact. Query letter with synopsis/outline. Include author bio.

Acceptance Policies. Unagented manuscripts: yes. Simultaneous submissions: no. Response time to initial inquiry: 3 months. Average time until publication: 6 months. **Advance:** n/a. **Royalty:** n/a, unless reprinted elsewhere.

Marketing Channels. Distribution houses; direct mail; independent reps. Subsidiary rights: all.

Additional Information. Catalog: upon request. Writer's guidelines: SASE.

SOHO PRESS, INC. 853 Broadway. New York, NY 10003. (212) 260-1900. Fax: (212) 260-1902. Submissions Editor: Laura McHruska. Founded: 1986. Number of titles published: cumulative—60, 1992—12. Hardback 80%, softback 20%.

Subjects of Interest. Fiction—ethnic groups (Arabs, African-Americans, Basques, Chinese, Czechoslovakians, Irish, Japanese, Koreans, Native Americans, Russians); contemporary; mainstream; literary; mystery; women's issues. Recent publications: *Silver Stallion* (Korean novel). Nonfiction—ethnic groups (Arabs, African-Americans, Basques, Chinese, Czechoslovakians, Irish, Japanese, Koreans, Native Americans, Russians); child care; family issues; literary; translations. Recent publications: *O Come Ye Back to Ireland* (autobiography); *Inspector Imanishi Investigates* (mystery in translation); *Taxi from Hell* (memoir in translation).

Initial Contact. Book proposal with 3 sample chapters. SASE required.

Acceptance Policies. Unagented manuscripts: yes. First novels: yes. Simultaneous submissions: yes. Response time to initial inquiry: 8 weeks. Average time until publication: 1 year. **Advance:** yes. **Royalty:** 10-12-15%; based on 5000, 7500, 10,000 copies sold.

Marketing Channels. Distribution houses; independent reps; special sales. Subsidiary rights: all.

Additional Information. Catalog: SASE.

STONE BRIDGE PRESS. PO Box 8208. Berkeley, CA 94707. (510) 524-8732. Fax: (510) 524-8711. Submissions Editor: Peter Goodman. Founded: 1989. Number of titles published: 1992—3. Softback 100%.

Subjects of Interest. Fiction—Japanese focus on contemporary, literary, short story collections; translations of Japanese literature. Recent publications: *Death March on Mount Hakkoda: A Documentary Novel* (translation). **Nonfiction**—Japan-related subjects, especially language learning, art, design, culture, business, education, religion (Buddhism, Zen), translations. Recent publications: *Going to Japan on Business; Going to Silicon Valley on Business* (in Japanese); *Kanji Pictographix*. Do not want: original haiku; travel diaries; mass-market fiction.

Initial Contact. Query letter with synopsis/outline; book proposal. Include sample chapters, author's resumé, and a demonstration of competence in Japan-related field.

Acceptance Policies. Unagented manuscripts: yes. Simultaneous submissions: yes, inform us. Response time to initial inquiry: 1 month. Average time until publication: 12-18 months. **Advance:** yes. **Royalty:** yes.

Marketing Channels. Publishers Group West; distributors; direct mail. Subsidiary rights: all.

Additional Information. Looking for competence and knowledge more than proven organizational ability. Tips: Go to Japanese bookstore like Kinokuniya (San Francisco, Los Angeles, New York) to see how Japanese books are done. Catalog: on request.

TECHNICIANS OF THE SACRED. 1317 N. San Fernando Blvd., Ste. 310. Burbank, CA 91504. Submissions Editor: Courtney Wills. Founded: n/i. Number of titles published: cumulative—5, 1992—12. Hardback 10%, softback 90%.

Subjects of Interest. Nonfiction—voodoo; neo-African religions. Do not want: anything else.

Initial Contact. Query letter with synopsis/outline. Include information on author. SASE required.

Acceptance Policies. Unagented manuscripts: yes. Simultaneous submissions: no. Response time to initial inquiry: 1 month. Average time until publication: 1 year. **Advance:** not offered. **Royalty:** 15%; based on wholesale price of book.

Marketing Channels. Distribution houses; independent reps. Subsidiary rights: none.

Additional Information. We are a very small press and our writers are usually involved with our organization in some way. We also publish the magazine, *Société*. Writer's guidelines: not available. Catalog: $8.

TEMPLE PUBLISHING, INC., ELLEN C. 5030 Champions Dr., Ste. 100. Lufkin, TX 75901. (409) 639-4707. Submissions Editor: Ellen Temple. Founded: 1980. Number of titles published: cumulative—15, 1992—3. Hardback 20%, softback 80%.

Subjects of Interest. Fiction—for young adults, ages 8-14; mysteries. Recent publications: *Maggie and a Horse Named Devildust; A Vampire Named Fred.* **Nonfiction**—Texas women's history and biography. Recent publications: *Citizens at Last: The Woman Suffrage Movement in Texas; A Texas Suffragist: Diaries and Writings of Jane Y. McCallum.*

Initial Contact. Query letter with synopsis/outline. Include 3 sample chapters. Discuss author's willingness to promote book in schools and libraries.

Acceptance Policies. Unagented manuscripts: yes. Simultaneous submissions: yes. Response time to initial inquiry: 2-3 months. Average time until publication: 1 year. **Advance:** n/i. **Royalty:** n/i.

Marketing Channels. Cooperative distribution. Subsidiary rights: reprint; book club.

Additional Information. Concentrating on books for the 8- to 14-year-old market. Catalog: call 1-800-677-2800, Ext. 589.

TEXAS A&M UNIVERSITY PRESS. Drawer C. Lewis Street. College Station, TX 77843. (409) 845-1436. Submissions Editor: Noel Parsons. Founded: 1974. Number of titles published: cumulative—300, 1992—33. Hardback 85%, softback 15%.

Subjects of Interest. Fiction—regional folklore. **Nonfiction**—regional; natural history; American history (also military); economics; environmental studies. Recent publications: *Czech Voices: Stories from Texas in the Amerikan Narodni Kalendar; A Life among the Texas Flora: Ferdinand Lindheimer's Letters to George Englemann; Coming to Terms: The German Hill Country of Texas; Rise of the Mexican American Middle Class: San Antonio, 1929-1941.*

Initial Contact. Query letter with synopsis/outline and sample chapters. Include how the proposed book contributes to the material already available in the field. SASE required.

Acceptance Policies. Unagented manuscripts: yes. Simultaneous submissions: no. Response time to initial inquiry: 3 weeks. Average time until publication: 1 year. **Advance:** negotiable. **Royalty:** varies.

Marketing Channels. Direct mail; independent sales; in-house staff. Subsidiary rights: all.

Additional Information. We are interested in all ethnic groups of Texas and the Southwest, including blacks and Native Americans. Catalog: upon request.

TEXAS WESTERN PRESS. (Imprints: Southwestern Studies). University of Texas at El Paso. El Paso, TX 79968-0633. (915) 747-5688. Submissions Editor: Dale L. Walker, director. Founded: 1952. Number of titles published: cumulative—250, 1992—10. Hardback 75%, softback 25%.

Subjects of Interest. Nonfiction—Southwestern history and cultures (Hispanic involvement in Southwestern U.S. history). Recent publications: *Demographic Dynamics of the U.S.-Mexico Border; Merejildo Grijalva, Apache Scout; Elfego Baca, New Mexico Lawman.* Do not want: poetry; fiction.

Initial Contact. Query letter with synopsis/outline. Include sample chapters, author bio, and publishing or research experience and interests.

Acceptance Policies. Unagented manuscripts: yes. Simultaneous submissions: yes; inform us and be willing to grant us a "hold" if our press is interested. Response time to initial inquiry: 30-60 days. Average time until publication: 9 months. **Advance:** none. **Royalty:** 10% of net.

Marketing Channels. Direct mail; in-house staff; special sales. Subsidiary rights: all.

Additional Information. Our interest is in Southwestern history and cultures. Our publishing program is limited to 8-10 books a year, a "Southwestern Studies" series of short, paperback books (100 pages average). We want nineteenth century material that is serious, scholarly, and footnoted. Tips: We need more Hispanic historians submitting queries on their works-in-progress. Send for guidelines. Catalog: SASE. Writer's guidelines: upon request.

THIRD WORLD PRESS. (Subsidiary of Positive Education). 7524 S. Cottage Grove Ave. Chicago, IL 60619. (312) 651-0700. Fax: (312) 651-7286. Submissions Editor: address to editorial department. Founded: 1967. Number of titles published: cumulative—60, 1992—10. Hardback 5%, softback 95%.

Subjects of Interest. Fiction—any and all books reflecting the black experience. Recent publications: *The Future and Other Stories; The Brass Bed, Jiva Telling Rites.* **Nonfiction**—any and all books reflecting the black experience. Recent publications: *Black Men; Issis Papers.* Do not want: books which do not reflect the black experience.

Initial Contact. Query letter with entire manuscript. SASE required.

Acceptance Policies. Unagented manuscripts: yes. First novels: yes. Simultaneous submissions: yes, inform us. Response time to initial inquiry: 3-6 months. Average time until publication: 1 year. **Advance:** not offered. **Royalty:** 8%.

Marketing Channels. Distribution houses; direct mail; in-house staff; special sales. Subsidiary rights: none.

Additional Information. We publish high-quality books on the black experience; we are not a multicultural publisher. Tips: Manuscript must be typed and checked for grammatical and typing errors. Read our books for content and base your submissions on that. Send SASE. Writer's guidelines: upon request. Catalog: upon request.

TREASURE CHEST PUBLICATIONS, INC. PO Box 5250. Tucson, AZ 85703. (602) 623-9558. (800) 969-9558. Fax: (602) 624-5888. Submissions Editors: Nancie S. Mahan, Sterling L. Mahan. Founded: 1975. Number of titles published: cumulative—35, 1992—6. Hardback 65%, softback 35%.

Subjects of Interest. Fiction—children's books and picture books; folklore. Recent publications: 3 children's historical "cut and color" books (Kachi, Dolii, Bozagolaa); *Chana, An Anazsazi Girl* (cut and color). **Nonfiction**—Arizona/Southwestern topics (history, folklore); Native Americans. Recent publications: *Arizona: A Cavalcade of History* (Arizona history); *Pueblo Stories and Storytellers; Navajo Sandpainting Art.* Do not want: poetry; prose.

Initial Contact. Book proposal. Include sample chapters, reference material, or source of information.

Acceptance Policies. Unagented manuscripts: yes. First novels: yes (children's). Simultaneous submissions: n/i. Response time to initial inquiry: 3 weeks. Average time until publication: 6-8 months. **Advance:** n/i. **Royalty:** n/i.

Marketing Channels. Distribution houses; direct mail; in-house staff. Subsidiary rights: none.

Additional Information. We are small, but growing! Our topics are strictly Southwestern and Indian related. Catalog: call or write.

Trillium Art Productions *see* **CRUMB ELBOW PUBLISHING.**

Tyee Press *see* **CRUMB ELBOW PUBLISHING.**

University Editions *see* **AEGINA PRESS, INC.**

UNIVERSITY OF ALABAMA PRESS. PO Box 870380. Tuscaloosa, AL 35487. (205) 348-5180. Fax: (205) 348-9201. Submissions Editors: Malcolm M. MacDonald (history, Political science); Nicole F. Mitchell (literary studies, criticism, religious studies, rhetoric, and communication). Founded: 1945. Number of titles published: cumulative—650 in print, 1992—40. Hardback 60%, softback 40%.

Subjects of Interest. Nonfiction—ethnic groups (Afro-Americans, Jews, Native Americans); history; literary criticism; political science; religious studies; anthropology; archaeology. Recent publications: *Chronicles of Faith: The Autobiography of Frederick D. Patterson.*

Initial Contact. Query letter with synopsis/outline. Include information about the physical dimensions of the proposed book: how many double-spaced manuscript pages? how many illustrations? SASE not required.

Acceptance Policies. Unagented manuscripts: yes. Simultaneous submissions: no. Response time to initial inquiry: 1 week. Average time until publication: 1 year. **Advance:** not offered. **Royalty:** 10%; based on net monies received.

Marketing Channels. Cooperative distribution; direct mail; in-house staff. Subsidiary rights: all.

Additional Information. We publish scholarly books, and we have excellent lists in African-American studies, Judaic studies, and many other areas. Tips: We do not publish either original fiction or poetry. Writer's guidelines: send for our brochure, "Guidelines for Authors." Catalog: write for our current seasonal catalog and complete list of books in print.

UNIVERSITY OF ALASKA PRESS. (Imprints: Rasmuson Historical Translation Series, Oral Biography Series, Classic Reprint Series, Monograph Series). First Floor, Gruening Bldg. UAF. Fairbanks, AK 99775-1580. (907) 474-6389. Fax: (907) 474-7225. Submissions Editors: C. Helfferich, managing editor; Claus Naske, director. Founded: 1967. Number of titles published: cumulative—40, 1992—8-12. Hardback 50%, softback 50%.

Subjects of Interest. Nonfiction—scholarly works relating to Alaska and the circumpolar regions. Recent publications: *Chills and Fever: Health and Disease in the Early History of Alaska; From the Writings of the Greenlanders.* Do not want: fiction; poetry; conference proceedings.

Initial Contact. Query letter with synopsis/outline. Include curriculum vitae. SASE not required.

Acceptance Policies. Unagented manuscripts: yes. Simultaneous submissions: no. Response time to initial inquiry: 30-60 days. Average time until publication: 9-18 months. **Advance:** not offered. **Royalty:** 7%; based on net sales.

Marketing Channels. Direct mail; independent reps; in-house staff; special sales. Subsidiary rights: all.

Additional Information. Regional material only. Writer's guidelines: upon request. Catalog: upon request.

UNIVERSITY OF CALIFORNIA AT LOS ANGELES, AMERICAN INDIAN STUDIES. 3220 Campbell Hall. 405 Hilgard Ave. Los Angeles, CA 90024-1548. Submissions Editor: Duane Champagne. Founded: 1974. Number of titles published: cumulative—25, 1992—1. Hardback 10%, softback 90%.

Subjects of Interest. Nonfiction—history; politics; economics; crafts; education; poetry. Recent publications: *The Light on the Tent Wall: A Bridging* (poetry); *Exemplar of Liberty* (Native American contributions to the evolution of democracy). Do not want: fiction.

Initial Contact. Entire manuscript. SASE not required.

Acceptance Policies. Unagented manuscripts: yes. Simultaneous submissions: no. Response time to initial inquiry: 3 weeks. Average time until publication: 1-2 years. **Advance:** not offered. **Royalty:** not offered.

Marketing Channels. Distribution houses; direct mail; in-house staff. Subsidiary rights: reprint; computer and other magnetic and electronic media.

Additional Information. Writer's guidelines: upon request. Catalog: upon request.

UNIVERSITY OF ILLINOIS PRESS. (Imprints: Illini Books, Prairie State Books). 54 E. Gregory Dr. Champaign, IL 61820. (217) 333-0950. Fax: (217) 244-8082. Submissions Editor: Richard L. Wentworth. Founded: 1918. Number of titles published: cumulative—1400, 1992—110. Hardback 90%, softback 10%.

Subjects of Interest. Nonfiction—immigration and ethnic history of Afro-Americans, Germans, Hispanics, Irish, Indians from India, Israelis, Italians, Japanese, Jews, Native Americans; women's studies. Recent publications: *The Butte Irish; Germans in the New World*; publisher of series sponsored by Statue-of-Liberty-Ellis Island Foundation. Do not want: works in languages other than English.

Initial Contact. Query letter with synopsis/outline. (Do not send entire manuscript.) SASE not required.

Acceptance Policies. Unagented manuscripts: yes. Simultaneous submissions: no. Response time to initial inquiry: 2 weeks. Average time until publication: 1 year. **Advance:** rarely. **Royalty:** yes; depends on sales potential.

Marketing Channels. Distribution houses; direct mail; independent reps; in-house staff; academic meetings. Subsidiary rights: all.

Additional Information. We specialize in American social history, with a special interest in women's history. We also publish many studies of ethnic groups in a single community.

UNIVERSITY OF NEBRASKA PRESS. (Imprints: Bison Books). 901 N. 17th. Lincoln, NE 68588-0520. (402) 472-3581. Submissions Editors: Willis Regier (director and literature editor); Daniel Ross (history); James Fultz (Bison Books, reprint series); Kay Graber (managing editor). Founded: 1941. Number of titles published: cumulative—2500, 1992—100. Hardback 50%, softback 50%.

Subjects of Interest. Nonfiction—history, literature, biography, autobiography, and anthropological studies of the American Indians. Recent publications: *The Sixth Grandfather: Black Elk's Teaching Given to John G. Neihardt; Ancestral Voice: Conversations with N. Scott Momaday*. Do not want: previously unpublished fiction; poetry.

Initial Contact. Query letter with synopsis/outline. SASE required.

Acceptance Policies. Unagented manuscripts: yes. Simultaneous submissions: no. Response time to initial inquiry: 2 weeks. Average time until publication: approximately 14 months after receipt of completed manuscript. Subsidy or co-publishing basis: only if the subsidy is from a bona fide sponsoring organization and subject to the same conditions and criteria that apply to other manuscripts. **Advance:** rarely. **Royalty:** yes; depends on nature of the book.

Marketing Channels. Direct mail; independent reps. Subsidiary rights: all, but subject to negotiation.

Additional Information. This press cosponsors the annual North American Indian Prose Award. Writer's guidelines: upon request. Catalog: upon request.

UNIVERSITY OF NEVADA PRESS. University of Nevada. Reno, NV 89557. (702) 784-6573. Fax: (702) 784-6200. Submissions Editor: Nicholas Cady. Founded: 1961. Number of titles published: cumulative—170, 1992—24. Hardback 60%, softback 40%.

Subjects of Interest. Fiction—Basque folklore; short story collections. Recent publications: *The Basque Hotel* (novel); *Contemporary Basque Fiction* (anthology). **Nonfiction**—Nevada history, biography, political science; Great Basin natural history; Basque culture, history, language; gambling; sociology; psychology. Recent publications: *Escape Via Berlin* (Basque president eludes Nazis in WW II); *View from the Witch's Cave* (Basque folktales). Do not want: how-to books.

Initial Contact. Short query letter with synopsis/outline and sample chapter. Include author's qualifications, target audience, and how this manuscript differs from similar published works. SASE not required.

Acceptance Policies. Unagented manuscripts: yes. First novels: yes. Simultaneous submissions: no. Response time to initial inquiry: 2 weeks. Average time until publication: 10 months. **Advance:** not offered. **Royalty:** 5-10%; based on net.

Marketing Channels. Independent sales; special sales; direct mail catalog. Subsidiary rights: all.

Additional Information. We want manuscripts relating to any ethnic group located in Great Basin area. Writer's guidelines: upon request. Catalog: upon request.

UNIVERSITY OF NORTH TEXAS PRESS. PO Box 13856. Denton, TX 76203-3856. (817) 565-2142. Fax: (817) 565-4284. Submissions Editor: Frances B. Vick. Founded: 1987. Number of titles published: cumulative—28, 1992—10. Hardback 33%, softback 67%.

Subjects of Interest. Nonfiction—Hispanic and black history; Native Americans; translations from Hispanic works. Recent publications: *Cold Anger: A Story of Faith and Power Politics; They Are Coming* (1992 publication).

Initial Contact. Query letter with synopsis/outline or book proposal with sample chapters. Include author's bio. SASE required.

Acceptance Policies. Unagented manuscripts: yes. Simultaneous submissions: yes, inform us. Response time to initial inquiry: 2 months. Average time until publication: 9-12 months. Subsidy or co-publishing basis: as a grant to the UNTP fund. **Advance:** not offered. **Royalty:** 10%; based on net.

Marketing Channels. Distribution houses; cooperative distribution; direct mail. Subsidiary rights: all.

Additional Information. Writer's guidelines: upon request. Catalog: upon request.

UNIVERSITY OF TEXAS PRESS. PO Box 7819. Austin, TX 78713. (512) 471-4278. Submissions Editor: Theresa May. Founded: 1950. Number of titles published: cumulative—1500+/-, 1992—85. Hardback 70%, softback 30%.

Subjects of Interest. Fiction—translations. Recent publications: *Goodbyes and Other Stories* (Juan Carlos Onetti); *Mae Franking's "My Chinese Marriage"* (Katherine Anne Porter). **Nonfiction**—ethnic groups include Middle Eastern cultures (Arabs, Israelis), Hispanics, Indians of Central/South America, Latin Americans, Mexican-Americans, Native Americans; anthropology; archaeology; environment/ecology; natural history; geography; history; literary; mythology; scholarly works; women's issues. Recent publications: *Guaman Poma; Return of the Whooping Crane; La Malinche in Mexican Literature: From History to Myth; The Sheltered Quarter: A Tale of a Boyhood in Mecca.* Do not want: contemporary fiction in English; poetry.

Initial Contact. Query letter with synopsis/outline and book proposal.

Acceptance Policies. Unagented manuscripts: yes (we prefer not to deal with agents). Simultaneous submissions: no. Response time to initial inquiry: 1 month. Average time until publication: 12-18 months. **Advance:** occasionally. **Royalty:** varies, based on actual monies received by the publisher.

Marketing Channels. Direct mail; independent reps; in-house staff; special sales. Subsidiary rights: all.

Additional Information. Standard university press review procedures; rarely publish edited collections. Tips: Study our list to see the kinds of things we're actually publishing. Catalog: upon request. Writer's guidelines: upon request.

VÉHICULE PRESS. (Imprint: Signal Editions). PO Box 125, Place du Parc Station. Montreal, Quebec, Canada. (514) 844-6073. Fax: (514) 844-7543. Submissions Editors: Linda Leith (fiction); Simon Dardick (nonfiction). Founded: 1973. Number of titles published: cumulative—115, 1992—14. Softback 100%.

Subjects of Interest. Fiction—short stories; contemporary/modern; folklore; literary; women's issues. **Nonfiction**—Judaic subjects; women's studies; translations (Yiddish, Spanish, French (Quebec). Recent publications: *An Everyday Miracle: Yiddish Culture in Montreal.*

Initial Contact. n/i. SASE required with International Reply Coupons (IRC) from the United States.

Acceptance Policies. Unagented manuscripts: yes. First novels: yes. Simultaneous submissions: no. Response time to initial inquiry: 4 months. Average time until publication: 12 months. **Advance:** yes. **Royalty:** 10%; based on retail cover price.

Marketing Channels. Distribution houses; direct mail. Subsidiary rights: all.

Additional Information. We generally accept manuscripts from Canadian authors only. Writer's guidelines: very fluid. Catalog: IRC.

VOLCANO PRESS, INC. (Imprint: Kazan Books). PO Box 270. Volcano, CA 95689-0270. (209) 296-3445. Fax: (209) 296-4515. Submissions Editor: Ruth Gottstein. Founded: 1976. Number of titles published: cumulative—25, 1992—4. Hardback 5%, softback 95%.

Subjects of Interest. Fiction—children's ethnic stories from varied cultures. Recent publications: *Mighty Mountain and the Three Strong Women; Berchick.* **Nonfiction**—ethnic women's issues; children's; women's health; domestic violence; men's issues;

nature/environment; sociology; self-help. Recent publications: *Mother Gave a Shout: Poems by Women and Girls*. Do not want: fiction; poetry.

Initial Contact. Query letter with synopsis/outline. SASE required.

Acceptance Policies. Unagented manuscripts: yes. Simultaneous submissions: yes. Response time to initial inquiry: 1 month. Average time until publication: 1 year. **Advance:** not offered. **Royalty:** varies.

Marketing Channels. Distribution houses; cooperative distribution; direct mail; independent reps; special sales. Subsidiary rights: all.

Additional Information. We look to publish women-oriented books that seek to enlighten, liberate, and delight. Tips: Have manuscript and short query letter typed very neatly. Always send SASE. Do not call regarding your manuscript. Writer's guidelines: upon request. Catalog: upon request.

WALKER AND COMPANY. 720 Fifth Ave. New York, NY 10017. (212) 265-3632. Fax: (212) 307-1764. Submissions Editors: Amy Shields, Emily Easton (juvenile, YA); Mary Herbert (adult nonfiction). Founded: 1961. Number of titles published: cumulative—30, 1992—n/i. Hardback n/i, softback n/i.

Subjects of Interest. Fiction—ethnic groups (Native Americans, Hispanics, Afro-Americans); children's; historical fiction; fantasy; folklore; holiday stories; mystery; romance; science fiction; Westerns. Recent publications: *Which Way Freedom?; Out from This Place.* Nonfiction—ethnic groups (Native Americans, Hispanics, Afro-Americans); anthropology; biography; child care; consumer; education; entertainment; family issues; gardening; handicrafts; history; minority issues; nature/environment; politics/world affairs; recreation; reference books; self-help; children's. Recent publications: *Long Hard Journey.* Do not want: contemporary fiction.

Initial Contact. Book proposal with sample chapters. SASE required.

Acceptance Policies. Unagented manuscripts: yes. First novels: yes. Simultaneous submissions: yes. Response time to initial inquiry: 6-8 weeks. Average time until publication: n/i. **Advance:** yes. **Royalty:** yes.

Marketing Channels. Direct mail; independent reps; in-house staff; wholesalers. Subsidiary rights: depends on project.

Additional Information. One of our books, *Long Hard Journey*, won the Coretta Scott King Award in 1989. Writer's guidelines: SASE. Catalog: SASE.

WASHINGTON STATE UNIVERSITY PRESS. Cooper Publications Building. Pullman, WA 99164-5910. (509) 335-3518. Fax: (509) 335-8568. Submissions Editor: Glen Lindeman. Founded: 1928. Number of titles published: cumulative—45, 1992—5. Hardback 20%, softback 80%.

Subjects of Interest. Nonfiction—ethnic studies. Recent publications: *Black Studies: Theory, Method, and Cultural Perspectives; Asian Americans: Comparative and Global Perspectives.* Do not want: fiction of any kind.

Initial Contact. Query letter with synopsis/outline or book proposal with sample chapters. SASE not required.

Acceptance Policies. Unagented manuscripts: yes. Simultaneous submissions: no. Response time to initial inquiry: 2-4 weeks. Average time until publication: 1-2 years. **Advance:** not offered. **Royalty:** based on profits from second printing.

Marketing Channels. Distribution houses; direct mail; independent reps; display ads; conferences.

Additional Information. We will consider submissions on any ethnic topic. Catalog: upon request.

WINSTON-DEREK PUBLISHERS, INC. (Imprints: MaggPie Productions, One Horn Press, Scythe Books). PO Box 90883. Nashville, TN 37209. (615) 329-1319. (615) 329-4824. Submissions Editors: Robert Earl (general editor); Maggie Ella Sims (fiction); Matalyn Rose (children); Sandra Smitson (religion). Founded: 1974. Number of titles published: cumulative—622, 1992—85. Hardback 25%, softback 75%.

Subjects of Interest. Fiction—children's/young adult, contemporary, folklore, historical novels, mainstream, women's issues, pre-Civil War, ancient Africa, all with an African-American focus. Recent publications: *Death and Duplicity* (police brutality in the black community). **Nonfiction**—African-American focus on civil and social unrest, child care/development, education, gay/lesbian issues, religion, how to. Recent publications: *The Black Biblical Heritage* (blacks in the Bible). Do not want: poetry.

Initial Contact. Query letter only or query letter with synopsis/outline. Include biographical sketch and other published titles if applicable. SASE required.

Acceptance Policies. Unagented manuscripts: yes. First novels: yes. Simultaneous submissions: no. Response time to initial inquiry: query letter, 4 weeks; manuscript, 6-8 weeks. Average time until publication: varies. Subsidy or co-publishing basis: depends upon manuscript and author's qualifications, etc. **Advance:** possibility. **Royalty:** 10%; based on retail price.

Marketing Channels. Distribution houses; independent reps; book fairs and conventions. Subsidiary rights: all.

Additional Information. We are a major distributor of African-American titles. Tips: We are well stocked with poetry. Writing must be literate and in standard English. Avoid racial derogatives. Do not call about publications. Writer's guidelines: SASE. Catalog: SASE, $1.05 postage.

WOMAN IN THE MOON (WIM). 2215-R Market St. Box 137-WC. San Francisco, CA 94114. (408) 253-3329. Fax: (408) 257-5683. Submissions Editor: Dr. SDiane Bogus. Founded: 1979. Number of titles published: cumulative—18, 1992—6. Hardback 40%, softback 60%.

Subjects of Interest. Nonfiction—ethnic (Afro-American emphasis); poetry; reference books; writing; religion (Buddhism); erotica and sexuality; enlightenment; prisoners; self-help; minority issues; gay/lesbian issues. Recent publications: *Poet's Workbook; Buddhism for My Friends; Who's Who in Mail Order; The Lesbian and Gay Wedding Album*. Do not want: novels; abuse; recovery; male-female material.

Initial Contact. Query letter with track record and poetic philosophy or entire manuscript or six poems. We require a $5 reading fee for submissions; submit only between April 1 and June 30. SASE required.

Acceptance Policies. Unagented manuscripts: yes. Simultaneous submissions: yes. Response time to initial inquiry: within a week. Average time until publication: 2 years possibly. **Advance:** not offered. **Royalty:** 1/2 press run to first authors; royalty to others.

Marketing Channels. Direct mail; independent reps; in-house staff. Subsidiary rights: first serialization; sound reproduction and recording; direct mail or direct sales; book club; translation and foreign; English language publication outside the United States and Canada.

Additional Information. We prefer the work of lesbians, gays, prisoners, and African-Americans. We sponsor two cash poetry contests. Write for guidelines. Tips: Be for real and formal. Be clear about your poetic vision and your own intention for your work. Be neat and professional. Writer's guidelines: included with catalog. Catalog: SASE, $.52 postage.

THE FEMINIST PRESS AT CUNY. 311 E. 94th St. New York, NY 10128. (212) 360-5790. Fax: (212) 348-1241. Submissions Editor: Susannah Driver. Founded: 1970. Number of titles published: cumulative—125, 1992—10. Hardback and softback published concurrently. Also publishes *Women's Studies Quarterly, a Journal.*

Subjects of Interest. Fiction—children's/young adult; all ethnic groups; plays; original anthologies; "lost" classics; translations. Recent publications: *Allegra Maud Goldman* (by a Jewish lesbian novelist); *Bamboo Shoots after the Rain* (Chinese fiction). **Nonfiction**—cross-cultural memoirs; all ethnic groups; translations; women's issues; poetry. Recent publications: *Journey to Freedom: A Biography of Sojourner Truth.* Do not want: work by first-time authors.

Initial Contact. Query letter or book proposal. Include other works published. SASE required.

Acceptance Policies. Unagented manuscripts: yes. Simultaneous submissions: yes. Response time to initial inquiry: 1 month. Average time until publication: n/i. **Advance:** $100 token amount. **Royalty:** 10%; based on all sales.

Marketing Channels. Distribution houses; direct mail; independent reps; in-house staff; special sales. Subsidiary rights: all.

Additional Information. We're a nonprofit, tax-exempt publisher with an educational mission. Tips: Read the catalog. Our books need to serve the classroom as well as the library and bookstore. Writer's guidelines: read the catalog. Catalog: upon request.

Worldwide *see* HARLEQUIN ENTERPRISES LIMITED.

WYRICK AND COMPANY. 12 Exchange St. Charleston, SC 29401. (803) 722-0881. Fax: (803) 722-6771. Submissions Editor: C.L. Wyrick, Jr. Founded: 1986. Number of titles published: cumulative—14, 1992—8. Hardback 30%, softback 70%.

Subjects of Interest. Fiction—contemporary works with an Afro-American and Southern Americana focus. **Nonfiction**—art, biography, comedy, cooking, gardening, history, nature, self-help, translations, and travel, all with an Afro-American and Southern Americana focus. Recent publications: *Porgy, a Gullah Version.*

Initial Contact. Book proposal with sample chapters. SASE required.

Acceptance Policies. Unagented manuscripts: yes. First novels: yes. Simultaneous submissions: yes. Response time to initial inquiry: 2-12 weeks. Average time until publication: 12-14 months. **Advance:** yes. **Royalty:** yes.

Marketing Channels. Distribution houses; direct mail; independent reps; special sales. Subsidiary rights: all.

Additional Information. Books of ethnic interest are not considered separately from other submissions. Tips: Examine our guidelines and publication list carefully. Writer's guidelines: #10 SASE. Catalog: #10 SASE.

YORK PRESS, LTD. PO Box 1172. Fredericton, New Brunswick, Canada E3B 5C8. (506) 458-8748. Submissions Editor: Dr. S. Elkhadem. Founded: 1975. Number of titles published: cumulative—65, 1992—8. Softback 100%.

Subjects of Interest. Fiction—ethnic groups (Arabs, Afro-Americans, Indians from India, Germans, Hispanics, Italians, Jews, Native Americans, Russians); avant-garde; contemporary; folklore; literary; short stories; women's issues. Recent publications: *Red, White and Blue* (contemporary); *Ulysses Trilogy* (translation from Arabic); *Missing in Action* (collection); *Three Egyptian Short Stories* (translation). Nonfiction—reference; history; proverbs; literary criticism; ethnic groups (Arabs, Afro-Americans, Indians from India, Germans, Hispanics, Italians, Jews, Native Americans, Russians); folklore; minority issues; scholarly works. Recent publications: *The York Companion to Themes and Motifs of World Literature, Mythology, History, and Folklore; Old Arabic Sayings, Similes, and Metaphors.*

Initial Contact. Query letter only. Include author's background, previous publications, and book reviews of previous works. SASE required.

Acceptance Policies. Unagented manuscripts: yes. First novels: yes. Simultaneous submissions: no. Response time to initial inquiry: 2 weeks. Average time until publication: 6 months. **Advance:** not offered. **Royalty:** 10%; based on all copies sold.

Marketing Channels. Distribution houses; direct mail. Subsidiary rights: all.

Additional Information. Tips: Do not send complete manuscript. Catalog: upon request.

ZEPHYR PRESS. 13 Robinson St. Somerville, MA 02145. (617) 628-9726. Submissions Editors: Ed Hogan (literature in translation); Leora Zeitlin (fiction). Founded: 1980. Number of titles published: cumulative—12, 1992—6. Hardback 45%, softback 55%.

Subjects of Interest. Fiction—literary fiction. Recent publications: *St. Veronica Gig Stories* (Jewish). Nonfiction—ethnic groups (Afro-Americans, Arabs, Slavic cultures, Filipinos, Germans, Hispanics, Indians from India, Indians of Central/South America, Irish, Israelis, Italians, Japanese, Jews, Koreans, Mexicans, Native Americans, Scots, Vietnamese); ecology; essays; biography; history; politics/world affairs; nature; peace; technology; men's and women's issues. Recent publications: *The Complete Poems of Anna Akhmatova* (Russian).

Initial Contact. Query letter and 10 sample pages. Enclose reply postcard if you wish confirmation on receipt of your query. SASE required.

Acceptance Policies. Unagented manuscripts: yes. First novels: yes. Simultaneous submissions: yes. Response time to initial inquiry: We will respond only if we have further interest. Average time until publication: 18 months. **Advance:** policy varies. **Royalty:** 10%; based on publisher's net sales.

Marketing Channels. Distribution houses; direct mail; special sales. Subsidiary rights: reprint; dramatization, motion picture, and broadcast; video; sound reproduction and recording; book club; translation and foreign; computer and other magnetic and electronic media; English language publication outside the United States and Canada.

Additional Information. Tips: Make sure you've got something special before you consider contacting a publisher. Your manuscript should have been seen by many others before a book editor sees it. Writer's guidelines: not available. Catalog: SASE.

Periodical Publishers

A single issue of a periodical (magazine, newspaper, or newsletter) is constructed from many different manuscripts, including articles, interviews, fiction, columns, reviews, poetry, etc. Some of this material is produced in-house by the publisher's staff, and some is purchased from freelance writers. The following information has been collected and organized to help you find and approach publishers of periodicals with an interest in ethnic material. These publishers are most likely to accept your inquiry and your submission.

How to Use the Information in This Section

The first paragraph of each entry identifies the publication and gives its location, submissions editor(s), and focus or type. Publications identified as having a "nonspecific ethnic audience" target a general audience or a variety of ethnic groups. Also included is information on the frequency of publication, circulation, and the number of manuscripts bought each year if the publication buys freelance material. Whether payment is made in cash or copies is also indicated.

Editorial Needs

This section identifies the publication's interests. However, when indicating nonfiction index topics for their publications, some editors selected more subjects than were named in their initial list of interests. In some cases, additional topics may indicate future interests; in others, they identify subcategories within the periodical's basic focus, such as celebrity profiles for a regional publication or ethnic issues for a family magazine. Check the subject index to see which publications are listed for your specific interest or expertise.

Editorial needs are listed for fiction and/or nonfiction. For periodicals that accept fiction, we have listed the forms or types such as short stories, excerpts, translations, etc., followed by the subject areas. Information on length and/or payment (if made in cash) follows in parentheses when that information varies for each form. When payment and/or word length are the same for all forms, a general statement at the end of the fiction section contains that information.

For nonfiction, we have indicated the forms accepted followed by the general subject interests. Information in parentheses may include specific subjects for each form, preferred length, and payment (when made in cash). Whenever information is the same for all forms, we have included it in a comprehensive sentence at the end of the section.

Initial contact

This information indicates how the editor wants to be contacted. You increase your chances for selling to a particular editor if you follow the suggestions listed here. Whether stated or not, always include a SASE.

Acceptance Policies

Byline offered: While most publications include an author's byline, some do not—an important issue for most writers and thus listed first.

Publishing rights: This information specifies the particular use of your manuscript the periodical is paying for. Most magazine editors purchase first North American serial rights—the right to publish your material first in their periodical for distribution in the United States and Canada. For information concerning other rights purchased, we suggest that you consult one of the many legal handbooks for writers or see the Books for Writers section of this book.

Payment made: Some smaller publications offer contributor's copies and publish your byline as payment. We have listed the exact number of copies offered whenever possible. When payment is offered in cash rather than copies, the timing is listed—most commonly on acceptance or on publication. For payments made in cash, the listing includes information on kill fees and expenses.

Kill fee: Some publications pay the writer a portion of the regular payment for articles that are assigned but later cancelled (or killed). Kill fees generally do not apply to unassigned articles.

Writer's expenses: Keep in mind that expenses are generally paid only when preapproved by the editor, so always clarify policies ahead of time. Editors rarely authorize payment of expenses incurred by authors unknown (and unproven) to them. Expenses are generally covered only for writers with proven ability and reliability.

Response time and time until publication: Always dependent upon a number of factors, this information provides an approximate idea of how long the publishing process takes after the editor has received your query, responded, and accepted the completed manuscript.

Simultaneous submissions: If the publisher says "yes," you may submit your manuscript to several different publications at the same time, but you must inform each publisher that the manuscript is being simultaneously submitted.

Seasonal material: This section tells you how many weeks or months in advance of a holiday or season you must send your material in order for it to be considered for publication within the next year.

Disk submissions: While the majority of publishers want your material submitted in the form of manuscript pages, many will now accept your finished submission on a disk compatible with their computer systems. For your first contact with a publication, always send a hard copy (typed or printed manuscript).

Photography Submissions

We've included the publication's preference for film type, format (black-and-white or color prints or transparencies), and size. Requests for additional information (listed under "Photographs should include") may cover model releases, captions, and identification of subjects. Payment for photographs may be made separately or in conjunction with the article submitted. Photographic rights may also be handled in the same manner.

Additional Information

This section of the entry reflects additional comments by the editor aimed specifically at the writer. Tips are suggestions that can help ensure your success in placing an article with a particular periodical. The best first step toward approaching any publication is to obtain its writer's guidelines and a sample copy.

Abbreviations

n/i means no information was given to us by the periodical.

n/a means that this information does not apply to the periodical.

AIM MAGAZINE. PO Box 20554. Chicago, IL 60620. (312) 874-6184. Submissions Editors: Dr. Myron Apilado (managing editor); Ruth Apilado (publisher); Mark Boone (fiction). Type: magazine for high school and college targeting a nonspecific ethnic audience. Frequency of publication: quarterly. Circulation: 7000. Number of manuscripts accepted per year: 80. Payment offered.

Editorial Needs. Fiction forms—short stories ($25); children's/young adult. For all forms: subjects include ethnic groups (Arabs, Afro-Americans, Indians from India, Chinese, Filipinos, Hispanics, Indians of Central/South America, Latin Americans), historical fiction.

Nonfiction forms—book excerpts; essays; fillers; poetry. For all forms: subjects include ethnic groups (Arabs, Afro-Americans, Indians from India, Chinese, Filipinos, Hispanics,

Indians of Central/South America, Latin Americans), essays, family issues, general interest, biography, history, social/political commentary.

Initial Contact. Entire manuscript. Include short bio. SASE required.

Acceptance Policies. Byline given: yes. Publishing rights: first North American serial rights. Payment made: upon publication. Kill fee: no. Expenses: no. Response time to initial inquiry: 1 month. Average time until publication: 2 months. Submit seasonal material 3 months in advance. Simultaneous submissions: yes. Disk submissions: no.

Photography Submissions. Format and film: n/i. Photographs should include: captions; identification of subjects. **Payment:** $10. Photographic rights: first rights.

Additional Information. We want to prove by the written word that people from different ethnic and racial backgrounds are more alike than not. Tips: Typewritten, well written. Writer's guidelines: upon request. Sample copy: $3.50.

ALOHA, THE MAGAZINE OF HAWAII AND THE PACIFIC. 49 S. Hotel St., #309. Honolulu, HI 96813. (808) 523-9871. Submissions Editor: Cheryl Chee Tsutsumi. Type: magazine targeting a nonspecific ethnic audience. Frequency of publication: every other month. Circulation: 65,000. Number of manuscripts accepted per year: 30. Payment offered.

Editorial Needs. Fiction forms—short stories (2000 words maximum, $150-$400).

Nonfiction forms—book excerpts; food/recipes; interview/profiles; poetry ($30); book/entertainment reviews; photo features. For all forms except poetry: 2000-3000 words; $150-$400.

Initial Contact. Query letter only. Clips are a must. SASE required.

Acceptance Policies. Byline given: yes. Publishing rights: first North American serial rights. Payment made: upon publication. Kill fee: usually 25-50%. Expenses: must be approved in advance. Response time to initial inquiry: 2 months. Average time until publication: up to 1 year. Submit seasonal material 12 months in advance. Simultaneous submissions: no. Disk submissions: Microsoft Word 4.0.

Photography Submissions. Format and film: transparencies; 5x7 or 8x10 (preferred) black-and-white prints. Photographs should include: captions; model releases; identification of subjects. **Payment:** $25 black-and white prints; $60 color; $125 spread; $175 color cover. Photographic rights: one-time rights.

Additional Information. *Aloha*, even with an international readership, directs its material to the residents of Hawaii in the belief that this will result in a true and accurate presentation. We are not a tourist or travel publication and not geared to such a readership. We welcome material reflecting the true Hawaiian experience. Tips: Use the *Chicago Manual of Style*. Writer's guidelines: SASE. Sample copy: SASE; $2.95.

AMERASIA JOURNAL. Asian American Studies Center. 3232 Campbell Hall. 405 Hilgard Ave. University of California. Los Angeles, CA 90024-1546. (213) 825-2968, 825-3415. Fax: (213) 206-9844. Submissions Editors: Russell Leong (chief editor); Glenn Omatsu (editor, ads, book review). Type: academic journal targeting a nonspecific ethnic audience. Frequency of publication: 3 times per year. Circulation: 1800. Number of manuscripts accepted per year: n/i. Payment not offered.

Editorial Needs. Fiction forms—book excerpts; short stories; translations.

Nonfiction forms—essays; interview/profiles; poetry; book/entertainment reviews; scholarly works and research essays on the social, historical fiction, and cultural aspects of Asian-Americans in the United States. For all forms: subjects include ethnic groups (Asian-

Americans, Indians from India, Chinese, Filipinos, Japanese, Koreans, Vietnamese), biography, culture, essays, history, humanities, immigration, minority issues, social/political commentary.

Initial Contact. Entire manuscript. SASE required.

Acceptance Policies. Byline given: yes. Publishing rights: n/i. Payment made: not offered. Response time to initial inquiry: 3 months. Average time until publication: 6 months. Simultaneous submissions: no. Disk submissions: 3 1/2 disk.

Additional Information. Writer's guidelines: upon request. Sample copy: upon request.

AMERICAN DANE. 3717 Harney St. Omaha, NE 68131-3844. (402) 341-5049. Fax: (402) 341-0830. Submissions Editors: Jerome L. Christensen, administrative editor; Jennifer C. Denning, editor in chief. Type: magazine targeting the Danish, Danish-American audience. Frequency of publication: monthly. Circulation: 10,000. Number of manuscripts accepted per year: 24. Payment offered.

Editorial Needs. Fiction forms—book excerpts; novellas; short stories; translations. For all forms: subjects include adventure, ethnic groups, folklore, holiday stories, humor, suspense; 3000 words maximum; payment varies.

Nonfiction forms—book excerpts (payment varies); essays (payment varies); features (payment varies); interview/profiles (payment varies); photo features ($20 maximum); poetry ($35 maximum); book/entertainment reviews (payment varies). For all forms: subjects include Danish adventure, humor, culture, folklore, immigration; 3000 word maximum.

Initial Contact. Query letter only or entire manuscript. SASE not required.

Acceptance Policies. Byline given: yes. Publishing rights: first rights; all rights revert to author. Payment made: upon publication. Kill fee: no. Expenses: no. Response time to initial inquiry: 2 weeks. Average time until publication: 1-18 months. Submit seasonal material 12-18 months in advance. Simultaneous submissions: yes. Disk submissions: no.

Photography Submissions. Format and film: 6 1/2 x 8 maximum black-and-white or color prints. Photographs should include: captions; identification of subjects. **Payment:** $20 maximum. Photographic rights: first rights.

Additional Information. Please submit material April through August as material is chosen in August and September for the following year. Tips: Remember our audience is conservative, family-oriented Danish-Americans. Writer's guidelines: write or call. Sample copy: write or call, $1.

AMERICAN INDIAN CULTURE AND RESEARCH JOURNAL. UCLA American Indian Studies Center. 3220 Campbell Hall. 405 Hilgard Ave. Los Angeles, CA 90024-1548. (213) 825-7315. (213) 206-7060. Submissions Editor: Duane Champagne. Type: academic journal targeting the Native American audience. Frequency of publication: quarterly. Circulation: 1250. Number of manuscripts accepted per year: 15-20. Payment made in copies.

Editorial Needs. Nonfiction forms—book reviews (500-1000 words); scholarly articles (length varies). For all forms: subjects include American Indian culture, history, current issues, agriculture, archaeology, arts and music, education, folklore, government/politics, law, medicine, minority issues, nature/environment, social/political commentary.

Initial Contact. Entire manuscript. Manuscripts are not returned to the author.

Acceptance Policies. Byline given: yes. Publishing rights: one-time rights; microfilm. Payment made: in copies. Response time to initial inquiry: 1 month. Average time until publication: 6 months. Simultaneous submissions: no. Disk submissions: required; 3 1/2; MacWrite II, WordPerfect, Microsoft Word.

Photography Submissions. Only to accompany articles. Do not submit initially; original photos/artwork will be requested after acceptance of manuscript. Format and film: prints. Photographs should include: captions; identification of subjects. **Payment:** not offered. Photographic rights: one-time rights.

Additional Information. We also publish academic books, monographs, and a poetry series. Writer's guidelines: upon request. Sample copy: upon request.

AMERICAN INDIAN LAW REVIEW. University of Oklahoma College of Law.
300 Timberdell Rd. Norman, OK 73019. (405) 325-2840, 325-5191. Fax: (405) 325-6282. Submissions Editors: Kathy Supernaw (editor in chief); Tamela Hughlett (managing editor). Type: academic legal journal targeting the Native American audience. Frequency of publication: 2 times per year. Circulation: 650. Number of manuscripts accepted per year: 8. Payment in copies.

Editorial Needs. Nonfiction forms—essays; book/entertainment reviews; scholarly articles. For all forms: subjects include American Indian legal and cultural issues.

Initial Contact. Entire manuscript. SASE required.

Acceptance Policies. Byline given: yes. Publishing rights: author has option of retaining rights. Payment made: 25 reprints and 2 copies. Response time to initial inquiry: 6 weeks. Average time until publication: 6-12 months. Simultaneous submissions: yes. Disk submissions: WordPerfect 4.2, 5.0, 5.1.

Additional Information. Writer's guidelines: SASE. Sample copy: $5 per issue.

ANTIETAM REVIEW. 82 W. Washington St., 3rd Fl. Hagerstown, MD 21740.
(301) 791-3132. Submissions Editors: Ann Knox (fiction); Crystal Brown (poetry); Benita Keller (photography); Susanne Kass (executive editor). Type: magazine targeting a nonspecific ethnic audience. Frequency of publication: annually. Circulation: 1500. Number of manuscripts accepted per year: 12 fiction, 18 poems, 12 photos. Payment and copies offered.

Editorial Needs. Fiction forms—book excerpts (literary, contemporary/modern).

Nonfiction forms—poetry; interview/profiles (literary figure). For all forms: copies are offered and payment varies.

Initial Contact. Entire manuscript. Include bio. SASE required.

Acceptance Policies. Byline given: yes. Publishing rights: first North American serial rights. Payment made: upon publication. Kill fee: no. Expenses: no. Response time to initial inquiry: 6 weeks. Average time until publication: varies. Simultaneous submissions: reluctantly. Disk submissions: no.

Photography Submissions. Format and film: any size black-and-white prints. Photographs should include: SASE and photographer's bio. **Payment:** $25. Photographic rights: first North American serial rights.

Additional Information. We are a regional magazine accepting submissions from natives or residents of Maryland, Virginia, West Virginia, Pennsylvania, Delaware, and District of Columbia. Tips: Get a sample copy of the magazine and a set of guidelines. We look for well-crafted fiction and poetry, and black-and-white photographs. Writer's guidelines: write or call. Sample copy: $3.00 for back issue, $5 for current issue.

APPALACHIAN HERITAGE. Berea College. Berea, KY 40404. (606) 986-9341, ext. 5260. Fax: (606) 986-9494. Submissions Editor: Sidney Saylor Farr. Type: magazine targeting the Southern Appalachian audience. Frequency of publication: quarterly. Circulation: 1000. Number of manuscripts accepted per year: 10-12. Payment in copies.

Editorial Needs. Fiction forms—short stories. For all forms: subjects focus is on Southern-Appalachian culture.

Nonfiction forms—essays; features. For all forms: focus is on Southern-Appalachian culture and social/political commentary; 3000 words maximum.

Initial Contact. Query letter only or article proposal with subject outline or entire manuscript. SASE required.

Acceptance Policies. Byline given: yes. Publishing rights: first North American serial rights. Payment made: 3 copies. Response time to initial inquiry: 3 weeks. Average time until publication: 6-12 months. Submit seasonal material 3-6 months in advance. Simultaneous submissions: yes. Disk submissions: MacWrite.

Photography Submissions. Format and film: black-and-white prints, negatives, transparencies. Photographs should include: n/i. **Payment:** not offered. Photographic rights: first-time rights.

Additional Information. Tips: Know the Southern Appalachian region; submission must be Appalachian in topic or subject. Writer's guidelines: upon request. Sample copy: $5.

ARAB STUDIES QUARTERLY. 556 Trapelo Rd. Belmont, MA. (617) 484-5483. Submissions Editor: Jamal Nassar. Type: academic journal targeting a nonspecific ethnic audience. Frequency of publication: quarterly. Circulation: n/i. Number of manuscripts accepted per year: 20. Payment not offered.

Editorial Needs. Nonfiction forms—book excerpts (800 words); book/entertainment reviews; articles (6000 words); scholarly works; reference. For all forms: subjects focus on the Arab world and Arab-American anthropology, art, culture, education, government/politics, humanities, immigration, Israel, Judaica, law, Muslims, Eastern cultures, social/political commentary.

Initial Contact. Entire manuscript. Submit on disk, using WordPerfect 5.0. SASE not required.

Acceptance Policies. Byline given: yes. Publishing rights: first rights. Payment made: none. Response time to initial inquiry: 3 months. Average time until publication: 8 months. Simultaneous submissions: no. Disk submissions: WordPerfect 5.0.

Additional Information. We are a scholarly journal concerned with the Arab world and Arab-Americans. Tips: Contact the editor for further information. Writer's guidelines: contained in the journal. Sample copy: check your local library.

ARARAT. 585 Sable River Rd. Saddle Brook, NJ 07662. (201) 776-7630. Submissions Editor: Leo Hamaliar. Type: magazine targeting the Armenian audience. Frequency of publication: quarterly. Circulation: n/i. Number of manuscripts accepted per year: 30. Payment offered.

Editorial Needs. Fiction forms—book excerpts; short stories; translations. For all forms: subjects focus on Armenian historical fiction, literary works.

Nonfiction forms—essays; interview/profiles; photo features; poetry; book/entertainment reviews. For all forms: subjects include Armenian archaeology, immigration, minority issues, politics/world affairs, social/political commentary.

Initial Contact. Query letter only. SASE required.

Acceptance Policies. Byline given: yes. Publishing rights: first North American serial rights. Payment made: upon publication. Response time to initial inquiry: 2 weeks. Average time until publication: 12-16 weeks. Simultaneous submissions: no. Disk submissions: no.

Photography Submissions. Format and film: black-and-white prints. Photographs should include: captions. **Payment:** $10. Photographic rights: n/i.

Additional Information. Subject matter usually related to Armenian life. Tips: Crisp, informal style preferred to journalistic prose.

ARBA SICULA. (Also publish *Sicilia Parra*). St. John's University. Jamaica, NY 11439. Submissions Editor: G. Cipolla. Type: newsletter and academic journal targeting the Sicilian-American and Italian-American audience. Frequency of publication: 2 issues yearly of *Arba Siccula*; 2 issues yearly of *Sicilia Parra*. Circulation: 1600. Number of manuscripts accepted per year: n/i. Payment not offered.

Editorial Needs. Fiction forms—short stories; translations. For all forms: focus is on Sicilian and Sicilian-American culture.

Nonfiction forms—essays; food/recipes; interview/profiles; photo features; poetry (Sicilian); reviews (on Sicily); social/political commentary. For all forms: focus is on Sicilian and Sicilian-American culture.

Initial Contact. Entire manuscript. SASE required.

Acceptance Policies. Byline given: n/i. Publishing rights: n/i. Payment made: not offered. Response time to initial inquiry: 1 month. Average time until publication: next publication date. Simultaneous submissions: yes. Disk submissions: IBM; Multimate, ASCII, WordPerfect 5.0.

ASIAN INSIGHTS MAGAZINE. 255 N. Market St., Ste. 270. San Jose, CA 95110. (408) 288-3443. Fax: (408) 292-5867. Submissions Editor: Corinna Pu. Type: magazine targeting a nonspecific ethnic audience. Frequency of publication: quarterly. Circulation: n/i. Number of manuscripts accepted per year: varies. Payment not offered currently.

Editorial Needs. Fiction forms—book excerpts; novellas; plays; serialized fiction; short stories; translations. For all forms: subjects include avant-garde, contemporary/modern, humor, literary, all with an Asian-American focus; 2500-4000 words.

Nonfiction forms—book excerpts; columns; essays; features (travel); fillers; food/recipes; interview/profiles; photo features; poetry; reviews (mostly by Asian-Americans); statistics. For all forms: subjects include art, Asian ethnic groups (Indians from India, Chinese, Filipinos, Japanese, Koreans, Thais, Vietnamese), cooking, culture, education, entertainment, family issues, film/television/video, government/politics, health/fitness, immigration, photography, social/political commentary.

Initial Contact. Query letter only or article proposal with subject outline or entire manuscript. Include your experience and previously published pieces. SASE not required.

Acceptance Policies. Byline given: yes. Publishing rights: one-time rights. Payment made: no payment offered at this time. As we grow we want to pay all contributors. Response time to initial inquiry: 2 weeks. Average time until publication: 1 month. Submit seasonal material 2-3 months in advance. Simultaneous submissions: yes, inform us. Disk submissions: 3 1/2 disk.

Photography Submissions. Format and film: 5x7 or 8x10 prints; transparencies. Photographs should include: captions; identification of subjects. **Payment:** not offered. Photographic rights: first-time rights.

Additional Information. We provide a forum of communication for Asian-Americans and the rest of the community. We are the first magazine of its kind. Sample copy: upon request.

ASIAN PERSPECTIVES. University of Hawaii Press. 2840 Kolowalu St. Honolulu, HI 96822. (808) 956-7500, 956-8415. Fax: (808) 956-4893. Submissions Editor: Michael W. Graves, *Asian Perspectives*, Univ. of Hawaii, Dept. of Anthropology, 2424 Maile Way, Honolulu, HI 96822. Type: academic journal targeting a nonspecific ethnic audience. Frequency of publication: 2 times per year. Circulation: 600-700. Number of manuscripts accepted per year: 12. Payment not offered.

Editorial Needs. Nonfiction forms—essays (archaeology, ethnoarchaeology; 10,000-word maximum); book reviews.

Initial Contact. Entire manuscript. SASE required.

Acceptance Policies. Byline given: yes. Publishing rights: first North American serial rights. Payment made: not offered. Response time to initial inquiry: 4 months. Average time until publication: 1 year. Simultaneous submissions: no. Disk submissions: IBM compatible; WordPerfect.

Photography Submissions. Format and film: n/i. Photographs should include: captions, identification of subjects. **Payment:** not offered. Photographic rights: first rights.

Additional Information. Writer's guidelines: upon request.

ASIAN WEEK. 809 Sacramento St. San Francisco, CA 94108. (415) 397-0220. Submissions Editor: Brad Walker. Type: newspaper targeting the Asian, Asian-American audience. Frequency of publication: weekly. Circulation: 35,000. Number of manuscripts accepted per year: varies. Payment offered.

Editorial Needs. Nonfiction forms—columns; essays; features; fillers; cartoons; interview/profiles; book/entertainment reviews. For all forms: subjects include Asian, Asian-American emphasis in the areas of art, business, culture, education, family issues, gay/lesbian issues, martial arts, health, minority issues, social/political commentary; 500-1000 words; payment varies.

Initial Contact. Query letter only. SASE not required.

Acceptance Policies. Byline given: yes. Publishing rights: first North American serial rights. Payment made: upon publication. Kill fee: no. Expenses: no. Response time to initial inquiry: 1-2 weeks. Average time until publication: varies. Simultaneous submissions: yes. Disk submissions: Macintosh; Microsoft Word.

Additional Information. Tips: Call us first. Writer's guidelines: varies with type of story. Sample copy: upon request.

ATALANTIK. 7630 Deer Creek Dr. Worthington, OH 43085. (614) 885-0550. Submissions Editor: Prabhat K. Dutta. Type: magazine targeting an audience of Indians from India. Frequency of publication: quarterly. Circulation: 400. Number of manuscripts accepted per year: 100. Payment in copies.

Editorial Needs. Fiction forms—book excerpts (1000 words); novellas (3000 words); plays (3000 words); serialized fiction (2000 words); short stories (2000 words); children's/young adult translations (2000 words). For all forms: subjects include adventure, contemporary/modern, ethnic groups (Afro-Americans, Indians from India), historical fiction, humor, literary, mainstream, mystery, romance, science fiction, surrealism, suspense, women's issues.

Nonfiction forms—book excerpts (1000 words); columns (500 words); essays (2000 words); features (500 words); interview/profiles (2000-5000 words); poetry (25 lines); book/entertainment reviews (500 words). For all forms: subjects include adventure, ethnic groups (Afro-Americans, Indians from India) biography, comedy, culture, education, entertainment, family issues, festivals, games/puzzles, history, human potential, humanities, immigration, mythology, nature/environment, philosophy, poetry, recreation, religion (Hinduism); social/political commentary, travel.

Initial Contact. Query letter only or entire manuscript. SASE required.

Acceptance Policies. Byline given: yes. Publishing rights: all rights. Payment made: in copies. Response time to initial inquiry: 2 months. Average time until publication: 6 months. Simultaneous submissions: yes. Disk submissions: no.

Photography Submissions. Format and film: 6x9 or smaller prints. Photographs should include: captions; identification of subjects. Payment: not offered. Photographic rights: all.

Additional Information. Tips: Manuscripts with themes about Indians from India are preferred. Writer's guidelines: upon request.

ATHENA. PO Box 5028. Thousand Oaks, CA 91360. Submissions Editor: Ronald K. Jones. Type: newspaper targeting a nonspecific ethnic audience. Frequency of publication: 2 times per year. Circulation: 10,000. Number of manuscripts accepted per year: 100-200. Payment in copies.

Editorial Needs. Fiction forms—book excerpts; novellas; plays; serialized fiction; short stories; translations. For all forms: subjects should focus on some aspect of domestic violence; 1500-2000 words.

Nonfiction forms—book excerpts (1200-2000 words); columns (legal aspects, 1000 words); essays (1000 words); features (1000 words); fillers (25 words); interview/profiles (1200 words); book reviews (1200 words). For all forms: subjects should focus on issues concerning domestic violence in ethnic communities (Arabs, Afro-Americans, Indians from India, Hispanics, Filipinos, Japanese), disabled, family issues, gay/lesbian issues, minority issues, relationships, social/political commentary, women's issues.

Initial Contact. Entire manuscript. SASE required.

Acceptance Policies. Byline given: yes. Publishing rights: first North American serial rights. Payment made: in copies. Response time to initial inquiry: 4 weeks. Average time until publication: 6-12 months. Simultaneous submissions: yes. Disk submissions: no.

Photography Submissions. Format and film: 4x6 black-and-white prints; contact sheets; negatives; transparencies. Photographs should include: identification of subjects. Payment: in copies. Photographic rights: n/i.

Additional Information. *Athena* is the only international newspaper focusing on victory over domestic violence. Tips: Concentrate on material dealing with woman-battering and child abuse. Writer's guidelines: $2, includes sample copy.

BAMBOO RIDGE: THE HAWAII WRITERS' QUARTERLY. PO Box 61781. Honolulu, HI 96839-1781. (808) 599-4823. Submissions Editors: Darrell Lum, Erick Chock. Type: magazine targeting the Asian-American audience. Frequency of publication: quarterly. Circulation: 1000. Number of manuscripts accepted per year: 40-60. Payment in copies and small honorarium.

Editorial Needs. **Fiction forms**—book excerpts; novellas; plays; serialized fiction; short stories; translations. For all forms: subjects include contemporary/modern, ethnic groups (Hawaiians, Japanese, Koreans, Thais, Vietnamese), literary, mainstream, women's issues; $20.

Nonfiction forms—essays ($20); poetry ($10-$20). For all forms: subjects include ethnic groups (Hawaiians, Japanese, Koreans, Thais, Vietnamese), minority issues.

Initial Contact. Query letter. Include 5 poems for poetry submission and 25 pages maximum for prose submission. SASE required.

Acceptance Policies. Byline given: yes. Publishing rights: first North American serial rights; first rights; one-time rights. Payment made: upon publication. Kill fee: no. Expenses: no. Response time to initial inquiry: 1-3 months. Average time until publication: 3-6 months. Simultaneous submissions: no. Disk submissions: no.

Additional Information. We are interested in writing that reflects the multiethnic culture of Hawaii. Tips: Read the magazine. Writer's guidelines: SASE. Sample copy: $4, plus $1 postage/handling.

BLACK ANGELS POETRY NEWSLETTER. PO Box 50892. Palo Alto, CA 94303. (415) 321-2489. Submissions Editor: Abimbola Adama. Type: newsletter targeting the Afro-American audience. Frequency of publication: quarterly. Circulation: begins publication January, 1992. Number of manuscripts accepted per year: uncertain. Payment in copies (pay is possible in the future).

Editorial Needs. **Fiction forms**—short stories (adult fables, fantasy, romance; very short, 1 per issue).

Nonfiction forms—essays; interview/profiles (African-American writers); poetry (chiefly African-American issues); book/entertainment reviews (African-American authors. For all forms: subjects include African-American education, essays, psycho-spirituality, self-help; length varies.

Initial Contact. Article proposal with subject outline. Include writer's track record and background. SASE required.

Acceptance Policies. Byline given: yes. Publishing rights: one-time rights. Payment made: in copies. Response time to initial inquiry: 2-4 weeks. Average time until publication: next quarter. Submit seasonal material 3 months in advance. Simultaneous submissions: yes. Disk submissions: WordPerfect 5.1, Ventura 1.1.

Photography Submissions. Format and film: half-tones. Photographs should include: captions; model releases; identification of subjects. **Payment:** not offered. Photographic rights: one-time rights.

Additional Information. *Black Angels* is a publication of quality poetry and fiction by and for African-American writers. Emphasis is on our culture but other subjects are also welcome. Tips: Write from your roots and send us your best. Writer's guidelines: SASE. Sample copy: $3.

BLACK COLLEGIAN, THE. 1240 S. Broad St. New Orleans, LA 70125. (504) 821-5694. Fax: (504) 821-5713. Submissions Editor: Kuumba Kazi-Ferrouillet. Type: magazine targeting the Afro-American college audience. Frequency of publication: every other month. Circulation: 125,000. Number of manuscripts accepted per year: 80. Payment offered.

Editorial Needs. **Nonfiction forms**—essays (750-1250 words); features (career development, 1250-1500 words); interview/profiles (celebrities, 1250-1500 words). For all forms: subjects include Afro-American issues, biography, history, human potential, Muslims, philosophy, scholarly works, social/political commentary; $250-$500.

Initial Contact. Entire manuscript. Include bio. SASE required.

Acceptance Policies. Byline given: yes. Publishing rights: first North American serial rights. Payment made: upon publication. Kill fee: no. Expenses: no. Response time to initial inquiry: 2 months. Average time until publication: 2-3 months. Submit seasonal material 4 months in advance. Simultaneous submissions: no. Disk submissions: WordPerfect.

Photography Submissions. Format and film: transparencies. Photographs should include: captions; model releases; identification of subjects. **Payment:** $25-$150. Photographic rights: one-time rights.

Additional Information. Tips: Please familiarize yourself with the publication prior to query. Writer's guidelines: SASE. Sample copy: SASE; $4.

BLACK ENTERPRISE. 130 Fifth Ave. New York, NY. (212) 242-8000. Fax: (212) 886-9610.
Submissions Editors: Alfred Edmond, Jr. (business, corporate issues); Kevin Thompson (small business); Carolyn Brown (personal finance, technology); Marjorie Whigham (lifestyle, leisure, travel). Type: business service magazine targeting the Afro-American audience. Frequency of publication: monthly. Circulation: 250,000. Number of manuscripts accepted per year: varies. Payment offered.

Editorial Needs. Nonfiction forms—features (money management, career development, entrepreneurship, developing small businesses, 2500 words, $800); interview/profiles (corporate executives, *B-E's* 100 companies); book reviews (black history, business).

Initial Contact. Query letter only. Include resumé and writing samples. SASE required.

Acceptance Policies. Byline given: yes. Publishing rights: all rights. Payment made: upon acceptance. Kill fee: yes. Expenses: yes. Response time to initial inquiry: 6-8 weeks. Average time until publication: varies. Submit seasonal material 4-5 months in advance. Simultaneous submissions: no. Disk submissions: IBM, Macintosh.

Additional Information. Our articles must be sophisticated and offer substantial how-to information. Tips: Write a strong query letter that emphasizes our readers' interests and needs. We do not accept unsolicited manuscripts. Writer's guidelines: upon request. Sample copy: upon request.

BLACK SCHOLAR: JOURNAL OF BLACK STUDIES & RESEARCH, THE. PO Box 2869. Oakland, CA 94609. (415) 547-6633.
Submissions Editor: Toni M. Tingle. Type: magazine and academic journal targeting the black, Hispanic, and Native American audience. Frequency of publication: quarterly. Circulation: 6000. Number of manuscripts accepted per year: varies. Payment in copies.

Editorial Needs. Fiction forms—short stories; translations.

Nonfiction forms—book and entertainment reviews.

Initial Contact. Entire manuscript. SASE required.

Acceptance Policies. Byline given: yes. Publishing rights: simultaneous rights. Payment made: in copies. Response time to initial inquiry: 1 month. Average time until publication: n/i. Submit seasonal material 2 months in advance. Simultaneous submissions: no. Disk submissions: WordPerfect 5.1.

Additional Information. We also publish a book supplement titled *Black Books Round-up*, which includes listings from most major publishing houses, as well as small black presses, and books by black authors of interest to black readers. Tips: Look through a copy of the magazine first before submitting material.

B'NAI B'RITH INTERNATIONAL JEWISH MONTHLY. 1640 Rhode
Island Ave., NW. Washington, DC 20036. (202) 857-6645. Submissions Editor: Jeff Rubin. Type: magazine targeting the Jewish audience. Frequency of publication: monthly. Circulation: 200,000. Number of manuscripts accepted per year: n/i. Payment offered.

Editorial Needs. Fiction forms—short stories (very rarely).

Nonfiction forms—book excerpts; features; interview/profiles; photo features; book/entertainment reviews. For all forms: subjects include Judaic culture, biography, history, politics/world affairs, Israel; 750-3000 words.

Initial Contact. Query letter only. Include clips. SASE required.

Acceptance Policies. Byline given: yes. Publishing rights: first North American serial rights. Payment made: n/i. Kill fee: yes. Expenses: n/i. Response time to initial inquiry: n/i. Average time until publication: n/i. Submit seasonal material 3 months in advance. Simultaneous submissions: n/i. Disk submissions: submission on Mac disks in ASCII or WordPerfect is appreciated.

Photography Submissions. We look for high-quality photography and other illustrations. Format and film: n/i. Photographs should include: n/i. **Payment:** n/i. Photographic rights: n/i.

Additional Information. Our magazine explores in depth the social, cultural, historical fiction, and political issues that affect the Jewish community in the United States and abroad. Tips: We strongly discourage the submission of fiction, political commentary, and nostalgia. Writer's guidelines: upon request. Sample copy: upon request.

BRIDGE; JOURNAL OF THE DANISH AMERICAN HERITAGE SOCIETY, THE. 1132 Newport Dr. SE. Salem, OR 97306. (503) 588-1331.
Submissions Editor: Egon Bodtker. Type: newsletter and academic journal targeting the Danish-American audience. Frequency of publication: 2 times per year. Circulation: 700. Number of manuscripts accepted per year: 20. Payment in copies.

Editorial Needs. Nonfiction forms—book reviews; history; biography. For all forms: subjects focus on Danish-American culture and people.

Initial Contact. Query letter only or article proposal with subject outline or entire manuscript. Include information about author. SASE not required.

Acceptance Policies. Byline given: n/i. Publishing rights: n/i. Payment made: 2 copies. Response time to initial inquiry: 2 weeks. Average time until publication: 6 months. Simultaneous submissions: yes. Disk submissions: no.

Photography Submissions. Format and film: any size black-and-white prints. Photographs should include: captions. **Payment:** not offered. Photographic rights: none.

Additional Information. We accept articles about Danish-North American history, culture, and individuals. Sample copy: upon request.

BRILLIANT STAR. Baha'i National Center. Wilmette, IL 60091. (708) 869-9039. Submissions Editors: Candace Moore Hill, general editor; Pepper Oldziey,
activities editor. Type: children's magazine targeting a nonspecific ethnic market. Frequency of publication: every other month. Circulation: 2500. Number of manuscripts accepted per year: 12. Payment in copies.

Editorial Needs. Fiction forms—plays (500-1000 words); short stories (250-500-750 words); translations.

Nonfiction forms—features; food/recipes; interview/profiles; photo features; poetry; book/entertainment reviews. For all forms: subjects include world unity, race unity, other cultures, ethnic groups (multicultural), holidays around the world (not Christmas), religion; 250-1000 words (appropriate to the age of the reader).

Initial Contact. Entire manuscript. SASE required.

Acceptance Policies. Byline given: yes. Publishing rights: n/i. Payment made: in copies. Response time to initial inquiry: 6-8 weeks. Average time until publication: 1 year. Simultaneous submissions: n/i. Disk submissions: no.

Additional Information. Our purpose is to teach Baha'i children the history and beliefs of the Baha'i faith. Tips: Write to a specific age level. No Christmas stories. Writer's guidelines: SASE. Sample copy: SASE (5 ounces).

CALAPOOYA COLLAGE. PO Box 309. Monmouth, OR 97361. (503) 838-6292. Submissions Editor: Tom Ferté. Type: magazine targeting a nonspecific ethnic audience. Frequency of publication: annually. Circulation: n/i. Number of manuscripts accepted per year: 100. Payment in copies.

Editorial Needs. Fiction forms—short stories (one per issue).

Nonfiction forms—columns (about poetry, 2000 words); essays (about poetry, 2000 words); poetry (120 poems per issue); reviews (poetry, 600 words).

Initial Contact. Entire manuscript. SASE required.

Acceptance Policies. Byline given: yes. Publishing rights: none, all rights belong to the author. Payment made: in copies. Response time to initial inquiry: 4-6 weeks. Average time until publication: annually in August. Simultaneous submissions: no. Disk submissions: no.

Additional Information. We publish poetry by all ethnic groups in the United States, including gays, and by Hindu, Muslim, Jewish, Chinese, Hispanic, etc., authors abroad. We also sponsor the annual $700 Carolyn Kizer Poetry Awards. Writer's guidelines: none available. Sample copy: $5.

CANADIAN JOURNAL OF NATIVE EDUCATION. Department of Educational Foundations. 5-109 Educ. N. Bldg. University of Alberta. Edmonton, Alberta, Canada T6G 2G5. (403) 492-2769. Fax: (403) 492-0762. Submissions Editor: Carl Urion. Type: academic journal targeting a Native American audience. Frequency of publication: biannually. Circulation: 450. Number of manuscripts accepted per year: 22. Payment not offered.

Editorial Needs. Nonfiction forms—essays; photo features; poetry; book/entertainment reviews. For all forms: subjects must focus on Native Americans.

Initial Contact. Article proposal with subject outline or entire manuscript. SASE required.

Acceptance Policies. Byline given: yes. Publishing rights: varies, author may or may not retain copyright. Payment made: none. Response time to initial inquiry: n/i. Average time until publication: 6-12 months. Submit seasonal material 8 months in advance. Simultaneous submissions: no. Disk submissions: ASCII or any other common text processor.

Photography Submissions. Format and film: contact sheets. Photographs should include: captions; model releases; identification of subject. **Payment:** not offered. Photographic rights: none.

CHICAGO REVIEW. 5801 S. Kenwood Ave. Chicago, IL 60637. Submissions Editors: Anne Myles (poetry); Gregory Sendi (fiction); Mark Morrison (nonfiction). Type: magazine targeting a nonspecific ethnic audience. Frequency of publication: quarterly. Circulation: 2000. Number of manuscripts accepted per year: 60. Payment in copies.

Editorial Needs. Fiction forms—book excerpts; short stories; translations. For all forms: style includes avant-garde; 5000 words.

Nonfiction forms—book excerpts; essays; interview/profiles; photo features; poetry (1-3 pages); reviews (books, theater, etc). For all forms: literary, cultural topics, and social/political commentary are the focus; 5000 words (except poetry).

Initial Contact. Entire manuscript. SASE required.

Acceptance Policies. Byline given: yes. Publishing rights: all rights. Payment made: in copies. Response time to initial inquiry: 3 months. Average time until publication: 1 month. Submit seasonal material 3 months in advance. Simultaneous submissions: no. Disk submissions: no.

Photography Submissions. Format and film: transparencies. Photographs should include: captions; identification of subjects. **Payment:** not offered. Photographic rights: all.

Additional Information. Writer's guidelines: upon request. Sample copy: $5.

CICADA. 329 E St. Bakersfield, CA 93304. (805) 323-4064. Submissions Editor: Frederick A. Raborg, Jr. Type: magazine targeting the Japanese audience. Frequency of publication: quarterly. Circulation: 600. Number of manuscripts accepted per year: 400 nonfiction, 4 fiction. Payment and copies offered.

Editorial Needs. Fiction forms—short stories; translations. For all forms: subjects include adult fables, adventure, avant-garde, Asian ethnic groups (Indians from India, Koreans, Japanese, Chinese, Filipinos, Thais, Vietnamese), genres, new age, surrealism; 1500-3000 words; $10 plus 1 copy payment.

Nonfiction forms—articles (about haiku or Japan, $10 plus copy); essays ($10 plus copy); poetry (no payment); reviews (copy). For all forms: subjects include ethnic groups (Indians from India, Koreans, Japanese, Chinese, Filipinos, Thais, Vietnamese), adventure, archaeology, art, comedy, erotica, family issues, gay/lesbian issues, martial arts, mythology, nature/environment, religion (Buddhism, Taoism, Zen), yoga.

Initial Contact. Entire manuscript. SASE required.

Acceptance Policies. Byline given: yes. Publishing rights: first North American serial rights. Payment made: upon publication. Kill fee: 50%. Expenses: no. Response time to initial inquiry: 2 weeks. Average time until publication: 6-12 months. Submit seasonal material 6 months in advance. Simultaneous submissions: prefer not. Disk submissions: no.

Photography Submissions. Format and film: 5x7 or 8x10 black-and-white prints. Photographs should include: captions; model releases; identification of subjects. **Payment:** $10-$25. Photographic rights: one-time rights.

Additional Information. We are open to all forms of literature pertaining to the Orient. Tips: Persist and study. Read a copy of *Cicada*. Writer's guidelines: SASE. Sample copy: $4.50.

COLLAGES & BRICOLAGES. 212 Founders Hall. Clarion University of Pennsylvania. Clarion, PA 16214. (814) 226-2340. Fax: (814) 226-2341. Submissions Editor: Marie-José Fortis. Type: magazine targeting a nonspecific ethnic audience. Frequency of publication: yearly. Circulation: 400. Number of manuscripts accepted per year: 15-20. Payment in copies.

Editorial Needs. Fiction forms—book excerpts; plays (short); short stories; translations. For all forms: subjects include adult fables, avant-garde, contemporary, erotica, fantasy, humor, literary, science fiction, surrealism, women's issues; 3000 word maximum.

Nonfiction forms—book excerpts; columns; essays; interview/profiles; photo features; poetry; book/entertainment reviews. For all forms: subjects include art, comedy, essays, film/television/video, gay/lesbian issues, minority issues, philosophy, politics/world affairs, sociology, war/peace issues, women's issues; 3000 word maximum.

Initial Contact. Entire manuscript. Include letter and short bio. SASE required.

Acceptance Policies. Byline given: yes. Publishing rights: one-time rights. Payment made: in copies. Response time to initial inquiry: 2 weeks to 3 months. Average time until publication: 6-9 months. Submit material only in the fall. Simultaneous submissions: yes. Disk submissions: IBM; WordPerfect 5.0, 5.25, or ASCII.

Photography Submissions. Format and film: black-and-white prints smaller than 11x18. Photographs should include: captions; identification of subjects. **Payment:** in copies. Photographic rights: none.

Additional Information. *Collages & Bricolages* is interested in the literary writer, the playful writer, the writer that knows how take risks. Tips: Believe in yourself. If rejected, keep trying. If you really want to write, never give up. Writer's guidelines: n/i. Sample copy: n/i.

CRAZY QUILT QUARTERLY. PO Box 63729. San Diego, CA 92163-2729. (619) 688-1023. Submissions Editor: Marsh Cassaday (fiction, drama); Jackie Ball (poetry); Jim Kitchen (nonfiction). Type: literary magazine targeting a nonspecific ethnic audience. Frequency of publication: quarterly. Circulation: 200. Number of manuscripts accepted per year: 100. Payment in copies.

Editorial Needs. Fiction forms—book excerpts (4000 words maximum); plays (one act, 20 pages maximum); short stories (3000-4000 words). For all forms: subjects include contemporary, all ethnic groups, fantasy, general interest, literary, mainstream, science fiction.

Nonfiction forms—essays (related to writers or writing, 2000-3000 words); features (biographies of ethnic writers); interview/profiles (writers, 2000 words); poetry (any style, short preferred).

Initial Contact. Entire manuscript. SASE required.

Acceptance Policies. Byline given: yes. Publishing rights: first rights. Payment made: 2 copies. Response time to initial inquiry: 6 weeks. Average time until publication: 18 months. Simultaneous submissions: yes. Disk submissions: WordPerfect.

Photography Submissions. Format and film: 3x5 prints. Photographs should include: n/i. **Payment:** 2 copies. Photographic rights: one-time rights.

Additional Information. We are a literary journal; no romances, Westerns or pornography. Writer's guidelines: SASE. Sample copy: $3 back issue, $5 current issue, plus $1 postage.

CROSSCURRENTS. Asian American Studies Center. 3232 Campbell Hall. 405 Hilgard Ave. University of California. Los Angeles, CA 90024. (213) 825-2968, 825-3415. Fax: (213) 206-9844. Submissions Editor: Glen Omatsu. Type: newsletter targeting a nonspecific ethnic audience. Frequency of publication: twice yearly. Circulation: 3000. Number of manuscripts accepted per year: very few unsolicited manuscripts. Payment not offered.

Editorial Needs. Nonfiction forms—columns; essays; features; interview/profiles; photo features. For all forms: subjects include ethnic groups (Asian-American, Indians from India, Filipinos, Koreans, Thais, Vietnamese), biography, history, immigration, minority issues, sociology, social/political commentary.

Initial Contact. Query letter only. SASE required.

Acceptance Policies. Byline given: yes. Publishing rights: n/i. Payment made: not offered. Response time to initial inquiry: n/i. Average time until publication: n/i. Simultaneous submissions: n/i. Disk submissions: n/i.

Additional Information. Sample copy: upon request.

CULTURAL SURVIVAL QUARTERLY. 53A Church St. Cambridge, MA 02138. (617) 495-2562. Fax: (617) 495-1396. Submissions Editor: send to Editor. Type: magazine targeting a nonspecific ethnic audience. Frequency of publication: quarterly. Circulation: 20,000. Number of manuscripts accepted per year: 60. Payment in copies.

Editorial Needs. Nonfiction forms—features (indigenous rights; 3000 words).

Initial Contact. Article proposal with subject outline. SASE required.

Acceptance Policies. Byline given: yes. Publishing rights: n/i. Payment made: in copies. Response time to initial inquiry: 2 months. Average time until publication: 2-12 months. Simultaneous submissions: yes. Disk submissions: n/i.

Photography Submissions. Format and film: 5x7 black-and-white or color prints. Photographs should include: captions. **Payment:** none. Photographic rights: n/i.

Additional Information. *CSQ* addresses issues of both immediate and long-term concerns to indigenous peoples. Tips: Find out what our theme line-up is for the year as each issue has a different focus.

DETROIT JEWISH NEWS. 27676 Franklin Rd. Southfield, MI 48034. (313) 354-6060. Fax: (313) 354-6069. Submissions Editor: Alan Hitsky. Type: newspaper targeting the Jewish audience. Frequency of publication: weekly. Circulation: 21,000. Number of manuscripts accepted per year: 6. Payment offered.

Editorial Needs. Fiction forms—short stories (1500 words; $40-$100).

Nonfiction forms—columns; essays; features; food/recipes; interview/profiles. For all forms: subjects include Judaica, the Jewish community, social/political commentary.

Initial Contact. Entire manuscript. SASE required.

Acceptance Policies. Byline given: yes. Publishing rights: all. Payment made: upon publication. Kill fee: no. Expenses: no. Response time to initial inquiry: 1 month. Average time until publication: 2 months. Submit seasonal material 2 months in advance. Simultaneous submissions: n/i. Disk submissions: no.

Additional Information. We are associated with the *Baltimore* and *Atlanta Jewish Times* and your article may appear in all of these. Writer's guidelines: upon request. Sample copy: $2.

DZIENNIK ZWIAZKOWY (POLISH DAILY NEWS). 5711 N. Milwaukee Ave. Chicago, IL 60646. (312) 763-3343. Fax: (312) 763-3825. Submissions Editor: n/i. Type: Polish-language newspaper targeting Poles and Polish-Americans. Frequency of publication: daily. Circulation: 25,000. Number of manuscripts accepted per year: varies. Payment offered.

Editorial Needs. Fiction forms—short stories; translations (into Polish). For all forms: subjects include Polish or Polish-American adventure, general interest, historical fiction, humor.

Nonfiction forms—columns; essays; features; fillers; food/recipes; interview/profiles; book/entertainment reviews. For all forms: subjects include Polish or Polish-American adventure, art, astronomy, biography, business/economics, family issues, education, festivals, government/politics, health/fitness, immigration, law, labor, medicine, science, sociology, sports, social/political commentary, transportation, travel; $8 per 8 1/2 x 11 double-spaced page.

Initial Contact. Query letter only or article proposal with subject outline.

Acceptance Policies. Byline given: yes. Publishing rights: work-for-hire. Payment made: upon publication. Kill fee: no. Expenses: yes. Response time to initial inquiry: 1 week. Average time until publication: n/i. Simultaneous submissions: yes. Disk submissions: no.

Photography Submissions. Format and film: n/i. Photographs should include: captions; identification of subjects. **Payment:** $5 per photo. Photographic rights: n/i.

Additional Information. All articles must be written in Polish.

EAGLE'S FLIGHT. 2501 Hunter's Hill Dr., Apt. 822. Enid, OK 73703. (405) 233-1118. Submissions Editors: Shyamkant Kulkarni (poetry, short story); Rekha Kulkarni (fiction). Type: magazine targeting a nonspecific ethnic audience. Frequency of publication: quarterly. Circulation: n/i. Number of manuscripts accepted per year: 4-6. Payment, copies, and subscription offered.

Editorial Needs. Fiction forms—short stories (literary, mainstream, romance; 2500 words; $5-$15).

Nonfiction forms—poetry (any subject, 20-30 lines, free subscription); reviews (novels, short stories, 200 words, free subscription).

Initial Contact. Query letter only or entire manuscript. SASE required.

Acceptance Policies. Byline given: yes. Publishing rights: first North American serial rights; one-time rights. Payment made: upon publication. Kill fee: no. Expenses: no. Response time to initial inquiry: 1-6 months. Average time until publication: 1-2 years. Simultaneous submissions: yes. Disk submissions: no.

Additional Information. Tips: Read our previous issues and study what we are publishing. Writer's guidelines: SASE, $1. Sample copy: SASE, $1.

EAST BAY MONITOR, A MULTICULTURAL NEWSPAPER. PO Box 258. San Ramon, CA 94583. (415) 833-8667. Submissions Editor: Maggie Malone. Type: newspaper targeting a nonspecific ethnic audience. Frequency of publication: monthly (becomes a weekly in 1992). Circulation: 22,000 (audited). Number of manuscripts accepted per year: 150+. Payment in copies.

Editorial Needs. Nonfiction forms—columns; features; interview/profiles; book reviews (500 words maximum). For all forms: subjects include ethnic groups (Afro-Americans, Asians, Indians from India, Cajuns, Creoles, Chinese, Filipinos, Hispanics, Japanese, Muslims, Native Americans), art, culture, festivals, human potential, immigration, minority issues, social/political commentary; the shorter the better.

Initial Contact. Entire manuscript. Include the phone number of your sources. SASE required.

Acceptance Policies. Byline given: yes. Publishing rights: one-time rights; rights then revert to author. Payment made: in copies. Response time to initial inquiry: 3 weeks. Average time until publication: 1-2 months. Submit seasonal material 2 months in advance. Simultaneous submissions: yes. Disk submissions: WordPerfect 5.0, any size floppy disk.

Additional Information. We don't run "the sky is falling" stories. If there are problems, tell us what is being done about them. Tips: Get your facts right and spell names correctly. Locate stories the major papers aren't covering. Writer's guidelines: read the newspaper. Sample copy: $1.

EL TECOLOTE. PO Box 40037. San Francisco, 94140. (415) 252-5957. Fax: (415) 863-9314. Submissions Editor: Juan Gonzales. Type: newspaper targeting the Hispanic audience. Frequency of publication: monthly. Circulation: n/i. Number of manuscripts accepted per year: 24. Payment in copies.

Editorial Needs. Nonfiction forms—features (profiles, 800 words); photo features (800 words); poetry (Latino affairs, any length); book/entertainment reviews (500 words); social/political commentary (400 words); community news (Latino affairs).

Initial Contact. Article proposal with subject outline. Include photo possibilities. SASE not required.

Acceptance Policies. Byline given: yes. Publishing rights: first rights. Payment made: in copies. Response time to initial inquiry: 30 days. Average time until publication: 30 days. Submit seasonal material 3 months in advance. Simultaneous submissions: no. Disk submissions: Macintosh SE; Microsoft Word.

Photography Submissions. Format and film: 5x7 black-and-white prints. Photographs should include: captions; model releases; identification of subjects. **Payment**: not offered. Photographic rights: first rights.

Additional Information. We would consider material in Spanish. Tips: Discuss idea with me personally. Writer's guidelines: upon request.

ESSENCE MAGAZINE. 1500 Broadway. New York, NY 10036. (212) 642-0600. Fax: (212) 921-5173. Submissions Editor: check our masthead. Type: magazine targeting African-American women. Frequency of publication: monthly. Circulation: 900,000. Number of manuscripts accepted per year: 200. Payment offered.

Editorial Needs. Fiction forms—book excerpts; short stories. For all forms: subjects include Black focus on contemporary/modern, general subjects, holiday stories, humor, literary, women's issues.

Nonfiction forms—book excerpts; essays; features; fillers; food/recipes; interview/profiles; poetry; book/entertainment reviews. For all forms: focus is on black.

Initial Contact. Query letter only. We do not accept unsolicited fiction. SASE required.

Acceptance Policies. Byline given: yes. Publishing rights: first North American serial rights. Payment made: upon acceptance. Kill fee: 25%. Expenses: yes. Response time to initial inquiry: 2 months. Average time until publication: 6 months. Submit seasonal material 6-12 months in advance. Simultaneous submissions: if informed. Disk submissions: prearrange.

Additional Information. It's best not to send us anything until one has studied the publication and requested our writer's guidelines. Tips: Do not send a manuscript; send queries only. We only accept manuscripts for the Interiors and Brothers columns. Writer's guidelines: SASE. Sample copy: buy current issue on newsstand.

FINNAM NEWSLETTER. Finnish-American Historical Society of the West. PO Box 5522. Portland, OR 97208. (503) 654-0448. Submissions Editor: address to Editor. Type: academic journal targeting the Finnish-American audience. Frequency of publication: quarterly. Circulation: 350-450. Number of manuscripts accepted per year: 2. Payment in copies.

Editorial Needs. Nonfiction forms—essays; photo featuress. For all forms: subjects include Finnish-American biography, history, culture, folklore, immigration, minority issues, and religion.

Initial Contact. Article proposal with subject outline or entire manuscript. SASE required.

Acceptance Policies. Byline given: n/i. Publishing rights: cooperative agreement not to publish under separate cover. Payment made: in copies. Response time to initial inquiry: 1 week. Average time until publication: 3-6 months. Simultaneous submissions: no. Disk submissions: MS DOS, Radio Shack OS9, or Color Comp III.

Photography Submissions. Format and film: contact sheets. Photographs should include: captions; identification of subjects. **Payment:** not offered. Photographic rights: none.

Additional Information. We are a nonprofit organization. In addition to the journal, we also publish historical monographs on the average on one per year, focusing on Finnish-Americans circa 1900-1947. Tips: Photos to be released for publication with credits as necessary. We edit to our style. Writer's guidelines: upon request. Sample copy: not available.

FISH DRUM MAGAZINE. 626 Kathryn Ave. Santa Fe, NM 87501. Submissions Editors: Robert Winson; Suzi Winson (women's issues and Brooklyn editor) 40 Prospect Park W., #2D, Brooklyn, NY 11215. Type: magazine targeting a nonspecific ethnic audience. Frequency of publication: 2-4 times per year. Circulation: 500. Number of manuscripts accepted per year: 80. Payment in copies.

Editorial Needs. Fiction forms—plays; short stories; translations. For all forms: works should be literary in tone.

Nonfiction forms—essays; photo features; poetry (emphasis); book/entertainment reviews. For all forms: subjects include ethnic groups (American Indians and Hispanics in the Southwest, Chinese, Eastern cultures), religion (Zen Buddhism), erotica, women's issues.

Initial Contact. Entire manuscript with only a brief cover letter. SASE required.

Acceptance Policies. Byline given: yes. Publishing rights: first serial rights. Payment made: in copies. Response time to initial inquiry: 2 weeks. Average time until publication: 6-12 months. Simultaneous submissions: no. Disk submissions: no.

Photography Submissions. Format and film: 5x7 maximum black-and-white prints. Photographs should include: n/i. **Payment:** not offered. Photographic rights: one-time rights.

Additional Information. We're a general literary magazine with a strong interest in news from outside the mainstream. We are particularly interested in Southwestern Indian and Hispanic work, lively modern poetry, and material on Zen Buddhism. Send women's prose and poetry to the Brooklyn editor. Tips: Be sure and see an issue of the magazine. Writer's guidelines: not available. Sample copy: $3.

FORT CONCHO AND THE SOUTH PLAINS JOURNAL. 213 E.
Avenue D. San Angelo, TX 76903-7099. (915) 657-4441. Submissions Editor: John
Neilson. Type: historical journal targeting a nonspecific ethnic audience. Frequency
of publication: quarterly. Circulation: 1000. Number of manuscripts accepted per
year: 4-8. Payment in copies.

Editorial Needs. Nonfiction forms—essays; features; fillers; interview/profiles; photo
features; book/entertainment reviews. For all forms: subjects include ethnic groups in Texas
(Afro-Americans, Hispanics, Irish, Italians, Jews, Native Americans), anthropology,
archaeology, architecture, biography, history, humanities, medicine, military, tribal issues.

Initial Contact. Entire manuscript. Include bio. SASE preferred.

Acceptance Policies. Byline given: yes. Publishing rights: all rights. Payment made: in
copies. Response time to initial inquiry: 6-8 weeks. Average time until publication: within 1
year. Simultaneous submissions: no. Disk submissions: no.

Photography Submissions. Format and film: 5x7 or 8x10 glossy black-and-white prints.
Photographs should include: identification of subjects. **Payment:** not offered. Photographic
rights: include credit line; photos will be returned.

Additional Information. We concentrate on Great Plains and Southwestern history. Articles
are 30 pages maximum, including illustrations and notes. Each issue is approximately 46
pages. Tips: We look for solidly researched and interestingly written manuscripts. Writer's
guidelines: upon request. Sample copy: upon request.

FRONTIERS: A JOURNAL OF WOMEN STUDIES. Mesa Vista Hall,
Room 2142. University of New Mexico. Albuquerque, NM 87131. (505) 277-1198.
Fax: (505) 277-0267. Submissions Editor: Louise Lamphere. Type: academic journal
targeting a nonspecific ethnic audience. Frequency of publication: 3 times per year.
Circulation: 1200. Number of manuscripts accepted per year: 40. Payment in copies.

Editorial Needs. Fiction forms—book excerpts; novellas; short stories; translations. For all
forms: subjects include all ethnic groups, adult fables, adventure, avant-garde, disabled,
genres, humor, folklore, women's issues; 15-20 pages.

Nonfiction forms—essays; book/entertainment reviews; academic articles. For all forms:
subjects include all ethnic groups, art, child care/development, culture, education, family
issues, film/television/video, folklore, gay/lesbian issues, biography, history, humanities,
minority issues, philosophy, photography, scholarly works, sociology, religion (Taoism),
social/political commentary, women's issues.

Initial Contact. Entire manuscript. Include 2 copies with your name on the title page only.
SASE required.

Acceptance Policies. Byline given: yes. Publishing rights: we hold first rights for
academic works; author retains rights on literary works. Payment made: in copies. Response
time to initial inquiry: 2-3 months. Average time until publication: 3-6 months. Simultaneous
submissions: yes. Disk submissions: WordPerfect, ASCII, or any other major DOS program.

Photography Submissions. Format and film: any size black-and-white or color prints;
transparencies. Photographs should include: captions; model releases; identification of
subjects. **Payment:** not offered. Photographic rights: none.

Additional Information. *Frontiers* is a bridge between the academic and feminist
communities emphasizing race, ethnicity, and class issues. Writer's guidelines: upon request.
Sample copy: send $8 to University Press of Colorado, PO Box 839, Niwot, CO 80544.

GWIAZDA POLARNA. 2619 Post Rd. Stevens Point, WI 54481. (715) 345-0744. Fax: (715) 345-1913. Submissions Editor: Malgorzata Terentiew. Type: Polish-language newspaper targeting the Polish audience. Frequency of publication: weekly. Circulation: 15,000. Number of manuscripts accepted per year: varies. Payment not offered.

Editorial Needs. Fiction forms—book excerpts; novellas; short stories; translations; children's/young adult. For all forms: subjects should be general and mainstream with a Slavic focus.

Nonfiction forms—book excerpts; columns; essays; features; fillers; food/recipes; interview/profiles; photo features; book/entertainment reviews. For all forms: subjects include Slavic ethnic groups, astrology, cooking/foods/nutrition, culture, entertainment, family issues, fashion, general interest, humanities, immigration, magic, minority issues, mythology, psychic, recreation, religion, self-help, social/political commentary.

Initial Contact. Entire manuscript. SASE required.

Acceptance Policies. Byline given: yes. Publishing rights: n/i. Payment made: none. Response time to initial inquiry: 6 weeks. Average time until publication: 6 weeks. Submit seasonal material 2 months in advance. Simultaneous submissions: yes. Disk submissions: no.

Photography Submissions. Format and film: prints. Photographs should include: captions. **Payment**: none. Photographic rights: none.

Additional Information. We are the oldest Polish-language paper in the United States. We do have an English section. Tips: Bear with us. Writer's guidelines: not available. Sample copy: call editorial office at (715) 345-0744.

GYPSY LITERARY MAGAZINE. 10708 Gay Brewer. El Paso, TX 79935. (915) 592-3701. Submissions Editors: Belinda Subraman, S. Ramnath. Type: magazine targeting a nonspecific ethnic audience. Frequency of publication: 2 times per year. Circulation: 2000. Number of manuscripts accepted per year: 80. Payment in copies.

Editorial Needs. Fiction forms—short stories; translations. For all forms: works should be literary in tone; 500-1500 words preferred.

Nonfiction forms—essays; interview/profiles; photo features; poetry; book/entertainment reviews. For all forms: subjects include ethnic groups (all cultures), humanities, nature/environment, psycho-spiritual, social/political commentary; 500-1500 words preferred.

Initial Contact. Entire manuscript. SASE required.

Acceptance Policies. Byline given: yes. Publishing rights: one-time rights. Payment made: in copies. Response time to initial inquiry: 2-9 weeks. Average time until publication: 6-12 months. Submit seasonal material 6 months in advance. Simultaneous submissions: prefer not. Disk submissions: no.

Photography Submissions. Format and film: 5x7 or 8x10 black-and-white prints. Photographs should include: captions; model releases; identification of subjects. **Payment**: in copies. Photographic rights: one-time rights.

Additional Information. Our slant is humanitarian. We will consider good writing from any culture or walk of life. Tips: We use only very short works (500-1500 words), but exceptions can be made. Query us. Writer's guidelines: SASE. Sample copy: $5 for writers.

HAWAI'I REVIEW. 1733 Donaghho Rd. Honolulu, HI 96822. (808) 956-8548. Submissions Editor: Galatea Maman. Type: literary journal targeting a nonspecific ethnic audience. Frequency of publication: 3 times per year. Circulation: 2000. Number of manuscripts accepted per year: 500. Payment and copies offered.

Editorial Needs. Fiction forms—book excerpts; novellas; plays; short stories; translations. For all forms: subjects include adult fables, adventure, contemporary, ethnic groups, genres, surrealism, women's issues; 7000 words maximum; $5 per page.

Nonfiction forms—book excerpts; columns; essays; features; fillers; interview/profiles; poetry; book/entertainment reviews. For all forms: any subject, universal topics best; 7000 words maximum; $5 per page.

Initial Contact. Entire manuscript. Include short bio. SASE required.

Acceptance Policies. Byline given: yes. Publishing rights: one-time rights. Payment made: upon publication. Kill fee: no. Expenses: no. Response time to initial inquiry: 1-4 months. Average time until publication: 4-5 months. Simultaneous submissions: no. Disk submissions: no.

Photography Submissions. Format and film: black-and-white contact sheets. Photographs should include: captions; model releases; identification of subjects. **Payment:** $25-$75. Photographic rights: one-time rights.

Additional Information. Tips: Make sure you have a great ending. It makes or breaks so many stories. Writer's guidelines: SASE. Sample copy: $4.

HAYDEN'S FERRY REVIEW. Matthews Center. Arizona State University. Tempe, AZ 85287-1502. (602) 965-1243. Fax: (602) 965-8484. Submissions Editor: address to Editor. Type: magazine targeting a nonspecific ethnic audience. Frequency of publication: 2 times per year. Circulation: 2000. Number of manuscripts accepted per year: 60. Payment offered.

Editorial Needs. Fiction forms—short stories (general subject matter; $25).

Nonfiction forms—essays (general interest; 450 words; $15); poetry ($15).

Initial Contact. Entire manuscript. Include brief bio. SASE required.

Acceptance Policies. Byline given: n/i. Publishing rights: first North American serial rights. Payment made: upon publication. Kill fee: no. Expenses: no. Response time to initial inquiry: 8-10 weeks. Average time until publication: 4 months. Submit seasonal material 4 months in advance. Simultaneous submissions: no. Disk submissions: Microsoft Word.

Photography Submissions. Format and film: any size black-and-white or color prints. Photographs should include: n/i. **Payment:** $15. Photographic rights: n/i.

Additional Information. We are a literary and art magazine. Writer's guidelines: SASE. Sample copy: $6.

HERITAGE FLORIDA JEWISH NEWS. PO Box 300742. Fern Park, FL 32730. (407) 834-8787. Fax: (407) 831-0507. Submissions Editor: Edith Schulman. Type: newspaper targeting the Jewish audience. Frequency of publication: weekly. Circulation: 5000. Number of manuscripts accepted per year: 50. Payment offered.

Editorial Needs. Nonfiction forms—essays; features; fillers; food/recipes; interview/profiles; photo features. For all forms: subjects include ethnic groups (Arabs, Jews), archaeology, cooking/foods/nutrition, family issues, medicine, politics/world affairs, religion, social/political commentary, travel; 1500 words maximum except for essays on social/political commentary, 3000 words; $.50 per inch.

Initial Contact. Entire manuscript. SASE required.

Acceptance Policies. Byline given: yes. Publishing rights: first rights; simultaneous rights. Payment made: following publication. Kill fee: no. Expenses: no. Response time to initial inquiry: n/i. Average time until publication: n/i. Submit seasonal material 3 months in advance. Simultaneous submissions: yes, in non-competing publications. Disk submissions: yes; send hard copy also.

Photography Submissions. Format and film: 3x5 or 5x7 black-and-white prints; contact sheets. Photographs should include: captions; identification of subjects. **Payment:** $5 per picture used. Photographic rights: n/i.

Additional Information. Tips: We are looking for material for our nine special issues. Writer's guidelines: call or write. Sample copy: $1.

HINDUISM TODAY. 1819 Second St. Concord, CA 94519. (510) 823-0237. Fax: (510) 827-0137. Submissions Editor: Arumugaswami. Type: tabloid newspaper targeting the Indians from India. Frequency of publication: monthly. Circulation: 30,000. Number of manuscripts accepted per year: 25. Payment offered.

Editorial Needs. Nonfiction forms—features; interview/profiles; photo features; children's/young adult. For all forms: subjects include ethnic groups (Indians from India, East-Asian cultures), astrology, child care/development, comedy/humor, education, religion (Hinduism), nature/environment, yoga.

Initial Contact. Article proposal with subject outline. Include previous published works.

Acceptance Policies. Byline given: yes. Publishing rights: yes. Payment made: upon publication. Kill fee: $25. Expenses: if arranged in advance. Response time to initial inquiry: 2 months. Average time until publication: 1-3 months. Simultaneous submissions: yes. Disk submissions: Macintosh 3 1/2 disk; MS DOS.

Photography Submissions. Format and film: prints. Photographs should include: identification of subjects. **Payment:** $10. Photographic rights: all rights.

Additional Information. We are a Hindu religious publication catering to the Indians from India. Tips: Get our guidelines; read a few issues. Writer's guidelines: upon request. Sample copy: upon request.

IL CAFFÈ. 840 Post, #626. San Francisco, CA 94109. (415) 928-4886. Fax: (415) 928-4886. Submissions Editor: R. T. Loverso. Type: magazine targeting the Italian-American audience. Frequency of publication: every other month. Circulation: 20,000. Number of manuscripts accepted per year: 12. Payment in copies.

Editorial Needs. Fiction forms—short stories (adult fables, adventure, avant-garde, contemporary, folklore, genre, holiday, humor, literary, sports, surrealism, women's issues, all with an Italian, Italian-American focus).

Nonfiction forms—columns (1500 words); essays (3000 words); features (1500 words); fillers (200 words); food/recipes (1000 words); interview/profiles (1500 words); photo features (half page); poetry (half page); book/entertainment reviews (800 words). For all forms: subjects include archaeology, architecture, art, astrology, business/economics, comics, computers, cooking, culture, dance, disabled, education, family issues, fashion, general interest, biography, history, humanities, law, metaphysics, music, minority issues, nature/environment, philosophy, religion, social/political commentary, all with an Italian-American focus.

Initial Contact. Entire Manuscript. SASE required.

Acceptance Policies. Byline given: yes. Publishing rights: first rights; second serial rights; one-time rights. Payment made: in copies. Response time to initial inquiry: 3 months. Average time until publication: 1-3 months. Submit seasonal material 2 months in advance. Simultaneous submissions: yes. Disk submissions: no.

Photography Submissions. Format and film: any size black-and-white or color prints; negatives; transparencies. Photographs should include: captions. **Payment:** not offered. Photographic rights: none.

Additional Information. Our publication deals with politics, economy, short stories, interviews, sports, and cooking, all related to Italians and the Italian-American culture. Writer's guidelines: upon request. Sample copy: upon request.

INDIA CURRENTS. PO Box 21285. San Jose, CA 95151. (408) 274-6966. Fax: (408) 274-2733. Submissions Editor: Arvind Kumar. Type: magazine targeting a nonspecific ethnic audience. Frequency of publication: monthly. Circulation: 25,000. Number of manuscripts accepted per year: 50. Payment offered.

Editorial Needs. Fiction forms—book excerpts (1000-1500 words, $20); short stories (1000-1500 words, $25); translations (1000-1500 words, $25).

Nonfiction forms—book excerpts (400-800 words); columns; essays (800 words); features (1000-2000 words); food/recipes (800 words); interview/profile (1000 words); photo features; book/entertainment reviews (300-400 words). For all forms: subjects include ethnic groups (Indians from India, East-Asian cultures), adventure, art, business/economics, comedy/humor, festivals, folklore, immigration, minority issues, music, philosophy, politics/world affairs, psycho-spirituality, recreation, religion (Buddhism, Hinduism, Islam), social/political commentary, and yoga, all of which must be related to India or Indian culture in the United States; payment averages $25.

Initial Contact. Entire manuscript. Indicate whether photographs are available. SASE required.

Acceptance Policies. Byline given: yes. Publishing rights: one-time rights. Payment made: upon publication. Kill fee: no. Expenses: no. Response time to initial inquiry: 6-8 weeks. Average time until publication: 6 months. Submit seasonal material 6 months in advance. Simultaneous submissions: yes. Disk submissions: PC compatible; Microsoft Word, Word Star, WordPerfect.

Photography Submissions. Format and film: 3x5 prints. Photographs should include: captions; identification of subjects. **Payment:** $10. Photographic rights: one-time rights.

Additional Information. *India Current's* readers are Indophiles of all different races and backgrounds. We are looking for new insights into Indian culture. Our articles do not presume prior knowledge on the part of the readers. Writer's guidelines: SASE. Sample copy: $2.

INDIAN LIFE MAGAZINE. PO Box 3765, Station B. Winnipeg, Manitoba, Canada R2W 3R6. (204) 661-9333. Fax: (204) 661-3982. Submissions Editor: Jim Uttley. Type: magazine targeting the Native American audience. Frequency of publication: every other month. Circulation: 65,000. Number of manuscripts accepted per year: 5. Payment offered.

Editorial Needs. Fiction forms—short stories (historical fiction, $.04 per word); legends (250-500 words, $.04 per word).

Nonfiction forms—book excerpts (social issues, 1000-1500 words, $.04 per word); fillers (legends, sayings, 200 words, $10); recipes (Indian, $10); interview/profiles (Native Americans, $.04 per word); photo features (500-800 words, $.04 per word, $10 per photo). For all forms: subjects include Native American handicrafts and Christian religion as it relates to the Indians.

Initial Contact. Query letter only. SASE required with IRC or Canadian postage.

Acceptance Policies. Byline given: yes. Publishing rights: first North American serial rights; all rights. Payment made: upon publication. Kill fee: no. Expenses: no. Response time to initial inquiry: 4 weeks. Average time until publication: 4 months. Submit seasonal material 6 months in advance. Simultaneous submissions: no. Disk submissions: no.

Photography Submissions. Format and film: 5x7 or 8x10 black-and-white or color prints. Photographs should include: captions; identification of subjects. **Payment:** $10 (black and white); $15 (color). Photographic rights: first rights.

Additional Information. *Indian Life Magazine* is a nondenominational Christian magazine designed to help the North American Indian church speak to the social, cultural, and spiritual needs of her own people. Tips: Keep it simple, but not childish. We aim at about an eighth grade reading level. Many of readers have not made it through high school. Writer's guidelines: upon request.

INDIAN LITERATURE. Sahitya Akademi. National Academy of Letters. India Rabindara Bhavan. 35 Ferozeshah Rd. New Delhi, India 110 001. 386-626.

Submissions Editor: Dr. D. S. Rao. Type: newspaper, newsletter, and academic journal targeting Indians. Frequency of publication: daily to quarterly depending on type of publication. Circulation: 4100. Number of manuscripts accepted per year: varies. Payment in copies.

Editorial Needs. Fiction forms—book excerpts (2000 words); play (1500 words); short stories (2000 words); translations (2000 words). For all forms: all works must be literary in style and relate to India's culture and peoples

Nonfiction forms—essays (literary criticism, 2000 words); interview/profiles (2000 words); poetry (literary, 1000 words); book/entertainment reviews (literary, 1500 words). For all forms: all works must relate to India's culture and peoples.

Initial Contact. Article proposal with subject outline or entire manuscript. SASE not required.

Acceptance Policies. Byline given: yes. Publishing rights: first North American serial rights; second serial rights; all rights; simultaneous rights; work-for-hire. Payment made: in copies. Response time to initial inquiry: 1 week. Average time until publication: 1 year. Simultaneous submissions: yes. Disk submissions: yes.

Photography Submissions. Format and film: any size and any format in black and white or color. Photographs should include: captions; model releases; identification of subjects. **Payment:** not offered. Photographic rights: one-time rights.

Additional Information. *Indian Literature* is a literary journal devoted to literature in the 22 languages of India. Tips: Only typewritten submissions, please. Sample copy: by subscription.

INDIA-WEST. 5901 Christie Ave., #301. Emeryville, CA 94608. (510) 652-0265.

Fax: (510) 652-7968. Submissions Editor: Bina Muraska. Type: newspaper targeting the Indians from India. Frequency of publication: weekly. Circulation: n/i. Number of manuscripts accepted per year: varies. Payment not offered.

Editorial Needs. Nonfiction forms—book excerpts; features; interview/profiles. For all forms: general subject matter which is related to India; 500-1000 words.

Initial Contact. Article proposal with subject outline. SASE required.

Acceptance Policies. Byline given: yes. Publishing rights: n/i. Payment made: none. Response time to initial inquiry: n/i. Average time until publication: n/i. Simultaneous submissions: n/i. Disk submissions: n/i.

INTERNATIONAL FICTION REVIEW, THE. Dr. S. Elkhadem. Department of German. University of New Brunswick. Frederickton, New Brunswick, Canada E3B 5A3. (506) 453-4636. Submissions Editor: Dr. Saad Elkhadem. Type: academic journal targeting a nonspecific ethnic audience. Frequency of publication: 2 times per year. Circulation: 500. Number of manuscripts accepted per year: 30. Payment not offered.

Editorial Needs. Nonfiction forms—essays (world fiction, 1500-4500 words); book reviews (fictional works, 500-750 words).

Initial Contact. Query letter only. SASE required.

Acceptance Policies. Byline given: yes. Publishing rights: first rights. Payment made: none. Response time to initial inquiry: 2 weeks. Average time until publication: 6 months. Simultaneous submissions: no.

Additional Information. We do not publish fiction, only works on fiction. Tips: Adhere to our style manual. Writer's guidelines: $2.50. Sample copy: $4 for back issues.

INTERNATIONAL MIGRATION REVIEW. Center for Migration Studies. 209 Flagg Pl. Staten Island, NY 10304. (718) 351-8800. Fax: (718) 667-4598. Submissions Editor: S. M. Tomasi, Ph.D. Type: academic journal targeting a nonspecific ethnic audience. Frequency of publication: quarterly. Circulation: 2300. Number of manuscripts accepted per year: 50. Payment not offered.

Editorial Needs. Nonfiction forms—essays (6500 words); book/entertainment reviews; original articles; conference reports; listings of new books.

Initial Contact. Entire manuscript. SASE not required.

Acceptance Policies. Byline given: yes. Publishing rights: all. Payment made: none. Response time to initial inquiry: 3 months. Average time until publication: 3-6 months. Simultaneous submissions: no. Disk submissions: WordPerfect 4.2, 5.0, 5.1.

Additional Information. Guidelines published on inside of back cover of every *IMR* issue. Tips: Submit original articles on the cutting edge of immigration and refugee studies. Writer's guidelines: in every issue. Sample copy: upon request.

INTIMACY/BLACK ROMANCE. (Also publishes *Intimacy/Bronze Thrills, Jive/Black Confessions, Secrets*). 355 Lexington Ave. New York, NY 10017. (212) 973-3222. Fax: (212) 986-5926. Submissions Editor: D. Boyd. Type: magazine targeting the Afro-American audience. Frequency of publication: every other month. Circulation: n/i. Number of manuscripts accepted per year: 350. Payment offered.

Editorial Needs. Fiction forms—short stories (romance, 5100-6000 words, $75-$100).

Nonfiction forms—features (relationship tips, beauty, health, and fashion articles, $100).

Initial Contact. Entire manuscript. SASE required.

Acceptance Policies. Byline given: yes. Publishing rights: simultaneous rights. Payment made: upon publication. Kill fee: no. Expenses: no. Response time to initial inquiry: 3-6 months. Average time until publication: 3-6 months. Simultaneous submissions: no. Disk submissions: no.

Photography Submissions. Format and film: n/i. Photographs should include: model releases; identification of subjects. **Payment:** negotiable. Photographic rights: all rights.

Additional Information. We publish true-to-life confessions with uplifting themes. The information about this publication also applies to our other magazines. Tips: Study magazine and request guidelines. Writer's guidelines: SASE. Sample copy: SASE.

Intimacy/Bronze Thrills see **INTIMACY/BLACK ROMANCE.**

JAPANOPHILE. PO Box 223. Okemos, MI 48864. (517) 349-1795. Submissions Editors: Vada Davis (column, *Japan in America*); Earl Snodgrass (poetry, short stories). Type: newspaper targeting those interested in Japanese culture. Frequency of publication: quarterly. Circulation: n/i. Number of manuscripts accepted per year: 20. Payment offered.

Editorial Needs. Fiction forms—short stories (1000-4000 words, $20).

Nonfiction forms—columns; essays; fillers; food/recipes; interview/profiles; photo features; poetry (translations); book/entertainment reviews. For all forms: subjects include material about Japan, Japanese-American culture.

Initial Contact. Article proposal with subject outline or entire manuscript. Include bio. SASE required.

Acceptance Policies. Byline given: yes. Publishing rights: one-time rights. Payment made: in copies. Response time to initial inquiry: 2 months. Average time until publication: immediate. Submit seasonal material 3 months in advance. Simultaneous submissions: yes. Disk submissions: no.

Photography Submissions. Format and film: 5x7 black-and-white prints. Photographs should include: n/i. **Payment:** n/i. Photographic rights: one-time use.

Additional Information. We need articles about Americans or other non-Japanese who are interested in Japan and its culture. Tips: Read two or three issues. Writer's guidelines: SASE. Sample copy: $4.

JEWISH REVIEW, THE. 6800 SW Beaverton-Hillsdale Hwy, Ste. C. Portland, OR 97225. (503) 292-4913. Fax: (503) 292-8965. Submissions Editor: Mara Woloshin. Type: newspaper targeting the Jewish audience. Frequency of publication: 2 times per month. Circulation: 6100. Number of manuscripts accepted per year: varies. Payment offered.

Editorial Needs. Fiction forms—serialized fiction; translations. For all forms: subjects include Jewish ethnic material for children/young adults, historical fiction, holiday stories, humor; $35-$100.

Nonfiction forms—columns; features (600-2000 words); fillers; food/recipes (600-2000 words); interview/profiles; photo features (150-500 words); book/entertainment reviews (1000-1500 words). For all forms: subjects related to Jewish issues include anthropology, archaeology, art, business/economics, comedy/humor, cooking, culture, education, family issues, festivals, film/television, video, folklore, gay/lesbian issues, government/politics, health/fitness, biography, history, human potential, immigration, Israel, Judaica, medicine, minority issues, politics/world affairs, religion, and science.

Initial Contact. Article proposal with subject outline. SASE required.

Acceptance Policies. Byline given: yes. Publishing rights: one-time rights. Payment made: upon publication. Kill fee: no. Expenses: no. Response time to initial inquiry: 3-5 weeks.

Average time until publication: 2+ weeks. Submit seasonal material 2-3 months in advance. Simultaneous submissions: yes. Disk submissions: no.

Photography Submissions. Format and film: 5x7 or 8x10 black-and-white prints. Photographs should include: captions; model releases; identification of subjects. **Payment:** $15-$85. Photographic rights: varies.

Additional Information. We print materials exclusively related to Jewish issues. Sample copy: upon request.

Jive/Black Confessions see **INTIMACY/BLACK ROMANCE.**

JOURNAL, THE. English Department. Ohio State University. 164 W. 17th Ave. Columbus, OH 43210. (614) 292-4076. Submissions Editors: Michelle Herman (fiction, nonfiction); Kathy Fagan (poetry, poetry book reviews). Type: literary magazine targeting a nonspecific ethnic audience. Frequency of publication: 2 times per year. Circulation: 1200. Number of manuscripts accepted per year: 80. Payment offered.

Editorial Needs. Fiction forms—book excerpts ($25); short stories ($25).

Nonfiction forms—book excerpts (literary); interview/profiles (poets and writers, 1000-1500 words); poetry; book reviews (poetry, 1000-1500 words, $25).

Initial Contact. Entire manuscript. Include cover letter. SASE required.

Acceptance Policies. Byline given: yes. Publishing rights: n/i. Payment made: upon publication. Kill fee: no. Expenses: no. Response time to initial inquiry: 2-3 months. Average time until publication: 2-3 months. Simultaneous submissions: no. Disk submissions: no.

Additional Information. Sample copy: upon request.

JOURNAL OF AMERICAN INDIAN EDUCATION. Arizona State University. Center for Indian Education. 415 Farmer Bldg. Tempe, AZ 85287-1311. (602) 965-6292. Submissions Editor: Dr. Karen Swisher. Type: academic journal targeting a nonspecific ethnic audience. Frequency of publication: 3 times per year. Circulation: 650. Number of manuscripts accepted per year: 12. Payment in copies.

Editorial Needs. Nonfiction forms—research manuscripts. For all forms: subjects include education and tribal issues concerning Native Americans; word length varies.

Initial Contact. Article proposal with subject outline. Include tribal affiliation. SASE required.

Acceptance Policies. Byline given: yes. Publishing rights: all rights. Payment made: in copies. Response time to initial inquiry: 1 week. Average time until publication: 2-3 months. Simultaneous submissions: no. Disk submissions: APA.

Additional Information. We solicit basic and applied research manuscripts related to American Indian/Alaskan Native education. Our circulation is international. Writer's guidelines: write or call. Sample copy: purchase through us.

JOURNAL OF THE AFRO-AMERICAN HISTORICAL AND GENEALOGICAL SOCIETY. PO Box 73068. Washington, DC 20056. Submissions Editors: Sandra Lawson (journal); Norman Peters (newsletter). Type: newsletter and academic journal targeting the Afro-American and Native American audience. Frequency of publication: quarterly. Circulation: n/i. Number of manuscripts accepted per year: 20. Payment in copies.

Editorial Needs. Nonfiction forms—book excerpts; columns; features; fillers; book/entertainment reviews. For all forms: subjects include Afro-American and Native American education, folklore, genealogy, biography, and history.

Initial Contact. Query letter only or article proposal with subject outline or entire manuscript. SASE required.

Acceptance Policies. Byline given: yes. Publishing rights: n/i. Payment made: in copies. Response time to initial inquiry: 6 months. Average time until publication: 1-2 years. Simultaneous submissions: no. Disk submissions: IBM compatible.

Photography Submissions. Format and film: black-and-white prints. Photographs should include: captions. **Payment:** not offered. Photographic rights: none.

Additional Information. Tips. Document all references.

LA GENTE DE AZTLAN. 112 D Kerckhoff Hall. 308 Westwood Plaza. Los Angeles, CA 90024. (213) 825-9836. Fax: (213) 206-0906. Submissions Editor: Gloria D. Hernandez. Type: news magazine targeting the Latino audience. Frequency of publication: 6 times per year. Circulation: 10,000. Number of manuscripts accepted per year: varies. Payment not offered.

Editorial Needs. Fiction forms—short stories (500 words).

Nonfiction forms—columns; interview/profiles; photo features; poetry; book/entertainment reviews.

Initial Contact. Entire manuscript. Include short biography and phone number. SASE required.

Acceptance Policies. Byline given: yes. Publishing rights: n/i. Payment made: none. Response time to initial inquiry: 2 weeks. Average time until publication: 3 weeks. Submit seasonal material 1 month in advance. Simultaneous submissions: yes. Disk submissions: Macintosh.

Photography Submissions. Format and film: contact sheets. Photographs should include: captions. **Payment:** not offered. Photographic rights: none.

Additional Information. We are a progressive news magazine. Tips: Contact the editor and get editor's approval before submission. Writer's guidelines: contact editor.

LANGUAGE BRIDGES QUARTERLY. PO Box 850792. Richardson, TX 75085. (214) 530-2782. Submissions Editors: Eva Ziem (managing editor); Zofia Przebindowska-Tousty (fiction editor); Ewa Gierat, Roxanne Conner-Sveiven, Joseph Lisowski, Anna Milo (associate editors). Type: bilingual magazine targeting the Polish and Polish-American audience. Frequency of publication: quarterly. Circulation: 250. Number of manuscripts accepted per year: 100. Payment in copies.

Editorial Needs. Fiction forms—book excerpts; novellas; plays; serialized fiction; short stories; translations. For all forms: subjects include general and historical fiction, humor, literary, science fiction, and short stories; any word length.

Nonfiction forms—book excerpts; columns; essays; features; fillers; interview/profiles; poetry; book/entertainment reviews. For all forms: any subject matter.

Initial Contact. Article proposal with subject outline or entire manuscript. SASE not required.

Acceptance Policies. Byline given: yes. Publishing rights: one-time rights. Payment made: in copies. Expenses: sometimes. Response time to initial inquiry: 2-3 weeks. Average time until publication: 3-6 months. Simultaneous submissions: yes. Disk submissions: 5 1/4; ASCII.

Photography Submissions. Format and film: 8 1/2 x 11 or smaller. Photographs should include: n/i. **Payment:** n/i. Photographic rights: n/i.

Additional Information. *LBQ* is the only fully bilingual Polish-English publication in the United States. All texts are printed in both languages. Tips: *LBQ* is trying to fulfill the increasing demand for cross-cultural dialogue in seeking common roots and discovering differences. Writer's guidelines: upon request. Sample copy: upon request.

LA OFERTA REVIEW. 2103 Alum Rock Ave. San Jose, CA 95116. (408) 729-6397. Fax: (408) 729-3278. Submissions Editor: n/i. Type: bilingual newspaper targeting the Hispanic audience. Frequency of publication: 2 times per week. Circulation: 10,000 per issue. Number of manuscripts accepted per year: n/i. Payment not offered.

Editorial Needs. Nonfiction forms—columns; fillers; photo features.

Initial Contact. Article proposal with subject outline. SASE required.

Acceptance Policies. Byline given: yes. Publishing rights: one-time rights. Payment made: none. Response time to initial inquiry: n/i. Average time until publication: n/i. Submit seasonal material 2 months in advance. Simultaneous submissions: no. Disk submissions: no

Photography Submissions. Format and film: contact sheets. Photographs should include: captions; model releases; identification of subjects. **Payment:** none. Photographic rights: none.

Additional Information. Sample copy: upon request.

LEFT CURVE. PO Box 472. Oakland, CA 94604. (510) 763-7193. Submissions Editors: Csaba Polony (general); Jack Hirschman (poetry); Luis Talamantez (Latinos and political prisoners). Type: magazine targeting a nonspecific ethnic audience. Frequency of publication: irregularly. Circulation: 1200. Number of manuscripts accepted per year: 3-4. Payment in copies.

Editorial Needs. Fiction forms—short stories; translations. For all forms: subjects include avant-garde, contemporary/modern, ethnic, historical fiction, literary, women's issues; 1500-2500 words; 3 copies.

Nonfiction forms—essays; interview/profiles; photo features; poetry; book/entertainment reviews. For all forms: subjects include all ethnic groups, architecture, art, culture, film/television/video, government/politics, humanities, immigration, minority issues, music, nature/environment, philosophy, photography, social/political commentary; 3000 words maximum; 5 copies.

Initial Contact. Query letter only or article proposal with subject outline. SASE required.

Acceptance Policies. Byline given: yes. Publishing rights: revert back to author. Payment made: in copies. Response time to initial inquiry: 3-6 months. Average time until publication: 3-6 months. Simultaneous submissions: no. Disk submissions: Macintosh.

Photography Submissions. Format and film: 8x10 maximum black-and-white prints. Photographs should include: captions; identification of subjects. **Payment:** in copies. Photographic rights: none.

Additional Information. Tips: Read a copy of *Left Curve* to get an idea of what we are about. Sample copy: $5.

LILITH. 250 W. 57th St., #2432. New York, NY 10107. (212) 757-0818. Submissions Editors: Susan Schnur (nonfiction); Julia Wolf Mazow (fiction); Alicia Ostriker (poetry). Type: magazine targeting the female Jewish audience. Frequency of publication: quarterly. Circulation: 9500. Number of manuscripts accepted per year: n/i. Payment offered.

Editorial Needs. Fiction forms—book excerpts; short stories; translations. For all forms: subjects include folklore, holiday stories, humor, all with a Jewish woman's focus.

Nonfiction forms—book excerpts; essays; features; food/recipes; interview/profiles; poetry; book/entertainment reviews; reference. For all forms: subjects include cooking, family issues, film/television/video, folklore, biography, history, holistic practices, immigration, Israel, Judaica, nature/environment, political/world affairs, relationships, religion, spirituality, social/political commentary, women's issues, all with a Jewish woman's focus.

Initial Contact. Query letter or article proposal with subject outline for nonfiction; entire manuscript for fiction. Include clips. SASE required.

Acceptance Policies. Byline given: yes. Publishing rights: one-time rights. Payment made: upon publication. Kill fee: no. Expenses: yes. Response time to initial inquiry: 1-3 weeks. Average time until publication: 3-12 months. Simultaneous submissions: yes. Disk submissions: n/i.

Additional Information. Writer's guidelines: SASE. Sample copy: $5, includes postage.

LIVING BLUES. Sam Hall. University of Mississippi. University, MS 38677. (601) 232-5518. Submissions Editor: Peter Lee. Type: magazine targeting the Afro-American audience. Frequency of publication: every other month. Circulation: 13,500. Number of manuscripts accepted per year: 40. Payment offered.

Editorial Needs. Nonfiction forms—features (blues music, $45-$75).

Initial Contact. Article proposal with subject outline. SASE required.

Acceptance Policies. Byline given: yes. Publishing rights: first rights. Payment made: upon publication. Kill fee: no. Expenses: no. Response time to initial inquiry: 1 month. Average time until publication: 2-6 months. Submit seasonal material 4-6 months in advance. Simultaneous submissions: no. Disk submissions: Macintosh compatible.

Photography Submissions. Format and film: black-and-white prints. Photographs should include: captions; identification of subjects. **Payment:** $10. Photographic rights: first rights.

Additional Information. Publication is for blues aficionados. Tips: Read the magazine first.

MACGUFFIN, THE. Schoolcraft College. 18600 Haggerty Rd. Livonia, MI 48152. (313) 462-4400, ext. 5292. Submissions Editors: Arthur Lindenberg (editor); Elizabeth Hebron (fiction). Type: magazine targeting a nonspecific ethnic audience. Frequency of publication: 3 times per year (April, June, November). Circulation: 500. Number of manuscripts accepted per year: 90. Payment in copies.

Editorial Needs. Fiction forms—short stories (contemporary/modern, general interest, literary, experimental, 4000 words maximum).

Nonfiction forms—essays; poetry (no Haiku, light verse, or concrete poetry, 400 lines maximum).

Initial Contact. Entire manuscript. Include short bio. SASE required.

Acceptance Policies. Byline given: yes. Publishing rights: first North American serial rights. Payment made: 2 copies. Response time to initial inquiry: 6-8 weeks. Average time until publication: 6-18 months. Simultaneous submissions: no. Disk submissions: no.

Photography Submissions. Format and film: any size black-and-white prints. Photographs should include: n/i. **Payment:** 2 copies. Photographic rights: first rights. We also accept black-and-white illustrations.

Additional Information. We publish the best short fiction, poetry, and essays we can find. Tips: Proofread for typos before sending. Writer's guidelines: upon request. Sample copy: $3.

MANOA: A PACIFIC JOURNAL OF INTERNATIONAL WRITING.

University of Hawaii. 1733 Donaghho Rd. Honolulu, HI 96822. (808) 956-3070. Fax: (808) 956-3083. Submissions Editors: Robert Shapard (fiction); Frank Stewart (poetry); Alan MacGregor (reviews). Type: literary magazine targeting a nonspecific ethnic audience. Frequency of publication: 2 times per year. Circulation: n/i. Number of manuscripts accepted per year: n/i. Payment in copies.

Editorial Needs. **Fiction forms**—book excerpts; novellas; plays; serialized fiction; short stories; translations. For all forms: interested in all subjects except genre or formalist writing, Pacific exotica, or picturesque impressions of the region; length open.

Nonfiction forms—book excerpts; essays (articles of current literary or cultural interest); features; interview/profiles; photo features; poetry (5-6 entries); book/entertainment reviews (arts or humanities related to Asia or the Pacific in some way).

Initial Contact. Entire manuscript. SASE required.

Acceptance Policies. Byline given: yes. Publishing rights: first rights. Payment made: in copies. Response time to initial inquiry: 8 weeks. Average time until publication: 6 months. Simultaneous submissions: no. Disk submissions: yes.

Photography Submissions. Accepts photography and other art work. Format and film: n/i. Photographs should include: n/i. **Payment:** n/i. Photographic rights: n/i.

Additional Information. We are a high-quality literary magazine. Our focus is not ethnic but international. We focus on one Pacific Rim country per issue, as well as publishing American writing regardless of author's ethnicity or subject matter. Tips: Look at a copy first. Writer's guidelines: upon request.

MARYLAND REVIEW. Department of English and Languages. University of Maryland, Eastern Shore. Princess Anee, MD 21853. (301) 651-2200. Fax: (301) 651-3685. Submissions Editor: Chester M. Hedgepeth, Jr. Type: academic journal targeting the Afro-American audience. Frequency of publication: annually. Circulation: 500. Number of manuscripts accepted per year: 15. Payment in copies.

Editorial Needs. **Fiction forms**—short stories (literary, mainstream, no genre, 5000-10,000 words).

Nonfiction forms—poetry (any subject).

Initial Contact. Entire manuscript. Include bio. SASE required.

Acceptance Policies. Byline given: yes. Publishing rights: n/i. Payment made: 2 copies. Response time to initial inquiry: 6-8 months. Average time until publication: 10-12 months. Simultaneous submissions: no. Disk submissions: no.

Additional Information. We are looking for entertaining stories with original themes and believable characters. We have a special interest in black literature, but we welcome all kinds. Tips: We read manuscripts from September through April. New issue published in the fall. Writer's guidelines: upon request. Sample copy: $6.

MENNONITE PUBLISHING HOUSE. 616 Walnut Ave. Scottdale, PA
15683-1999. (412) 887-8500. Submissions Editor: we publish several periodicals,
each with its own editor (order *When You Write* guidelines). Type: several
publications targeting all ethnic groups involved with the Mennonite religion.
Frequency of publication: varies with publication. Circulation: varies with publication.
Number of manuscripts accepted per year: varies with publication. Payment offered.

Editorial Needs. Fiction forms—see *When You Write* guidelines (includes children's, short
stories). For all forms: $.05 per word maximum.

Nonfiction forms—see *When You Write* guidelines. Includes essays, meditations, poetry ($1
per line maximum), Christian doctrine, life and scriptural exposition.

Initial Contact. Entire manuscript. SASE required.

Acceptance Policies. Byline given: yes. Publishing rights: one-time rights. Payment made:
upon acceptance. Kill fee: no. Expenses: no. Response time to initial inquiry: 8 weeks.
Average time until publication: 9 months. Submit seasonal material 6 months in advance.
Simultaneous submissions: yes. Disk submissions: no.

Photography Submissions. Format and film: black-and-white prints. Photographs should
include: captions; identification of subjects. **Payment:** up to $50. Photographic rights: one-
time rights.

Additional Information. Our audience is the Mennonite Church. Writers need to develop
their works accordingly. Tips: See *When You Write*. Writer's guidelines: upon request. Sample
copy: upon request.

MIDDLE EASTERN DANCER. PO Box 181572. Casselberry, FL 32718-
1572. (407) 831-3402. Fax: (407) 290-6528. Submissions Editor: Jeanette Spencer.
Type: magazine targeting a specific ethnic audience interested in Middle Eastern
culture. Frequency of publication: monthly. Circulation: 2500+. Number of
manuscripts accepted per year: 100. Payment or copies offered.

Editorial Needs. Fiction forms—plays (short); serialized fiction; short stories. For all
forms: subjects include adult fables, adventure, ethnic groups, folklore, general interest, genre,
holiday stories, humor, new age, women's issues; $20 assigned, $10 unsolicited.

Nonfiction forms—columns; essays; features; fillers; food/recipes; interview/profiles; photo
features; poetry ($5); book/entertainment reviews. For all forms: subjects include adventure,
ethnic groups (Arab culture, Greek culture), archaeology, architecture, art,
business/economics, cooking, culture, dance, entertainment, family issues, festivals, folklore,
handicrafts, biography, history, law, music, psycho-spirituality, travel, social/political
commentary, women's issues.

Initial Contact. Query letter only or article proposal with subject outline or entire
manuscript. Include background and credentials. SASE required.

Acceptance Policies. Byline given: yes. Publishing rights: one-time rights. Payment made:
upon acceptance. Kill fee: no. Expenses: no. Response time to initial inquiry: 3-4 weeks.
Average time until publication: varies. Submit seasonal material 3-4 months in advance.
Simultaneous submissions: yes, but not within the dance community. Disk submissions:
WordPerfect 5.0 or 5.1, or MS DOS.

Photography Submissions. Format and film: black-and-white prints (preferred, but can
accept color); contact sheets. Photographs should include: captions; model releases;
identification of subjects. **Payment:** $5. Photographic rights: one-time rights.

Additional Information. We're reader-friendly, with a fairly educated, traveled group of mostly women readers, but with a good number of male readers, too. Tips: Material must relate to Middle Eastern dance and culture. Writer's guidelines: SASE. Sample copy: $1.

MIDSTREAM, A MONTHLY JEWISH REVIEW. 110 E. 59th St. New York, NY 10022. (212) 759-6208. Submissions Editors: Joel Charmichael, Melinda Solow, Estuer Raul. Type: magazine targeting the Jewish audience. Frequency of publication: monthly. Circulation: n/i. Number of manuscripts accepted per year: n/i. Payment offered.

Editorial Needs. Fiction forms—novellas; short stories; translations. For all forms: subjects should focus on Jewish ethnicity; $.05 per word.

Nonfiction forms—essays ($.05 per word); features ($.05 per word); poetry ($25); book/entertainment reviews ($.07 per word). For all forms: subjects include biography, general interest, government/politics, humanities, Israel, Judaica, mythology, philosophy, politics/world affairs, religion, scholarly works, social/political commentary, women's issues, all focused on Zionism, Judaism, and Israel.

Initial Contact. Article proposal with subject outline; entire manuscript. SASE required.

Acceptance Policies. Byline given: yes. Publishing rights: n/i. Payment made: upon publication. Kill fee: no. Expenses: no. Response time to initial inquiry: 3 weeks. Average time until publication: 1-3 months. Simultaneous submissions: no. Disk submissions: Macintosh, IBM; Microsoft Word, WordPerfect.

Additional Information. Tips: Do not call us, we will contact you. Writer's guidelines: SASE. Sample copy: SASE.

MIGRATION WORLD MAGAZINE. Center for Migration Studies. 209 Flagg Pl. Staten Island, NY 10304. (718) 351-8800. Fax: (718) 667-4598. Submissions Editor: Lydio F. Tomasi, Ph.D. Type: magazine targeting a nonspecific ethnic audience. Frequency of publication: every other month. Circulation: 2500. Number of manuscripts accepted per year: 60. Payment not offered.

Editorial Needs. Nonfiction forms—essays; profiles; photo features; book/entertainment reviews; agency perspectives; legal columns.

Initial Contact. Entire manuscript. SASE required.

Acceptance Policies. Byline given: yes. Publishing rights: all. Payment made: none. Response time to initial inquiry: 1 month. Average time until publication: 3 months. Simultaneous submissions: no. Disk submissions: WordPerfect 4.2, 5.0, 5.1.

Photography Submissions. Format and film: any size black-and-white prints. Photographs should include: identification of subjects. **Payment**: none. Photographic rights: n/i.

Additional Information. Guidelines are published on inside back cover of every *MW* issue. Tips: Submit article on the most recent immigrant and refugee groups. Writer's guidelines: in every issue. Sample copy: upon request.

MIORITA, A JOURNAL OF ROMANIAN STUDIES. FLLL, DEW 482. University of Rochester. Rochester, NY 14627. (716) 275-4251, ext. 4258. Submissions Editor: C. M. Carlton. Type: academic journal targeting the Romanian audience. Frequency of publication: irregularly. Circulation: 300. Number of manuscripts accepted per year: 6. Payment not offered.

Editorial Needs. Fiction forms—book excerpts (10 pages); short stories; translations. For all forms: subjects focus on Romanian culture.

Nonfiction forms—book excerpts (Romanian culture, language, literature, etc.); poetry; book reviews. For all forms: subjects must reflect Romanian culture in all its manifestations at home and abroad.

Initial Contact. Query letter only. SASE required.

Acceptance Policies. Byline given: yes. Publishing rights: n/i. Payment made: none. Response time to initial inquiry: varies. Average time until publication: varies. Simultaneous submissions: yes. Disk submissions: Macintosh PC.

NACHIKETA. PO Box 1142. Berkeley, CA 94701. (510) 547-3219. Submissions Editor: Ved Prakash Vatuk. Type: children's publication targeting Indians from India. Frequency of publication: every other month. Circulation: 2000. Number of manuscripts accepted per year: 50. Payment in copies.

Editorial Needs. Fiction forms—short stories and translations of Indian folktales for children.

Nonfiction forms—essays; fillers; photo features; poetry; book reviews. For all forms: subjects must target Indian children.

Initial Contact. Query letter only or article proposal with subject outline or entire manuscript. SASE required.

Acceptance Policies. Byline given: yes. Publishing rights: first North American serial rights. Payment made: in copies. Response time to initial inquiry: 1 month. Average time until publication: 2-4 months. Submit seasonal material 4 months in advance. Simultaneous submissions: yes. Disk submissions: no.

Photography Submissions. Format and film: 4x6 prints. Photographs should include: captions; identification of subjects. **Payment**: none. Photographic rights: remain with the photographer.

Additional Information. We want to educate kids with non-preachy writing. Writer's guidelines: SASE. Sample copy: $1.

NAJDA NEWSLETTER. PO Box 7152. Berkeley, CA 94707. (510) 549-3512. Submissions Editor: G. Rathbun. Type: newsletter targeting the Arab, Muslim, and Arab-American audience. Frequency of publication: quarterly. Circulation: n/i. Number of manuscripts accepted per year: varies. Payment not offered.

Editorial Needs. Fiction forms—book excerpts; short stories; translations. For all forms: subjects focus on Arabs, Muslims, Arab-Americans; 2000 words.

Nonfiction forms—book excerpts; columns; essays; features; fillers; food/recipes; interview/profiles; photo features; poetry; book/entertainment reviews. For all forms: subjects include Arab-Muslim women, Palestinian-Israeli conflict, Arab-American affairs; 2000 words maximum.

Initial Contact. Query letter only. SASE required.

Acceptance Policies. Byline given: yes. Publishing rights: n/i. Payment made: none. Response time to initial inquiry: 1-2 months. Average time until publication: 2-4 months. Submit seasonal material 3 months in advance. Simultaneous submissions: yes. Disk submissions: Macintosh DD or HD; Microsoft Word.

Photography Submissions. Format and film: maximum 3x5 prints. Photographs should include: captions; identification of subjects (if necessary). **Payment:** none. Photographic rights: none.

NATIVE NEVADAN, THE. 98 Colony Rd. Reno, NV 89502. (702) 329-2936.
Fax: (702) 359-9501. Submissions Editor: Andreé Zouty. Type: magazine targeting the Native American audience. Frequency of publication: monthly. Circulation: n/i. Number of manuscripts accepted per year: 50. Payment in copies.

Editorial Needs. Fiction forms—book excerpts; serialized fiction; short stories. For all forms: subjects include adventure, avant-garde, ethnic, folklore, historical fiction, humor, women's issues, all with a focus on Native Americans; 1000 words.

Nonfiction forms—book excerpts; columns; essays; features; fillers; interview/profiles; poetry; book/entertainment reviews. For all forms: subjects include art, business/economics, comedy/humor, comics, culture, dance, education, family issues, festivals, general interest, government/politics, history, human potential, law, medicine, minority issues, mythology, nature/environment, philosophy, politics/world affairs, social/political commentary, spirituality, sports, women's issues, all with a focus on Native Americans; no specific length.

Initial Contact. Query letter. Include tribal affiliation, if any. SASE required.

Acceptance Policies. Byline given: yes. Publishing rights: one-time rights. Payment made: in copies. Response time to initial inquiry: 1 week. Average time until publication: 1 month. Submit seasonal material 1 month in advance. Simultaneous submissions: yes. Disk submissions: Macintosh.

Photography Submissions. Format and film: black-and-white contact sheets. Photographs should include: captions; identification of subjects. **Payment:** none. Photographic rights: none.

Additional Information. Tips: Positive aspects of Native Americans should be highlighted. Writer's guidelines: upon request. Sample copy: upon request.

NATIVE PEOPLES MAGAZINE. 5333 N. 7th St., Ste. C-224. Phoenix, AZ
85004. (602) 252-2236. Fax: (602) 265-3113. Submissions Editors: Gary Avey (editor); Margaret Clark Price (associate editor). Type: magazine targeting the multicultural, native peoples of the Americas. Frequency of publication: quarterly. Circulation: 50,000. Number of manuscripts accepted per year: 40. Payment offered.

Editorial Needs. Nonfiction forms—book excerpts (in advance of publication only); essays (800 words); features (1800-2500 words); photo features; poetry ($.25 per word). For all forms: subjects include arts and lifeways of native peoples of the Americas.

Initial Contact. Query letter only. SASE required.

Acceptance Policies. Byline given: yes. Publishing rights: first North American serial rights. Payment made: upon publication. Kill fee: no. Expenses: no. Response time to initial inquiry: 6 weeks. Average time until publication: 3 months. Simultaneous submissions: no. Disk submissions: IBM; WordPerfect. Include hard copy.

Photography Submissions. Format and film: transparencies. Photographs should include: info captions. **Payment:** $250 cover; $150 two pages; $100 full page; $75 half page. Photographic rights: one-time rights.

Additional Information. *Native Peoples* is an extremely high-quality, full-color publication dedicated to the sensitive portrayal of the arts and lifeways of the native people of the Americas. The magazine is affiliated with nine national museums throughout the United States. Writer's guidelines: upon request.

NEWS FROM INDIAN COUNTRY. Rt 2, Box 2900-A. Hayward, WI 54843.

(715) 634-5226. Fax: (715) 634-3243. Submissions Editor: Paul DeMain. Type: newspaper targeting the Native American audience. Frequency of publication: 2 times per month. Circulation: 6500. Number of manuscripts accepted per year: 50. Payment offered.

Editorial Needs. Nonfiction forms—columns; features; fillers; food/recipes; photo features; poetry. For all forms: subjects include Native American archaeology, business/economics, child care/development, comedy/humor, culture, general interest, government/politics, humanities, nature/environment, philosophy, social/political commentary, spirituality.

Initial Contact. Query letter only. SASE required.

Acceptance Policies. Byline given: yes. Publishing rights: work-for-hire assignments. Payment made: upon publication. Kill fee: no. Expenses: yes. Response time to initial inquiry: 3 weeks. Average time until publication: 3 weeks. Submit seasonal material 3 months in advance. Simultaneous submissions: yes. Disk submissions: Macintosh compatible, 3 1/2.

Photography Submissions. Format and film: 3x5 prints. Photographs should include: captions. **Payment:** $15 per photo. Photographic rights: none.

Additional Information. We are geared towards the Native American community, teachers, and libraries.

NIMROD CONTEMPORARY PROSE AND POETRY JOURNAL. The

Arts and Humanities Council of Tulsa. 2210 S. Main. Tulsa, OK 74114. (918) 584-3333. Submissions Editor: Fran Ringold. Type: magazine targeting a nonspecific ethnic audience. Frequency of publication: 2 times per year. Circulation: 3500. Number of manuscripts accepted per year: 80. Payment in copies.

Editorial Needs. Fiction forms—short stories (7500 words); translations (7500 words).

Nonfiction forms—essays (writers and writing, 7500 words maximum); interview/profiles (writers, 7500 words maximum); poetry (any subject, 1800 words maximum).

Initial Contact. Entire manuscript. Include a one-page cover letter with short bio, name, address, and phone. Author's bio is printed in the back of the book. SASE required.

Acceptance Policies. Byline given: writer's name appears on story, poetry, and prose. Publishing rights: first North American serial rights. Payment made: 3 copies. Response time to initial inquiry: 3-12 weeks. Average time until publication: 6-12 months. Submit seasonal material 6 months in advance. Simultaneous submissions: no. Disk submissions: no.

Additional Information. Past issues include *Oklahoma Indian Markings, From the Soviets, China Today, India: A Wealth of Diversity, Clap Hands and Sing: Writers of Age.* In 1992 we will publish an international issue featuring works by authors from Eastern Europe and the Caribbean. In 1993 the focus of our thematic (spring) issue will be Australian writing. In 1994 a study of Canadian writing is planned. Send a #10 SASE for information on deadlines and guidelines for our thematic issues. Tips: We offer a contest with monetary awards. Send #10 SASE for guidelines. Writer's guidelines: SASE. Sample copy: $6.95.

NOTEBOOK/CUADERNO: A LITERARY JOURNAL. PO Box 15607.

Rio Rancho, NM 87174. Submissions Editor: Y. Zentella. Type: literary journal targeting a nonspecific ethnic audience. Frequency of publication: annually. Circulation: 200. Number of manuscripts accepted per year: 15. Payment in copies.

Editorial Needs. Fiction forms—short stories (3000 word average); translations.

Nonfiction forms—columns (labor, environment, 1500-2000 words); essays (alternative political commentary, 1500-2000 words); interview/profile (ethnic writers, artists, and others, 1500-2000 words); book reviews (ethnic and assorted themes).

Initial Contact. Entire manuscript. Include bio. SASE required.

Acceptance Policies. Byline given: yes. Publishing rights: first North American serial rights. Payment made: in copies. Response time to initial inquiry: 6-12 weeks. Average time until publication: 1 year. Simultaneous submissions: yes, inform us. Disk submissions: no.

Photography Submissions. Format and film: 3x5 black-and-white prints. Photographs should include: captions; text. **Payment:** in copies. Photographic rights: one-time rights.

Additional Information. Writer's guidelines: upon request. Sample copy: current issue not available. Next issue will be published in December, 1991.

NOW AND THEN. Center for Appalachian Studies and Serivces. PO Box 1-A. East Tennessee State University. Johnson City, TN 37603. Submissions Editors: Jo Carson (poetry); Ed Snodderly (music); Pat Arnow (all other categories). Type: magazine targeting the Appalachian audience. Frequency of publication: 3 times per year. Circulation: 2000. Number of manuscripts accepted per year: 36. Payment in copies.

Editorial Needs. Fiction forms—plays; short stories. For all forms: subjects include ethnic groups (Appalachians, Afro-Americans, Native Americans), adult fables, contemporary/modern, folklore, general interest, historical fiction, humor, literary, mainstream, women's issues, all pertaining to the Appalachian region and peoples.

Nonfiction forms—columns; essays; features; interview/profiles; photo features; poetry; book reviews. For all forms: subjects include ethnic groups (Afro-Americans, Native Americans, Appalachians), comedy/humor, culture, dance, education, family issues, film/television/video, handicrafts, biography, history, humanities, immigration, music mythology, all pertaining to the Appalachian region and its peoples.

Initial Contact. Entire manuscript. SASE required.

Acceptance Policies. Byline given: yes. Publishing rights: one-time rights. Payment made: in copies. Response time to initial inquiry: 4 months. Average time until publication: 6 months. Simultaneous submissions: yes. Disk submissions: no.

Photography Submissions. Format and film: 5x7, 8x10 black-and-white prints; contact sheets; transparencies; color prints for cover only. Photographs should include: captions; model releases; identification of subjects. **Payment:** $25 maximum. Photographic rights: one-time rights.

Additional Information. Writer's guidelines: upon request. Sample copy: $3.50.

OBSIDIAN II: BLACK LITERATUE IN REVIEW. Department of English, Box 8105. North Carolina State University. Raleigh, NC 27695-8105. Submissions Editors: Gerald Barrax (poetry); Karla F. C. Holloway (associate); Joyce Pettis (criticism); Susie R. Powell (fiction, drama). Type: academic journal targeting the Afro-American audience. Frequency of publication: quarterly. Circulation: 10,000. Number of manuscripts accepted per year: varies. Payment in copies.

Editorial Needs. Fiction forms—plays (any subject); short stories (any subject.

Nonfiction forms—essays (scholarly articles dealing with black literature, word length open); interview/profiles (black writers); book reviews (scholarly reviews of black literature).

Initial Contact. Entire manuscript. Materials should be submitted on disk (if possible), with two hard copies. Details included in our guidelines. SASE required.

Acceptance Policies. Byline given: yes. Publishing rights: release of copyright will accrue to the author upon publication. Payment made: in copies. Response time to initial inquiry: 1 month. Average time until publication: varies. Simultaneous submissions: no. Disk submissions: Macintosh in Microsoft Word, Macwrite, or ASCII; IBM in ASCII. Check our guidelines for details.

Additional Information. We are a scholarly journal and all essays must adhere to MLA guidelines. We encourage the submission of fiction and poetry also. Tips: Adhere to our guidelines. Writer's guidelines: SASE. Sample copy: $5.

OXFORD MAGAZINE. English Department. Bachelor Hall. Miami University. Oxford, OH 45056. (513) 529-5256. Submissions Editors: Kathryn Lacey (fiction); Collin Brooke (poetry). Type: magazine targeting Appalachia and a nonspecific ethnic audience. Frequency of publication: 2 times per year. Circulation: 500+. Number of manuscripts accepted per year: 90. Payment and subscription offered.

Editorial Needs. Fiction forms—short stories; translations. For all forms: subjects include ethnic groups (all cultures), adult fables, adventure, avant-garde, contemporary/modern, folklore, general interest, historical fiction, humor, mainstream, Western, women's issues; $2.50 per page.

Nonfiction forms—essays ($2.50 per page); poetry ($5 per poem). For all forms: subjects include ethnic groups (all cultures, emphasis on Appalachians), art, disabled, family issues, folklore, gay/lesbian issues, biography, history, men's issues, minority issues, nature/environment, religions (Buddhism, Hinduism, Islam, Jewish, Taoism, Zen), surrealism, travel, war/peace issues, women's issues.

Initial Contact. Entire manuscript. SASE required.

Acceptance Policies. Byline given: yes. Publishing rights: one-time rights. Payment made: upon publication. Kill fee: no. Expenses: no. Response time to initial inquiry: 8-10 weeks. Average time until publication: 6 weeks. Submit seasonal material 2 months in advance. Simultaneous submissions: yes. Disk submissions: no.

Additional Information. We wish to diversify content and audience. Tips: Pick up a copy and read it. Writer's guidelines: upon request. Sample copy: $4.

POLONIAN. 165 Eleventh St. San Francisco, CA 94103. (415) 864-6100. Fax: (415) 431-6450. Submissions Editor: Dalegor Wladsyslaw Suchecki. Type: newsletter targeting a Polish audience. Frequency of publication: monthly. Circulation: n/i. Number of manuscripts accepted per year: 50. Payment offered.

Editorial Needs. Nonfiction forms—book excerpts (only Polish-Americans); columns; essays; features; fillers; food/recipes; interview/profiles; photo features; poetry; book/entertainment reviews; social/political commentary. For all forms: subjects should emphasize the Polish community in Northern California; 500 words.

Initial Contact. Entire manuscript. SASE required.

Acceptance Policies. Byline given: yes. Publishing rights: n/i. Payment made: n/i. Response time to initial inquiry: n/i. Average time until publication: n/i. Submit seasonal material 1 month in advance. Simultaneous submissions: yes. Disk submissions: Ventura, Wordstar.

Photography Submissions. Format and film: velox. Photographs should include: captions; identification of subjects. **Payment:** $250 maximum. Photographic rights: n/i.

Additional Information. Publication is by and for Polish-Americans and about their activities.

POLONIA'S VOICE: THE POLISH AMERICAN JOURNAL. 1275

Harlem Rd. Buffalo, NY 14206. (716) 893-5771. Fax: (716) 893-5783. Submissions Editors: Stanislaus Kmiec (culture); Daniel Haskin (fine arts); Sophie Hodorowicz-Knab (heritage); Steve Litwin (polka); Benjamin Fiorse, S.J. (religion); Thomas Tarapacki (sports). Type: newspaper targeting the Polish-American audience. Frequency of publication: monthly. Circulation: 19,000. Number of manuscripts accepted per year: 6. Payment offered.

Editorial Needs. Nonfiction forms—columns (Polish/Polonia relations, 600 words, $20); essays (600 words, $20); features (bios on Polish-Americans, 750 words, $25).

Initial Contact. Query letter only. SASE required.

Acceptance Policies. Byline given: yes. Publishing rights: one-time rights. Payment made: quarterly. Kill fee: no. Expenses: no. Response time to initial inquiry: 2-3 weeks. Average time until publication: 2-3 months. Submit seasonal material 4 months in advance. Simultaneous submissions: no. Disk submissions: DOS.

Additional Information. We are looking for remembrances of growing up as a Polish-American. Tips: Keep it short! Three pages, double spaced. Writer's guidelines: upon request. Sample copy: upon request.

RACKHAM JOURNAL OF THE ARTS AND HUMANITIES. 411 Mason

Hall. University of Michigan. Ann Arbor, MI 48109. Submissions Editors: Thomas Mussio, Mary Lacey. Type: academic journal targeting a nonspecific ethnic audience. Frequency of publication: annually. Circulation: n/i. Number of manuscripts accepted per year: 8-15. Payment in copies.

Editorial Needs. Fiction forms—short stories (literary); translations.

Nonfiction forms—essays; poetry. For all forms: subjects include anthropology, folklore, humanities, philosophy, photography, social/political commentary.

Initial Contact. Entire manuscript. SASE required.

Acceptance Policies. Byline given: yes. Publishing rights: n/i. Payment made: 2 copies. Response time to initial inquiry: 1 month. Average time until publication: next issue. Simultaneous submissions: no. Disk submissions: no.

Photography Submissions. Format and film: maximum 5x8 prints. Photographs should include: n/i. **Payment:** none. Photographic rights: none.

Additional Information. If essays, they must be rigorous and informed with a strong, useful bibliography and notes. If fiction, it must be mature and practiced.

RESPONSE: A CONTEMPORARY JEWISH REVIEW. 27 W. 20th St.,

9th Floor. New York, NY 10011. (212) 675-1168. Fax: (212) 929-3459. Submissions Editor: Paul Lerner (managing editor). Type: magazine targeting the Jewish audience. Frequency of publication: quarterly. Circulation: 1500. Number of manuscripts accepted per year: 30. Payment in copies.

Editorial Needs. Fiction forms—short stories; translations.

Nonfiction forms—essays (Judaic focus, 2000-3000 words); poetry (must have Judaic content, any length); book reviews (1000 words).

Initial Contact. Query letter only or entire manuscript. Include curriculum vitae. SASE required.

Acceptance Policies. Byline given: yes. Publishing rights: n/i. Payment made: 5 copies. Response time to initial inquiry: 6 weeks. Average time until publication: 8 weeks. Submit seasonal material 5 months in advance. Simultaneous submissions: yes. Disk submissions: Macintosh; Microsoft Word.

Additional Information. We prefer to publish students or young, undiscovered writers. Editorially, we are pluralistic and progressive. Writer's guidelines: write or call. Sample copy: $4.

ROHWEDDER: INTERNATIONAL JOURNAL OF LITERATURE AND ART. PO Box 29490. Los Angeles, CA 90029. Submissions Editors: Nancy Antell (fiction); Robert Dassanowsky-Harris (poetry); Julien Foreman (art); H. J. Schacht (managing editor). Type: magazine trageting a nonspecific ethnic audience. Frequency of publication: irregularly (1 or 2 times per year). Circulation: 500-1000. Number of manuscripts accepted per year: 40-80. Payment in copies.

Editorial Needs. Fiction forms—short stories (all subjects); translations (all subjects).

Nonfiction forms—essays ('92 feminist writers and theory, '92/'93 contemporary media); fillers; interview/profiles; photo features (black-and-white); poetry (5 poems).

Initial Contact. Query letter only. SASE required.

Acceptance Policies. Byline given: yes. Publishing rights: one-time rights. Payment made: in copies. Response time to initial inquiry: 2 weeks. Average time until publication: next issue. Simultaneous submissions: yes. Disk submissions: yes.

Photography Submissions. Format and film: black-and-white prints. Photographs should include: n/i. **Payment:** none. Photographic rights: one-time rights.

Additional Information. Writer's guidelines: upon request. Sample copy: upon request.

SAN JOSE STUDIES. English Department. San Jose State University. San Jose, CA 95192. (408) 924-4476. Submissions Editors: Fauneil J. Rinn (fiction, essays); O. C. Williams (poetry). Type: academic journal targeting a nonspecific ethnic audience. Frequency of publication: 3 times per year. Circulation: 500. Number of manuscripts accepted per year: 35-40. Payment in copies.

Editorial Needs. Fiction forms—short stories (general topics suitable for an academic journal).

Nonfiction forms—book excerpts (must stand on its own, 15-25 pages); essays (any subject of interest to educated layperson, 10-25 pages); interview/profiles (intellectually influential person, 10-25 pages); poetry (3-6 poems); cartoons (with academic focus). For all forms: all subjects (except erotica, human potential, new age, psychic material) are fine if well researched.

Initial Contact. Entire manuscript. SASE required.

Acceptance Policies. Byline given: yes. Publishing rights: rights revert to author after publication. Payment made: in copies. Response time to initial inquiry: 6-8 weeks. Average time until publication: 6-12 months. Simultaneous submissions: no. Disk submissions: no.

Additional Information. Our audience is mostly academic, and we think of our publication as directed to the educated layperson with interdisciplinary interest. Our journal has a record of concern for work that reflects the contributions and interests of ethnic minorities. We are planning a special issue of drama, poetry, fiction, essays, and art by and about Chicanas and Chicanos in the local area. Send for guidelines. Tips: We are a refereed journal and offer a $100 prize. Writer's guidelines: upon request. Sample copy: $3.50.

SAQI: SOUTH ASIA QUARTERLY INTERNATIONAL. PO Box 5582.
Berkeley, CA 94704. (415) 848-8200. Submissions Editor: C. J. Wallia, Ph.D. Type: magazine targeting the South Asian audience. Frequency of publication: quarterly. Circulation: n/i. Number of manuscripts accepted per year: 40. Payment in copies.

Editorial Needs. Fiction forms—book excerpts; novellas; plays; serialized fiction; short stories; translations. For all forms: subjects include adult fables, avant-garde, folklore, general interest, historical fiction, humor, literary, new age, women's issues, all with a South Asian focus.

Nonfiction forms—book excerpts, columns; essays; features; fillers; interview/profiles; photo features; poetry; book/entertainment reviews. For all forms: subjects include comedy/humor, education, entertainment, folklore, holistic practices, human potential, humanities, immigration, medicine, men's issues, new age/metaphysical, minority issues, music, philosophy, politics/world affairs, psycho-spirituality, religion (Buddhism, Islam, Sikhism, Hinduism, Christianity, Judaism), scholarly works, social/political commentary, travel, women's issues, yoga, all with a South Asian focus.

Initial Contact. n/i. SASE required.

Acceptance Policies. Byline given: yes. Publishing rights: first rights. Payment made: in copies. Response time to initial inquiry: 3-6 weeks. Average time until publication: 3-6 months. Simultaneous submissions: yes. Disk submissions: IBM PC; ASCII.

SARMATIAN REVIEW, THE. PO Box 79119. Houston, TX 77279-9119.
(713) 467-5836. Submissions Editor: Dr. E. M. Thompson. Type: academic journal targeting the Eastern European audience. Frequency of publication: 3 times per year. Circulation: privileged information. Number of manuscripts accepted per year: 10-15. Payment in copies.

Editorial Needs. Nonfiction forms—columns; essays. For all forms: subjects include general interest, biography, history, ethnic groups (Eastern Europeans, Poles, Jews), economic commentary, social/political commentary, all relevant to East European affairs and their impact on the United States; 300-10,000 words.

Initial Contact. Entire manuscript. SASE required.

Acceptance Policies. Byline given: yes. Publishing rights: we permit reprints if source is given and we receive a copy. Payment made: in copies. Response time to initial inquiry: 1-3 months. Average time until publication: 2 months to 2 years. Submit seasonal material 4 months in advance. Simultaneous submissions: no. Disk submissions: Macintosh; MacWrite or Microsoft Word.

Additional Information. Sample copy: Write to Claire Allen, associate editor.

SCANDINAVIAN REVIEW. 725 Park Ave. New York, NY 10021. (212) 879-
9779. Fax: (212) 249-3444. Submissions Editor: address to Editor. Type: magazine targeting the Scandinavian audience. Frequency of publication: 3 times per year. Circulation: n/i. Number of manuscripts accepted per year: 30. Payment offered.

Editorial Needs. Fiction forms—short stories (travel/adventures, women's issues, in English); translations (from the Nordic languages, $100-$300).

Nonfiction forms—features; interview/profiles; photo features (4-5 photos). For all forms: subjects include adventure, antiques, architecture, art, business/economics, child care/development, culture, fashion, festivals, government/politics, humanities, men's issues, nature/environment, social/political commentary, women's issues, all with a focus on modern life in the Scandinavian countries; 1500-2000 words.

Initial Contact. Query letter only or article proposal with subject outline. SASE required.

Acceptance Policies. Byline given: yes. Publishing rights: second serial rights. Payment made: upon publication. Kill fee: no. Expenses: no. Response time to initial inquiry: 2 weeks. Average time until publication: 3 months. Submit seasonal material 1 month in advance. Simultaneous submissions: yes. Disk submissions: no.

Photography Submissions. Format and film: black-and-white or color prints; transparencies. Photographs should include: captions. **Payment**: $25-$100. Photographic rights: one-time rights.

Additional Information. Subject matter is contemporary life in the Nordic countries: Denmark, Finland, Iceland, Norway, and Sweden. Writer's guidelines: upon request. Sample copy: upon request.

Secrets see **INTIMACY/BLACK ROMANCE.**

SHAMAN'S DRUM: A JOURNAL OF EXPERIENTIAL SHAMANISM.
PO Box 430. Willits, CA 95490. (707) 459-0486. Submissions Editor: Timothy White. Type: magazine targeting a nonspecific ethnic audience. Frequency of publication: quarterly. Circulation: 20,000. Number of manuscripts accepted per year: 20. Payment offered.

Editorial Needs. **Fiction forms**—book excerpts (3000 words maximum, $150); short stories (2000 words maximum, $100).

Nonfiction forms—book excerpts (shamanism, 6000 words maximum, $300); features (shamanism, native spirituality, 6000 words maximum, $300); photo features (shamanism, native spirituality, 6000 words maximum, $600); book/entertainment reviews (assigned only); poetry (shamanism, word length varies, $50).

Initial Contact. Entire manuscript. Include availability of photos. SASE required.

Acceptance Policies. Byline given: yes. Publishing rights: first North American serial rights; second serial rights. Payment made: upon acceptance. Kill fee: no. Expenses: no. Response time to initial inquiry: 2 months. Average time until publication: 6 months. Simultaneous submissions: no. Disk submissions: no.

Photography Submissions. Format and film: prints; contact sheets; transparencies. Photographs should include: captions; identification of subjects. **Payment**: $30-$60. Photographic rights: one-time.

Additional Information. Only interested in articles about shamanism or native spiritual healing traditions. Tips: Emphasize firsthand experiences and observations. Writer's guidelines: SASE. Sample copy: $4.

SHOFAR.
43 Northcote Dr. Melville, NY 11747. (516) 643-4598. Submissions Editor: Gerald. H. Grayson. Type: newspaper targeting Jewish children, 8-13. Frequency of publication: monthly, October through May. Circulation: n/i. Number of manuscripts accepted per year: varies. Payment and copies offered.

Editorial Needs. **Fiction forms**—short stories (Judaic theme, 500-700 words, $.10 per word and 5 copies).

Nonfiction forms—features (special holiday issues, 500-700 words, $.10 per word and 5 copies); poetry; photo features; cartoons; games/puzzles.

Initial Contact. Entire manuscript. SASE required.

Acceptance Policies. Byline given: yes. Publishing rights: first North American serial rights. Payment made: upon publication. Kill fee: no. Expenses: no. Response time to initial inquiry: 6-8 weeks. Average time until publication: varies. Submit seasonal material at least 4 months in advance. Simultaneous submissions: yes. Disk submissions: no.

Photography Submissions. Format and film: black-and-white prints. Photographs should include: captions; identification of subjects. **Payment:** yes. Photographic rights: first rights (with manuscript).

Additional Information. All materials must be on a Jewish theme. Tips: Queries welcome. Writer's guidelines: upon request. Sample copy: 9x12 SASE, $1.05 postage.

Sicilia Parra see **ARBA SICULA.**

SOCIÉTÉ. Technicians of the Sacred. 1317 N. San Fernando Blvd., Ste. 310. Burbank, CA 91504. Submissions Editor: Courtney Willis. Type: magazine targeting people interested in Neo-African religions. Frequency of publication: 3 times per year. Circulation: 2000. Number of manuscripts accepted per year: varies. Payment in copies.

Editorial Needs. Nonfiction forms—essays; fillers; food/recipes; interview/profiles; book reviews. For all forms: subjects include ethnic groups (Afro-Americans, Latin Americans), anthropology, archaeology, art, culture, education, folklore, gay/lesbian issues, handicrafts, human potential, magic, men's issues, minority issues, mythology, nature/environment, psychology, psycho-spirituality, relationships, religion (Taoism, Zen), self-help, sociology, travel, tribal issues, yoga, all focusing on Neo-African religious/magical systems.

Initial Contact. Entire manuscript. SASE required.

Acceptance Policies. Byline given: no. Publishing rights: second serial rights. Payment made: in copies. Response time to initial inquiry: 4 weeks. Average time until publication: n/i. Simultaneous submissions: yes. Disk submissions: no.

Photography Submissions. Format and film: black-and-white prints. Photographs should include: n/i. **Payment:** none. Photographic rights: none.

Additional Information. This is the first and only journal of Neo-African religious/magical systems. Writer's guidelines: not available. Sample copy: not available.

SOKOL MINNESOTA SLOVO. 383 Michigan St. St. Paul, MN 55102. (612) 290-0542. Submissions Editor: Sharon Wyberg. Type: newsletter targeting the Czech and Slovak audience. Frequency of publication: monthly. Circulation: 800. Number of manuscripts accepted per year: n/i. Payment not offered.

Editorial Needs. Nonfiction forms—n/i. For all forms: subjects must relate to Czech and Slovak issues.

Initial Contact. n/i. SASE required.

Acceptance Policies. Byline given: yes. Publishing rights: n/i. Payment made: none. Response time to initial inquiry: n/i. Average time until publication: n/i. Simultaneous submissions: n/i. Disk submissions: n/i.

South Asia Quarterly International see **SAQI.**

SOUTH DAKOTA REVIEW. English Department. University of South Dakota. Vermillion, SD 57069. (605) 677-5220. Submissions Editor: John R. Milton. Type: literary, academic journal targeting a nonspecific ethnic audience. Frequency of publication: quarterly. Circulation: n/i. Number of manuscripts accepted per year: 50+. Payment in copies.

Editorial Needs. Fiction forms—novellas; short stories; translations.

Nonfiction forms—essays; poetry.

Initial Contact. Entire manuscript. Include brief bio. SASE required.

Acceptance Policies. Byline given: yes. Publishing rights: first North American serial rights; second serial rights. Payment made: in copies. Response time to initial inquiry: 3 weeks. Average time until publication: 3 months. Simultaneous submissions: no. Disk submissions: no.

Additional Information. We are somewhat, but not entirely, oriented to the American West. Tips: We want exceptionally good writing. Writer's guidelines: not available. Sample copy: $5.

SOUTHERN CALIFORNIA ANTHOLOGY. WPH 404, MC 4034. University of Southern California. Los Angeles, CA 90089-4034. Submissions Editor: Melissa Hartman. Type: literary magazine targeting a nonspecific ehtnic audience. Frequency of publication: annually. Circulation: 1200. Number of manuscripts accepted per year: 25. Payment in copies.

Editorial Needs. Fiction forms—short stories (avant-garde, ethnic groups, general interest, historical fiction, literary, modern, women's issues, 5000 words maximum).

Nonfiction forms—interview/profiles; poetry (poetry prize awarded, $750, $250, $100, or copies).

Initial Contact. Entire manuscript. SASE required if material is to be returned.

Acceptance Policies. Byline given: yes. Publishing rights: first North American serial rights. Payment made: in copies. Response time to initial inquiry: 8 weeks. Average time until publication: publish in June. Simultaneous submissions: no. Disk submissions: Microsoft Word.

Additional Information. Writer's guidelines: SASE. Sample copy: $7.95.

TOZAI TIMES. 5810 E. Olympic Blvd. Los Angeles, CA 90022. (213) 723-6245. Fax: (213) 722-7865. Submissions Editor: Joy Yamauchi. Type: newsmagazine targeting the Japanese-American audience. Frequency of publication: monthly. Circulation: 10,000. Number of manuscripts accepted per year: varies. Payment offered.

Editorial Needs. Fiction forms—short stories (ethnic, folklore, historical fiction, holiday stories, humor). For all forms: subjects should focus on Japanese-Americans or Asian-Americans.

Nonfiction forms—essays; features; food/recipes; interview/profiles; book/entertainment reviews. For all forms: subjects include ethnic groups (Asians), comedy/humor, culture, family issues, folklore, martial arts, medicine, women's issues, with a focus on a Japanese-American or Asian-American angle; length varies according to content; $25-$150.

Initial Contact. Article proposal with subject outline or entire manuscript. SASE required.

Acceptance Policies. Byline given: yes. Publishing rights: first rights. Payment made: upon publication. Kill fee: no. Expenses: yes. Response time to initial inquiry: 1 month.

Average time until publication: 2-3 months. Submit seasonal material 3 months in advance. Simultaneous submissions: no. Disk submissions: Page Maker 4.

Photography Submissions. Format and film: black-and-white prints. Photographs should include: captions; model releases; identification of subjects. **Payment:** varies. Photographic rights: first rights.

Additional Information. We're published in English and looking for human interest and profiles for second, third, and fourth generation Japanese-Americans. Tips: Avoid stereotypes; look to the inner story. Writer's guidelines: call or write. Sample copy: SASE.

[VEINTE] 20 DE MAYO SPANISH NEWSPAPER. 1824 Sunset Blvd., Ste. 202. Los Angeles, CA 90026. (213) 483-8511. Fax: (213) 483-6474.

Submissions Editors: Esteban Fernandez (general editor); Angel Torres (sports); Oscar Borras (boxing); Cesar Remon (entertainment); Gina Perez (city editor); Maria C. de los Prados (social events). Type: Spanish language newspaper targeting the Hispanic audience. Frequency of publication: weekly. Circulation: 10,000. Number of manuscripts accepted per year: varies. Payment in copies.

Editorial Needs. Nonfiction forms—columns; essays; features; food/recipes; interview/profiles; photo features; poetry; book/entertainment reviews. For all forms: subjects should focus on the Southern California Hispanic community.

Initial Contact. Article proposal with subject outline. SASE required.

Acceptance Policies. Byline given: n/i. Publishing rights: n/i. Payment made: in copies. Response time to initial inquiry: 1 month. Average time until publication: 2-3 weeks. Submit seasonal material 1 month in advance. Simultaneous submissions: yes. Disk submissions: no.

Photography Submissions. Format and film: any size prints. Photographs should include: captions. **Payment:** none. Photographic rights: none.

Additional Information. We are designed to serve the interest of the Hispanic community in Southern California. Our editorial pages analyze the political spectrum of Latin America, the United States, and the world as it is perceived by its Hispanic writers and reporters. Tips: Send a maximum of 2 pages (8 1/2 x 11) typed, double spaced. Writer's guidelines: rate card. Sample copy: upon request.

WHISPERING WIND. 8009 Wales St. New Orleans, LA 70126-1952. (504) 241-5866. Submissions Editor: Jack Heriard. Type: newspaper targeting the Native American audience. Frequency of publication: every other month. Circulation: 4000. Number of manuscripts accepted per year: 12. Payment in copies.

Editorial Needs. Nonfiction forms—photo features (American Indians); book reviews (600 words maximum). For all forms: subjects include Native American anthropology, culture, ethnology, folklore, handicrafts, biography, history, martial arts, mythology.

Initial Contact. Entire manuscript. SASE required.

Acceptance Policies. Byline given: yes. Publishing rights: first North American serial rights; second serial rights. Payment made: in copies. Response time to initial inquiry: 2-4 weeks. Average time until publication: 1-2 years. Simultaneous submissions: yes. Disk submissions: IBM compatible; ASCII.

Photography Submissions. Format and film: 4x6 black-and-white or color prints. Photographs should include: captions; identification of subjects. **Payment:** none. Photographic rights: none.

Additional Information. All articles (other than book reviews) must be referenced with an included bibliography. Tips: All articles must relate to the arts, crafts, material culture, or history of the American Indian. Writer's guidelines: upon request. Sample copy: $4.

Film and TV Markets

The film production companies listed in this section may specialize in developing and producing material for television, feature film, video, or documentaries. Their particular ethnic interests may differ widely, but their demand for quality writing and exceptional stories is consistent for all. The information provided in this section has been compiled to help scriptwriters easily target markets for scripts dealing with ethnic elements, themes, or issues. Companies that did not indicate specific entries for media forms, ethnic focus, and/or script genres have not been listed in the film index.

How to Use the Information in This Section

The first part of the entry identifies the name of the film company, its address, phone and fax numbers (when provided), the name of a contact person and his or her title, and the year the company was founded.

Subjects of Interest

This paragraph details information about the ethnic focus and genre for scripts that the film company will consider. Depending on its particular needs, a company could list one, several, or all of the following genres: action-driven, biographies, character-driven, children's/young adult, drama, entertainment, epics, fantasy, general interest, historical period pieces, mysteries, romantic adventure, true stories, Westerns, and women's films. Some listings include titles of recent film projects produced by the company as well as titles of ethnic projects in development. Finally, the information following the heading "Do not want" spells out what the producers absolutely do not want to see. Scriptwriters should pay special attention to this portion of the entry.

Initial Contact

This information outlines how the producer/production company wishes to have the scriptwriter make initial contact. Most prefer a query letter. Some ask that you also send a treatment. Many also expect you to request their release form or to complete and include your own before sending your script. Check the company's entry to see if there's a specific person to contact to request the form. Note whether or not the company requires you to contact them through an agent. Always send a SASE for return of your materials.

Acceptance Policies

This section lists information on whether or not the company will accept unagented scripts and, if so, under what specific conditions. Also included is information on whether or not the company will consider multiple submissions, the approximate length of time from initial query to the company's response, and the approximate time from a positive response to the optioning of script. The average dollar amount of an option offered by the company and a listing of the production rights it purchases is also provided when available.

Additional Information

The information listed under this heading includes direct comments from the producer or representative of the film or TV production company to you, the scriptwriter. These comments contain information that may be vital in helping you assess whether or not you've correctly interpreted the company's need and whether your script fills that need. Also included is information on how to obtain writer's guidelines, if available.

Abbreviations

n/i means no information was given to us by the film company.

n/a means that this information does not apply to the film company.

AFRA-FILM ENTERPRISES. Division of Mosfilm Studios, USSR. 8730 Wilshire Blvd., Ste. 201. Beverly Hills, CA 90211. (213) 854-6504. Fax: (213) 804-3002. Contact Persons: Anatoly A. Fradis, president; Mila N. Taubhina, executive assistant. Founded: 1980.

Subjects of Interest. Ethnic focus—Russians, Poles, and other Eastern European cultures. Script genres—romantic adventure; action-driven; thrillers. Recent film projects: *Back in the USSR* (Largo Entertainment); *Inner Circle* (Numero Uno, Columbia). Ethnic projects in development: *Ice Runner; Ments and Cops*. Do not want: anything other than the above-mentioned subjects.

Initial Contact. Query letter with treatment. Include phone and fax numbers. Release form required: contact Anatoly A. Fradis. SASE required.

Acceptance Policies. Unagented manuscripts: yes. Simultaneous submissions: yes. Response time to initial inquiry: 1 month. Response time to option script: n/i. **Option amount:** $10,000. Production rights purchased: all.

AMERICAN CORSAIR. PO Box 38816. Los Angeles, CA 90038. Contact Person: Stuart Beckman, vice-president development. Founded: 1980

Subjects of Interest. Ethnic focus—Cubans; Native Americans; Eskimos; Afro-Americans. **Script genres**—romantic adventure; action-driven; any good story. Recent film projects: *Garwood* (ABC). Ethnic projects in development: yes.

Initial Contact. Query letter with outline. Please, no full scripts. Release form required: no. SASE required.

Acceptance Policies. Unagented manuscripts: yes. Simultaneous submissions: yes. Response time to initial inquiry: 1 month. Response time to option script: 1 month. **Option amount:** WGA minimum. Production rights purchased: all.

Additional Information. We want stories that have a good, strong structure with a beginning, middle, and end.

BLAKE PRODUCTIONS, TIMOTHY. 1643 Sunset Plaza Dr. Los Angeles, CA 90069. (213) 657-4136. Contact Persons: Patrick Strong, vice-president; Ira Tatur, development. Founded: 1989.

Subjects of Interest. Ethnic focus—Hispanics, Native Americans. **Script genres**—character-driven; mystery. Ethnic projects in development: none at present. Do not want: violence to women; sexually exploitive films.

Initial Contact. Query letter only. Include any credits. Release form required: yes; WGA or in letter. SASE required.

Acceptance Policies. Unagented manuscripts: yes, with release. Simultaneous submissions: yes. Response time to initial inquiry: 3 weeks. Response time to option script: 6-8 weeks. **Option amount:** varies. Production rights purchased: all.

Additional Information. Tips: Be sure it's your best work; no works-in-progress or first drafts.

BRAVERMAN PRODUCTIONS, INC. 3000 Olympic Blvd. Santa Monica, CA 90404. (213) 315-4710. Contact Persons: Charles Braverman, president; Diane Wynter, director of development. Founded: 1967.

Subjects of Interest. Ethnic focus—West Africans; Afro-Americans; Hispanics; Native Americans; West Indians; Russians. **Script genres**—true crime; biographies; romantic adventure; action-driven; character-driven; psychological thriller. Recent film or TV projects: *Brotherhood of Justice; Richard Lewis' I'm in Pain Concert; Teddy Pendergast Plays Tahoe.* Ethnic projects in development: none at present.

Initial Contact. Query letter with treatment if unrepresented. Entire script through agent only. SASE required.

Acceptance Policies. Unagented manuscripts: no. Simultaneous submissions: yes. Response time to initial inquiry: 6-8 weeks. Response time to option script: varies. **Option amount:** n/i. Production rights purchased: all.

CHILDREN'S TELEVISION WORKSHOP. New Show Projects. 1 Lincoln Plaza, 3rd floor; New York, NY 10023. (212) 875-6485. Fax: (212) 875-6104. Contact Persons: Victoria Strong, Alyce Myatt. Founded: company in business 23 years; New Show Projects commercial division is two years old.

Subjects of Interest. **Ethnic focus**—all cultures. **Script genres**—NSP is interested in a variety of genres (epics, character-driven, period pieces, children's, coming-of-age). Central to story should be a youth or child who is "empowered" during course of story. Recent film or TV projects: several projects in commercial development. Ethnic projects in development: several projects in development. Do not want: period drama about Civil War themes.

Initial Contact. Query letter only. Release form required: yes. SASE required.

Acceptance Policies. Unagented manuscripts: only after query letter. Simultaneous submissions: no. Response time to initial inquiry: 1 month. Response time to option script: 1-2 months. **Option amount:** varies; based on credits. Production rights purchased: yes.

Additional Information. In addition to searching for new scripts for option, we are constantly seeking to expand our database of minority writers for possible work on various projects in development. Tips: We are looking for original and professional scripts for MOWs, family programming series pilots, features.

ENTERTAINMENT PRODUCTIONS, INC. 2210 Wilshire Blvd., Ste. 744.
Santa Monica, CA 90403. (213) 456-3143. Fax: (213) 828-0427. Contact Persons: Story Editor. Founded: 1971.

Subjects of Interest. **Ethnic focus**—all cultures. **Script genres**—entertainment-type only. Recent film projects: *Why Me?* Ethnic projects in development: various ethnic themes. Do not want: scripts not geared for worldwide markets.

Initial Contact. Query letter with synopsis. Release form required: writer's release in any form will be acceptable. SASE required.

Acceptance Policies. Unagented manuscripts: yes; only with writer's release form. Simultaneous submissions: yes. Response time to initial inquiry: 1 month. Response time to option script: 1 day. **Option amount:** varies; based on marketplace. Production rights purchased: all.

Additional Information. Tips: State why script has great potential.

EVENSTAR PICTURES. 8233 Manchester Ave., Ste. 5. Playa del Rey, CA
90293. (213) 306-0368, 851-1402. Contact Persons: Brian Allman, Gail Viola. Founded: 1986.

Subjects of Interest. **Ethnic focus**—Afro-Americans; Hispanics; Asians. **Script genres**—all feature film ideas; preferably completed screenplays or published novels. Recent film or TV projects: *Apartment Zero* (feature). Ethnic projects in development: none currently.

Initial Contact. Telephone us to pitch idea before sending complete manuscript. SASE preferred.

Acceptance Policies. Unagented manuscripts: yes. Simultaneous submissions: yes. Response time to initial inquiry: 1 week. Response time to option script: 2-3 weeks. **Option amount:** percentage against a fair purchase price. Production rights purchased: all, but subject to negotiation.

Additional Information. Tips: Quality writing most important! Write a good script.

HOMETOWN FILMS. Paramount Pictures. 5555 Melrose Ave. Los Angeles, CA 90038. (213) 956-5955. Contact Persons: Michael Sheehy, senior vice-president; Bridget Adaitis, vice-president.

Subjects of Interest. **Ethnic focus**—all cultures. **Script genres**—romantic adventure; character-driven; psychological thriller; Westerns; mystery; fantasy; children's; coming-of-age. Recent film or TV projects: *Internal Affairs*. Ethnic projects in development: *Killing of the Saints*.

Initial Contact. Through agent only.

Acceptance Policies. Unagented manuscripts: no. Simultaneous submissions: yes. Response time to initial inquiry: n/i. Response time to option script: n/i. **Option amount:** n/i. Production rights purchased: all.

HUDLIN BROS., INC. Division of Tri-Star Pictures. Tribeca Film Center. 375 Greenwich St. New York, NY 10013. (212) 941-4004. Fax: (212) 941-4099. Contact Persons: Reginald Hudlin, president, writer/producer/director; Warrington Hudlin, writer/producer/director; Monica Breckenridge, director of development.

Subjects of Interest. **Ethnic focus**—African-American. **Script genres**—all. Ethnic projects in development: yes.

Initial Contact. Entire script. Include cover letter which lists the writer's name, address, and telephone number. Release form required: yes. SASE required if script is to be returned.

Acceptance Policies. Unagented manuscripts: yes. Simultaneous submissions: yes. Response time to initial inquiry: varies. Response time to option script: n/i. **Option amount:** n/i. Production rights purchased: n/i.

Additional Information. We will accept any unsolicited screenplay from an established agent licensed by the state. In addition, we will accept unsolicited screenplays from current members of the Black Filmmaker Foundation. Members must sign a release form which we provide. Writer's guidelines: upon request.

ITV PRODUCTIONS, LTD. 3941 Madison Ave. Culver City, CA 90232. Contact Person: David Shapiro, president. Founded: 1986.

Subjects of Interest. **Ethnic focus**—Indians of Asia. **Script genres**—romantic adventure; character-driven. Recent film or TV projects: *Mandulala*. Ethnic projects in development: "fish-out-of-water" theme. Do not want: any of the other genres.

Initial Contact. Query letter only with paragraph describing story. Release form required: contact Lisa. SASE required.

Acceptance Policies. Unagented manuscripts: yes. Simultaneous submissions: yes. Response time to initial inquiry: 4 weeks. Response time to option script: 3 months. **Option amount:** nothing for the first 6 months; $500 for second 6 months; $1000 for second year. Production rights purchased: all.

JKR PRODUCTIONS. 12140 W. Olympic Blvd. Los Angeles, CA 90064. (213) 826-3666. Contact Person: James Ruxin. Founded: 1985.

Subjects of Interest. **Ethnic focus**—universal human needs expressed through a specific culture. **Script genres**—preference for drama; romantic adventure; action-driven; character-driven. Recent film or TV projects: *Neon City; Defense Play*. Do not want: expensive high-tech; copy-cat scripts; gimmicks.

Initial Contact. Entire script. Include synopsis/treatment. SASE required only if return is necessary.

Acceptance Policies. Unagented manuscripts: yes. Simultaneous submissions: yes. Response time to initial inquiry: n/i. Response time to option script: n/i. **Option amount:** varies with material. Production rights purchased: varies with material, but at least dramatization, motion picture, broadcast rights, and video distribution.

KSCI-TV CHANNEL 18. International Channel Network. 12401 W. Olympic Blvd. Los Angeles, CA 90064. (213) 478-1818. Fax: (213) 479-8118. Contact Persons: Scott T. Wyskocil, network producer; Martie Quan, community relations manager; Robin D. Thornton, network promotions manager. Founded: current Asian/International format, 1986.

Subjects of Interest. **Ethnic focus**—Asian-Americans; Filipinos. **Script genres**—period pieces; documentaries; children's. Recent TV projects: *Korean American Pioneers; Domestic Violence in the Asian Pacific Communities; Moving the Image; Nisei Week: Then and Now; Tiananmen Square: Two Years Later*. Ethnic projects in development: yes. Do not want: exploitative, sensational, insensitive portrayals.

Initial Contact. Query letter with treatment. Release form required: no. SASE required.

Acceptance Policies. Unagented manuscripts: yes. Simultaneous submissions: yes. Response time to initial inquiry: 30 days. Response time to option script: varies. **Option amount:** negotiable. Production rights purchased: negotiable.

LCJ PRODUCTIONS. PO Box 5548. Mission Hills, CA 91604. (818) 367-8519. Contact Person: Lilyan Chauvin, executive producer-director. Founded: 1979.

Subjects of Interest. **Ethnic focus**—all cultures. **Script genres**—character-driven; psychological thriller; mystery. Ethnic projects in development: relationship between blacks and whites. Do not want: horror.

Initial Contact. Entire script through agent only. SASE required.

Acceptance Policies. Unagented manuscripts: yes. Simultaneous submissions: sometimes. Response time to initial inquiry: n/i. Response time to option script: 2 weeks. **Option amount:** varies. Production rights purchased: all.

Additional Information. We are open to ideas. Tips: Don't push us. Don't bug us.

MRUVKA ENTERTAINMENT, ALAN. 9073 Nemo St., 3rd Floor. Los Angeles, CA 90069. (213) 271-5400. Fax: (213) 271-3479. Contact Person: Peter Karlin. Founded: 1990.

Subjects of Interest. **Ethnic focus**—Afro-Americans; Chicanos; Latinos; Chinese; Japanese. **Script genres**—romantic adventure; epic; action-driven; character-driven; psychological thriller; horror; mystery. Recent film or TV projects: n/i. Ethnic projects in development: yes.

Initial Contact. Entire script. Release form required: call first. SASE required.

Acceptance Policies. Unagented manuscripts: yes. Simultaneous submissions: yes. Response time to initial inquiry: 2 weeks. Response time to option script: varies. **Option amount:** n/i. Production rights purchased: all.

NELVANA ENTERTAINMENT. Division of Nelvana Limited. 9000 Sunset Blvd., Ste. 911. Los Angeles, CA 90069. (213) 278-8466. Fax: (213) 278-4872. Contact Persons: Michael Hirsh, chairman; Patrick Loubert, president; Toper Taylor, vice-president, West Coast. Founded: 1971.

Subjects of Interest. Ethnic focus—Afro-Americans; Hispanics; Asians; Native Americans; Eastern European cultures. Script genres—mostly children's works in varying genres. Recent film or TV projects: *Burglar; Whoopi Goldberg; Brer Rabbit.* Ethnic projects in development: yes.

Initial Contact. Query letter through agent only. Release form required: yes; write or call. SASE not required.

Acceptance Policies. Unagented manuscripts: no. Simultaneous submissions: yes. Response time to initial inquiry: 2-4 weeks. Response time to option script: 1 month. **Option amount:** varies; based on pre-sale, etc. Production rights purchased: all.

Additional Information. We are an animation company primarily. Tips: We are looking for pre-sold ideas for Saturday morning and high-concept ideas for feature films.

POLAKOFF PRODUCTIONS, CAROL. Division of Aaron Spelling Productions. 5700 Wilshire Blvd., Ste. 575. Los Angeles, CA 90036. Contact Persons: Carol Polakoff, producer; Marc B. Lorber, director of development.

Subjects of Interest. Ethnic focus—Afro-Americans; Asians; Hispanics; Filipinos. Script genres—romantic adventure; psychological thriller; mystery; true stories. Recent TV projects: *Cuba, in the Shadow of Doubt; Held Hostage, the Sis and Jerry Levin Story; Seattle Cannery Murders.* Ethnic projects in development: yes. Do not want: works with no concept; action/adventure scripts; film scripts.

Initial Contact. Writers with agent through agent only. Writers without agent through query letter only. Release form required: we will send letter for those writers without agents. SASE required.

Acceptance Policies. Unagented manuscripts: rarely. Simultaneous submissions: yes. Response time to initial inquiry: 2 weeks. Response time to option script: varies. **Option amount:** varies; based on credits, rights, length of option, etc. Production rights purchased: all.

Additional Information. We are looking for socially just pieces that tell a story with a strong ethnic or female lead. Tips: Be honest about the material and its content.

POTOCKA PRODUCTIONS, LTD., M. M. UL. Zwyciezcow 8ml. 03-941 Warszawa, Poland. (22)17-59-63. Contact Person: Andrzej Gutowski, vice-president, producer. Founded: 1989.

Subjects of Interest. Ethnic focus—European themes with an international appeal to audiences. Script genres—romantic adventure; epic; character-driven; psychological thriller; mystery; period pieces; documentary; docudrama; fantasy. Recent film projects: *A Very Polish Practice* (TV project for the BBC; satire on Polish daily life). Do not want: fantasy stories dealing with themes commonly dealt with in Hollywood; James Camoran style scripts; teen-oriented films.

Initial Contact. Query letter with treatment. Release form required: no. SASE required.

Acceptance Policies. Unagented manuscripts: yes. Simultaneous submissions: yes. Response time to initial inquiry: 2-4 weeks. Response time to option script: n/i. **Option amount:** n/i. Production rights purchased: n/i.

Additional Information. We are a production company. We work mainly on scripts that have full or partial backing. Tips: Polish and English language scripts preferred.

PRODUCER AND MANAGEMENT ENTERTAINMENT GROUP. 6255 Sunset Blvd., 20th Floor. Hollywood, CA 90028. (213) 466-5318. Fax: (213) 466-1892. Contact Person: Michael Flint. Founded: 1991.

Subjects of Interest. Ethnic focus—all groups. **Script genres**—action-adventure; karate movies; love stories; everything uplifting. Recent film projects: n/i. Ethnic projects in development: yes. Do not want: Westerns; documentaries; docudramas.

Initial Contact. Query letter with treatment. Include past credits and resumé. Release form required: n/i. SASE required.

Acceptance Policies. Unagented manuscripts: yes. Simultaneous submissions: yes. Response time to initial inquiry: 1 week. Response time to option script: 1 month. **Option amount:** none, but a fair deal if the movie gets made. Production rights purchased: all.

Additional Information. Michael Fleet spent five years as head of story department at Paramount; Neville Johnson, president of the company, has been an entertainment attorney for 16 years. We are interested in low budget ($1-$3 million) features. Tips: We want to appeal to wide audiences. We want to make the ethnic Frank Capra or Alfred Hitchcock movie. Obviously, we expect good writing and dialogue.

RAINBOW RIDGE FILMS. Lantana 3000. 3000 Olympic Blvd., #1425. Santa Monica, CA 90404. (213) 315-4712. Contact Persons: Michael Barclay, president; Tex Rudloff, vice-president of production; Al Gomez, vice-president development. Founded: 1989.

Subjects of Interest. Ethnic focus—Hispanics; Chicanos; Native Americans; South American Indians; Afro-Americans. **Script genres**—all. Recent ethnic film projects in development: *Teachings of the Grandfathers; Song of the Deer.*

Initial Contact. Query letter only or query letter with treatment. Release form required: n/i. SASE required.

Acceptance Policies. Unagented manuscripts: yes. Simultaneous submissions: yes. Response time to initial inquiry: 1-2 weeks. Response time to option script: 3-6 weeks. **Option amount:** to be discussed in person or on phone. Production rights purchased: all.

SPANISH TRAIL PRODUCTIONS. 100 Universal City Plaza. Universal City, CA 91608. Contact Person: Paul Little. Founded: 1989.

Subjects of Interest. Ethnic focus—n/i. **Script genres**—n/i. Recent TV and cable projects: n/i. Ethnic projects in development: yes.

Initial Contact. Through agent only. Release form required: no. SASE not required.

Acceptance Policies. Unagented manuscripts: no. Simultaneous submissions: yes. Response time to initial inquiry: 2 weeks. Response time to option script: varies. **Option amount:** varies; based on writer's credits, projected market, material, potential budget. Production rights purchased: all.

Additional Information. We are primarily a TV and cable production company looking for series and MOW scripts and stories. Tips: Material must be submitted through an agent.

TFG ENTERTAINMENT. c/o Warner Hollywood Studios. 1041 N. Formosa Blvd. West Hollywood, CA 90046. (213) 850-2633. Contact Person: address to producer or development executive. Founded: 1990.

Subjects of Interest. **Ethnic focus**—Afro-Americans; Chicanos; Cubans; South Americans. **Script genres**—romantic adventure; character-driven; psychological thriller, mystery. Recent film or TV projects: *Hotel California* (in development). Ethnic projects in development: yes. Do not want: horror; exploitation.

Initial Contact. Query letter with treatment. Entire script only through an agent. Include credits and bio. Release form required: n/i. SASE required.

Acceptance Policies. Unagented manuscripts: yes. Simultaneous submissions: n/i. Response time to initial inquiry: 2 weeks. Response time to option script: varies. **Option amount:** varies. Production rights purchased: all.

WYNTER FILMS. 1734 Taft Ave., #2. Los Angeles, CA 90028. (213) 466-6038. Contact Person: Diane Wynter. Founded: 1989.

Subjects of Interest. **Ethnic focus**—women's films by minority women writers with ethnic focus on Afro-Americans, West Africans, Hispanics, Native Americans, West Indians, Soviets. **Script genres**—stories by and about women; stories that uplift and present positive role models for all ages; romantic adventure; character-driven; psychological thriller; docudrama; children's; coming-of-age. Recent film projects: *Vows* (production of the American Film Institute, directed by Diane Wynter). Ethnic projects in development: teenage black over-achiever battling the New York school system. Do not want: gratuitous violence; negative minority images; negative portrayal of women.

Initial Contact. Entire script through agent only. If unrepresented send query letter with treatment. Release form required: n/i. SASE required.

Acceptance Policies. Unagented manuscripts: yes. Simultaneous submissions: yes. Response time to initial inquiry: 6-8 weeks. Response time to option script: 12 weeks. **Option amount:** n/i. Production rights purchased: all.

Protection, Trademarks, and ISBNs

How Do You Protect Your Work?

Copyright law in the United States changed significantly when the Copyright Act of 1976 took effect on January 1, 1978. For works copyrighted prior to 1978, the previous law still applies, except that the renewal term is now 47 rather than 28 years. For more information on early copyrights, write to the Copyright Office and request circulars R15a and R15t.

Works created in 1978 or after are automatically protected by copyright from the moment of creation (as soon as they are "fixed in tangible form"). Copyright ordinarily lasts for the author's life plus 50 years (or in the case of multiple authors of the same work, 50 years after the death of the last surviving author).

You need take no action to copyright your work other than to put it in written form, whether that form is printed or stored on electronic media. However, including a notice of copyright on the first or title page of documents is common practice. Notice serves as a clear statement that the work is not in the public domain (available for any use, reproduction, etc.) and is protected under the Copyright Act of 1976, not under the previous law that required either publication or registration. Notice also has relevance for international copyright law.

Copyright gives you, the author or creator, the exclusive right to do, or to authorize others to do, the following:
- Reproduce the work
- Prepare derivative works based on the content or characters of the original work

- Distribute the work for public sale, rent or lease copyright for the term of publication, or transfer specific rights (as to magazine publishers)
- Perform the work, as with music, drama, motion pictures, etc.
- Display the work in the case of visual art

No one else has the right to do any of these things without your express written permission or your agreed-upon transfer of specific rights.

In order to claim copyright, you need only be the original creator. Your notice of copyright should contain all of the following elements:
- The symbol © or the word "Copyright" or the abbreviation "Copr."
- The year of first publication or creation in tangible form
- The name of the owner of the copyright, for example: "Copyright 1991 by Jane Buck" or "© 1991 John Doe"

Material you cannot copyright includes works that have not been fixed in tangible form, such as improvised speeches; titles, names, short phrases, slogans, familiar symbols or designs, ornamentation or lettering, or listings of ingredients or contents; ideas, procedures, methods, systems, processes, concepts, principles, discoveries, or devices as distinguished from a description, explanation, or illustration; and works consisting entirely of information that is common property, such as calendars, height and weight charts, etc.

You can register your copyright by requesting the proper form from the Copyright Office (TX for manuscripts), completing the form, and returning it with the required payment ($20 in 1991). Registration offers these advantages:
- Establishes a public record of the copyright claim
- Is usually necessary before infringement suits can be filed in court
- Gives the copyright owner certain legal advantages in court regarding presentation of evidence and the extent of damages the court will award

Copyright forms are available from the Copyright Office at no charge; write to Copyright Office, Library of Congress, Washington, DC 20559, or call (202) 707-9100. You may duplicate forms, but the photocopy must be identical to the original.

For a copy of the actual copyright law, send $3.75 to the Superintendent of Documents, U.S. Government Printing Office, Washington, DC 20401-9371, or contact your nearest government printing office and request Copyright Office Circular 92, stock number 030-002-00168-3.

What Are Trademarks and How Are They Used?

Trademarks are not copyrights. Rather, they are a separate means of protecting business or product names, titles, logos, symbols, or designs. Most companies are diligent about protecting their trademarks because once allowed to enter common usage, trademarks become generic and are no longer protected as the sole property of a company. Thus the term escalator, once a brand name for a moving staircase, is now part of our everyday language.

To exercise your responsibility as a writer, you should be aware of trademarks and the rules that govern their use. They should be used only as adjectives, be capitalized, and be followed by the appropriate generic noun, as in Kleenex tissues.

In nonfiction articles that discuss specific products, this requirement generally poses no problem. But in fiction, when characters stop off for a couple of Cokes, writing that "Bill and Ted bought Coca-Cola soft drinks at the corner store" calls too much attention to a minor action. For fiction, the terminology is too self-conscious.

In nonfiction written for national publications, you would be wise to follow the letter of the law. For fiction, where trademark references are much less common, strict adherence may not be as important, though technically you can still be asked by a company to either use the proper form or not mention their product. At the very least, however, trademark names must always be capitalized.

For more information or a list of common trademarks, write the U. S. Trademark Association, 6 East 45th Street, New York, NY 10017, or call (212) 986-5880.

What Is an ISBN?

The ISBN number is a worldwide identification code that distinguishes different works of like titles and facilitates book ordering. The system is administered by R. R. Bowker for the International Standard Book Numbering Agency. Published books are assigned numbers by the agency or, in most instances, by the publisher from a series of numbers assigned to that publisher by the ISBN Agency.

If you are a self-publisher, you will need to apply for your own ISBN number. If you intend to publish more than one book, you should apply for more than one number, as receipt of your designated numbers is often a drawn-out process, and the part of the number that designates the publisher will change with each new issue.

For information or to apply, write to the ISBN Agency (U. S.), 121 Chanlon Road, New Providence, NJ 07974, or call (908) 665-6770.

A Writer's Glossary

Advance. Your payment from the publisher prior to the publication of your book. The amount is then deducted from your royalties.

All rights. Magazines that purchase all rights to your material own the right to publish it wherever and whenever they choose without additional payment to you. Also, you lose the right to sell reprint rights to another publication. Book publishers that negiotiate all rights do so as a function of your contract, which spells out how or what you will be paid for each separate right. (*See also* **subsidiary rights.**)

Anthology. A collection of writings, usually by more than one author, published in a single book. Anthology rights are different from first time or one-time rights and should be negotiated separately.

ASCII. A way of storing a computer file without formatting so that it can be read by most word-processing programs.

Assignment. When an editor asks you to write an article for which you will be paid upon completion. Acceptance of the finished piece is implied in the request.

Avant-garde. An article or story with nontraditional ideas and often written in an unusual format.

Backlist. A list of the publisher's books that were not published during the current season, but which are still in print.

Bio. A short biography of those details of your life and experience directly related to your credibility as an author in your specific field.

Byline. The credit that lists you by name as the author with your published work.

Chapbook. A short collection of poetry or stories published in a very small edition.

Children's. Writing for children ages 2 through 12. Often called juvenile literature.

Clips. Copies from newspapers or magazines of your previously published works. Clips are often requested by editors as examples of your writing.

Compatible. Refers to different computers that can read the same computer disk.

Co-publishing. An agreement between publisher and author to split the costs of publication, often resulting in a higher author's royalty. Also known as cooperative publishing and sometimes employed by universities and well-established presses that obtain funds from sources other than the author. Do not confuse co-publishing with vanity or subsidy publishing. Read your contract carefully.

Copyright. A legal protection of your work. (For more information, see the section on "Protection, Trademarks, and ISBNs.")

Cover letter. Rarely sent with a proposal and not to be confused with a query, this letter can accompany a submission and be a response to an editor's questions or a brief communication of material you want the editor to know.

Cover price. The retail price of your published book. Cover price may be used as the basis for determining your royalty.

Disk. A flat, magnetic recording surface used to store computer data.

Feature. The lead article in a magazine, a special department at the magazine.

Filler. Short and often amusing or intriguing items used in newspapers and magazines to finish out a column or page.

First run. The number of book copies first printed by a publisher, before any reprintings are done.

First North American serial rights. The right to first publication of material in a periodical in the United States and Canada.

Freelance submissions. Manuscripts submitted by writers who are not on the staff of a publication and who, as independents, manage their own work and submit to a variety of markets.

Genre. In commercial fiction, the specific categories of writing, such as mysteries, romances, or Westerns. In scholarly terms, genre can mean types of writing, such as poetry or essays.

Hard copy. Printed copy as opposed to a computer file.

Honorarium. A small amount of money offered as payment.

Illustrations. Drawings, lithographs, or visual art forms, but not photographs.

Imprint. A division within a publishing house which publishes a special category of books and is named differently than the parent company.

IRC. Coupons you enclose with work sent to publishers outside the United States and its territories to be used as postage for the return your material. IRC coupons can be purchased at U. S. post offices.

Juvenile *see* **children's.**

Kill fee. A portion of the total payment for an assigned article that is paid to you in lieu of full payment when the editor decides not to run your article. To insure payment, you must have the kill fee included in your contract or specified in writing.

Literary fiction. Relies more on stylistic elements, details of character and atmosphere, and character's thoughts than on physical action. Often experimental in style and subject.

Literary agent. A person who represents you, the author, in finding a publisher or arranging contract terms on a literary project.

Mainstream fiction. A more in-depth treatment of characters, situations, and plots than the genre novel, or a book promoted as a potential best-seller by a publisher's marketing campaign.

Manuscript. Your unpublished, written work.

Mass market paperback. A paperback book on a popular subject, published with a cover designed to attract the "impulse" buyer at the drugstore, market, or bookstore.

Midlist. Books that the publisher decides to bring out but does not heavily promote. These books are not expected to be best sellers but are often thought to have some literary or educational value. Not a good situation for an author.

Model release. Written permission given to a photographer to use a picture of you for a specific stated purpose or purposes. A guardian must sign for a minor child.

Multiple submissions. Copies of the same manuscript that you send to several publishers for consideration at the same time.

Net receipts. Money the publisher receives from sales of your book. An important part of negotiating your contract is the basis upon which royalties are paid. Payment used to be based on a percentage of the cover price. More common now is a royalty based on the amount of money a book publisher receives from the wholesale price of the book, often after all promotional and incidental expenses are deducted.

Novella or novelette. A short novel or long story of about 7000 to 15,000 words.

On spec *see* **speculation or spec.**

One-time rights. Gives the publisher permission to publish your story or book one time only. All other rights remain with you, the author.

Outline. A general summary of your project broken down into major headings and subheadings (or chapter headings) and often included with your book proposal or sent with your query to magazines or newspapers.

Page rate. Rather than pay by the inch or by the word, many magazine publishers pay by the published page; the term does not refer to manuscript pages.

Payment on acceptance. The editor reads your article, decides to publish it, and sends you a check along with (or soon after) notification of your article's acceptance; the preferred method for writers.

Payment on publication. The editor reads your article, accepts it for publication, publishes it, and then sends your check, often weeks or months later. If a publisher pays on publication, try to negotiate for a kill fee should the publisher later decide not to publish your article.

Photo feature. A piece that focuses on beautiful, interesting, or compelling photos. Written text supports the photos.

Periodical. A publication, not including newspapers, produced in serial issues at regular or stated intervals with the intent of continued publication.

Proposal. The sales tool you send to book publishers to convince them to accept your nonfiction manuscript. Often includes a query, outline, information on the intended audience, and bio. Several good books discuss how to assemble a proposal.

Query. A letter to an editor meant to raise interest in a work you propose to write.

Reprint rights. Permission to publish material that has already been published in another periodical or book. You retain this right only if you have not sold all rights or produced a work-for-hire. When offering reprint rights to publishers, always inform them where and when the material was originally published.

Royalties. A negotiated amount of money paid to you, the author, by the publisher. The royalty can be figured on the cover price or the publisher's net receipts. (*See also* **cover price** and **net receipts.**)

SASE. Self-addressed stamped envelope. Include one with your query or proposal.

Second serial rights. Permission for a periodical to reprint your work after it has been previously published in another magazine. *See also* **reprint rights.**

Sidebar. A short piece that complements or expands a feature article.

Simultaneous submissions. Sending the same manuscript or article to several publishers at the same time. Inform publishers in your query letter to avoid problems should more than one accept your material. *See also* **multiple submissions.**

Slant. The approach, angle, tone, or point of view you use in writing an article.

Speculation or spec. The condition when you agree to write an article with no promise from the editor that it will be accepted when it is finished.

Subsidiary rights. Rights granted to the publisher by your contract, allowing the publisher to sell your manuscript anywhere and in any form, including for serial (periodical) publication, book clubs, anthologies, and radio, television, and video reproduction. Negotiate these rights carefully.

Subsidy publishing. You pay a company the full costs of publishing your book, and then you receive 40 percent of the retail price of the books sold and 80 percent of subsidiary rights, if sold. Also known as vanity publishing, these presses often have poor reputations for editing, production, and promotion.

Syndication rights. A story, article, or column series sold to a business service that makes a wide variety of features available to many publications.

Synopsis. A narrative summary of your fiction manuscript that includes major plot points and dramatic scenes and is from one to fifteen pages long, depending on the length of the manuscript.

Trade. A book, often in paperback, on a general-interest subject directed toward a general rather than a professional audience and sold primarily in bookstores.

Transparencies. Positive color slides; not color prints.

Unsolicited manuscript. A manuscript you send to a publisher without its being requested. In many cases, unsolicited submissions are returned unopened or thrown out. Send a query or proposal first.

Work-for-hire. Work you do for a company or publisher as part of your employment, whether in a permanent or contract (temporary) position. You are paid for your writing, and the company owns the copyright and other rights. Specific legal conditions govern determination of a work-for-hire.

Writer's guidelines. The publisher's instructions on what subjects, forms, lengths, etc., are appropriate for the material you submit. Send for guidelines whenever they are available.

Young adult (YA). Books written for readers ages 12 through 18.

Multicultural Resources

This list is by no means exhaustive. Comprehensive information on multicultural resources is available in various resources, including *Guide to Multicultural Resources*, published by Praxis Publications, P.O. Box 9869, Madison, WI 53715.

Multicultural Publishers Exchange
P.O. Box 9869
Madison, WI 53715
(608) 244-5633
Contact: Charles Taylor, Editor

The Association of American Cultures
1225 19th Street, NW, Ste. 340
Washington, DC 20036-2411
(202) 463-8222
Contact: Victoria Sharpley, Executive Director

Center for Studies of Ethnicity and Race in America
University of Colorado
SERA Campus Box 339
Boulder, CO 80309
(303) 494-8852
Contact: Dr. Evelyn Hu-Dehart, Director

Afro-American

Afro-American Resource Center
P.O. Box 746
Howard University
Washington, DC 20059
(202) 636-7242
Contact: E. Ethelbert Miller

Black Think Tank
1801 Bush Street, #127
San Francisco, CA 94109
(415) 474-1707
Contact: Julia Hare, Ed.D.

Center for Afro-American Studies
University of California at Los Angeles
405 Hilgard Avenue, 160 Haines Hall
Los Angeles, CA 90024-1545
(213) 825-7403, 825-7404
Contact: Toyomi Igus, Senior Editor

International Black Writers Conference
P.O. Box 1030
Chicago, IL 60690
(312) 924-3818
Contact: Mable Terrell

NAACP (National Headquarters)
1397 Fulton Street
Brooklyn Heights, NY 11201
(718) 789-3043
Contact: Benjamin Hooks

Western States Black Research Center
2617 Montclair Street
Los Angeles, CA 90018
(213) 737-3292
Contact: Dr. Mayme Clayton

Asian-American Resources

Asian American Legal Defense and Education Fund
99 Hudson Street, 12th Floor
New York, NY 10013
(212) 966-5932
Contact: Margaret Fung, Executive Editor

Asian American Studies Library
University of California at Berkeley
3407 Dwinelle
Berkeley, CA 94720
(415) 642-2218
Contact: Wei Chi Poon, Head Librarian

Chinese Historical Society of America
650 Commercial Street
San Francisco, CA 94111
(415) 391-1188
Contact: Philip Choy, President

Department of Asian and Asian-American Studies
California State University at Long Beach
1250 Bellflower Blvd.
Long Beach, CA 90840
(213) 985-5493
Contact: Dr. San-pao Li

Independent Scholars of Asia
2321 Russell, #3A
Berkeley, CA 94705
(415) 849-3791
Contact: Ruth-Inge Heinze, Ph.D.

New York Chinatown History Project
70 Mulberry Street, 2nd Floor
New York, NY 10013
(212) 619-4785
Contact: Fau Chuw Matsuda, Executive Director

Hispanic-American Resources

Center for Inter-American and Border Studies
University of Texas at El Paso
El Paso, TX 79968-0605
(915) 747-5000
Contact: Dr. Richard Bath, Director

Mexican-American Cultural Center
P.O. Box 28185
San Antonio, TX 78228
(512) 732-2156
Contact: Rosendo Urrabazo, C.M.S.

Mexican American Commission
Box 94965 - State Capitol
Lincoln, NE 68509
(402)471-2791
Contact: Jake Gonzales, Jr.

Pan American Development Foundation
1889 F. Street, NW
Washington, DC 20006
(202) 458-3972
Contact: Jeanine Hess, Public Relations

The Puerto Rican Legal Defense and Education Fund, Inc.
99 Hudson Street
New York, NY 10013
(212) 219-3360
Contact: Ruben Franco, Director

Native American

American Indian Inter-Tribal Cultural Organization
Twinbrook Station, Box 775
Rockville, MD 20851
(202) 662-5764
Contact: Katherine Frick

Cherokee National Historical Society
P.O. Box 515
Tahlequah, OK 74465
(918) 456-6007
Contact: Myrna Moss

Indian Law Resource Center
601 E. Street, SE
Washington, DC 20003
(202) 547-2800
Contact: Curtis Burkey, Director

Iroquois Indian Museum
Box 158
Schoharie, NY 12157
(518) 295-8553
Contact: Director

Native American Research Information Service
555 Constitution Avenue
Norman, OK 73037
Contact: Dr. Duane Hale

R.A.I.N. for all Indigenous Nations, Inc.
RD 1, Box 308A
Petersburg, NY
(518) 658-3055
Contact: Hank Hazelton

Books for Writers

Most of the following writing- and publishing-related books are available from the Writers Connection bookstore. Those not sold through Writers Connection are marked with an asterisk (*). Inquire at your local bookstore or check your library for copies or information. Writers Connection members are entitled to a 15% discount off the retail prices of books ordered from our bookstore. Availability and prices are subject to change; call (408) 973-0227 for current information. To order by mail, use the order form on page 259.

Fiction

CREATING UNFORGETTABLE CHARACTERS
Linda Seger
Invaluable character techniques for all fiction writers, from scripts to novels. 1990.
F46—$12.95

FICTION WRITER'S RESEARCH HANDBOOK, THE
Mona McCormick
How to locate historical data using various sources. 1988.
F44—$9.95

HOW TO CREATE LIVING CHARACTERS (booklet)
Phyllis Taylor Pianka
A handbook of methods for drawing believable characters. 1983.
F31—$2.35

HOW TO WRITE A DAMN GOOD NOVEL
James N. Frey
A step-by-step no-nonsense guide to dramatic storytelling. 1987.
F32—$14.95

HOW TO WRITE A SYNOPSIS (booklet)
Phyllis Taylor Pianka
A guide to writing the all-important novel synopsis. 1990.
F11—$2.35

HOW TO WRITE DYNAMIC DIALOGUE (booklet)
Phyllis Taylor Pianka
Ways to use believable dialogue to improve your writing. 1990.
F15—$2.35

HOW TO WRITE ROMANCES
Phyllis Taylor Pianka
Everything you need to know about writing and selling the romance novel, including a sample query and synopsis. 1988.
F33—$13.95

HOW TO WRITE TALES OF HORROR, FANTASY & SCIENCE FICTION
J. N. Williamson
How-to essays from 26 top speculative fiction writers. 1987. Now in paperback.
F16—$12.95

MYSTERY WRITER'S HANDBOOK
Mystery Writers of America, revised edition
Top mystery writers share tricks of the trade. 1982.
F17—$11.95

PLOTTING THE NOVEL (booklet)
Phyllis Taylor Pianka
Plot patterns; the seven elements of plot and how to use them. 1990.
F20—$2.35

WRITING THE MODERN MYSTERY
Barbara Norville
How to research, plot, write, and sell a modern mystery. 1986.
F29—$15.95

WRITING THE NOVEL FROM PLOT TO PRINT
Lawrence Block
Every step is fully described. 1985.
F30—$10.95

Nonfiction

FREELANCE INTERVIEW TIPS AND TRICKS (booklet)
Pat Kite
Techniques for landing the interview and methods for putting the interviewee at ease for best results. 1991.
NF6—$3.25

HOW TO SELL 75% OF YOUR FREELANCE WRITING
Gordon Burgett
The best book on marketing. 1990.
NF10—$12.95

HOW TO WRITE A BOOK PROPOSAL
Michael Larsen
A step-by-step guide by a leading literary agent. 1990.
NF11—$10.95

HOW TO WRITE A QUERY (booklet)
Phyllis Taylor Pianka
A guide to writing queries and proposals for articles and books. 1990.
NF12—$2.35

HOW TO WRITE THE STORY OF YOUR LIFE
Frank Thomas
A step-by-step guide to recording your life; 500 "memory sparkers" and 100 topic ideas. 1989.
NF39—$11.95

QUERY LETTERS/COVER LETTERS
Gordon Burgett
How to write the most compelling queries, cover letters. 1986.
NF24—$9.95

SYNDICATING YOUR COLUMN (booklet)
Pat Kite
Tips and directions for getting columns syndicated into weekly or daily newspapers. 1987.
NF33—$5.00

THE TRAVEL WRITER'S GUIDE
Gordon Burgett
Comprehensive compilation of travel writing tips, facts, and techniques. 1991.
NF48—$14.95

WRITING FAST, FUN MONEY FILLERS (booklet)
Pat Kite
How to make money on short paragraphs. 1988.
NF30—$3.25

Desktop/Publishing

DESKTOP PUBLISHER'S LEGAL HANDBOOK, THE
Daniel Sitarz
How to make best use of your rights as a publisher and avoid infringing rights of others. 1989.
DP15—$19.95.

HOW TO GET AN AGENT (booklet)
Phyllis Taylor Pianka
How to select and work with an agent. 1990.
DP11—$2.35

HOW TO SELF-PROMOTE YOUR BOOK (booklet)
Kite/Nelson
Tips on self-publicizing for new authors. 1989.
DP7—$3.55

LITERARY AGENTS
Debby Mayer
A writer's guide; includes interviews with well-known agents. 1983.
DP9—$6.95

SELF-PUBLISHING MANUAL, THE
Dan Poynter
New, revised edition of a complete guide to the self-publishing process. 1991.
DP13—$19.95

Specialized Markets

CHILDREN'S PICTURE BOOK, THE
Ellen Roberts
How to write it; how to sell it. 1986.
SM12—$18.95

CHILDREN'S WRITER'S & ILLUSTRATOR'S MARKET
Lisa Carpenter
Constructing a story, handling illustration, and getting published. Updated annually.
SM9—$16.95

HOW TO WRITE AND ILLUSTRATE CHILDREN'S BOOKS
Bicknell/Trotman
Covers constructing a story, illustrating, and getting published. 1991.
SM10—$22.50

HUMOR AND CARTOON MARKETS
Edited by Bob Staake
Over 500 listings of magazines, newsletters, greeting card companies, comic book publishers, advertising agencies, and syndicates for humor writers and illustrators. Updated annually.
SM1—$16.95

INTRODUCTION TO CHRISTIAN WRITING, AN
Ethel Herr
Effective techniques and marketing strategies for Christian writers. 1988.
SM6—$8.95

NONFICTION FOR CHILDREN
Ellen Roberts
How to create and sell "real-world" subjects to children from preschoolers to teenagers. 1986.
SM13—$16.95

WRITING FOR THE EDUCATIONAL MARKET
Barbara Gregorich
A complete resource manual for writing/publishing in the various educational applications. 1990.
SM18—$13.95

WRITING FOR THE ETHNIC MARKETS
Meera Lester
Provides writing tips, marketing strategies, and listings of book and magazine publishers and film and TV companies that buy ethnic material. 1991.
SM19—$14.95

WRITING TO INSPIRE
Gentz/Roddy
A quide to writing and publishing for the expanding religious market. 1987.
SM5—$14.95

WRITING YOUNG ADULT NOVELS
Irwin/Eyerly
How to write the stories today's teens want to read. 1988.
SM11—$14.95

Scriptwriting

HOW TO SELL YOUR SCREENPLAY
Carl Sautter
Comprehensive explanation from a seasoned professional of how to sell your screenplay. 1988.
SC18—$22.95

HOW TO WRITE FOR TELEVISION
Madeline DiMaggio
Tips and techniques from a successful scriptwriter. 1990.
SC23—$10.95

MAKING A GOOD SCRIPT GREAT
Linda Seger
How to get a script back on track and preserve the original creativity; a guide for writing and rewriting. 1987.
SC8—$11.95

PRACTICAL SCREENWRITING HANDBOOK
Michael McCarthy
Light but thorough "how-to" guide for motion pictures and feature films, from title page to "the end." 1980.
SC2—$12.95

SCREENPLAY
Syd Field
The foundations of screenwriting; a step-by-step guide from concept to finished script. 1984.
SC9—$9.95

SCREENWRITER'S WORKBOOK, THE
Syd Field
Exercises and step-by-step instruction for creating a successful screenplay; a workshop approach. 1984.
SC10—$9.95

Resource/Reference

AMERICAN SLANG *
Robert L. Chappman, Ph.D., ed.
Dictionary of slang words and phrases with meanings, examples, dates, and origins. 1987.
Check local bookstores. Published by Harper and Row, New York.

ASSOCIATED PRESS STYLEBOOK AND LIBEL MANUAL
Addison-Wesley
Authoritative word on rules of grammar, punctuation, and the general meaning and usage of over 3,000 terms; insight into journalistic techniques. 1987.
RR1—$10.95

CALIFORNIA AND HAWAII PUBLISHING MARKETPLACE
Writers Connection
Comprehensive directory of publishers, magazines, agents, newspapers, organizations, and conferences. 1990.
RR48—$16.95

CHICAGO MANUAL OF STYLE
University of Chicago Press
A comprehensive, authoritative guide to journalistic and reference techniques. 1982.
RR41—$37.50

COPYEDITING, A PRACTICAL GUIDE
Karen Judd
A comprehensive field guide to copyediting, publishing. 1990.
RR23—$19.95

DIRECTORY OF POETRY PUBLISHERS *
Len Fulton, ed.
Over 2000 poetry markets with indexes. Updated annually.
Available from Dustbooks, PO Box 100, Paradise, CA 95967.

EDITING YOUR NEWSLETTER
Mark Beach
A complete guide to writing and producing a successful newsletter—on schedule and within budget. 1988.
RF.2—$18.50

FINDING FACTS FAST
Alden Todd
Comprehensive research techniques to save you hours; a gold mine of information sources and research techniques. 1979.
RR40—$5.95

GET IT ALL DONE AND STILL BE HUMAN
Tony and Robbie Fanning
New revised edition of time management strategies for writers and others. 1990.
RR24—$9.95

GRANTS AND AWARDS *
PEN American Center
A directory listing of grants and prizes available to American writers. 1990/91.
Available from PEN American Center, 568 Broadway, New York, NY 10012.

HOW TO BULLET-PROOF YOUR MANUSCRIPT
Bruce Henderson
How to check manuscripts for potential libel and other legal problems. 1986.
RR20—$9.95

HOW TO WRITE WITH A COLLABORATOR
Hal Z. Bennett
How to team up with another writer, an expert, or a celebrity to co-author books, articles, and short stories. 1988.
RR3—$11.95

INTERNATIONAL DIRECTORY OF LITTLE MAGAZINES & SMALL PRESSES *
Len Fulton, ed.
A standard worldwide publishing and market reference for writers. Updated biannually.
Available from Dustbooks, PO Box 100, Paradise, CA 95967.

JUST OPEN A VEIN
William Brohaugh
A collection of essays by writers, for writers. 1987.
RR6—$15.95

LITERARY AGENTS OF NORTH AMERICA *
Author Aid/Research Associates International
Comprehensive five-index listing of agencies, contacts, and commission rates, plus profiles of agency heads, number of clients, and fee schedules. Updated annually.
Contact AA/RAI, 340 East 52nd Street, New York, NY 10022; or call 1-212-758-4213.

LITERARY MARKET PLACE (LMP) *
R.R.Bowker
The most widely used national directory of book publishers, editorial services, and agents, with complete reference book listing. Updated annually.
Available at most public libraries, or contact R.R. Bowker, 1-800-521-8110.

MENTOR GUIDE TO PUNCTUATION, THE
William C. Paxson
Quick and easy answers to punctuation problems. Organized for easy access. 1986.
RR9—$4.95

NORTHWEST PUBLISHING MARKETPLACE
Writers Connection
Comprehensive directory of writers' markets and more for Alaska, Idaho, Montana, Oregon, Washington, and Wyoming. 1991.
RR50—$14.95

NOVEL & SHORT STORY WRITER'S MARKET
Robin Gee
Marketing information on fiction publishers with interviews of fiction writers, publishers, and editors. Updated annually.
RR15—$19.95

PROFESSIONAL WRITERS GUIDE, THE
Bower/Young
An indispensable, comprehensive guide on all aspects of the writing business. 1990.
RR47—$16.95

REWRITE RIGHT!
Jan Venolia
Most writing can be improved by the simple process of reviewing and rewriting. 1987.
RR5—$6.95

SOUTHWEST PUBLISHING MARKETPLACE
Writers Connection
Comprehensive directory of writers' markets and more for Arizona, Colorado, Nevada, New Mexico, Texas, and Utah. 1990.
RR49—$14.95

12 KEYS TO WRITING BOOKS THAT SELL
Kathleen Krull
Develop a more professional attitude toward writing and marketing your book. 1989.
RR25—$12.95

WRITE RIGHT!
Jan Venolia
The best summary of grammar available for writers. 1988.
RR32—$5.95

WRITER'S DIGEST GUIDE TO MANUSCRIPT FORMATS, THE
Writer's Digest
Illustrated, easy-to-follow guide to all types of manuscript formats, including books, articles, poems, and plays. 1987.
RR44—$17.95

WRITER'S GUIDE TO COPYRIGHT, A
Poets & Writers
A summary of the current copyright law for writers, editors, and teachers. 1990.
RR29—$6.95

WRITER'S HANDBOOK, THE *
Sylvia K. Burack, ed.
Essentials and techniques from many successful writers, plus listings of markets for manuscripts. Updated annually.
Check local bookstores or contact The Writer, Inc., 120 Boylston Street, Boston, MA 02116.

WRITER'S LEGAL COMPANION, THE
Brad Bunnin
How to deal successfully with copyrights, contracts, libel, taxes, agents, publishers, legal relationships, and marketing strategies. 1988.
RR8—$14.95

WRITER'S MARKET
Writer's Digest
Where and how to sell what you write; thousands of markets for fiction and nonfiction articles, books, plays, scripts, short stories, and more. Updated annually. 1991.
RR25—$25.95

WRITING AFTER FIFTY
Leonard L. Knott
How to start a writing career after you retire. 1985.
RR37—$12.95

WRITING DOWN THE BONES
Natalie Goldberg
Guidelines for freeing the writer within. 1986.
RR38—$9.95

YEARBOOK OF EXPERTS, AUTHORITIES, & SPOKESPERSONS, THE *
Mitchell P. Davis, ed.
An encyclopedia of ads and listings of sources for interviews, programs, etc., with index by subject or topic. Updated annually.
Available from Broadcast Interview Source, 2233 Wisconsin Avenue, NW, Washington, DC 20007, (202) 333-4904.

Book Subject Index

This index is alphabetized using the letter-by-letter system and is divided into two sections: fiction and nonfiction.

When indicating fiction and nonfiction index topics, some publishers selected more subjects that were named in their initial list of interests. Additional topics may indicate future interests or identify subcategories with the publication's basic focus, such as folklore in Native American books or children's books for a publisher of multicultural materials.

Publishers indicating an interest in almost all fiction or nonfiction categories are listed under General Interest in the index.

Because this is an ethnic book, all entries accept ethnic material. Publishers who indicated they accept material from and for all ethnic cultures are listed under the subheading All Groups in the index heading Ethnic/Cultural Focus. Other publishers have their ethnic interests listed under the particular group(s) under the subheading Specific Groups.

Fiction

Adventure
Avon Books 63
Crumb Elbow Publishing 73
Jordan Enterprises 85
Pelican Publishing Company, Inc. 94
Philomel Books (children's) 95
Scholastic, Inc. 97
Third World Press (Afro-American) 101

Avant-Garde
Calyx Books 67
Crumb Elbow Publishing 73
Esoterica Press 76
Third World Press (Afro-American) 101
York Press, Ltd. 108

Children's/Young Adult
Aegina Press, Inc. 59
African American Images 60
Associated Publishers, Inc., The 62
Avon Books 63
Beacon Press 63
Carolrhoda Books, Inc. 68
China Books 70
Chronicle Books 70
Crumb Elbow Publishing 73
Dial Books for Young Readers 74

Esoterica Press 76
Farrar, Straus & Giroux, Inc. 77
Folklore Institute (Indians from India) 77
Herald Press (Mennonite, Amish) 80
Holiday House 81
Jordan Enterprises 85
Kar-Ben Copies, Inc. (Jewish) 86
Lions Books Publisher (YA) 87
Little, Brown and Company 87
Lodestar Books 88
New Day Press, Inc. (Afro-American) 91
Open Hand Publishing, Inc. (Afro-American) 93
Pelican Publishing Company, Inc. 94
New Day Press, Inc. (Afro-American) 91
Press of MacDonald & Reinecke, The 95
Scholastic, Inc. 97
Seal Press 97
Third World Press (Afro-American) 101
Volcano Press, Inc. 105
Walker and Company 106
Winston-Derek Publishers, Inc. (Afro-American 107
Women's Studies Quarterly, A Journal 108

Contemporary/Modern
Avon Books 63
Bear Flag Books (California) 64
Bilingual Press/Editorial Bilingue
  (Hispanic) 65
Calyx Books 67
Eastern Caribbean Institute 75
Italica Press 85
Jordan Enterprises 85
Scholastic, Inc. (children's/YA) 97
Soho Press, Inc. 98
Third World Press
  (Afro-American) 101
Véhicule Press 105
Winston-Derek Publishers, Inc.
  (Afro-American) 107
Wyrick and Company 108
York Press, Ltd. 108
Zephyr Press 109

Erotica
Esoterica Press 76
Orient Paperbacks (Indians from
  India) 94
Zephyr Press 109

Ethnic/Cultural Focus
All Ethnic Groups
Aegina Press, Inc. 59
Avalon Books 62
Avon Books 63
Calyx Books 67
Carolrhoda Books, Inc. 68
Chronicle Books (children's) 70
Crumb Elbow Publishing 73
Harlequin Enterprises, Ltd. 79
Heyday Press (California) 80
Holiday House (children's) 81
Jordan Enterprises 85
Little, Brown and Company 87
Los Hombres Press 88
Louisiana University Press
  (Southern US) 89
Pelican Publishing Company,
  Inc. 94
New Day Press, Inc. (Afro-
  American) 91
Philomel Books (children's) 95
Press of MacDonald & Reinecke,
  The 95
Scholastic, Inc. (children's/YA) 97
Soho Press, Inc. 98
Volcano Press, Inc. 105

Women's Studies Quarterly, A
  Journal 108
York Press, Ltd. 108
Zephyr Press 109
Specific Groups
Afro-Americans/Blacks
African American Images 60
Associated Publishers, Inc.,
  The 62
Black Angels Press 66
Esoterica Press 76
Guernica Editions 78
Jordan Enterprises 85
Lions Books Publisher 87
Lodestar Books (children's) 88
Louisiana University Press 89
New Day Press, Inc. 91
Open Hand Publishing, Inc. 93
Seal Press 97
Third World Press 101
Winston-Derek Publishers,
  Inc. 107
Wyrick and Company 108
Afro-Caribbeans
Eastern Caribbean Institute 75
Arabs/Arab-Americans
Guernica Editions 78
Asians/Asian-Americans
Beacon Press 63
China Books (Chinese, Chinese-
  Americans) 70
Cross Cultural Publications, Inc.
  (Chinese, Japanese) 72
Lion Book Publishers 87
Lodestar Books (children's) 88
Scholastic, Inc. (children's/YA) 97
Seal Press 97
Europeans
Bergli Books, Ltd. 65
Hispanics
Beacon Press 63
Bilingual Press/Editorial
  Bilingue 65
Ediciones Universal (Cubans) 75
Esoterica Press 76
Lodestar Books (children's) 88
Seal Press 97
Iranians/Iranian-Americans
Mage Publishers 89

Indians from India/Indo-Americans
Cross Cultural Publications, Inc. 72
Folklore Institute 77
Lion Book Publishers 87
Orient Paperbacks 94
Italians/Italian-Americans
Dante University Press 73
Guernica Editions (emphasis) 78
Italica Press 85
Lodestar Books (children's) 88
Jews
Beacon Press 63
Kar-Ben Copies, Inc. (children's) 86
Lodestar Books (children's) 88
Seal Press 97
Véhicule Press 105
Mennonite/Amish
Herald Press 80
Native Americans
Alaska Native Language Center 61
Avanyu Publishing, Inc. 63
Esoterica Press 76
Heyday Press (California) 80
Indian Country Communications, Inc. 83
Lodestar Books (children's) 88
Seal Press 97

Fantasy
Aegina Press, Inc. 59
Calyx Books 67
Crumb Elbow Publishing 73
Holiday House (children's) 81
Jordan Enterprises 85
New Day Press, Inc. (Afro-American) 91
Philomel Books (children's) 95
Third World Press (Afro-American) 101
Walker and Company 106

First Novels
Aegina Press, Inc. 59
Avalon Books 62
Avon Books 63
Bear Flag Books 64
Bilingual Press/Editorial Bilingue (Hispanic) 65
Calyx Books 67

Carolrhoda Books, Inc. (children's) 68
China Books 70
Crumb Elbow Publishing 73
Dial Books for Young Readers 74
Ediciones Universal 75
Esoterica Press 76
Farrar, Straus & Giroux, Inc. (children's) 77
Guernica Editions 78
Harlequin Enterprises, Ltd. 79
Herald Press (Mennonite, Amish) 80
Holiday House (children's) 81
Indian Country Communications, Inc. 83
Jordan Enterprises 85
Little, Brown and Company (children's) 87
Los Hombres Press 88
Mage Publishers (Iran) 89
New Day Press, Inc. (Afro-American children's) 91
Orient Paperbacks (Indian, Asian) 94
Pelican Publishing Company, Inc. 94
Philomel Books (children's) 95
Press of MacDonald & Reinecke, The 95
Scholastic, Inc. (children's) 97
Seal Press 97
Soho Press, Inc. 98
Third World Press (Afro-American) 101
Véhicule Press 105
Walker and Company 106
Winston-Derek Publishers, Inc. (Afro-American) 107
York Press, Ltd. 108
Zephyr Press 109

Folklore
Alaska Native Language Center 61
Avanyu Publishing, Inc. 63
Bear Flag Books 64
Calyx Books 67
Carolrhoda Books, Inc. (children's) 68
China Books 70
Chronicle Books (children's) 70
Crumb Elbow Publishing 73
Ediciones Universal 75

Folklore continued
Esoterica Press 76
Folklore Institute (India) 70
Heyday Press (California) 80
Holiday House (children's) 81
Jordan Enterprises 85
Lions Books Publisher 87
Mage Publishers (Iranian) 89
New Day Press, Inc. (Afro-American
  children's) 91
Pelican Publishing Company,
  Inc. 94
Philomel Books (children's) 95
Third World Press
  (Afro-American) 101
Véhicule Press 105
Volcano Press, Inc. 105
Walker and Company 106
Winston-Derek Publishers, Inc.
  (Afro-American) 107
York Press, Ltd. 108

Gay/Lesbian Issues
Guernica Editions 78
Los Hombres Press 88
Woman in the Moon 107
Zephyr Press 109

Historical Fiction
Aegina Press, Inc. 59
Avanyu Publishing, Inc. 63
Avon Books 63
Bear Flag Books (California) 64
Carolrhoda Books, Inc.
  (children's) 68
China Books 70
Cross Cultural Publications, Inc. 72
Crumb Elbow Publishing 73
Esoterica Press 76
Harlequin Enterprises, Ltd.
  (romance) 79
Herald Press (Mennonite,
  Amish) 80
Heyday Press (California) 80
Holiday House (children's) 81
Italica Press (Italian) 85
Mage Publishers (Iranian) 89
New Day Press, Inc. (Afro-American
  children's) 91
Open Hand Publishing, Inc. (Afro-
  American) 93
Pelican Publishing Company,
  Inc. 94
Philomel Press (children's) 95

Scholastic, Inc. (children's) 97
Third World Press
  (Afro-American) 101
Walker and Company 106
Winston-Derek Publishers, Inc.
  (Afro-American) 107
Zephyr Press 109

Holiday Stories
Bergli Books, Ltd. 65
Chronicle Books (children's) 70
Crumb Elbow Publishing 73
Ediciones Universal 75
Kar-Ben Copies, Inc. (Jewish
  children's) 86
Little, Brown and Company
  (children's) 87
Pelican Publishing Company,
  Inc. 94
Philomel Books (children's) 95
Third World Press
  (Afro-American Kwanzaa) 101
Walker and Company 106

Horror
Aegina Press, Inc. 59
Crumb Elbow Publishing 73
Lions Books Publisher 87
Philomel Books (children's) 95
Scholastic, Inc. (children's) 97

Humor
Aegina Press, Inc. 59
Bergli Books, Ltd. 65
Crumb Elbow Publishing 73
Jordan Enterprises 85
Mage Publishers (Iranian) 89
Orient Paperbacks (Indians from
  India) 94
Pelican Publishing Company,
  Inc. 94
Philomel Books (children's) 95
Third World Press
  (Afro-American) 101

Literary
Aegina Press, Inc. 59
Bilingual Press/Editorial Bilingue
  (Hispanic) 65
Calyx Books 67
China Books 70
Crumb Elbow Publishing 73
Dante University Press 73
Eighth Mountain Press, The 75
Esoterica Press 76

Heyday Press (California) 80
Italica Press (Italian) 85
Jordan Enterprises 85
Louisiana University Press 89
Mage Publishers (Iranian)) 89
Orient Paperbacks (Indians from
    India) 94
Pelican Publishing Company,
    Inc. 94
Press of MacDonald & Reinecke,
    The 95
Scholastic, Inc. (children's) 97
Seal Press 97
Soho Press, Inc. 98
Third World Press
    (Afro-American) 101
Véhicule Press 105
Wyrick and Company 108
York Press, Ltd. 108
Zephyr Press 109

Mainstream
Aegina Press, Inc. 59
Avon Books 63
Crumb Elbow Publishing 73
Soho Press, Inc. 98
Winston-Derek Publishers, Inc.
    (Afro-American) 107
Wyrick and Company 108

Mystery
Aegina Press, Inc. 59
Avalon Books (mystery) 62
Avon Books 63
Crumb Elbow Publishing 73
Herald Press (Mennonite, Amish),
    children's) 80
Scholastic, Inc. (children's/YA) 97
Seal Press 97
Soho Press, Inc. 98
Walker and Company 106

New Age
Aegina Press, Inc. 59
Avon Books 63
Black Angels Press 66
Crumb Elbow Publishing 73

Plays/Drama
Bilingual Press/Editorial Bilingue
    (Hispanic) 65
Calyx Books 67
Fairleigh Dickinson University
    Press 76
Guernica Editions 78

Howard University Press 82
Jordan Enterprises 85
Third World Press
    (Afro-American) 101
Women's Studies Quarterly, A
    Journal 108

Romance
Aegina Press, Inc. 59
Avalon Books 62
Avon Books 63
Crumb Elbow Publishing 73
Herald Press (Mennonite,
    Amish) 80
Jordan Enterprises 85
Walker and Company 106

Science Fiction
Aegina Press, Inc. 59
Avon Books 63
Crumb Elbow Publishing 73
Jordan Enterprises 85
Third World Press
    (Afro-American) 101
Walker and Company 106

Short Story Collections
Aegina Press, Inc. 59
Beacon Press 63
Bergli Books, Ltd. 65
Bilingual Press/Editorial Bilingue
    (Hispanic) 65
Calyx Books 67
China Books 70
Crumb Elbow Publishing 73
Eastern Caribbean Institute 75
Herald Press (Mennonite,
    Amish) 80
Indian Country Communications,
    Inc. 83
Jordan Enterprises 85
Mage Publishers (Iranian)) 89
Los Hombres Press 88
New Day Press, Inc. (Afro-American
    children's) 91
Pelican Publishing Company,
    Inc. 94
Philomel Books (children's) 95
Press of MacDonald & Reinecke,
    The 95
Seal Press 97
Third World Press
    (Afro-American) 101
Véhicule Press 105

Short Story Collections continued
Women's Studies Quarterly, A
  Journal (anthologies) 108
York Press, Ltd. 108
Zephyr Press 109

Sports
Crumb Elbow Publishing 73
Jordan Enterprises 85
Lion Books Publisher 87
Pelican Publishing Company,
  Inc. 94

Suspense
Aegina Press, Inc. 59
Avon Books 63
Crumb Elbow Publishing 73

Suspense
Harlequin Enterprises, Ltd.
  (romantic) 79

Translations
Alaska Native Language Center 61
Bilingual Press/Editorial Bilingue
  (Spanish) 65
Calyx Books 67
Carolrhoda Books, (children's) 68
Dante University Press (Italian) 73
Indian Country Communications,
  Inc. 83
Italica Press (Italian) 85
Jordan Enterprises 85
Louisiana University Press 89
Open Hand Publishing, Inc. (Afro-
  American) 93
Philomel Books (children's) 95
Soho Press, Inc. 98
Véhicule Editions (Yiddish, Spanish,
  French) 105
Zephyr Press 109

Westerns
Avalon Books 62
Avanyu Publishing, Inc. 63
Crumb Elbow Publishing 73
Heyday Press (California) 80
Walker and Company 106

Women's Books
Aegina Press, Inc. 59
Avon Books 63
Bergli Books, Ltd. 65
Bilingual Press/Editorial Bilingue
  (Hispanic) 65
Calyx Books 67

China Books 70
Eighth Mountain Press, The 75
Esoterica Press 76
Guernica Editions 78
Herald Press (Mennonite,
  Amish) 80
Heyday Press (California) 80
Italica Press (Italian) 85
Jordan Enterprises 85
Mage Publishers (Iranian)) 89
Press of MacDonald & Reinecke,
  The 95
Soho Press, Inc. 98
Third World Press
  (Afro-American) 101
Véhicule Press 105
Winston-Derek Publishers, Inc.
  (Afro-American) 107
York Press, Ltd. 108
Zephyr Press 109

Nonfiction

Adventure
Aegina Press 59
Avanyu Publishing, Inc. 63
Avon Books 63
Council for Indian Education 71

Agriculture
China Books 70
Countrywoman's Press, The 72

Anthropology
Avanyu Publishing, Inc. 63
Avon Books 63
Bear Flag Books (Native
  American) 64
Center for Migration Studies of New
  York, Inc. 69
Council for Indian Education 71
Denali Press, The 74
Fairleigh Dickinson University
  Press 76
Folklore Institute (India) 77
Hemingway Western Studies
  Series 79
Heyday Press (California) 80
Howard University Press
  (cultural) 82
Karnak House (African) 86
Louisiana University Press 89

Texas A&M University Press 100
University of Alabama Press,
    The 102
University of Alaska Press 102
University of California at Los
    Angeles, American Indian
    Studies 103
University of Illinois Press 103
University of Nebraska Press 103
University of Nevada Press 104
Walker and Company 106
Washington State University
    Press 106

Antiques
Avanyu Publishing, Inc. 63
Avon Books 63
China Books 70

Archaeology
Avanyu Publishing, Inc. 63
Avon Books 63
Bear Flag Books 64
China Books 70
Council for Indian Education 71
Fairleigh Dickinson University
    Press 76
Italica Press 85
Karnak House (African) 86
Texas A&M University Press 100
University of Alabama Press,
    The 102
University of Alaska Press 102
University of California at Los
    Angeles, American Indian
    Studies 103
University of Illinois Press 103
University of Nevada Press 104

Architecture
China Books 70
Italica Press 85
Mage Publishers (Iranian)) 89
Pelican Publishing Company,
    Inc. 94
Texas A&M University Press 100
Zephyr Press 109

Art
Avanyu Publishing, Inc. 63
Avon Books 63
China Books 70
Council for Indian Education 71
Fairleigh Dickinson University
    Press 76

Howard University Press 82
Jordan Enterprises 85
Mage Publishers (Iranian)) 89
Pelican Publishing Company,
    Inc. 94
Texas A&M University Press 100
University of California at Los
    Angeles, American Indian
    Studies 103
Wyrick and Company 108
Zephyr Press 109

Astrology
Avon Books 63
Orient Paperbacks 94

Astronomy
Avon Books 63

Aviation
Avon Books 63
Pelican Publishing Company,
    Inc. 94
University of Alabama Press,
    The 102

Biography
Aegina Press 59
African American Images 60
Associated Publishers, Inc., The
    (Afro-Americans) 62
Avanyu Publishing, Inc. 63
Avon Books 63
Bear Flag Books 64
Blair, Publisher, John F. 66
Carolrhoda Books, Inc.
    (children's) 68
China Books 70
Council for Indian Education 71
Dante University Press (Italians) 73
Denali Press, The 74
Eastern Caribbean Institute 75
Enslow Publishers, Inc. 76
Fairleigh Dickinson University
    Press 76
Heyday Press (California) 80
Hill Books, Lawrence 81
Holiday House (children's) 81
Howard University Press 82
Karnak House (African) 86
Lion Books Publisher 87
Louisiana University Press 89
Noble Press, The 92
Orient Paperbacks 94

Biography continued
Pelican Publishing Company,
  Inc. 94
Philomel Books (children's) 95
Scholastic, Inc. (children's/YA) 97
Soho Press, Inc. 98
Texas A&M University Press 100
Third World Press
  (Afro-American) 101
University of Alabama Press,
  The 102
University of Alaska Press 102
University of Illinois Press 103
University of Nebraska Press 103
University of North Texas Press 105
Walker and Company 106
Winston-Derek Publishers, Inc.
  (Afro-American) 107
Women's Studies Quarterly, A
  Journal (cross-cultural
  memoirs) 108
Wyrick and Company 108
Zephyr Press 109

Business/Economics
Aegina Press 59
Avon Books 63
Center for Migration Studies of New
  York, Inc. 69

Business/Economics
China Books 70
Eastern Caribbean Institute 75
Pelican Publishing Company,
  Inc. 94
Texas A&M University Press 100
Third World Press
  (Afro-American) 101

Child Care/Development
Avon Books 63
Herald Press (Mennonite,
  Amish) 80
Noble Press, The 92
Pelican Publishing Company,
  Inc. 94
Soho Press, Inc. 98
Third World Press
  (Afro-American) 101
Walker and Company 106
Winston-Derek Publishers, Inc.
  (Afro-American) 107

Children's Nonfiction
Aegina Press 59

African American Images 60
Avon Books 63
Carolrhoda Books, Inc. 68
China Books 70
Chronicle Books 70
Council for Indian Education 71
Dial Books for Young Readers 74
Enslow Publishers, Inc. 76
Farrar, Straus and Giroux, Inc. 77
Holiday House (children's) 81
Little, Brown and Company 87
Lodestar Books 88
New Day Press, Inc. 91
Pelican Publishing Company,
  Inc. 94
Philomel Press (children's) 95
Scholastic, Inc. 97
Third World Press
  (Afro-American) 101
Volcano Press, Inc. 105
Walker and Company 106
Winston-Derek Publishers, Inc.
  (Afro-American) 107

Comedy/Humor
Aegina Press 59
Avon Books 63
Bergli Books, Ltd. 65
Council for Indian Education 71
Pelican Publishing Company,
  Inc. 94
Third World Press
  (Afro-American) 101
Wyrick and Company 108

Comics
Avon Books 63
Third World Press
  (Afro-American) 101

Computers
Aegina Press 59
Avon Books 63
Orient Paperbacks 94

Consumer Issues
Avon Books 63
Jonathan David Publishers, Inc. 85
Orient Paperbacks 94
Walker and Company 106

Cooking/Foods/Nutrition
Avon Books 63
Blair, Publisher, John F.
  (Southeastern US) 66
China Books 70

Countrywoman's Press, The 72
Ediciones Universal 75
Esoterica Press 76
Herald Press (Mennonite,
   Amish) 80
Jonathan David Publishers, Inc.
   (Jewish) 85
Orient Paperbacks 94
Pelican Publishing Company,
   Inc. 94
R&M Publishing Company 96
Third World Press
   (Afro-American) 101
University of North Texas Press 105
Wyrick and Company 108

Crafts
Avanyu Publishing, Inc. 63
Chronicle Books (children's) 70
Council for Indian Education 71
Countrywoman's Press, The 72
Karnak House (African) 86
Lion Books Publisher 87
Naturegraph Publishers, Inc. 91
Texas A&M University Press 100
Third World Press
   (Afro-American) 101
University of California at Los
   Angeles, American Indian
   Studies 103
Walker and Company 106

Dance
Esoterica Press 76
Karnak House (African) 86
Third World Press
   (Afro-American) 101

Disabilities
Avon Books 63
Noble Press, The 92
Philomel Books (children's) 95
Seal Press 97
University of Illinois Press 103

Education
Aegina Press 59
Avanyu Publishing, Inc. 63
Avon Books 63
Beacon Press 63
Bergli Books, Ltd. 65
Bilingual Press/Editorial Bilingue
   (Hispanic) 65
China Books 70
Council for Indian Education 71

Esoterica Press 76
Howard University Press 82
Karnak House (African) 86
New Day Press, Inc. (Afro-American
   children's) 91
Noble Press, The 92
Philomel Press (children's) 95
R&M Publishing Company 96
Texas A&M University Press 100
Third World Press
   (Afro-American) 101
University of Alabama Press,
   The 102
University of California at Los
   Angeles, American Indian
   Studies 103
University of North Texas Press 105
Walker and Company 106
Winston-Derek Publishers, Inc.
   (Afro-American) 107

Entertainment
Avon Books 63
Bergli Books, Ltd. 65
Third World Press
   (Afro-American) 101
Walker and Company 106

Environment/Ecology see also Nature
Avanyu Publishing, Inc. 63
Avon Books 63
Beacon Press 63
Council for Indian Education 71
Countrywoman's Press, The 72
Herald Press 80
Heyday Press (California) 80
Noble Press, The 92
Texas A&M University Press 100
Third World Press
   (Afro-American) 101
University of Alabama Press,
   The 102
University of Nevada Press 104
Volcano Press, Inc. 105
Walker and Company 106
Zephyr Press 109

Erotica
Esoterica Press 76
Orient Paperbacks 94
Woman in the Moon 107
Zephyr Press 109

Essays

Avon Books 63
Beacon Press 63
Bergli Books, Ltd. 65
China Books 70
Eastern Caribbean Institute 75
Eighth Mountain Press, The 75
Guernica Editions 78
Herald Press (Mennonite) 80
Howard University Press 82
Jordan Enterprises 85
Louisiana University Press 89
Third World Press
  (Afro-American) 101
York Press, Ltd. 108
Zephyr Press 109

Ethnic/Cultural Focus

All Ethnic Groups

Ahsahta Press
  (Western America) 60
Blair, Publisher, John F.
  (Southeastern US) 66
Calyx Books 67
Center for Migration Studies of
  New York, Inc. 69
Crumb Elbow Publishing 73
Dial Books for Young Readers 74
Hemingway Western Studies
  Series (Intermountain West) 79
Heyday Press (California) 80
Holiday House (children's) 81
Jordan Enterprises 85
Little, Brown and Company
  (children's) 87
Los Hombres Press 88
Louisiana University Press
  (Southern US) 89
Pelican Publishing Company,
  Inc. 94
Philomel Press (children's) 95
Social Justice 98
Texas A&M University Press
  (Texas, Southwest) 100
Volcano Press, Inc. 105
Women's Studies Quarterly, A
  Journal 108
Wyrick and Company (Southern
  US) 108

Specific Groups

Afro-Americans/Blacks

Aegina Press 59

African American Images 60
Associated Publishers, Inc.,
  The 62
Avon Books 63
Beacon Press 63
Bear Flag Books (in CA) 64
Carolina Wren Press 68
Chronicle Books (children's) 70
Clarity Press, Inc. 71
Eastern Caribbean Institute 75
Ediciones Universal 75
Enslow Publishers, Inc. 76
Esoterica Press 76
Fairleigh Dickinson University
  Press 76
Guernica Editions 78
Hill Books, Lawrence 81
Howard University Press 82
Jordan Enterprises 85
Karnak House (African) 86
Lion Books Publisher 87
Lodestar Books (children's) 88
Louisiana University Press 89
New Day Press, Inc. 91
Noble Press, The 92
Open Hand Publishing, Inc. 93
R&M Publishing Company 96
Scholastic, Inc. (children's/YA) 97
Seal Press 97
Soho Press, Inc. 98
Technicians of the Sacred 99
Texas A&M University Press 100
Third World Press 101
University of Alabama Press,
  The 102
University of Illinois Press 103
University of North Texas
  Press 104
Walker and Company 106
Washington State University 106
Winston-Derek Publishers,
  Inc. 107
Woman in the Moon 107
York Press, Ltd. 108
Zephyr Press 109

Arabs/Arab-Americans

Clarity Press, Inc. 71
Esoterica Press 76
Fairleigh Dickinson University
  Press 76
Guernica Editions 78
Hill Books, Lawrence 81

Soho Press, Inc. 98
York Press, Ltd. 108
Zephyr Press 109
Asians/Asian-Americans
Enslow Publishers, Inc. 76
Lion Books Publisher 87
Lodestar Books (children's) 88
Scholastic, Inc. (children's/YA) 97
Seal Press 97
Texas A&M University Press 100
Washington State University
   Press 106
Basques
Ahsahta Press 60
Bear Flag Books (in CA) 64
Hemingway Western Studies
   Series 79
Soho Press, Inc. 98
University of Nevada Press 104
Chinese/Chinese-Americans
Ahsahta Press 60
Asian Humanities Press 62
Avon Books 63
Beacon Press 63
Bear Flag Books (in CA) 64
Center for East Asian Studies
   (China) 69
China Books 70
Chronicle Books (children's) 70
Cross Cultural Publications,
   Inc. 72
Hemingway Western Studies
   Series 79
Kodansha International 86
Lion Books Publisher 87
Scholastic, Inc. (children's/YA) 97
Soho Press, Inc. 98
University of Illinois Press 103
University of Nevada Press 104
Washington State University
   Press 106
Czechoslovakians
Soho Press, Inc. 98
Zephyr Press 109
Europeans
Bergli Books, Ltd. (Swiss) 65
Texas A&M University Press
   (Eastern Europeans) 100
Filipinos/Filipino-Americans
Asian Humanities Press 62
Beacon Press 63
Bear Flag Books (in CA) 64

Scholastic, Inc. (children's/YA) 97
Zephyr Press 109
Germans/German-Americans
Texas A&M University Press 100
University of Illinois Press 103
York Press, Ltd. 108
Zephyr Press 109
Greeks/Greek-Americans
Texas A&M University Press 100
Hawaiians
Ahsahta Press 60
Hispanics
Ahsahta Press 60
Avanyu Publishing, Inc. 63
Avon Books 63
Beacon Press 63
Bear Flag Books (in CA) 97
Bilingual Press/Editorial Bilingue
   (in US) 65
Carolina Wren Press 68
Chronicle Books (children's) 70
Council for Indian Education 71
Denali Press, The 74
Ediciones Universal 75
Enslow Publishers, Inc. 76
Esoterica Press 76
Hemingway Western Studies
   Series 79
Howard University Press 82
Lodestar Books (children's) 88
Open Hand Publishing, Inc. 93
Scholastic, Inc. (children's/YA) 97
Texas A&M University Press 100
University of Alabama Press,
   The 102
University of Illinois Press 103
University of North Texas
   Press 104
Walker and Company 106
Washington State University
   Press 106
York Press, Ltd. 108
Zephyr Press 109
Hungarians/Hungarian-Americans
Zephyr Press 109
Indians from Asia/Indo-Americans
Asian Humanities Press 62
Avon Books 63
Cross Cultural Publications,
   Inc. 72
Folklore Institute 77
Orient Paperbacks 94

Indians from Asia/Indo-Americans continued
    Scholastic, Inc. (children's/YA) 97
    York Press, Ltd. 108
    Woman in the Moon 107
    Zephyr Press 109
Indians of Central/South America
    Avon Books 63
    Beacon Press 63
    Chronicle Books (children's) 70
    Esoterica Press 76
    Hemingway Western Studies
        Series 79
    Howard University Press 82
    Lodestar Books (children's) 88
    Texas A&M University Press 100
    University of Alabama Press,
        The 102
    University of Illinois Press 103
    Woman in the Moon 107
    Zephyr Press 109
Iranians/Iranian-Americans
    Mage Publishers 89
Irish/Irish-Americans
    Beacon Press 63
    Fairleigh Dickinson University
        Press 76
    Soho Press, Inc. 98
    Texas A&M University Press 100
    University of Illinois Press 103
    Zephyr Press 109
Israelis
    Avon Books 63
    Beacon Press 63
    Fairleigh Dickinson University
        Press 76
    Hill Books, Lawrence 81
    Jonathan David Publishers,
        Inc. 85
    University of Illinois Press 103
    York Press, Ltd. 108
    Zephyr Press 109
Italians/Italian-Americans
    Dante University Press (Italian-
        Americans) 73
    Esoterica Press 76
    Fairleigh Dickinson University
        Press 76
    Guernica Editions 78
    Italica Press 85
    Louisiana University Press 89
    Texas A&M University Press 100

Italians/Italian-Americans
    University of Illinois Press 103
    University of Nevada Press 104
    York Press, Ltd. 108
    Zephyr Press 109
Japanese/Japanese-Americans
    Ahsahta Press 60
    Asian Humanities Press 62
    Beacon Press 63
    Bear Flag Books (in CA) 64
    Center for East Asian Studies
        (Japan) 69
    Chronicle Books (children's) 70
    Cross Cultural Publications,
        Inc. 72
    Fairleigh Dickinson University
        Press 76
    Kodansha International 86
    Soho Press, Inc. 98
    University of Illinois Press 103
    Washington State University
        Press 106
    Woman in the Moon 107
    Zephyr Press 109
Jews
    Aegina Press 59
    Avon Books 63
    Beacon Press 63
    Denali Press, The 74
    Eighth Mountain Press, The 75
    Fairleigh Dickinson University
        Press 76
    Hippocrene Books, Inc. 81
    Jonathan David Publishers,
        Inc. 85
    Kar-Ben Copies, Inc.
        (children's) 86
    Lodestar Books (children's) 88
    Louisiana University Press 89
    Seal Press 97
    Texas A&M University Press 100
    University of Alabama Press,
        The 102
    University of Illinois Press 103
    Véhicule Press 105
    Woman in the Moon 107
    York Press, Ltd. 108
    Zephyr Press 109
Koreans/Korean Americans
    Asian Humanities Press 62
    Beacon Press 63
    Bear Flag Books (in CA) 64

Center for East Asian Studies
  (Korea) 69
Kodansha International 86
Soho Press, Inc. 98
Zephyr Press 109
Latin Americans
Beacon Press 63
Avon Books 63
Bilingual Press/Editorial
  Bilingue 65
Chronicle Books (children's) 70
Denali Press, The 74
Ediciones Universal (Cubans) 75
Esoterica Press 76
Fairleigh Dickinson University
  Press 76
Hill Books, Lawrence 81
Howard University Press 82
Louisiana University Press 89
Seal Press 97
Technicians of the Sacred 99
Texas A&M University Press 100
University of Alabama Press,
  The 102
Washington State University
  Press 106
Woman in the Moon 107
York Press, Ltd. 108
Mexicans/Mexican-Americans
Bear Flag Books (CA issues) 64
Bilingual Press/Editorial Bilingue
  (Hispanic) 65
Chronicle Books (children's) 70
Scholastic, Inc. (children's/YA) 97
Texas A&M University Press 100
University of Alabama Press,
  The 102
University of North Texas
  Press 104
Woman in the Moon 107
York Press, Ltd. 108
Zephyr Press 109
Mongolians
Center for East Asian Studies 69
Native Americans
Ahsahta Press 60
Alaska Native Language
  Center 61
Avanyu Publishing, Inc. 63
Avon Books 63
Beacon Press 63
Bear Flag Books 64

Carolina Wren Press 68
Chronicle Books (children's) 70
Council for Indian Education 71
Crumb Elbow Publishing 73
Denali Press, The 74
Esoterica Press 76
Fairleigh Dickinson University
  Press 76
Heyday Press (California) 80
Hill Books, Lawrence 81
Howard University Press 82
Indian Country Communications,
  Inc. 83
Lodestar Books (children's) 88
Louisiana University Press 89
Naturegraph Publishers, Inc. 91
Noble Press, The 92
Press of MacDonald & Reinecke,
  The 95
Scholastic, Inc. (children's/YA) 97
Seal Press 97
Soho Press, Inc. 98
Texas A&M University Press 100
University of Alabama Press,
  The 102
University of Alaska Press 102
University of California at Los
  Angeles, American Indian
  Studies 103
University of Illinois Press 103
University of Nebraska Press 103
University of Nevada Press 104
Walker and Company 106
Washington State University
  Press 106
York Press, Ltd. 108
Zephyr Press 109
Poles/Polish Americans
Fairleigh Dickinson University
  Press 76
Hippocrene Press, Inc. 81
Texas A&M University Press 100
University of Illinois Press 103
Zephyr Press 109
Russians/Russian-Americans
Beacon Press 63
Fairleigh Dickinson University
  Press 76
Soho Press, Inc. 98
Texas A&M University Press 100
University of Alaska Press 102
Woman in the Moon 107

Russians/Russian-Americans continued
  Zephyr Press 109
Scandinavians/Scandianvian-Americans
  Fairleigh Dickinson University
    Press 76
  Texas A&M University Press 100
  Zephyr Press 109
Scots/Scottish-Americans
  Fairleigh Dickinson University
    Press 76
  Texas A&M University Press 100
  University of Alabama Press,
    The 102
  Zephyr Press 109
Slavic Peoples
  Fairleigh Dickinson University
    Press 76
  Texas A&M University Press 100
  Zephyr Press 109
Thais/Thai-Americans
  Beacon Press 63
  Fairleigh Dickinson University
    Press 76
  Kodansha International 86
  Texas A&M University Press 100
Vietnamese/Vietnamese-Americans
  Asian Humanities Press 62
  Beacon Press 63
  Chronicle Books (children's) 70
  Fairleigh Dickinson University
    Press 76
  Kodansha International 86
  Scholastic, Inc. (children's/YA) 97
  Texas A&M University Press 100
  Zephyr Press 109

Family Issues
  African American Images 60
  Avon Books 63
  Herald Press (Mennonite,
    Amish) 80
  Noble Press, The 92
  Pelican Publishing Company,
    Inc. 94
  Seal Press 97
  Soho Press, Inc. 98
  Texas A&M University Press 100
  Third World Press
    (Afro-American) 101

  Volcano Press, Inc. 105
  Walker and Company 106
Fashion
  Avon Books 63
  Third World Press
    (Afro-American) 101
Film/Television/Video
  Aegina Press 59
  African American Images 60
  Avon Books 63
  Fairleigh Dickinson University
    Press 76
  Guernica Editions 78
Film/Television/Video
  Third World Press
    (Afro-American) 101
Folklore
  Alaska Native Language Center 61
  Avanyu Publishing, Inc. (Native
    American) 63
  Bear Flag Books 64
  Blair, Publisher, John F.
    (Southeastern US) 66
  Ediciones Universal 75
  Esoterica Press 76
  Folklore Institute (India) 77
  Heyday Press (California) 80
  Lions Books Publisher 87
  Louisiana University Press 89
  Technicians of the Sacred 99
  Texas A&M University Press 100
  University of Alabama Press,
    The 102
  University of California at Los
    Angeles, American Indian
    Studies 103
  University of Illinois Press 103
  University of Nevada Press 104
  University of North Texas Press 105
  York Press, Ltd. 108

Games/Puzzles
  Esoterica Press 76
  Orient Paperbacks 94
  University of Nevada Press
    (gambling) 104
Gardening
  Avon Books 63
  Countrywoman's Press, The 72
  Heyday Press (California) 80
  Walker and Company 106

Wyrick and Company (Southern
 US) 108

Gay/Lesbian Issues
Avon Books 63
Beacon Press 63
Eighth Mountain Press, The 75
Esoterica Press 76
Guernica Editions 78
Los Hombres Press 88
Orient Paperbacks 94
Seal Press 97
Winston-Derek Publishers, Inc.
 (Afro-American) 107
Woman in the Moon 107
Zephyr Press 109

General Interest
Aegina Press 59
Avon Books 63
Crumb Elbow Publishing 73
Kodansha International 86
Little, Brown and Company
 (children's) 87
Jordan Enterprises 85
Louisiana University Press 89
Walker and Company 106
Washington State University
 Press 106

Geology
University of Nevada Press 104

Government/Politics
Avon Books 63
Center for Migration Studies of New
 York, Inc. 69
Clarity Press, Inc. 71
Hill Books, Lawrence 81
Howard University Press 82
Kodansha International 86
Louisiana University Press 89
Pelican Publishing Company,
 Inc. 94
R&M Publishing Company 96
Texas A&M University Press 100
Third World Press
 (Afro-American) 101
University of Alabama Press,
 The 102
University of Alaska Press 102
University of California at Los
 Angeles, American Indian
 Studies 103
University of North Texas Press 105

Zephyr Press 109
Health/Fitness
Aegina Press 59
Avon Books 63
Naturegraph Publishers, Inc. 91
Orient Paperbacks 94
Seal Press 97
Third World Press
 (Afro-American) 101
University of California at Los
 Angeles, American Indian
 Studies 103
Volcano Press, Inc. 105

History
Aegina Press 59
African American Images 60
Associated Publishers, Inc., The
 (Afro-Americans) 62
Avanyu Publishing, Inc. 63
Avon Books 63
Beacon Press 63
Bear Flag Books 64
Blair, Publisher, John F.
 (Southeastern US) 66
China Books 70
Eastern Caribbean Institute 75
Esoterica Press 76
Fairleigh Dickinson University
 Press 76
Herald Press (Mennonite,
 Amish) 80
Heyday Press (California) 80
Howard University Press 82
Italica Press 85
Louisiana University Press
 (Southern US) 89
Pelican Publishing Company,
 Inc. 94
R&M Publishing Company 96
Social Justice 98
Texas A&M University Press 100
Third World Press
 (Afro-American) 101
University of Alabama Press,
 The 102
University of Alaska Press 102
University of California at Los
 Angeles, American Indian
 Studies 103
University of Illinois Press 103
University of Nebraska Press 103
University of Nevada Press 104

History continued
University of North Texas Press 105
Walker and Company 106
Wyrick and Company 108
Zephyr Press 109

Hobbies
Avon Books 63
R&M Publishing Company 96

Holistic Practices
Aegina Press 59
Asian Humanities Press 62
Esoterica Press 76
Noble Press, The 92
Orient Paperbacks 94
Third World Press
(Afro-American) 101

Human Potential
Aegina Press 59
African American Images 60
Avon Books 63
New Day Press, Inc. (Afro-American
children's) 91
Orient Paperbacks 94
Third World Press
(Afro-American) 101

Immigrants/Immigration
Bergli Books, Ltd. 65
Center for Migration Studies of New
York, Inc. 69
China Books 70
Eastern Caribbean Institute 75
Esoterica Press 76
Fairleigh Dickinson University
Press 76
Kodansha International 86
Louisiana University Press 89
Social Justice 98
Texas A&M University Press 100
Third World Press
(Afro-American) 101
University of Alabama Press,
The 102
University of Illinois Press 103
University of Nevada Press 104
York Press, Ltd. 108

Labor
Avon Books 63
China Books 70
Crumb Elbow Publishing 73
Esoterica Press 76

Louisiana University Press 89
Texas A&M University Press 100
Third World Press
(Afro-American) 101
University of Illinois Press 103
Zephyr Press 109

Law
Avon Books 63
Fairleigh Dickinson University
Press 76
Woman in the Moon 107
Texas A&M University Press 100
Third World Press
(Afro-American) 101
University of Alaska Press 102
University of California at Los
Angeles, American Indian
Studies 103

Literary
Aegina Press 59
Avon Books 63
Bilingual Press/Editorial Bilingue
(Hispanic) 65
Ediciones Universal 75

Literary
Esoterica Press 76
Fairleigh Dickinson University
Press 76
Guernica Editions 78
Herald Press (Mennonite,
Amish) 80
Heyday Press (California) 80
Howard University Press 82
Italica Press 85
Louisiana University Press 89
Pelican Publishing Company,
Inc. 94
Press of MacDonald & Reinecke,
The 95
Soho Press, Inc. 98
Texas A&M University Press 100
Third World Press
(Afro-American) 101
University of Alabama Press,
The 102
University of California at Los
Angeles, American Indian
Studies 103
University of Illinois Press 103
University of North Texas Press 105
York Press, Ltd. 108

Zephyr Press 109

Magic
Avon Books 63
Technicians of the Sacred
(voodoo) 99

Martial Arts
China Books 70

Medicine
Associated Publishers, Inc., The 62
Avon Books 63
China Books 70
Orient Paperbacks 94
Pelican Publishing Company,
Inc. 94
University of Alaska Press 102
University of California at Los
Angeles, American Indian
Studies 103
Volcano Press, Inc. 105

Men's Issues
Avon Books 63
Beacon Press 63
Esoterica Press 76
Third World Press
(Afro-American) 101
Volcano Press, Inc. 105
Zephyr Press 109

Metaphysics/New Age
Asian Humanities Press 62
Black Angels Press 66
Kodansha International 86
Technicians of the Sacred 99
Woman in the Moon 107

Military
Associated Publishers, Inc., The 62
Avon Books 63
Hippocrene Books, Inc. 81
Louisiana University Press 89
Orient Paperbacks 94
University of Alabama Press,
The 102
University of Illinois Press 103
University of North Texas Press 105

Minority Issues
Aegina Press 59
Avon Books 63
Beacon Press 63
Bilingual Press/Editorial Bilingue
(Hispanic) 65
Clarity Press, Inc. 71

Denali Press, The 74
Esoterica Press 76
Fairleigh Dickinson University
Press 76
Guernica Editions 78
Heyday Press (California) 80
Hill Books, Lawrence 81
Howard University Press 82
Louisiana University Press 89
New Day Press, Inc. (Afro-American
children's) 91
Noble Press, The 92
Pelican Publishing Company,
Inc. 94
Texas A&M University Press 100
Third World Press
(Afro-American) 101
University of Alabama Press,
The 102
University of California at Los
Angeles, American Indian
Studies 103
University of Illinois Press 103
University of North Texas Press 105
Walker and Company 106
Woman in the Moon 107
York Press, Ltd. 108

Music
Associated Publishers, Inc., The 62
Avon Books 63
Esoterica Press 76
Seal Press 97
Third World Press
(Afro-American) 101
University of California at Los
Angeles, American Indian
Studies 103
University of Illinois Press 103

Mythology
Fairleigh Dickinson University
Press 76
Heyday Press (California) 80
Technicians of the Sacred 99
University of Alabama Press,
The 102

Nature
Avanyu Publishing, Inc. 63
Avon Books 63
Beacon Press 63
Council for Indian Education 71
Countrywoman's Press, The 72

Nature continued
Herald Press (Mennonite, Amish) 80
Heyday Press (California) 80
Naturegraph Publishers, Inc. 91
Noble Press, The 92
Third World Press (Afro-American) 101
University of Alabama Press, The 102
University of Nevada Press 104
Volcano Press, Inc. 105
Walker and Company 106
Wyrick and Company 108
Zephyr Press 109

Philosophy
Aegina Press 59
Asian Humanities Press 62
Avon Books 63
Beacon Press 63
China Books 70
Fairleigh Dickinson University Press 76
Jordan Enterprises 85
Kodansha International 86
Orient Paperbacks 94
Third World Press (Afro-American) 101

Poetry
Aegina Press 59
Ahsahta Press 60
Bilingual Press/Editorial Bilingue (Hispanic) 65
Black Angels Press 66
Holiday House (children's) 81
Jordan Enterprises 85
Los Hombres Press (haiku) 88
Lotus Press 88
Open Hand Publishing, Inc. 93
Press of MacDonald & Reinecke, The 95
Women's Studies Quarterly, A Journal 108

Politics/World Affairs
Avon Books 63
Beacon Press 63
China Books 70
Clarity Press, Inc. 71
Eastern Caribbean Institute 75
Fairleigh Dickinson University Press 76

Hill Books, Lawrence 81
Howard University Press 82
Kodansha International 86
Louisiana University Press 89
Noble Press, The 92
Social Justice 98
Texas A&M University Press 100
Third World Press (Afro-American) 101
University of California at Los Angeles, American Indian Studies 103
University of North Texas Press 105
Walker and Company 106
Zephyr Press 109

Psychology
Aegina Press 59
Esoterica Press 76
Seal Press 97
Third World Press (Afro-American) 101

Psycho-Spirituality
Avon Books 63
Technicians of the Sacred 99

Poetry
Calyx Books 67
Carolina Wren Press 68
Eighth Mountain Press, The 75
Guernica Editions 78

Recreation
Avon Books 63
Bear Flag Books 64
Blair, Publisher, John F. (Southeastern US) 66
Council for Indian Education 71
Countrywoman's Press, The 72
Esoterica Press 76

Recreation
Louisiana University Press 89
Volcano Press, Inc. 105
Walker and Company 106

Reference Books
Alaska Native Language Center 61
Avanyu Publishing, Inc. 63
Avon Books 63
China Books 70
Council for Indian Education 71
Denali Press, The 74
Herald Press Mennonite, Amish) 80

Hippocrene Books, Inc. (foreign
language dictionaries) 81
Jonathan David Publishers, Inc.
(Judaica) 85
Noble Press, The 92
University of California at Los
Angeles, American Indian
Studies 103
University of North Texas Press 105
Walker and Company 106
York Press, Ltd. 108

Religion

All Religions

Aegina Press 59
Avon Books 63
Beacon Press 63
Jordan Enterprises 85
Pelican Publishing Company,
Inc. 94
Texas A&M University Press (as
practiced by ethnic groups in
Texas, Southwest) 100
Third World Press
(Afro-American) 101
University of Alabama Press,
The 102
University of California at Los
Angeles, American Indian
Studies 103
Washington State University
Press 106
Winston-Derek Publishers, Inc.
(Afro-American) 107

Specific Religions

Buddhism

Asian Humanities Press 62
China Books 70
Folklore Institute 77
Kodansha International 86
Orient Paperbacks 94
Woman in the Moon 107

Christianity

Cross Cultural Publications,
Inc. 72
Fortress Press 77
Herald Press (Mennonite,
Amish) 80
Woman in the Moon 107

Hinduism

Asian Humanities Press 62

Cross Cultural Publications,
Inc. 72
Fortress Press 77
Kodansha International 86
Orient Paperbacks 94

Islam

Cross Cultural Publications,
Inc. 72
Clarity Press, Inc. 71
Guernica Editions 78
York Press, Ltd. 108

Judaism

Fortress Press 77
Jonathan David Publishers,
Inc. 85
Kar-Ben Copies, Inc.
(children's) 86

Taoism

Asian Humanities Press 62
China Books 70
Kodansha International 86
Washington State University
Press 106

Zen

Asian Humanities Press 62
Kodansha International 86

Reprints

Avanyu Publishing, Inc. 63
Beacon Press 63

Rural Lifestyle

Avon Books 63
China Books 70
Council for Indian Education 71
Countrywoman's Press, The 72
Louisiana University Press 89
University of Alaska Press 102
Zephyr Press 109

Scholarly Works

Aegina Press 59
Asian Humanities Press 62
Avanyu Publishing, Inc. 63
Beacon Press 63
Bilingual Press/Editorial Bilingue
(Hispanic) 65
Clarity Press, Inc. 71
Denali Press, The 74
Ediciones Universal 75
Fairleigh Dickinson University
Press 76
Fortress Press (theology,
religion) 77

Scholarly Works continued
Herald Press 80
Howard University Press 82
Italica Press 85
Louisiana University Press 89
Texas A&M University Press 100
University of Alabama Press,
  The 102
University of Alaska Press 102
University of California at Los
  Angeles, American Indian
  Studies 103
University of Illinois Press 103
University of Nebraska Press 103
University of North Texas Press 105
York Press, Ltd. 108

Science
Avon Books 63
Carolrhoda Books, Inc. (chilren's) 68
University of Alabama Press,
  The 102
University of Alaska Press 102

Self-Help
Aegina Press 59
African American Images 60
Avon Books 63
Black Angels Press 66
Council for Indian Education 71
Esoterica Press 76
Herald Press (recovery) 80
Jonathan David Publishers, Inc.
  (Judaica) 85
Orient Paperbacks 94
Pelican Publishing Company,
  Inc. 94
Seal Press 97
Third World Press
  (Afro-American) 101
Volcano Press, Inc. 105
Walker and Company 106
Woman in the Moon 107
Wyrick and Company 108

Sociology
Avon Books 63
African American Images 60
Fairleigh Dickinson University
  Press 76
Hemingway Western Studies
  Series 79
Howard University Press 82
R&M Publishing Company 96

Social Justice 98
Texas A&M University Press 100
Third World Press
  (Afro-American) 101
University of California at Los
  Angeles, American Indian
  Studies 103
University of Illinois Press 103
Volcano Press, Inc. 105

Sports
Associated Publishers, Inc., The 62
Avon Books 63
Jonathan David Publishers, Inc. 85
Pelican Publishing Company,
  Inc. 94
Seal Press 97
University of Illinois Press 103

Surrealism
Esoterica Press 76
Fairleigh Dickinson University
  Press 76
York Press, Ltd. 108

Technology
Avon Books 63
University of Alabama Press,
  The 102
Zephyr Press 109

Textbooks
Aegina Press 59
Asian Humanities Press 62
Associated Publishers, Inc. (Afro-
  American) 62
Bear Flag Books (for CA) 64
China Books 70
Cross Cultural Publications,
  Inc. 72

Trade Publications
Aegina Press 59
Avanyu Publishing, Inc. 63
China Books 70
Noble Press, The 92
Orient Paperbacks 94

Translations
Alaska Native Language Center 61
Asian Humanities Press 62
Beacon Press 63
Bilingual Press/Editorial Bilingue
  (Spanish) 65
Calyx Books 67

Translations
Carolina Wren Press 68
China Books 70
Crumb Elbow Publishing 73
Dante University Press
    (Italian) 73
Guernica Editions 78
Herald Press 80
Heyday Press 80
Hill Books, Lawrence 81
Howard University Press 82
Indian Country Communications,
    Inc. (Ojibway/English) 83
Italica Pres (Italian, Latin) 85
Jordan Enterprises 85
Karnak House (African) 86
Louisiana University Press 89
Open Hand Publishing, Inc. 93
Texas A&M University Press 100
University of Alaska Press 102
York Press, Ltd. 108
Wyrick and Company 108
Zephyr Press 109

Travel
Aegina Press 59
Avon Books 63
Bear Flag Books 64
Bergli Books, Ltd. 65
Blair, Publisher, John F.
    (Southeastern US) 66
China Books 70
Countrywoman's Press, The 72
Denali Press, The 74
Heyday Press (California) 80
Hippocrene Books, Inc. 81
Italica Press 85
Moon Publications, Inc. 90
Noble Press, The 92
Pelican Publishing Company,
    Inc. 94
University of North Texas Press 105
Wyrick and Company 108
Zephyr Press 109

Tribal Life
Council for Indian Education 71
Texas A&M University Press 100
University of California at Los
    Angeles, American Indian
    Studies 103

War/Peace Issues
Avon Books 63

Blair, Publisher, John F. (Civil
    War) 66
Herald Press (against war) 80
Zephyr Press 109

Women's Issues
Aegina Press 59
Avon Books 63
Beacon Press 63
Bilingual Press/Editorial Bilingue
    (Hispanic) 65
Calyx Books 67
Carolina Wren Press 68
China Books 70
Eighth Mountain Press, The 75
Esoterica Press 76
Guernica Editions 78
Heyday Press (California) 80
Hill Books, Lawrence 81
Howard University Press 82
Noble Press, The 92
Press of MacDonald & Reinecke,
    The 95
Seal Press 97
Social Justice 98
Texas A&M University Press 100
Third World Press
    (Afro-American) 101
University of Alabama Press,
    The 102
University of Illinois Press 103
University of North Texas Press 105
Véhicule Press 105
Volcano Press, Inc. 105
Woman in the Moon 107
Women's Studies Quarterly, A
    Journal 108
Zephyr Press 109

Yoga
Asian Humanities Press 62
Kodansha International 86
Orient Paperbacks 94

Periodical Subject Index
Magazines, Newspapers, and Newsletters

This index is alphabetized using the letter-by-letter system and is divided into two sections: fiction and nonfiction.

When indicating fiction and nonfiction index topics, some editors selected more subjects that were named in their initial list of interest. Additional topics may indicate future interests or identify subcategories with the publication's basic focus such as ethnic issues for a family magazine.

Publishers indicating an interest in almost all fiction or nonfiction categories are listed under General Interest in the index.

Because this is an ethnic book, all entries accept ethnic material. Publishers who indicated they accept material from and for all ethnic cultures are listed under the subheading All Groups in the index heading Ethnic/Cultural Focus. Other publishers have their ethnic interests listed under the particular group(s) under the subheading Specific Groups.

Fiction

Adult Fables
Black Angels Poetry Newsletter 121
Cicada 125
Collages & Bricolages 126
Frontiers: A Journal of Women
    Studies 131
Hawai'i Review 133
Il Caffè 134
Middle Eastern Dancer 144
Now and Then 149
Oxford Magazine 150
SAQI: South Asia Quarterly
    International 153

Adventure
Atalantik (Indians from India) 119
Brilliant Star (Baha'i, children's) 123
Cicada 125
Dziennik Zwiazkowy (Polish Daily
    News) 128
Frontiers: A Journal of Women
    Studies 131
Hawai'i Review 133
Il Caffè 134
Mennonite Publishing House 144
Middle Eastern Dancer 144
Native Nevadan, The (Native
    American) 147

Oxford Magazine 150
Scandinavian Review (travel) 153

Avant-Garde
Asian Insights Magazine 118
Chicago Review 125
Cicada 125
Collages & Bricolages 126
Frontiers: A Journal of Women
    Studies 131
Hawai'i Review 133
Il Caffè 134
Left Curve 141
MacGuffin, The (experimental) 142
Native Nevadan, The (Native
    American) 147
Notebook/Cuaderno: A Literary
    Journal 148
Oxford Magazine 150
SAQI: South Asia Quarterly
    International 153
Southern California Anthology 156

Children's/Young Adult
Aim Magazine 113
Atalantik (Indians from India) 119
Brilliant Star (Baha'i) 123
Gwiazda Polarna (Polish) 132
Jewish Review, The 138
Mennonite Publishing House 144
Nachiketa 146
Shofar (Jewish) 154

Contemporary/Modern

Antietam Review 116
Asian Insights Magazine 118
Atalantik (Indians from India) 119
Bamboo Ridge: The Hawaii Writers'
   Quarterly 120
Cicada 125
Collages & Bricolages 126
Crazy Quilt Quarterly 126
ESSENCE Magazine
   (Black women) 129
Frontiers: A Journal of Women
   Studies 131
Hawai'i Review 133
Il Caffè 134
Left Curve 141
MacGuffin, The 142
Now and Then 149
Oxford Magazine 150
Southern California Anthology 156

Erotica

Cicada 125
Collages & Bricolages 126
Fish Drum Magazine 130
Notebook/Cuaderno: A Literary
   Journal 148

Ethnic/Cultural Focus

All Ethnic Groups

Antietam Review 116
Appalachian Heritage 117
Brilliant Star (Baha'i, children's) 123
Calapooya Collage 124
Chicago Review 125
Collages & Bricolages 126
Crazy Quilt Quarterly 126
Eagle's Flight 128
Frontiers: A Journal of Women
   Studies 131
Hawai'i Review 133
Left Curve 141
Now and Then (Appalachia) 149
Oxford Magazine (Appalachia) 150
South Dakota Review (West) 156
Southern California Anthology 156

Specific Groups

Afro-Americans/Blacks

Aim Magazine 113
Athena 120
Black Angels Poetry
   Newsletter 121

Black Scholar, The 122
ESSENCE Magazine
   (Black women) 129
Intimacy/Black Romance 137
Mennonite Publishing House 144
Notebook/Cuaderno: A Literary
   Journal 148
Obsidian II: Black Literature in
   Review 149
Shaman's Drum 154

Arabs/Arab-Americans

Aim Magazine 113
Athena 120
Heritage Florida Jewish News 133
Middle Eastern Dancer 144
Najda Newsletter 146
Notebook/Cuaderno: A Literary
   Journal 148

Armenians/Armenian-Americans

Ararat 117

Asian Indians see Indians from India

Asians/Asian-Americans

Aloha, The Magazine of Hawaii and
   the Pacific 114
Amerasia Journal 114
Asian Insights Magazine 118
Bamboo Ridge: The Hawaii Writers'
   Quarterly 120
Cicada 125
Mennonite Publishing House 144
Tozai Times 156

Basques

Shaman's Drum 154

Chinese/Chinese-Americans

Aim Magazine 113
Fish Drum Magazine 130
Shaman's Drum 154

Danes/Danish-Americans

American Dane 115
Scandinavian Review 153

Filipinos/Filipino-Americans

Aim Magazine 113
Athena 120

Finns/Finnish-Americans

Scandinavian Review 153

Hawaiians

Aloha, The Magazine of Hawaii and
   the Pacific 114
Bamboo Ridge: The Hawaii Writers'
   Quarterly 120
Tozai Times 156

Hispanics
Aim Magazine 113
Athena 120
Fish Drum Magazine 130
La Oferta Review 141
Mennonite Publishing House 144
Notebook/Cuaderno: A Literary
Journal 148

Iceland
Scandinavian Review 153

Indians from India/Indo-Americans
Aim Magazine 113
Atalantik 119
Athena 120
India Currents 135
Nachiketa (children's) 146
Notebook/Cuaderno: A Literary
Journal 148
SAQI: South Asia Quarterly
International 153
Shaman's Drum 154

Indians of Central/South America
Aim Magazine 113
Notebook/Cuaderno: A Literary
Journal 148

Israelis
Jewish Review, The 138
Midstream, A Monthly Jewish
Review 145
Response: A Contemporary Jewish
Review 151
Shaman's Drum 154

Italians/Italian Americans
Arba Sicula 118
Il Caffè 134

Japanese/Japanese-Americans
Athena 120
Bamboo Ridge: The Hawaii Writers'
Quarterly 120
Cicada 125
Fish Drum Magazine 130
Japanophile 138
Shaman's Drum 154
Tozai Times 156

Jews
B'nai B'rith International Jewish
Monthly 123
Heritage Florida Jewish News 133
Jewish Review, The 138
Lilith (women) 142
Midstream, A Monthly Jewish
Review 145

Response: A Contemporary Jewish
Review 151
Shofar (children's) 154

Koreans/Korean-Americans
Bamboo Ridge: The Hawaii Writers'
Quarterly 120
Shaman's Drum 154

Latin Americans
Aim Magazine 113
La Gente de Aztlan 140
Notebook/Cuaderno: A Literary
Journal 148

Mexicans/Mexican-Americans
La Gente de Aztlan 140
La Oferta Review 141
Notebook/Cuaderno: A Literary
Journal 148

Native Americans
Athena 120
Fish Drum Magazine 130
Indian Life 135
Mennonite Publishing House 134
Native Nevadan, The 147
Notebook/Cuaderno: A Literary
Journal 148
Shaman's Drum 154

Poles/Polish Americans
Dziennik Zwiazkowy (Polish Daily
News) 128
Gwiazda Polarna 132
Language Bridges 140

Romanians/Romanian-Americans
Miorita, A Journal of Romanian
Studies 145

Nordic Peoples
Scandinavian Review 153

Norwegians/Norwegian Americans
Scandinavian Review 153

Scandinavians/Scandinavian-
Americans
Scandinavian Review 153

Vietnamese/Vietnamese-Americans
Bamboo Ridge: The Hawaii Writers'
Quarterly 120
Shaman's Drum 154

Fantasy
Cicada 125
Collages & Bricolages 126
Frontiers: A Journal of Women
Studies 131
Hawai'i Review 133

Fantasy continued
Middle Eastern Dancer 144

Folklore
Brilliant Star (Baha'i, children's) 123
Frontiers: A Journal of Women
Studies 131
Hawai'i Review 133
Il Caffè 134
India Currents 135
Indian Life (American Indian) 135
Lilith (Jewish women) 142
Middle Eastern Dancer 144
Native Nevadan, The (Native
American) 147
Notebook/Cuaderno: A Literary
Journal 148
Now and Then 149
Oxford Magazine 150
SAQI: South Asia Quarterly
International 153
Tozai Times (Japanese-
American) 156

General Interest
Atalantik (Indians from India) 119
Cicada 125
Dziennik Zwiazkowy (Polish Daily
News) 128
Frontiers: A Journal of Women
Studies 131
Gwiazda Polarna (Poles) 132
Hawai'i Review 133
Hayden's Ferry Review 133
Il Caffè 134
Language Bridges (Poles) 140
MacGuffin, The 142
Manoa: A Pacific Journal of
International Writing 143
Mennonite Publishing House 144
Middle Eastern Dancer 144
Now and Then 149
Oxford Magazine 150
Rohwedder, International Journal of
Literature and Art 152
San Jose Studies 152
SAQI: South Asia Quarterly
International 153
Southern California Anthology 156

Historical Fiction
Aim Magazine 113
Ararat 117
Atalantik (Indians from India) 119

Brilliant Star (Baha'i, children's) 123
Cicada 125
Frontiers: A Journal of Women
Studies 131
Il Caffè 134
Indian Life (Native Americans) 135
Japanophile 138
Jewish Review, The 138
Language Bridges (Poles) 140
Left Curve 141
Mennonite Publishing House 144
Middle Eastern Dancer 144
Nachiketa (children's) 146
Native Nevadan, The (Native
American) 147
Notebook/Cuaderno: A Literary
Journal 148
Now and Then 149
Oxford Magazine 150
SAQI: South Asia Quarterly
International 153
Southern California Anthology 156
Tozai Times (Japanese-
American) 156

Holiday Stories
ESSENCE Magazine
(Black women) 129
Il Caffè 134
Japanophile 138
Jewish Review, The 138
Lilith (Jewish) 142
Mennonite Publishing House 144
Middle Eastern Dancer 144
Shofar (Jewish children's) 154
Tozai Times (Japanese-
American) 156

Humor
Asian Insights Magazine 118
Atalantik (Indians from India) 119
Cicada 125
Collages & Bricolages 126
Dziennik Zwiazkowy (Polish Daily
News) 128
ESSENCE Magazine
(Black women) 129
Frontiers: A Journal of Women
Studies 131
Hawai'i Review 133
Il Caffè 134
India Currents 135
Jewish Review, The 138
Language Bridges (Poles) 140

Lilith (Jewish) 142
Middle Eastern Dancer 144
Nachiketa (children's) 146
Native Nevadan, The (Native
    American) 147
Now and Then 149
Oxford Magazine 150
SAQI: South Asia Quarterly
    International 153
Tozai Times (Japanese-
    American) 156

Literary
Antietam Review 116
Ararat 117
Asian Insights Magazine 118
Atalantik (Indians from India) 119
Bamboo Ridge: The Hawaii Writers'
    Quarterly 120
Calapooya Collage 124
Chicago Review 125
Cicada 125
Collages & Bricolages 126
Crazy Quilt Quarterly 126
Eagle's Flight 128
ESSENCE Magazine
    (Black women) 129
Fish Drum Magazine 130
Frontiers: A Journal of Women
    Studies 131
Gypsy Literary Magazine 132
Hawai'i Review 133
Il Caffè 134
India Currents 135
Indian Literature (Indians of
    India) 136
Japanophile 138
Journal, The 139
Language Bridges (Poles) 140
Left Curve 141
Lilith (Jewish) 142
MacGuffin, The 142
Maryland Review 143
Nimrod Contemporary Prose and
    Poetry Journal 148
Notebook/Cuaderno: A Literary
    Journal 148
Now and Then 149
Obsidian II: Black Literature in
    Review 149
Rackham Journal of the Arts and
    Humanities 151

SAQI: South Asia Quarterly
    International 153
Southern California Anthology 156

Mainstream
Atalantik (Indians from India) 119
Bamboo Ridge: The Hawaii Writers'
    Quarterly 120
Calapooya Collage 124
Cicada 125
Crazy Quilt Quarterly 126
Eagle's Flight 128
Gwiazda Polarna (Polish) 132
Hawai'i Review 133
Il Caffè 134
Japanophile 138
Maryland Review 143
Now and Then 149
Oxford Magazine 150

Metaphysic/New Age
Cicada 125
Middle Eastern Dancer 144
SAQI: South Asia Quarterly
    International 153

Mystery/Horror
Atalantik (Indians from India) 119
Cicada 125
Middle Eastern Dancer 144

Plays/Drama
Asian Insights Magazine 118
Atalantik (Indians from India) 119
Athena 120
Bamboo Ridge: The Hawaii Writers'
    Quarterly 120
Collages & Bricolages 126
Crazy Quilt Quarterly 126
Fish Drum Magazine 130
Hawai'i Review 133
Il Caffè 134
Indian Literature (Indians of
    India) 136
Language Bridges (Poles) 140
Manoa: A Pacific Journal of
    International Writing 143
Middle Eastern Dancer 144
Now and Then 149
Whispering Wind
    (Native American) 157

Romance
Atalantik (Indians from India) 119
Black Angels Poetry Newsletter 121

Romance continued
Cicada 125
Eagle's Flight 128
Middle Eastern Dancer 144

Science Fiction
Atalantik (Indians from India) 119
Cicada 125
Collages & Bricolages 126
Crazy Quilt Quarterly 126
Hawai'i Review 133
Il Caffè 134
Language Bridges (Poles) 140
Middle Eastern Dancer 144

Short Stories
Aim Magazine 113
Aloha, The Magazine of Hawaii and the
    Pacific 114
Amerasia Journal 114
American Dane 115
Appalachian Heritage 117
Ararat 117
Arba Sicula 118
Asian Insights Magazine 118
Atalantik (Indians from India) 119
Athena 120
Bamboo Ridge: The Hawaii Writers'
    Quarterly 120
Black Angels Poetry Newsletter 121
Black Scholar, The 122
B'nai B'rith International Jewish
    Monthly 123
Chicago Review 125
Cicada 125
Collages & Bricolages 126
Crazy Quilt Quarterly 126
Detroit Jewish News 127
Dziennik Zwiazkowy (Polish Daily
    News) 128
Eagle's Flight 128
Fish Drum Magazine 130
Frontiers: A Journal of Women
    Studies 131
Gwiazda Polarna (Polish) 132
Gypsy Literary Magazine 132
Hawai'i Review 133
Hayden's Ferry Review 133
Il Caffè 134
India Currents 135
Indian Life (American-Indian
    legends) 135

Indian Literature (Indians of
    India) 136
Intimacy/Black Romance 137
Japanophile 138
Journal, The 139
La Gente de Aztlan 140
Language Bridges (Poles) 149
Lilith (Jewish) 142
MacGuffin, The 142
Manoa: A Pacific Journal of
    International Writing 143
Maryland Review 143
Mennonite Publishing House 144
Middle Eastern Dancer 144
Midstream, A Monthly Jewish
    Review 145
Miorita, A Journal of Romanian
    Studies 145
Nachiketa (children's) 146
Najda Newsletter (Arab) 146
Native Nevadan, The (Native
    American) 147
Nimrod Contemporary Prose and
    Poetry Journal 148
Now and Then 149
Obsidian II: Black Literature in
    Review 149
Oxford Magazine 150
Rackham Journal of the Arts and
    Humanities 151
Response: A Contemporary Jewish
    Review 151
San Jose Studies 152
Scandinavian Review 153
Shaman's Drum 154
South Dakota Review 156
Tozai Times (Japanese-
    American) 156

Sports
Il Caffè 134
Japanophile 138
Rohwedder, International Journal of
    Literature and Art 152
Southern California Anthology 156

Surrealism
Atalantik (Indians from India) 119
Cicada 125
Collages & Bricolages 126
Hawai'i Review 133
Il Caffè 134
Notebook/Cuaderno: A Literary
    Journal 148

Translations
Amerasia Journal 114
American Dane 115
Ararat (Armenian) 117
Arba Siscula 118
Athena 120
Black Scholar, The 122
Chicago Review 125
Cicada 125
Dziennik Zwiazkowy (Polish Daily
News) 128
Fish Drum Magazine 130
*Frontiers: A Journal of Women
Studies* 131
Gwiazda Polarna (Polish) 132
Gypsy Literary Magazine 132
Hawai'i Review 133
Il Caffè (Italian) 134
India Currents 135
Indian Literature (Indians of
India) 136
Jewish Review, The 138
Language Bridges (Polish) 140
Left Curve 141
Lilith (Jewish) 142
*Manoa: A Pacific Journal of
International Writing* 143
*Midstream, A Monthly Jewish
Review* 145
*Miorita, A Journal of Romanian
Studies* 145
Nachiketa (children's folklore) 146
Najda Newsletter (Arab) 146
*Nimrod Contemporary Prose and
Poetry Journal* 148
Oxford Magazine 150
*Rackham Journal of the Arts and
Humanities* 151
*Response: A Contemporary Jewish
Review* 151
*Rohwedder, International Journal of
Literature and Art* 152
*SAQI: South Asia Quarterly
International* 153
Scandinavian Review 153
South Dakota Review 156
Southern California Anthology 156

Westerns
Oxford Magazine 150

Women's Issues
Atalantik (Indians from India) 119

Athena 120
*Bamboo Ridge: The Hawaii Writers'
Quarterly* 120
Collages & Bricolages 126
ESSENCE Magazine
(Black women) 129
*Frontiers: A Journal of Women
Studies* 131
Hawai'i Review 133
Il Caffè 134
Japanophile 138
Lilith (Jewish) 142
Mennonite Publishing House 144
Middle Eastern Dancer 144
Native Nevadan, The (Native
American) 147
*Notebook/Cuaderno: A Literary
Journal* 148
Now and Then 149
*Obsidian II: Black Literature in
Review* 149
*SAQI: South Asia Quarterly
International* 153
Scandinavian Review 153
Southern California Anthology 156

Nonfiction

Adventure
American Dane 115
Atalantik (Indians from India) 119
Cicada 125
Dziennik Zwiazkowy (Polish Daily
News) 128
India Currents 135
Middle Eastern Dancer 144
Oxford Magazine 150
Scandinavian Review (travel) 153

Agriculture
*American Indian Culture and Research
Journal* 115
Arab Studies Quarterly 117
*Fort Concho and the South Plains
Journal* 131
*Frontiers: A Journal of Women
Studies* 131

Anthropology
*American Indian Culture and Research
Journal* 115
Arab Studies Quarterly 117

Anthropology continued
Asian Perspectives 119
Fort Concho and the South Plains
    Journal 131
Frontiers: A Journal of Women
    Studies 131
International Migration Review 137
Jewish Review, The 138
Migration World Magazine 148
Native Peoples Magazine 147
Notebook/Cuaderno: A Literary
    Journal 148
Rackham Journal of the Arts and
    Humanities 151
Shaman's Drum 154
Société 155
Whispering Wind
    (Native American) 157

Antiques
Scandinavian Review 153

Archaeology
American Indian Culture and Research
    Journal 115
Arab Studies Quarterly 117
Ararat 117
Asian Perspectives 119
Cicada 125
Fort Concho and the South Plains
    Journal 131
Heritage Florida Jewish News 133
Il Caffè 134
Jewish Review, The 138
Middle Eastern Dancer 144
News From Indian Country 148
Société 155

Architecture
American Indian Culture and Research
    Journal 115
Arab Studies Quarterly 117
Finnam Newsletter 130
Fort Concho and the South Plains
    Journal 131
Il Caffè 134
Japanophile 138
Left Curve 141
Middle Eastern Dancer 144
Notebook/Cuaderno: A Literary
    Journal 148
Polonia's Voice: The Polish-American
    Journal 151
Scandinavian Review 153

Société 155

Art
Aloha, The Magazine of Hawaii and the
    Pacific 114
American Indian Culture and Research
    Journal 115
Arab Studies Quarterly 117
Asian Insights Magazine 118
Asian Week 119
Cicada 125
Collages & Bricolages 126
Dziennik Zwiazkowy (Polish Daily
    News) 128
East Bay Monitor 128
Frontiers: A Journal of Women
    Studies 131
Il Caffè 134
India Currents 135
Jewish Review, The 138
Language Bridges (Polish) 140
Left Curve 141
Middle Eastern Dancer 144
Native Nevadan, The (Native
    American) 147
Notebook/Cuaderno: A Literary
    Journal 148
Oxford Magazine 150
Polonian 150
Polonia's Voice: The Polish-American
    Journal 151
Scandinavian Review 153
Société 155

Astrology
Cicada 125
Gwiazda Polarna (Polish) 132
Hinduism Today 134
Il Caffè 134
Polonian 150

Astronomy
Cicada 125
Dziennik Zwiazkowy (Polish Daily
    News) 128
Polonian 150
Polonia's Voice: The Polish-American
    Journal 151

Biography
Aim Magazine 113
Amerasia Journal 114
Atalantik (Indians from India) 119
Cicada 125
Crazy Quilt Quarterly 126

CrossCurrents 127
Dziennik Zwiazkowy (Polish Daily
News) 128
Finnam Newsletter 130
Fort Concho and the South Plains
Journal 131
Frontiers: A Journal of Women
Studies 131
Il Caffè 134
Japanophile 138
Lilith (Jewish women) 142
Midstream, A Monthly Jewish
Review 145
Native Nevadan, The (Native
American) 147
Notebook/Cuaderno: A Literary
Journal 148
Oxford Magazine 150
Polonian 150

Book/Entertainment Reviews
Aloha, The Magazine of Hawaii and the
Pacific 114
Amerasia Journal 114
American Indian Culture and Research
Journal (book) 115
American Dane 115
American Indian Law Review 116
Arab Studies Quarterly 117
Ararat 117
Asian Perspectives 119
Asian Week 119
Arba Sicula (Italian/Sicilian) 118
Black Angels Poetry Newsletter 121
Black Enterprise 122
Black Scholar, The 122
B'nai B'rith International Jewish
Monthly 123
Canadian Journal of Native
Education 124
Chicago Review 125
Cicada 125
Collages & Bricolages 126
Dziennik Zwiazkowy (Polish Daily
News) 128
Eagle's Flight (book) 128
East Bay Monitor (book) 128
El Tecolote 129
ESSENCE Magazine
(Black women) 129
Fish Drum Magazine 130
Fort Concho and the South Plains
Journal 131

Frontiers: A Journal of Women
Studies 131
Gwiazda Polarna (Polish) 132
Gypsy Literary Magazine 132
Hawai'i Review 133
Il Caffè 134
India Currents 135
Indian Literature (Indians of
India) 136
International Fiction Review, The 137
International Migration Review 137
Jewish Review, The 138
Journal The, (poetry) 139
Journal of Afro-American Historical
and Genealogical Society 139
La Gente de Aztlan 140
Language Bridges (Polish) 140
Manoa: A Pacific Journal of
International Writing 143
Middle Eastern Dancer 144
Midstream, A Monthly Jewish
Review 145
Migration World Magazine 145
Miorita, A Journal of Romanian
Studies 145
Nachiketa (children's books) 146
Najda Newsletter (Arab) 146
Native Nevadan, The (Native
American) 147
Notebook/Cuaderno: A Literary
Journal (book) 148
Now and Then (book) 149
Obsidian II: Black Literature in
Review 149
Response: A Contemporary Jewish
Review 151
Société (book) 155
Tozai Times (Japanese-
American) 156
[Veinte] 20 de Mayo Spanish
Newspaper 157
Whispering Wind
(Native American) 157

Business/Economics
Aloha, The Magazine of Hawaii and the
Pacific 114
Asian Week 119
Black Enterprise 122
Dziennik Zwiazkowy (Polish Daily
News) 128
Finnam Newsletter 130
Il Caffè 134

Business/Economics continued
India Currents 135
International Migration Review 137
Japanophile 138
Jewish Review, The 138
Middle Eastern Dancer 144
Migration World Magazine 148
Native Nevadan, The (Native
  American) 147
News From Indian Country 148
Polonian 150
Polonia's Voice: The Polish-American
  Journal 151
Scandinavian Review 153
[Veinte] 20 de Mayo Spanish
  Newspaper 157

Child Care/Development
Dziennik Zwiazkowy (Polish Daily
  News) 128
Frontiers: A Journal of Women
  Studies 131
Hinduism Today 134
News From Indian Country 148
Scandinavian Review 153

Children's Nonfiction
Brilliant Star (Baha'i) 123
Finnam Newsletter 130
Shofar (Jewish) 154
Whispering Wind
  (Native American) 157

Comedy/Humor
American Dane 115
Asian Week 119
Atalantik (Indians from India) 119
Cicada 125
Collages & Bricolages 126
Dziennik Zwiazkowy (Polish Daily
  News) 128
India Currents 135
Jewish Review, The 138
Language Bridges (Polish) 140
La Oferta Review 141
Middle Eastern Dancer 144
Native Nevadan, The (Native
  American) 147
News From Indian Country 148
Oxford Magazine 150
Polonian 150
SAQI: South Asia Quarterly
  International 153

Tozai Times (Japanese-
  American) 156

Comics/Cartoons
Il Caffè 134
Japanophile 138
Native Nevadan, The (Native
  American) 147
Shofar (Jewish children's) 154
Whispering Wind
  (Native American) 157

Cooking/Foods/Nutrition
Aloha, The Magazine of Hawaii and the
  Pacific 114
Arba Sicula (Italian/Sicilian) 118
Asian Insights Magazine 118
Detroit Jewish News 127
Dziennik Zwiazkowy (Polish Daily
  News) 128
Gwiazda Polarna (Polish) 132
Heritage Florida Jewish News 133
Il Caffè 134
India Currents 135
Indian Life (Native-American
  recipes) 135
Japanophile 138
Jewish Review, The 138
Lilith (Jewish) 142
Middle Eastern Dancer 144
Najda Newsletter (Arab) 146
News From Indian Country 148
Notebook/Cuaderno: A Literary
  Journal 148
Polonian 150
[Veinte] 20 de Mayo Spanish
  Newspaper 157

Crafts
Brilliant Star (Baha'i, children's) 123
Indian Life (Native American) 135
Now and Then 149
Polonian 150
Whispering Wind
  (Native American) 157

Dance
American Indian Culture and Research
  Journal 115
Finnam Newsletter 130
Il Caffè 134
India Currents 135
Japanophile 138
Middle Eastern Dancer 144

Native Nevadan, The (Native American) 147
Notebook/Cuaderno: A Literary Journal 148
Now and Then (Appalachian) 149
Polonian 150
Polonia's Voice: The Polish-American Journal 151
Scandinavian Review 153

Disabilities
Il Caffè 134
Mennonite Publishing House 144
Oxford Magazine 150
Polonian 150

Education
American Indian Culture and Research Journal 115
Arab Studies Quarterly 117
Asian Insights Magazine 118
Asian Week 119
Atalantik (Indians from India) 119
Black Angels Poetry Newsletter 121
Canadian Journal of Native Education 124
Dziennik Zwiazkowy (Polish Daily News) 128
Finnam Newsletter 130
Frontiers: A Journal of Women Studies 131
Hinduism Today 134
Il Caffè 134
Japanophile 138
Jewish Review, The 138
Journal of American Indian Education 139
Journal of Afro-American Historical and Genealogical Society 139
Nachiketa (children's) 146
Native Nevadan, The (Native American) 147
Polonian 150
SAQI: South Asia Quarterly International 153
Société 155

Entertainment
Asian Insights Magazine 118
Atalantik (Indians from India) 119
Dziennik Zwiazkowy (Polish Daily News) 128
Finnam Newsletter 130
Gwiazda Polarna (Polish) 132

Il Caffè 134
India Currents 135
Japanophile 138
Middle Eastern Dancer 144

Environment/Ecology *see also* **Nature**
Atalantik (Indians from India) 119
Language Bridges (Polish) 140
Native Nevadan, The (Native American) 147
Native Peoples Magazine 147
News From Indian Country 148
Société 155

Essays
Aim Magazine 113
Amerasia Journal 114
American Dane 115
American Indian Law Review 116
Appalachian Heritage 117
Ararat 117
Arba Sicula (Italian/Sicilian) 118
Asian Insights Magazine 118
Asian Perspectives 119
Asian Week 119
Bamboo Ridge: The Hawaii Writers' Quarterly 120
Black Angels Poetry Newsletter 121
Black Collegian, The 121
Calapooya Collage 124
Canadian Journal of Native Education 124
Chicago Review 125
Cicada 125
Collages & Bricolages 126
Crazy Quilt Quarterly 126
CrossCurrents 127
Detroit Jewish News 127
Dziennik Zwiazkowy (Polish Daily News) 128
ESSENCE Magazine (Black women) 129
Finnam Newsletter 130
Fish Drum Magazine 130
Fort Concho and the South Plains Journal 131
Gypsy Literary Magazine 132
Hawai'i Review 133
Hayden's Ferry Review 133
Il Caffè 134
India Currents 135
Indian Literature (Indians of India) 136

Essays continued

*International Fiction Review,
The* 137
International Migration Review 137
Japanophile 138
Language Bridges (Polish) 140
Left Curve 141
Lilith (Jewish) 142
Living Blues (music) 142
MacGuffin, The 142
*Manoa: A Pacific Journal of
International Writing* 143
Mennonite Publishing House 144
Middle Eastern Dancer 144
Migration World Magazine 145
Nachiketa (children's) 146
Najda Newsletter (Arab) 146
Native Peoples Magazine 147
*Nimrod Contemporary Prose and
Poetry Journal* 148
Now and Then 149
Oxford Magazine 150
Polonian 150
*Rackham Journal of the Arts and
Humanities* 151
*Response: A Contemporary Jewish
Review* 151
*Rohwedder, International Journal of
Literature and Art* 152
Société 155
South Dakota Review 156
Tozai Times 156
*[Veinte] 20 de Mayo Spanish
Newspaper* 157
Whispering Wind
(Native American) 157

Ethnic/Cultural Focus

All Ethnic Groups

Antietam Review 116
Appalachian Heritage 117
Brilliant Star (Baha'i, children's) 123
Calapooya Collage 124
Chicago Review 125
Collages & Bricolages 126
Cultural Survival Quarterly 127
*Frontiers: A Journal of Women
Studies* 131
Hawai'i Review 133
*International Fiction Review,
The* 137
Left Curve 141

Native Peoples Magazine 147
Now and Then (Appalachia) 149
Oxford Magazine (Appalachia) 150
South Review (West) 156

Specific Groups

Afro-Americans/Blacks
Aim Magazine 113
Atalantik (Indians from India) 119
Athena 120
Black Angels Poetry Newsletter 121
Black Collegian, The 121
Black Enterprise 122
Black Scholar, The 122
East Bay Monitor 128
ESSENCE Magazine
(Black women) 129
*Fort Concho and the South Plains
Journal* 131
Intimacy/Black Romance 137
*Journal of Afro-American Historical
and Genealogical Society* 139
Living Blues 142
Mennonite Publishing House 144
*Notebook/Cuaderno: A Literary
Journal* 148
Now and Then 149
Société 155

Arabs/Arab-Americans
Aim Magazine 113
Arab Studies Quarterly 117
Athena 120
Middle Eastern Dancer 144
Najda Newsletter 146
*Notebook/Cuaderno: A Literary
Journal* 148

Armenians/Armenian-Americans
Ararat 117

Asian Indians *see* Indians from India
Asians/Asian Americans
*Aloha, The Magazine of Hawaii and
the Pacific* 114
Asian Insights Magazine 118
Asian Perspectives 119
Asian Week 119
*Bamboo Ridge: The Hawaii Writers'
Quarterly* 120
Cicada 125
CrossCurrents 127
East Bay Monitor 128
Mennonite Publishing House 144
Native Peoples Magazine 147

Obsidian II: Black Literature in
  Review 149
Tozai Times 156

Cajun/Creole
East Bay Monitor 128

Chinese/Chinese-Americans
Aim Magazine 113
East Bay Monitor 128
Fish Drum Magazine 130

Czechoslovakians
Sarmatian Review, The 153
Sokol Minnesota Slovo 155

Danes/Danish-Americans
American Dane 115
Scandinavian Review 153

Eastern Europeans
Sarmatian Review, The 153

Filipinos
Aim Magazine 113
Athena 120
CrossCurrents 127
East Bay Monitor 128

Finns/Finnish Americans
Finnam Newsletter 130
Scandinavian Review 153

Greeks
Middle Eastern Dancer 144

Hawaiians
Aloha, The Magazine of Hawaii and
  the Pacific 114
Bamboo Ridge: The Hawaii Writers'
  Quarterly 120
Japanophile 138

Hispanics
Aim Magazine 113
Athena 120
East Bay Monitor 128
El Tecolote 129
Fish Drum Magazine 130
Fort Concho and the South Plains
  Journal 141
Mennonite Publishing House 144
Notebook/Cuaderno: A Literary
  Journal 148
[Veinte] 20 de Mayo Spanish
  Newspaper 157

Icelanders
Scandinavian Review 153

Indians from India/Indians of India
Aim Magazine 113
Atalantik (Indians from India) 119

Athena 120
East Bay Monitor 128
Hinduism Today 134
India Currents 135
Indian Literature 136
India-West 136
Nachiketa (children's; include
  Jains, Parsis) 148
Notebook/Cuaderno: A Literary
  Journal 148
SAQI: South Asia Quarterly
  International 153

Indians of Central/South America
Aim Magazine 113
EastBay Monitor 128
Notebook/Cuaderno: A Literary
  Journal 148

Irish/Irish-Americans
Fort Concho and the South Plains
  Journal 131

Israelis/Israel
Arab Studies Quarterly 117
B'nai B'rith International Jewish
  Monthly 123
Detroit Jewish News 127
Jewish Review, The 138
Lilith 142
Midstream, A Monthly Jewish
  Review 145
Response: A Contemporary Jewish
  Review 151

Italians/Italian-Americans
Arba Sicula (Italians/Sicilians) 118
Fort Concho and the South Plains
  Journal 131
Il Caffè 134
Notebook/Cuaderno: A Literary
  Journal 148

Japanese/Japanese-Americans
Athena 120
Bamboo Ridge: The Hawaii Writers'
  Quarterly 120
Cicada 125
CrossCurrents 127
East Bay Monitor 128
Fish Drum Magazine 130
Japanophile 138
Tozai Times 156

Jews
Arab Studies Quarterly 117
B'nai B'rith International Jewish
  Monthly 123

Jews continued
  Detroit Jewish News 127
  *Fort Concho and the South Plains
    Journal* 131
  Heritage Florida Jewish News 133
  Jewish Review, The 138
  Language Bridges 140
  Lilith 142
  *Midstream, A Monthly Jewish
    Review* 145
  *Response: A Contemporary Jewish
    Review* 151
  Sarmation Review, The 153
  Shofar (children's) 154
Koreans/Korean-Americans
  *Bamboo Ridge: The Hawaii Writers'
    Quarterly* 120
  CrossCurrents 127
Latin Americans
  Aim Magazine 113
  El Tecolote 129
  La Gente de Aztlan 140
  *Notebook/Cuaderno: A Literary
    Journal* 148
  *[Veinte] 20 de Mayo Spanish
    Newspaper* 157
Mexicans
  East Bay Monitor 128
  La Gente de Aztlan 140
  *Notebook/Cuaderno: A Literary
    Journal* 148
  *[Veinte] 20 de Mayo Spanish
    Newspaper* 157
Native Americans
  *American Indian Culture and
    Research Journal* 115
  American Indian Law Review 116
  Athena 120
  *Canadian Journal of Native
    Education* 124
  East Bay Monitor 128
  Fish Drum Magazine 130
  *Fort Concho and the South Plains
    Journal* 131
  *Journal of American Indian
    Education* 139
  Mennonite Publishing House 144
  Native Nevadan, The 147
  News From Indian Country 148
  *Notebook/Cuaderno: A Literary
    Journal* 148
  Now and Then 149

  Whispering Wind 157
Nordic Peoples
  Scandinavian Review 153
Norwegians/Norwegian-Americans
  Scandinavian Review 153
Poles/Polish Americans
  Dziennik Zwiazkowy (Polish Daily
    News) 128
  Gwiazda Polarna 132
  Language Bridges 140
  Polonian 150
  *Polonia's Voice: The Polish American
    Journal* 151
  Sarmation Review, The 153
Romanians
  *Miorita, A Journal of Romanian
    Studies* 145
Slavic Peoples
  *Polonia's Voice: The Polish American
    Journal* 151
  Sarmation Review, The 153
**Scandinavians/Scandinavian-
  Americans**
  Finnam Newsletter 130
  Scandinavian Review 153
Thais/Thai-Americans
  *Bamboo Ridge: The Hawaii Writers'
    Quarterly* 120
  CrossCurrents 127

Family Issues
  Aim Magazine 113
  Asian Insights Magazine 118
  Asian Week 119
  Atalantik (Indians from India) 119
  Athena 120
  Cicada 125
  Dziennik Zwiazkowy (Polish Daily
    News) 128
  Heritage Florida Jewish News 133
  Il Caffè 134
  Jewish Review, The 138
  La Oferta Review 141
  Lilith (Jewish) 142
  Mennonite Publishing House 144
  Middle Eastern Dancer 144
  Native Nevadan, The 147
  Now and Then 149
  Oxford Magazine 150
  Polonian 150
  Tozai Times 156

Fashion

Gwiazda Polarna 132
Il Caffè 134
Intimacy/Black Romance 137
Polonian 150
Scandinavian Review 153

Festivals/Holidays

Asian Insights Magazine 118
Asian Week 119
Atalantik 119
Dziennik Zwiazkowy 128
East Bay Monitor 128
Finnam Newsletter 130
India Currents 135
Jewish Review, The 138
La Oferta Review 141
Middle Eastern Dancer 144
Native Nevadan, The 147
Polonian 150
Scandinavian Review 153
Shofar (Jewish children's) 154

Film/Television/Video

Asian Insights Magazine 118
Asian Week 119
Collages & Bricolages 126
Frontiers: A Journal of Women
    Studies 131
Jewish Review, The 138
Left Curve 141
Lilith 142
Middle Eastern Dancer 144
Now and Then 149
Obsidian II: Black Literature in
    Review 149
Polonian 150

Folkore

American Dane 115
American Indian Culture and Research
    Journal 115
Brilliant Star (Baha'i, children's) 123
Canadian Journal of Native
    Education 124
Finnam Newsletter 130
Frontiers: A Journal of Women
    Studies 131
India Currents 135
Japanophile 138
Jewish Review 138
Lilith (Jewish) 142
Middle Eastern Dancer 144
Nachiketa (children's) 146

Now and Then 149
Oxford Magazine 150
Polonian 150
Polonia's Voice: The Polish-American
    Journal 151
Rackham Journal of the Arts and
    Humanities 151
SAQI: South Asia Quarterly
    International 153
Sociètè 155
Tozai Times (Japanese-
    American) 156
Whispering Wind
    (Native American) 157

Games/Puzzles

Atalantik (Indians from India) 119
Brilliant Star (Baha'i, children's) 123
Polonian 150
Shofar (Jewish children's) 154
Whispering Wind
    (Native American) 157

Gay/Lesbian Issues

Asian Week 119
Athena 120
Calapooya Collage 124
Cicada 125
Collages & Bricolages 126
Fish Drum Magazine 130
Frontiers: A Journal of Women
    Studies 131
Jewish Review, The 138
Notebook/Cuaderno: A Literary
    Journal 148
Oxford Magazine 150
Sociètè 155

Genealogy

Journal of Afro-American Historical
    and Genealogical Society 139
Migration World Magazine 145
Now and Then (Appalachian) 149
Polonian 150
SAQI: South Asian Quarterly
    International 153

General Interest

Aim Magazine 113
Asian Insights Magazine 118
Asian Week 119
Atalantik (Indians from India) 119
Cicada 125

General Interest continued
Dziennik Awiazkowy (Polish Daily
News) 128
Gwiazda Polarna (Polish) 132
Hayden's Ferry Review 133
Il Caffè 134
India Currents 135
India-West 136
MacGuffin, The 142
Mennonite Publishing House 144
Midstream, A Monthly Jewish
Review 145
News From Indian Country 148
Polonian 150
Rohwedder, International Journal of
Literature and Art 152
San Jose Studies 152
Sarmatian Review, The 153

Government/Politics
American Indian Culture and Research
Journal 115
Arab Studies Quarterly 117
Asian Insights Magazine 118
Asian Week 119
Fort Concho and the South Plains
Journal 131
Jewish Review, The 138
Left Curve 141
Midstream, A Monthly Jewish
Review 145
Native Nevadan, The (Native
American) 147
News From Indian Country 148
Polonian 150
Scandinavian Review 153

Health/Fitness
Asian Insights Magazine 118
Dziennik Zwiazkowy (Polish Daily
News) 128
Finnam Newsletter 130
Intimacy/Black Romance 137
Jewish Review, The 138
Middle Eastern Dancer 144
Polonian 150

History
Aim Magazine 113
Aloha, The Magazine of Hawaii and the
Pacific 114
Amerasia Journal 1141
American Indian Culture and Research
Journal 115

Asian Insights 118
Asian Week 119
Atalantik (Indians from India) 119
Black Collegian, The 121
B'nai B'rith International Jewish
Monthly 121
Brilliant Star (Baha'i, children's) 123
Cicada 125
CrossCurrents 127
Finnam Newsletter 130
Fort Concho and the South Plains
Review 131
Frontiers: A Journal of Women
Studies 131
Il Caffè 134
Japanophile 138
Jewish Review, The 138
Journal of Afro-American Historical
and Genealogical Society 139
Langague Bridges (Polish) 140
Lilith 142
Middle Eastern Dancer 144
Native Nevadan, The 147
Native Peoples Magazine 147
Notebook/Cuaderno: A Literary
Journal 148
Now and Then (Appalachian) 149
Oxford Magazine 150
Polonian 150
Sarmatian Review, The 153
Whispering Wind
(Native American) 157

Hobbies
Brilliant Star 123
Middle Eastern Dancer 144
Polonian 150
Sociètè 155

Holistic Practices
Lilith 142
Notebook/Cuaderno: A Literary
Journal 148
SAQI: South Asia Quarterly
International 153

Human Potential
Atalantik (Indians from India) 119
Black Collegian, The 121
Cicada 125
East Bay Monitor 128
Jewish Review, The 138
Native Nevadan, The 147
San Jose Studies 152

SAQI: South Asia Quarterly International 153

Immigrants/Immigration
Amerasia Journal 114
American Dane 115
Arab Studies Quarterly 117
Ararat 117
Asian Insights Magazine 118
Asian Week 119
Atalantik 119
Collages & Bricolges 126
CrossCurrents 127
Dziennik Zwiazkowy 128
East Bay Monitor 128
Finnam Newsletter 130
Gwiazda Polarna 132
India Currents 135
International Migration Review 137
Jewish Review, The 138
Language Bridges 140
Left Curve 141
Lilith 142
Migration World Magazine 145
Now and Then 149
Polonian 150
SAQI: South Asia Quarterly International 153

Labor
Amerasia Journal 114
Asian Week 119
Dziennik Zwiazkowy (Polish Daily News) 128
Il Caffè 134
International Migration Review 137
Left Curve 141
Migration World Magazine 145
Notebook/Cuaderno: A Literary Journal 148
Polonian 150

Law
American Indian Culture and Research Journal 115
American Indian Law Review 116
Arab Studies Quarterly 117
Dziennik Zwiazkowy (Polish Daily News) 128
Frontiers: A Journal of Women Studies 131
Il Caffè 134
Migration World Magazine (legal column) 145

Native Nevadan, The (Native American) 147
Polonian 150

Literary
American Indian Culture and Research Journal 115
Arab Studies Quarterly 117
Ararat 117
Asian Insights Magazine 118
Atalantik (Indians from India) 119
Bamboo Ridge: The Hawaii Writers' Quarterly 120
Chicago Review 125
Cicada 125
Collages & Bricolages 126
Crazy Quilt Quarterly 126
Finnam Newsletter 130
Fish Drum Magazine 130
Gwiazda Polarna (Polish) 132
India Currents 135
International Fiction Review, The 137
Journal, The 139
Language Bridges (Polish) 140
Left Curve 141
Lilith (Jewish) 142
MacGuffin, The 142
Notebook/Cuaderno: A Literary Journal 148
Now and Then 149
Obsidian II: Black Literature in Review 149
Polonian 150
SAQI: South Asia Quarterly International 153

Magic
Atalantik (Indians from India) 119
Gwiazda Polarna (Polish) 132
Il Caffè 134
Polonian 150
Société 155

Martial Arts
Asian Week 119
Cicada 125
Polonian 150
Tozai Times (Japanese-American) 156
Whispering Wind (Native American) 157

Medicine
American Indian Culture and Research
  Journal 115
Dziennik Zwiazkowy (Polish Daily
  News) 128
Finnam Newsletter (folk) 130
Fort Concho and the South Plains
  Journal 131
Heritage Florida Jewish News 133
Il Caffè 134
Jewish Review, The 138
Native Nevadan, The (Native
  American) 147
Polonian 150
SAQI: South Asia Quarterly
  International 153
Tozai Times (Japanese-
  American) 156

Men's Issues
Cicada 125
Il Caffè 134
Mennonite Publishing House 144
Notebook/Cuaderno: A Literary
  Journal 148
Obsidian II: Black Literature in
  Review 149
Oxford Magazine 150
SAQI: South Asia Quarterly
  International 153
Scandinavian Review 153
Société 155

Metaphysics/New Age
Cicada 125
Il Caffè 134
SAQI: South Asia Quarterly
  International 153
Shaman's Drum 154

Minority Issues
Aim Magazine 113
Amerasia Journal 114
American Indian Culture and Research
  Journal 115
Ararat 117
Asian Insights Magazine 118
Asian Week 119
Athena 120
Bamboo Ridge: The Hawaii Writers'
  Quarterly 120
Black Enterprise 122
Collages & Bricolages 126
CrossCurrents 127

East Bay Monitor 128
Finnam Newsletter 130
Fort Concho and the South Plains
  Journal 131
Frontiers: A Journal of Women
  Studies 131
Gwiazda Polarna (Polish) 132
Il Caffè 134
India Currents 135
Jewish Review, The 138
Language Bridges (Polish) 140
Left Curve 141
Mennonite Publishing House 144
Migration World Magazine 145
Native Nevadan, The (Native
  American) 147
Notebook/Cuaderno: A Literary
  Journal 148
Obsidian II: Black Literature in
  Review 149
Oxford Magazine 150
SAQI: South Asia Quarterly
  International 153
Société 155

Music
American Indian Culture and Research
  Journal 115
Finnam Newsletter 130
Fish Drum Magazine 130
Il Caffè 134
India Currents 135
Left Curve 141
Living Blues 142
Middle Eastern Dancer 144
Now and Then (Appalachian) 149
Polonian 150
Polonia's Voice: The Polish-American
  Journal 151
SAQI: South Asia Quarterly
  International 153

Mythology
American Indian Culture and Research
  Journal 115
Atalantik (Indians from India) 119
Cicada 125
Finnam Newsletter 130
Gwiazda Polarna (Polish) 132
Il Caffè 134
Midstream, A Monthly Jewish
  Review 145
Nachiketa (children's) 146

Native Nevadan, The (Native
American) 147
*Notebook/Cuaderno: A Literary
Journal* 148
Now and Then (Appalachian) 149
Oxford Magazine 150
*SAQI: South Asia Quarterly
International* 153
Shaman's Drum 154
Société 155
Whispering Wind
(Native American) 157

Nature *see also* **Environment/Ecology**
*American Indian Culture and Research
Journal* 115
Brilliant Star (Baha'i, children's) 123
Cicada 125
*Dziennik Zwiazkowy (Polish Daily
News)* 128
*Frontiers: A Journal of Women
Studies* 131
Gypsy Literary Magazine 132
Hinduism Today 134
Il Caffè 134
India Currents 135
Language Bridges (Polish) 140
Left Curve 141
Lilith (Jewish) 142
*Midstream, A Monthly Jewish
Review* 145
Native Nevadan, The (Native
American) 147
News From Indian Country 148
*Notebook/Cuaderno: A Literary
Journal* 148
Oxford Magazine 150
*Rackham Journal of the Arts and
Humanities* 151
*SAQI: South Asia Quarterly
International* 153
Scandinavian Review 153

Philosophy
Arab Studies Quarterly 117
Atalantik (Indians from India) 119
Black Collegian, The 121
Cicada 125
Collages & Bricolages 126
Native Nevadan, The (Native
American) 147
*Notebook/Cuaderno: A Literary
Journal* 148
Now and Then (Appalachian) 149

Oxford Magazine 150
*SAQI: South Asia Quarterly
International* 153
Shaman's Drum 154
Société 155
Whispering Wind
(Native American) 157

Photo Features
American Dane 115
Ararat 115
Asian Insights Magazine 118
Collages & Bricolages 126
CrossCurrents 127
*Dziennik Zwiazkowy (Polish Daily
News)* 128
El Tecolote 129
Finnam Newsletter 130
Fish Drum Magazine 130
*Fort Concho and the South Plains
Journal* 131
Gwiazda Polarna (Polish) 132
Gypsy Literary Magazine 132
Heritage Florida Jewish News 133
Hinduism Today 134
Il Caffè 134
India Currents 135
Indian Life (Native Americans) 135
Jewish Review, The 138
La Gente de Aztlan 140
La Oferta Review 141
Left Curve 141
*Manoa: A Pacific Journal of
International Writing* 143
Middle Eastern Dancer 144
Migration World Magazine 145
Nachiketa (children's) 146
Najda Newsletter (Arab) 146
Native Peoples Magazine 147
*Notebook/Cuaderno: A Literary
Journal* 148
Now and Then (Appalachia) 149
*Rohwedder, International Journal of
Literature and Art* 152
*SAQI: South Asia Quarterly
International* 153
Scandinavian Review 153
Shaman's Drum 154
*[Veinte] 20 de Mayo Spanish
Newspaper* 157
Whispering Wind
(Native American) 157

Poetry
Aim Magazine 113
Aloha, The Magazine of Hawaii and the
    Pacific 114
Amerasia Journal 114
American Dane 115
Antietam Review 116
Ararat 117
Arba Sicula (Italian/Sicilian) 118
Asian Insights Magazine 118
Atalantik (Indians from India) 119
Bamboo Ridge: The Hawaii Writers'
    Quarterly 120
Black Angels Poetry Newsletter 121
Calapooya Collage 124
Canadian Journal of Native
    Education 124
Chicago Review 125
Cicada 125
Crazy Quilt Quarterly 126
Eagle's Flight 128
El Tecolote 129
ESSENCE Magazine
    (Black women) 129
Fish Drum Magazine 130
Gypsy Literary Magazine 132
Hayden's Ferry Review 133
Il Caffè 134
Indian Literature (Indians from
    India) 136
Japanophile 138
Journal, The 139
Language Bridges (Polish) 140
Lilith (Jewish) 142
MacGuffin, The 142
Manoa: A Pacific Journal of
    International Writing 143
Maryland Review 143
Mennonite Publishing House 144
Middle Eastern Dancer 144
Midstream, A Monthly Jewish
    Review 145
Miorita, A Journal of Romanian
    Studies 145
Nachiketa (children's) 146
Najda Newsletter (Arab) 146
Native Nevadan, The (Native
    American) 147
Native Peoples Magazine 147
News From Indian Country 148
Nimrod Contemporary Prose and
    Poetry Journal 148

Notebook/Cuaderno: A Literary
    Journal 148
Now and Then (Appalachian) 149
Obsidian II: Black Literature in
    Review 149
Oxford Magazine 150
Rackham Journal of the Arts and
    Humanities 151
Response: A Contemporary Jewish
    Review 151
Rohwedder, International Journal of
    Literature and Art 152
SAQI: South Asia Quarterly
    International 153
Shaman's Drum 154
Shofar (Jewish children's) 154
South Dakota Review 156
Southern California Anthology 156
[Veinte] 20 de Mayo Spanish
    Newspaper 157
Whispering Wind
    (Native American) 157

Politics/World Affairs
American Indian Culture and Research
    Journal 115
Arab Studies Quarterly 117
Ararat 117
Asian Insights Magazine 118
Asian Week 119
Black Collegian, The 121
B'nai B'rith International Jewish
    Monthly 123
Brilliant Star (Baha'i, children's) 123
Collages & Bricolages 126
Dziennik Zwiazkowy (Polish Daily
    News) 128
Frontiers: A Journal of Women
    Studies 131
Heritage Florida Jewish News 133
Il Caffè 134
India Currents 135
Jewish Review, The 138
Language Bridges (Polish) 140
Left Curve 141
Lilith 142
Midstream, A Monthly Jewish
    Review 145
Native Nevadan, The (Native
    American) 147
News From Indian Country 148
Polonian 150

Response: A Contemporary Jewish Review 151
SAQI: South Asia Quarterly International 153
[Veinte] 20 de Mayo Spanish Newspaper 157

Psychology
Arab Studies Quarterly 117
Cicada 125
Frontiers: A Journal of Women Studies 131
Il Caffè 134
Notebook/Cuaderno: A Literary Journal 148
SAQI: South Asia Quarterly International 153
Société 155

Psycho-Spirituality
Atalantik (Indians from India) 119
Black Angels Poetry Newsletter 121
Brilliant Star (Baha'i, children's) 123
Cicada 125
Gwiazda Polarna (Poles) 132
Gypsy Literary Magazine 132
India Currents 135
Lilith (spirituality) 142
Middle Eastern Dancer 144
Native Nevadan, The (Native American) 147
News From Indian Country 148
SAQI: South Asia Quarterly International 153
Shaman's Drum 154
Société 155

Recreation
Dziennik Zwiazkowy (Polish Daily News) 128
Finnam Newsletter 130
Gwiazda Polarna (Polish) 132
India Currents 135
Middle Eastern Dancer 144
Polonian 150

Religion

All Religions
American Indian Culture and Research Journal 115
Brilliant Star (Baha'i, children's) 123
Finnam Newsletter 130
Gwiazda Polarna (Polish) 132
Il Caffè 134

Specific Religions
Buddhism
Asian Week 119
Atalantik (Indians from India) 119
Cicada 125
Fish Drum Magazine 130
India Currents 135
Nachiketa (children's) 146
SAQI: South Asia Quarterly International 153
Tozai Times 156
Christianity
Indian Life (Native Americans) 135
Mennonite Publishing House 144
Polonia's Voice: The Polish-American Journal 151
SAQI: South Asia Quarterly International 153
Hinduism
Cicada 125
Hinduism Today 134
India Currents 135
Nachiketa (children's) 146
SAQI: South Asia Quarterly International 153
Islam
Arab Studies Quarterly 117
Black Collegian, The 121
India Currents 135
Nachiketa (children's) 146
Najda Newsletter (Arab) 146
SAQI: South Asia Quarterly International 153
Judaism
Heritage Florida Jewish News 133
Jewish Review, The 138
Lilith 142
Midstream, A Monthly Jewish Review 145
Response: A Contemporary Jewish Review 151
SAQI: South Asia Quarterly International 153
Neo-African Religions
Société 155
Sikhism
SAQI: South Asia Quarterly International 153

Taoism
Cicada 125
Frontiers: A Journal of Women
Studies 131
Japanophile 138
Zen
Cicada 125
Fish Drum Magazine 130
Japanophile 138
Société 155

Scholarly Works
Amerasia Journal 114
American Indian Culture and Research
Journal 115
American Indian Law Review 116
Arab Studies Quarterly 117
Black Collegian, The 121
Frontiers: A Journal of Women
Studies 131
International Fiction Review,
The 137
Japanophile 138
Midstream, A Monthly Jewish
Review 145
Obsidian II: Black Literature in
Review 149
San Jose Studies 152
SAQI: South Asia Quarterly
International 153
Sarmatian Review, The 153
Société 155

Science
Arab Studies Quarterly 117
Dziennik Zwiazkowy (Polish Daily
News) 128
Il Caffè 134
Jewish Review, The 138

Self-Help
Black Angels Poetry Newsletter 121
Dziennik Zwiazkowy (Polish Daily
News) 128
Gwiazda Polarna (Polish) 132
Mennonite Publishing House 144
Notebook/Cuaderno: A Literary
Journal 148
SAQI: South Asia Quarterly
International 153
Société 155

Social/Political Commentary
Aim Magazine 113

Amerasia Journal 114
American Indian Culture and Research
Journal 115
Appalachian Heritage 117
Arab Studies Quarterly 117
Ararat 117
Arba Sicula (Italian/Sicilian) 118
Asian Insights Magazine 118
Asian Week 119
Atalantik (Indians from India) 119
Black Collegian, The 121
Canadian Journal of Native
Education 124
Chicago Review 125
Collages & Bricolages 126
CrossCurrents 127
Detroit Jewish News 127
East Bay Monitor 128
El Tecolote 129
ESSENCE Magazine
(Black women) 129
Fish Drum Magazine 130
Frontiers: A Journal of Women
Studies 131
Gwiazda Polarna (Polish) 132
Gypsy Literary Magazine 132
Hawai'i Review 133
Heritage Florida Jewish News 133
Il Caffè 134
India Currents 135
India-West 136
La Gente de Aztlan 140
Language Bridges (Polish) 140
Left Curve 141
Lilith (Jewish) 142
Manoa: A Pacific Journal of
International Writing 143
Middle Eastern Dancer 144
Midstream, A Monthly Jewish
Review 145
Migration World Magazine 145
Najda Newsletter (Arab) 146
Native Nevadan, The (Native
American) 147
News From Indian Country 148
Notebook/Cuaderno: A Literary
Journal 148
Rackham Journal of the Arts and
Humanities 151
Rohwedder, International Journal of
Literature and Art 152
SAQI: South Asia Quarterly
International 153

Sarmatian Review, The 153
Société 155
[Veinte] 20 de Mayo Spanish Newspaper 157
Whispering Wind (Native American) 157

Sociology
Aim Magazine 113
Amerasia Journal 114
American Indian Culture and Research Journal 115
Arab Studies Quarterly 117
Atalantik (Indians from India) 119
CrossCurrents 127
Dziennik Zwiazkowy (Polish Daily News) 128
Frontiers: A Journal of Women Studies 131
Il Caffè 134
International Migration Review 137
Polonian 150
SAQI: South Asia Quarterly International 153
Société 155

Sports
Aloha, The Magazine of Hawaii and the Pacific 114
Dziennik Zwiazkowy (Polish Daily News) 128
Finnam Newsletter 130
Native Nevadan, The (Native American) 147
[Veinte] 20 de Mayo Spanish Newspaper 157

Translations
Dziennik Zwiazkowy (Polish Daily News) 128
Fish Drum Magazine 130
Frontiers: A Journal of Women Studies 131
Gwiazda Polarna (Polish) 132
Language Bridges (Polish) 140
Lilith 142
Midstream, A Monthly Jewish Review 145
Miorita, A Journal of Romanian Studies 145
Najda Newsletter (Arab) 146
Scandinavian Review 153

Transportation
Dziennik Zwiazkowy (Polish Daily News) 128
Polonia's Voice: The Polish-American Journal 151

Travel
Aloha, The Magazine of Hawaii and the Pacific 114
Asian Insights Magazine 118
Atalantik (Indians from India) 119
Cicada 125
Dziennik Zwiazkowy (Polish Daily News) 128
Heritage Florida Jewish News 133
Il Caffè 134
Japanophile 138
La Oferta Review 141
MacGuffin, The (some) 142
Middle Eastern Dancer 144
Oxford Magazine 150
SAQI: South Asia Quarterly International 153
Scandinavian Review 153
Société 155

Tribal Life
American Indian Culture and Research Journal 115
Collages & Bricolages 126
Fort Concho and the South Plains Journal 131
Journal of American Indian Education 139
Société 155

War/Peace Issues
American Indian Culture and Research Journal 115
Arab Studies Quarterly 117
Asian Week 119
Cicada 125
Collages & Bricolages 126
Polonia's Voice: The Polish-American Journal 151

Women's Issues
Athena 120
Collages & Bricolages 126
ESSENCE Magazine (Black women) 129
Frontiers: A Journal of Women Studies 131
Japanophile 138

Women's Issues continued
La Gente de Aztlan 140
Lilith (Jewish) 142
Mennonite Publishing House 144
Middle Eastern Dancer 144
Najda Newsletter (Arab) 146
Native Nevadan, The (Native
    American) 147
*Obsidian II: Black Literature in
    Review* 149
Oxford Magazine 150
*SAQI: South Asia Quarterly
    International* 153
Scandinavian Review 153
Tozai Times (Japanese-
    American) 156

Yoga
Cicada 125
Hinduism Today 134
India Currents 135
*SAQI: South Asia Quarterly
    International* 153
Société 155

Film and TV Markets

This index is alphabetized using the letter-by-letter system and is divided into three sections: Media Forms, Ethnic Focus, and Script Genres.

Media Forms

Documentaries
Braverman Productions, Inc. 161
Evenstar Pictures 162
KSCI-TV Channel 18 164
Potocka Productions,
Ltd., M. M. 165
Rainbow Ridge Films 166
Wynter Films 167

Motion Pictures
Afra Film Enterprises 160
American Corsair 161
Blake Productions, Timothy 161
Braverman Productions, Inc. 161
Children's Television Workshop 162
Entertainment Productions, Inc. 162
Evenstar Pictures 162
Hometown Films 163
Hudlin Bros., Inc. 163
Mruvka Entertainment, Alan 164
Producer and Management
Entertainment Groups 166
Rainbow Ridge Films 166
Wynter Films 167

Television
American Corsair 161
Braverman Productions, Inc. 161
Children's Television Workshop 162
Evenstar Pictures 162
Hudlin Bros., Inc. 163
ITV Productions, Ltd. 163
KSCI-TV Channel 18 164
JKR Productions 163
LCJ Productions 164
Mruvka Entertainment, Alan 164
Nelvana Entertainment 165
Polakoff Productions, Carol 165
Potocka Productions,
Ltd., M. M. 165
Spanish Trail Productions 166
TFG Entertainment 167

Wynter Films 167

Video
Braverman Productions, Inc. 161
Spanish Trail Productionss 166
Wynter Films 167

Ethnic Focus

All Ethnic Groups
Children's Television
Workshop 162
Entertainment Productions,
Inc. 162
Hometown Films 163
JKR Productions 163
Producer and Management
Entertainment Group 166

Specific Groups
Afro-Americans/Blacks
American Corsair 161
Braverman Productions, Inc., Inc.
(also West Africans) 161
Evenstar Pictures 162
Mruvka Entertainment, Alan 164
Hudlin Bros., Inc. 163
Nelvana Entertainment 165
Polakoff Productions, Carol 165
TFG Entertainment 167
Wynter Films (also West
Africans) 167
Asians/Asian-Americans
Evenstar Pictures 162
KSCI-TV Channel 18 164
Nelvana Entertainment 165
Polakoff Productions, Carol 165
Chinese
Mruvka Entertainment, Alan 164
Cubans
American Corsair 161
TFG Entertainment 167

Eastern European Cultures
Afra Film Enterprises 160
Braverman Productions, Inc., Inc.
(Russians) 161
Potocka Productions,
Ltd., M. M. 165
Eskimos
American Corsair 161
Filipinos
KSCI-TV Channel 18 164
Polakoff Productions, Carol 165
**Hispanics (include Chicanos,
Latinos)**
Blake Productions, Timothy 161
Braverman Productions, Inc. 161
Evenstar Pictures 162
Mruvka Entertainment, Alan 164
Nelvana Entertainment 165
Polakoff Productions, Carol 165
Rainbow Ridge Films 166
TFG Entertainment 167
Indians of Asia
ITV Productions, Ltd. 163
Wynter Films 167
Japanese
Mruvka Entertainment, Alan 164
Native Americans
American Corsair 161
Blake Productions, Timothy 161
Braverman Productions, Inc. 161
Nelvana Entertainment 165
Rainbow Ridge Films 166
Wynter Films 167
South Americans
TFG Entertainment 167
West Indians
Braverman Productions, Inc. 161
Wynter Films 167

Script Genres

Action-Driven
Afra Film Enterprises 160
American Corsair 161
Braverman Productions, Inc. 161
JKR Productions 163
Mruvka Entertainment, Alan 164
Producer and Management
Entertainment Group (karate) 166

Biographies
Braverman Productions, Inc. 161

Character-Driven
Blake Productions, Timothy 161
Braverman Productions, Inc. 161
Hometown Films 163
ITV Productions, Ltd. 163
JKR Productions 163
LCJ Productions 164
Mruvka Entertainment, Alan 164
Potocka Productions,
Ltd., M. M. 165
TFG Entertainment 167

Children's/Young Adults
Children's Television Workshop 162
Hometown Films
(coming-of-age) 163
KSCI-TV Channel 18 164
Nelvana Entertainment
(all subjects) 165

Drama
JKR Productions 163
Potocka Productions, Ltd., M. M.
(docudrama) 165
Producer and Managemeant
Entertainment Group (love
stories) 166

Entertainment
Entertainment Productions, Inc. 162

Epics
Mruvka Entertainment, Alan 164
Potocka Productions,
Ltd., M. M. 165

Fantasy
Hometown Films 163

General Interest
Evenstar Pictures 162
Hudlin Bros, Inc. 163
Potocka Productions,
Ltd., M. M. 165
Rainbow Ridge Films 166

Historical Period Pieces
KSCI-TV Channel 18 164
Potocka Productions,
Ltd., M. M. 165

Mysteries
Blake Productions, Timothy 161
Hometown Films 163

LCJ Productions 164
Mruvka Entertainmeant, Alan
   (horror) 164
Polakoff Productions, Carol 165
TFG Entertainment 167

Romantic Adventures
Afra Film Enterprises 160
Braverman Productions, Inc. 161
Hometown Films 163
ITV Productions, Ltd. 163
JKR Productions 163
Mruvka Entertainment, Alan 164
Polakoff Productions, Carol 165
Potocka Productions,
   Ltd., M. M. 165
TFG Entertainment 167

Thrillers (Psychological)
Afra Film Enterprises 160
American Corsair 161
Braverman Productions, Inc. 161
Hometown Films 163
LCJ Productions 164
Mruvka Entertainment, Alan 164
Polakoff Productions, Carol 165
Potocka Productions,
   Ltd., M. M. 165
TFG Entertainment 167

True Stories
Braverman Productions, Inc., Inc.
   (true crime) 161
Polakoff Productions, Carol 165

Westerns
Hometown Films 163

Women's Films
Wynter Films 167

Comprehensive Index

This index is alphabetized using the letter-by-letter system. Magazine, newsletter, and newspaper listings are in italics.

A

Aegina Press, Inc. 59
Afra-Film Enterprises 160
African American Images 60
Ahsahta Press 60
Aim Magazine 113
Alaska Native Language Center 61
Aloha, The Magazine of Hawaii and the Pacific 114
Amerasia Journal 114
American Corsair 161
American Dane 115
American Indian Culture and Research Journal 115
American Indian Law Review 116
Anand Paperbacks *see* Orient Paperbacks 94
Antietam Review 116
Appalachian Heritage 117
Arab Studies Quarterly 117
Ararat 117
Arba Sicula 118
Arte Publico Press 61
Asian Humanities Press 62
Asian Insights Magazine 118
Asian Perspectives 119
Asian Week 119
Associated Publishers, Inc., The 62
Atalantik 119
Athena 120
Avalon Books 62
Avanyu Publishing, Inc. 63
Avon Books 63

B

Bamboo Ridge: The Hawaii Writers' Quarterly 120
Beacon Press 63

Bear and Company, Inc. 64
Bear Flag Books 64
Bear Wallow Publishing Company, The 65
Bergli Books, Ltd. 65
Bilingual Press/Editorial Bilingue 65
Bison Books *see* University of Nebraska Press 103
Black Angels Poetry Newsletter 121
Black Angels Press 66
Black Collegian, The 121
Black Enterprise 122
Black Scholar: Journal of Black Studies & Research, The 122
Blair, Publisher, John F. 66
Blake Productions, Timothy 161
B'nai B'rith International Jewish Monthly 123
Braverman Productions, Inc. 161
Bridge; Journal of the Danish American Heritage Society, The 123
Brilliant Star 123
Buddha Rose Publications 67

C

Calapooya Collage 124
Calyx Books 67
Canadian Journal of Native Education 124
Carolina Wren Press 68
Carolrhoda Books, Inc. 68
Center for East Asian Studies 69
Center for Migration Studies of New York, Inc. 69
Chicago Review 125
Children's Book Press 69
Children's Television Workshop 162
China Books & Periodicals, Inc. 70
Chronicle Books 70

Cicada 125
Clarity Press 71
Classic Reprint Series *see* University
    of Alaska Press 102
Cleis Press 71
Collages & Bricolages 126
Council for Indian Education 71
Countrywoman's Press, The 72
Crazy Quilt Quarterly 126
Crime and Social Justice Associates
    see Social Justice 98
Cross Cultural Publications, Inc. 72
CrossCurrents 127
Crossing Press, The 72
Crumb Elbow Publishing 73
Cultural Survival Quarterly 127

D

Dante University Press 73
Denali Press, The 74
Destiny Books *see* Inner Traditions
    International 83
Detroit Jewish News 127
Dial Books for Young Readers 74
*Dziennik Zwiazkowy (Polish Daily
    News)* 128

E

Eagle's Flight 128
*East Bay Monitor, A Multicultural
    Newspaper* 128
Eastern Caribbean Institute 75
Ediciones Universal 75
Eighth Mountain Press, The 75
El Tecolote 129
Enslow Publishers, Inc. 76
Entertainment Productions, Inc. 162
Esoterica Press 76
Essence Magazine 129
Evenstar Pictures 162

F

Fairleigh Dickinson University
    Press 76
Farrar, Straus & Giroux, Inc. 77
Finnam Newsletter 130
First Avenue Editions *see*
    Carolrhoda Books, Inc. 68
Fish Drum Magazine 130
Folklore Institute 77
*Fort Concho and the South Plains
    Journal* 131
Fortress Press 77
*Frontiers: A Journal of Women
    Studies* 131

G

Gold Eagle *see* Harlequin
    Enterprises Limited 79
Golden West Publishers 78
Greenhaven Press, Inc. 78
Guernica Editions 78
Gwiazda Polarna 132
Gypsy Literary Magazine 132

H

Harlequin Enterprises Limited 79
Hawai'i Review 133
Hayden's Ferry Review 133
Healing Arts Press *see* Inner
    Traditions International 83
Hemingway Western Studies
    Series 79
Herald Press 80
Heritage Florida Jewish News 133
Heyday Books 80
Hill Books, Lawrence 81
Hinduism Today 134
Hippocrene Books, Inc. 81
Holiday House 81
Hometown Films 163
Howard University Press 82
Hudlin Bros., Inc. 163

I

Il Caffé 134
Illini Books *see* University of Illinois Press 103
Illuminations Press 82
India Currents 135
Indian Country Communications, Inc. 83
Indian Life Magazine 135
Indian Literature 136
India-West 136
Inner Traditions International 83
In One Ear Press 84
International Fiction Review, The 137
International Migration Review 137
Intimacy/Black Romance 137
Intimacy/Bronze Thrills see Intimacy/Black Romance 137
ISM Press 84
Italica Press 85
ITV Productions, Ltd. 163

J

Japanophile 138
Jewish Review, The 138
Jive/Black Confessions see Intimacy/Black Romance 137
JKR Productions 163
Jonathan David Publishers, Inc. 85
Jordan Enterprises Publishing Company 85
Journal, The 139
Journal of American Indian Education 139
Journal of the Afro-American Historical and Genealogical Society 139

K

Kar-Ben Copies, Inc. 86
Karnak House 86
Kazan Books *see* Volcano Press, Inc. 105

Kodansha Interntational 86
KSCI-TV Channel 18 164

L

La Gente de Aztlan 140
Language Bridges Quarterly 140
La Oferta Review 141
LCJ Productions 164
Left Curve 141
Lilith 142
Lion Books Publisher 87
Little, Brown and Company 87
Living Blues 142
Lodestar Books 88
Lollipop Power Books *see* Carolina Wren Press 68
Los Hombres Press 88
Lotus Press, Inc. 88
Louisiana University Press 89

M

MacGuffin, The 142
Mage Publishers 89
Maggpie Productions *see* Winston-Derek Publishers, Inc. 107
Manoa: A Pacific Journal of International Writing 143
Maryland Review 143
Mennonite Publishing House 144
Middle Eastern Dancer 144
Midstream, A Monthly Jewish Review 145
Migration World Magazine 145
Miorita, A Journal of Romanian Studies 145
Monograph Series *see* University of Alaska Press 102
Moon Publications, Inc. 90
Mr. Cogito Press 90
Mruvka Entertainment, Alan 164
Muir Publications, John 90

N

Nachiketa 146
Najda Newsletter 146
Native Nevadan, The 147
Native Peoples Magazine 147
Naturegraph Publishers, Inc. 91
Nelvana Entertainment 165
New Day Press, Inc. 91
New Seed Press 92
News From Indian Country 148
Nimrod Contemporary Prose and
Poetry Journal 148
Noble Press, The 92
Northland Publishing Company,
Inc. 92
Notebook/Cuaderno: A Literary
Journal 148
Now and Then 149

O

Obsidian II: Black Literature in
Review 149
One Horn Press see Winston-Derek
Publishers, Inc. 107
Open Hand Publishing, Inc. 93
Oral Biography Series see University
of Alaska Press 102
Oregon Fever Books see Crumb
Elbow Publishing 73
Oregon State University Press 93
Orient Paperbacks 94
Oxford Magazine 150

P

Park Street Press see Inner
Traditions International 83
Pelican Publishing Company,
Inc. 94
Penway Books see Lotus
Press, Inc. 88
Philomel Books 95
Polakoff Productions, Carol 165

Polonian 150
Polonia's Voice: The Polish American
Journal 151
Potocka Productions,
Ltd., M. M. 165
Prairie State Books see University of
Illinois Press 103
Press of MacDonald & Reinecke,
The 95
Prism Editions see Naturegraph
Publishers, Inc. 91
Producer and Management
Entertainment Group 166
Publishers Associates 96

R

Rackham Journal of the Arts and
Humanities 151
Rainbow Ridge Films 166
R&M Publishing Company 96
Rasmusson Historical Translation
Series see University of Alaska
Press 102
Red Crane Books 97
Research Centrex see Crumb Elbow
Publishing 73
Response: A Contemporary Jewish
Review 151
Rohwedder: International Journal of
Literature and Art 152

S

San Jose Studies 152
SAQI: South Asia Quarterly
International 153
Sarmatian Review, The 153
Scandinavian Review 153
Scholastic, Inc. 97
Scythe Books see Winston-Derek
Publishers, Inc. 107
Seal Press 97
Secrets see Intimacy/
Black Romance 137
Shaman's Drum: A Journal of
Experiential Shamanism 154

Shofar 154
Sicilia Parra see Arba Sicula 118
Signal Editions *see* Véhicule
  Press 105
Silhouette Imprints *see* Crumb
  Elbow Publishing 73
Silhouette *see* Harlequin
  Enterprises Limited 79
Social Justice 98
Société 155
Soho Press, Inc. 98
Sokol Minnesota Slovo 155
South Asia Quarterly International see
  SAQI 153
South Dakota Review 156
Southern California Anthology 156
Spanish Trail Productions 166
Stone Bridge Press 99

T

Technicians of the Sacred 99
Temple Publishing, Inc., Ellen 100
Texas A&M University Press 100
Texas Western Press 100
TFG Entertainment 167
Third World Press 101
Tozai Times 156
Treasure Chest Publications,
  Inc. 101
Trillium Art Productions *see* Crumb
  Elbow Publishing 73
Tyee Press *see* Crumb Elbow
  Publishing 73

U

University Editions *see* Aegina
  Press, Inc. 59
University of Alabama Press 102
University of Alaska Press 102
University of California at Los
  Angeles, American Indian
  Studies 103
University of Illinois Press 103
University of Nebraska Press 103

University of Nevada Press 104
University of North Texas Press 104
University of Texas Press 105

V

Véhicule Press 105
[Veinte] 20 de Mayo Spanish
  Newspaper 157
Volcano Press 105

W

Walker and Company 106
Washington State University
  Press 106
Whispering Wind 157
Winston-Derek Publishers, Inc. 107
Woman in the Moon (WIM) 107
Women's Studies Quarterly, A
  Journal 108
Worldwide *see* Harlequin
  Enterprises Limited 79
Wynter Films 167
Wyrick and Company 108

Y

York Press, Ltd. 108

Z

Zephyr Press 109

About the Author

Meera Lester, whose work has been published worldwide, specializes in writing for ethnic markets. Her writing about India, Indians and Indo-Americans, and their history, cultures, and religions has appeared in a variety of newspapers and magazines including *India Currents, Indian Voice, India West, India Times, Hinduism Today, Danik Prabhat* (daily newspaper of the city of Meerut, Uttar Pradesh, India), and others. Her reviews of books about Philippine and Native American cultures have appeared in *Small Press* magazine, while her reviews of other types of books and articles have appeared in publications ranging from small local community publications to major metropolitan newspapers such as the *San Francisco Chronicle* and the *San Jose Mercury News*. She is the editor of *High Technology Careers* magazine, former editor of *Professional Careers* and the *Paul Masson Summer Series* magazines, and associate producer of the documentary videotapes *Selling to Hollywood* and *Writing for Hollywood*.

In 1983, she co-founded Writers Connection, a California-based company serving writers and other publishing professionals. In addition to overseeing all book publishing by the small press arm of her company, she directs the writing/publishing seminar program and the Selling to Hollywood conference, held the second week in August each year.

She has appeared as a guest speaker on such radio programs as KCBS, KGO, and KNBR in San Francisco and has either directed or been a guest lecturer at a number of writer's conferences over the years. Currently, she is rewriting her epic novel about a cross-cultural love affair and contemplating a return to India and Nepal.

About Writers Connection

Writers Connection was founded in 1983 by Steve and Meera Lester to serve writers and publishing professionals in California. Writers Connection serves more than 2,000 members and provides a wide range of services, including seminars, a referral service to help writers connect with professional writers and editors who offer consultations or critique services, a bookstore offering a wide selection of titles on writing- and publishing-related topics, the annual Selling to Hollywood weekend conference, and a 16-page monthly newsletter.

With the establishment of the small press arm of the company, Writers Connection will be increasing its publishing activity. At present the company publishes the *Marketplace* series books and is co-producer of the *Writing for Hollywood* and *Selling to Hollywood* documentary videotapes. *Writing for the Ethnic Markets* is the company's latest book.

Writers Connection membership offers discounts on seminars, conferences, and book and tape purchases, and facilitates access to a wide range of resource material.

The monthly *Writers Connection* newsletter features current information on markets, events, contests, and industry news as well as articles on various aspects of writing and publishing. Members receive the newsletter free, and subscriptions are available to nonmembers.

The company's seminar offerings target professional writers as well as hobbyists, average three to six hours in length, and cover subjects such as "Constructing the Novel," "Writing Mystery and Suspense," "Basic Grammar," "Travel Writing," "Writing from Points of Power and Passion," "Writing the Nonfiction Best Seller," and "Editing for Technical and Business Communicators."

If you would like to join Writers Connection or subscribe to the monthly newsletter, an order form appears on page 259. The form may also be used to request seminar information, a free sample newsletter, or additional information about Writers Connection and future editions of the *Marketplace* directories and other books from Writers Connection Press.

Timely and useful information for writers delivered to you each month in the *Writers Connection* newsletter

Features and how-to tips for writers, self-publishers, freelancers, technical and business writers, editors, and scriptwriters

Plus

Publishing and film industry news and market listings
Contests for writers and poets
Events on the West Coast and nationwide
Issues of concern to writers
Writers' software and computer news

Here are just a few article titles from past issues:

How to Define a Blockbuster Novel—And Write One
Writing for the Screen: How to Make Your Own First Break
Mid-List Crisis: Promoting Your Novel after Publication
Audio-Visual Writer's Primer: Guide to a Growing Market for Writers
Strategies for Creativity: Learning to Write from Your Creative Center
Publicize or Perish: Suggestions for Small Presses and Self-Publishers

All this and services, opportunities, consultant referrals for writers, and **updates to the Publishing Marketplace directories**

Special Offer:

One full year (12 issues) for just $18
Use the the order form on page 259 or call (408) 973-0227
Offer good through December 31, 1992

Find hundreds of freelance writing opportunities in the Publishing Marketplace Series

Compiled and edited by a writer and experienced research librarian, the Marketplace books provide writers with a wealth of information on markets and resources in the western United States. Each book includes:

Book Publishers—Select from small, mid-size, and large presses. Find submission editors, subjects of interest, acceptance policies, contact information, and marketing channels.

Magazines—Locate hundreds of new markets. Discover submission editors, editorial needs, acceptance policies, contact information, and tips.

Newspapers—Find submission and book review editors. Learn submission, book review, and travel editors and circulation.

Literary Agents—Choose the right agent for your book or script. Evaluate subjects of interest, agency policies, contact information, represented titles, and tips.

Professional Organizations—Maximize your contacts. Locate national and state branches, contacts, purpose, dues, membership criteria, activities, and newsletters.

Writers Conferences—Gain insights, information, and contacts. Discover locations, frequency, fees, themes, subjects, and format.

Reference Books—Expand your sources of information. An annotated bibliography of writing and publishing books.

Indexes—Find what you need quickly. Separate subject index for books and magazines and also comprehensive and state indexes.

Use these comprehensive directories of submission information, editorial guidelines, and reference sources to get your material to the right person, in the right format, for the right market.

The *California and Hawaii Publishing Marketplace*.
292 pages, $16.95, ISBN: 0-9622592-1-7

The *Northwest Publishing Marketplace* listings for Alaska,
Idaho, Montana, Oregon, Washington, and Wyoming.
192 pages, $14.95, ISBN: 0-9622592-3-3

The *Southwest Publishing Marketplace* listings for Arizona,
Colorado, Nevada, New Mexico, Texas, and Utah.
176 pages, $14.95, ISBN: 0-9622592-2-5

"They [the books] are reasonably priced, easy to use, and provide
information that is not readily available in other sources."

Booklist, January 1991

"Superb new guides from Writers Connection. These books are invaluable
resources, not only for writers but for anyone in publishing."

Patricia Holt, Book Review Editor,
for the *San Francisco Chronicle*.

"These regional [Publishing Marketplace] directories are . . . sources of
practical assistance to the professional or aspiring writer. The publishing
sector listings and descriptions are very comprehensive . . . these
compilations are valuable reference items and superb resources."

Publishers Reports, April 1991

Be among the first to increase your sales to markets in these rapidly
growing writing/publishing regions. To order your copies, use the
form on page 259 or call (408) 973-0227.

How does a writer break into Hollywood? Find an agent? Write the stories Hollywood wants?

Nineteen top Hollywood pros answer these questions and more in the hottest resource for scriptwriters—the *Writing for Hollywood* and *Selling to Hollywood* videotapes. In the broadcast quality style of network television, these tapes provide an insider's look at the complex and intriguing process of writing and selling screenplays for motion pictures and television.

Selling to Hollywood

86 minutes

Writing for Hollywood

83 minutes

- **Breaking In**
  written and unwritten rules of the game
  using the "spec" script to open doors
- **Protecting Your Material**
  registering scripts with WGA
  sending follow-up letters to pitches
- **Agents**
  selling without an agent
  how to find and work with an agent
- **Selling to the Studios and Independents**
  rejection/acceptance factors
  the development process
- **"Hot" Scripts**
  elements of the equation
  writing with original voice & style
- **Pitching**
  elements of a good pitch
  log lines, set pieces, plot points
- **Opportunities and Alternatives**
  production deals with studios
  getting character-driven pieces to the stars

- **The Prewriting Process**
  stepping out the scenes
  determining the major turning points
- **Structure**
  the three-act structure
  the character's journey from A to Z
- **Dialog & Characterization**
  creating interesting characters
  advancing the story
- **Rewriting**
  time sequence in scriptwriting
  questions to ask during the rewrite
- **Story Analysis and Script Evaluation**
  how professional analysts evaluate scripts
  researching for accurate period pieces
- **Collaboration**
  how to become your own worst enemy
  collaborators as allies
- **TV Sitcoms**
  the sitcom structure
  creating cliffhangers

You don't have to live in Hollywood to be a successful screenwriter. Learn how to write the stories Hollywood wants and discover how to sell them to an increasingly competitive industry where million-dollar deals are made over lunch.

Produced by Paul Edwards Production Group and Writers Connection. Individual VHS tapes are priced at $79.95 each; the set is $129.95. Writers Connection member price is $71.95 per tape; $116.95 for the set. To order, use the order form on page 259 or call (408) 973-0227.

Order Form

Information/Membership/Subscription

☐ Send me a Writers Connection newsletter/seminar catalog

☐ Enroll me as a Writers Connection member
includes subscription—$40 per year $_____

☐ Send me 12 issues of the *Writers Connection* newsletter
without membership—$18 (includes tax & shipping) $_____

Books/Tapes

Check the items you wish. Price code: **member**/nonmember price.

☐ Send me _____ copies of **Writing for the
Ethnic Markets**—**$12.71**/$14.95 each $_____

☐ Send me _____ copies of the **Northwest Publishing
Marketplace**—**$12.71**/$14.95 each $_____

☐ Send me _____ copies of the **California and Hawaii
Publishing Marketplace**—**$14.41**/$16.95 each $_____

☐ Send me _____ copies of the **Southwest Publishing
Marketplace**—**$12.71**/$14.95 each $_____

☐ Send me _____ copies of the **Writing for Hollywood** VHS
videotape—**$71.95**/$79.95 each $_____

☐ Send me _____ copies of the **Selling to Hollywood** VHS
videotape—**$71.95**/$79.95 each $_____

☐ Send me _____ sets of both videotapes at the special
package price—**$116.95**/$129.95 per set $_____

☐ Send me the following titles from the books for writers
listing. Writers Connection members can deduct 15 percent.
Please enter code, title, and price for each book below.

_____ $_____

_____ $_____

                               Book/tape subtotal $_____

             Calif. residents add 8.25% sales tax $_____

Add $3.00 per book/tape ($6 max.), $.75 per newsletter for shipping $_____

                                         Total $_____

Name_____

Address_____

City_____ State_____ Zip_____

Daytime phone _____ Membership number_____

☐ Check or money order enclosed

Please charge my: ☐ Visa ☐ MasterCard   Account #_____

  Expiration date _____ Signature_____

Please return to: **Writers Connection**
1601 Saratoga-Sunnyvale Rd., Suite 180, Cupertino, CA 95014
Phone orders using a Visa or MasterCard are accepted: **(408) 973-0227**